ISBN 978-1-332-13386-4
PIBN 10289284

For support please visit www.forgottenbooks.com

1 MONTH OF
FREE
READING

at

www.ForgottenBooks.com

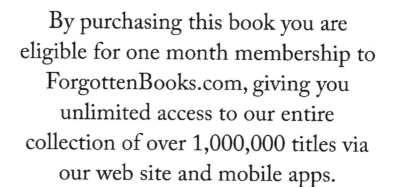

By purchasing this book you are eligible for one month membership to ForgottenBooks.com, giving you unlimited access to our entire collection of over 1,000,000 titles via our web site and mobile apps.

To claim your free month visit:

www.forgottenbooks.com/free289284

English
Français
Deutsche
Italiano
Español
Português

www.forgottenbooks.com

Mythology Photography **Fiction**
Fishing Christianity **Art** Cooking
Essays Buddhism Freemasonry
Medicine **Biology** Music **Ancient**
Egypt Evolution Carpentry Physics
Dance Geology **Mathematics** Fitness
Shakespeare **Folklore** Yoga Marketing
Confidence Immortality Biographies
Poetry **Psychology** Witchcraft
Electronics Chemistry History **Law**
Accounting **Philosophy** Anthropology
Alchemy Drama Quantum Mechanics
Atheism Sexual Health **Ancient History**
Entrepreneurship Languages Sport
Paleontology Needlework Islam
Metaphysics Investment Archaeology
Parenting Statistics Criminology
Motivational

CONTRIBUTIONS TO INTERNATIONAL LAW
AND DIPLOMACY
Edited by L. OPPENHEIM, M.A., LL.D.
Late Membre de l'Institut de Droit International,
Whewell Professor of International Law in the University of Cambridge,
Honorary Member of the Royal Academy of Jurisprudence at Madrid,
Corresponding Member of the American Institute of International Law

A GUIDE TO
DIPLOMATIC PRACTICE

A GUIDE

TO

DIPLOMATIC PRACTICE

BY THE

RT. HON. SIR ERNEST SATOW

G.C.M.G., LL.D., D.C.L.

FORMERLY ENVOY EXTRAORDINARY AND MINISTER PLENIPOTENTIARY
ASSOCIÉ DE L'INSTITUT DE DROIT INTERNATIONAL

VOL. II

SECOND AND REVISED EDITION

LONGMANS, GREEN AND CO.
39 PATERNOSTER ROW, LONDON, E.C. 4
NEW YORK, TORONTO,
BOMBAY, CALCUTTA AND MADRAS
1922

Made in Great Britain.

CONTENTS

BOOK III

INTERNATIONAL MEETINGS AND TRANSACTIONS

CHAPTER XXV

CONGRESSES

CHAPTER XXVI

CONFERENCES

CHAPTER XXVII

TREATIES AND OTHER INTERNATIONAL COMPACTS

TREATY, CONVENTION, ADDITIONAL ARTICLES, ACTE FINAL

CHAPTER XXVIII

TREATIES AND OTHER INTERNATIONAL COMPACTS (*contd.*)

DECLARATION, AGREEMENT, ARRANGEMENT

CHAPTER XXIX

TREATIES AND OTHER INTERNATIONAL COMPACTS (*contd.*)

PROTOCOL, PROCÈS-VERBAL, EXCHANGE OF NOTES, RÉVERSALES

CHAPTER XXX

TREATIES AND OTHER INTERNATIONAL COMPACTS (*contd.*)

COMPROMIS D'ARBITRAGE, MODUS VIVENDI

CONTENTS

CHAPTER XXXI

TREATIES AND OTHER INTERNATIONAL COMPACTS (*contd.*)

RATIFICATION, ADHESION AND ACCESSION

CHAPTER XXXII

GOOD OFFICES (BONS OFFICES)

CHAPTER XXXIII

MEDIATION

CHAPTER XXXIV

APPENDIX I

APPENDIX II

APPENDIX III

ERRATA

VOL. II

P. 47, note.—50 should be 52.

P. 161.—Karnebeck should be Karnebeek.

P. 291, l. 5.—Prorogation should be Prolongation.

P. 294, l. 19.—Affair should be affari.

P. 388, l. 5.—1919 should be 1819.

A GUIDE TO DIPLOMATIC PRACTICE

BOOK III.

INTERNATIONAL MEETINGS AND TRANSACTIONS

CHAPTER XXV

CONGRESSES

§ 439. From the point of view of International Law there is no essential difference between Congresses and Conferences. Both are meetings of plenipotentiaries for the discussion and settlement of international affairs. The presence sometimes of sovereigns at the place where they have been carried on does not alter their character. Analysis of the questions dealt with at one or other of such assemblies as were of greater historical importance may assist in determining on what occasions one or the

B

other term should be employed. Both have included meetings, first, for the determination of political questions; second, for treating of matters of a social-economic character.

Congresses have usually been convoked for the negotiation of a peace between belligerent Powers and the redistribution of territory which in most cases is one of the conditions of peace. At a Congress, as a rule, more than two Powers have been represented, and for this reason the inclusion of the Peace of the Pyrenees (§ 443) and the Peace of Amiens (§ 458) seems to be incorrect. Probably Troppau, Laybach and Verona (§§ 463-5) ought also to be excluded from the list. Ordinarily Congresses have been held at a neutral spot, or at some place expressly neutralized for the purpose of the meeting. In earlier times there were often mediators, who presided over the discussions, whether carried on orally or in writing. Before the dissolution of the Holy Roman Empire, in 1806, the principal representative of the Emperor discharged the functions of president. In the nineteenth century, Congresses, properly so-called, were mostly held at the capital of one of the Powers concerned, and then the Chancellor or Minister for Foreign Affairs presided. It will be found that on these occasions, besides the specially deputed plenipotentiaries, the local diplomatic representatives of the respective Powers were also appointed.

We relegate to a footnote the sarcastic description of a Congress by Rousseau.[1]

A semi-official article published in 1814, during the earlier days of the Congress of Vienna, which was

---

[1] " Il se forme de temps en temps parmi nous des espèces de diètes générales sous le nom de congrès, où l'on se rend solennellement de tous les Etats de l'Europe pour s'en retourner de même ; où l'on s'assemble pour ne rien dire ; où toutes les affaires publiques se traitent en particulier ; où l'on délibère en commun si la table sera ronde ou carrée, si la salle aura plus ou moins de portes, si un tel plénipotentiaire aura le visage ou le dos tourné vers la fenêtre, si tel autre fera deux pouces de chemin de plus ou de moins dans une visite, et sur mille questions de pareille importance, inutilement agitées depuis trois siècles, et très-dignes assurément d'occuper les politiques du nôtre."

written by Metternich,[1] contains the following remarks—

" Il ne faut pas de grandes lumières en politique pour s'apercevoir que ce Congrès ne pouvait se modeler sur aucun de ceux qui l'ont précédé. Les réunions antérieures qui ont porté le nom de Congrès, avaient pour objet, de vider un procès pour quelque sujet déterminé entre deux ou plusieurs puissances belligérantes ou prêtes à se faire la guerre, et dont l'issue devait être un traité de paix. Cette fois-ci, la paix est faite à l'avance, et les parties se réunissent à titre d'amis qui, quoique n'ayant pas tous le même intérêt, veulent travailler de concert à compléter et affermir le Traité existant, et les objets de la négociation sont une suite multipliée de questions en partie préparées par les décisions antérieures, en partie entièrement indécises. Les puissances qui ont conclu la paix de Paris, n'étant, certainement, en droit de déterminer le sens qu'il fallait attacher au mot de Congrès, pris dans une acceptation toute nouvelle, et, par conséquent, de prescrire la forme qui paraissait la plus convenable pour atteindre le but qu'elles se proposaient, usèrent de ce droit d'une manière également avantageuse à toutes les parties intéressées, et, par conséquent, au bien-être de l'empire [2] entier, en engageant les plénipotentiaires réunis à Vienne, à traiter les arrangements qu'ils ont à faire, par la voie la plus prompte et la plus efficace, suivant la voie confidentielle."[3]

As models of the procedure which should be followed on these occasions, the Congress of Berlin of 1878, and the Conference of Berlin of 1884–5, occupy the first place.

§ 440. The following is a list of the more important Congresses, from the middle of the seventeenth century onwards.

1. Münster and Osnabrück, which resulted in the Peace of Westphalia, in 1648.
2. Pyrenees, 1659.
3. Oliva, 1660.
4. Aix-la-Chapelle, 1668.

[1] See Oesterreichs Theilnahme an den Befreiungskriegen 463.
[2] The original German has Europa.
[3] d'Angeberg, 362.

5. Nijmegen, 1676–9.
6. Frankfort, 1681.
7. Rijswijk, 1697.
8. Carlowitz, 1699.
9. Utrecht, 1712–13.
10. Cambray, 1720–5.
11. Soissons, 1728–9.
12. Aix-la-Chapelle, 1748 (and Breda)
13. Fokchany, 1772.
14. Bukharest, 1773.
15. Teschen, 1779.
16. Rastadt, 1797.
17. Amiens, 1801–2.
18. Prague, 1813.
19. Châtillon, 1814.
20. Vienna, 1814–15.
21. Aix-la-Chapelle, 1818.
22. Troppau, 1820.
23. Laybach, 1821.
24. Verona, 1822.
25. Panama, 1826.[1]
26. Lima, 1847–8.[2]
27. Paris, 1856.
28. Berlin, 1878.[3]

A short account of these Congresses, with the exception of Nos. 25 and 26, follows. For those two, see Pradier-Fodéré, *Cours de Droit Diplomatique*, ii. 323, 326. The negotiations at Hubertusburg for treaties of peace between Frederick the Great, on the one side, and Maria-Theresa and the Elector of Saxony on the other, which ended the Seven Years War, are sometimes spoken of as having the character of a Congress (Garden, *Hist. générale des Traités*, iv. 195 ; Schäfer, *Geschichte*

[1] See W. F. Johnson, *America's Foreign Relations*, i. 358.
[2] *ibid.*, ii, 205.
[3] Cf. Lists given by Calvo, iii. 409 ; Holtzendorf, iii. 680 ; and de Martens-Geffcken, i. 179 *n*.

des Sieben-jährigen Krieges, iii. 669 ; Carlyle, *Hist. of Frederick II*, 1st edit., vi. 329. For the general subject see Holtzendorf, *Handbuch des Völkerrechts*, 1887, iii. 679 ; Nys, *Le Droit International*, iii. 7 ; Oppenheim, *International Law*, 2nd edit., i. 533 ; Calvo, *Le Droit International*, 4ème édit., iii. 405 ; de Martens-Geffcken, 5ème édit., 178 ; Pradier-Fodéré, *Cours de Droit Diplomatique*, ii. 303).

§ 441. *Congress of Münster and Osnabrück.*

The Congress of Münster and Osnabrück, which resulted in the Peace of Westphalia, signed October 14/24, 1648, was held in pursuance of a preliminary treaty concluded at Hamburg, December 25, 1641, n.s., between envoys of the Emperor, the Queen of Sweden and the King of France, under the mediation of the King of Denmark. But for the war with Sweden that broke out in January, 1644, he would probably have mediated at Osnabrück also. The motive of the arrangement for carrying on the negotiations simultaneously at two separate places was mainly the avoidance of disputes respecting precedence between France and Sweden,[1] and of contact between the Swedish plenipotentiaries and the Papal *Nuncio*, Fabio Chigi, who was appointed one of the mediators. The other mediating Power was Venice, represented by Luigi Contarini. As the distance between the two cities is but thirty miles, no very great difficulty was to be anticipated in the communications between the two sets of negotiators.

The Congress was to have opened March 25, 1642, but as the ratifications of the preliminary treaty were not exchanged until twelve months later, it was agreed to defer the commencement of the proceedings to July 1/11, 1643, partly because all the belligerents hoped to secure military successes, and because of difficulties raised by the Emperor. (Koch and Schoell, i. 761). But the

[1] It was arranged that the plenipotentiaries of France were to have precedence at Munster and to yield it to those of Sweden at Osnabrück (Vast, i. 2).

French plenipotentiaries, who were the latest to arrive, did not make their appearance until March and April 1644, and more than eighteen months elapsed before it was found possible to set to work. The official opening took place December 4, 1644, by the delivery of the proposals of the Emperor, the King of France, and the King of Spain.[1] Apart from a dispute at the outset respecting the admission of the members of the Empire to the negotiations, much delay was caused by wrangling over questions of precedence. Disputes arose about titles and aboutm atter sof etiquette, such as who was entitled to receive the first visit.

Monsieur *Davaux* et Monsieur *Servien* [2] étant Ambassadeurs Plenipotentiaires de France pour la paix à Munster, les Deputez des Villes Anseatiques leur firent demander audiance à l'Hostel de Monsieur *Davaux* premier Ambassadeur où ils furent reçûs en 1645. & on leur fit dire qu'aprés cette audiance ils pourroient voir le même jour ou le lendemain Monsieur *Servien* chez luy, Monsieur *Servien* se trouva à cette premiere audiance, ils addresserent leurs complimens à tous les deux, and ils crurent avoir satisfoit à ce qu'ils devoient aux Ambassadeurs de France, & allerent ensuite rendre visite aux Ambassadeurs d'Espagne qui les reçurent de la même maniere, le lendemain ils demanderent audiance à Monsieur *Servien* en particulier, il la leur assigna & les fit recevoir par ses domestiques qui les conduisirent dans une chambre, où aprés avoir attendu long-temps seuls, on leur vint dire que Monsieur *Servien* ne les pouvoit voir parce qu'il avoit appris qu'ils avoient manqué à ce qu'ils lui devoient en visitant les Ambassadeurs d'Espagne ensuite de la visite qu'ils avoient renduë à *Monsieur Davaux* avant que de venir chez luy qui avoit la même qualité que *Monsieur Davaux,* qu'ils avoient manqué en cela à ce qu'ils devoient au Roy son Maitre & qu'il ne doutoit pas qu'ils en fussent désavouëz par leurs superieurs.

" Ces Deputez voulurent se justifier en disant qu'ils n'avoient qu'une seule lettre pour les deux Ambassadeurs de France & qu'ils avoient satisfait à leur commission en la rendant à tous les deux & les visitant avant les Ambassadeurs d'Espagne, que *Monsieur Davaux* leur avoit répondu pour l'un et pour

[1] A Waddington, *La Républ. des Prov. Unies* ii. 80.
[2] Callières, 188. The spelling and punctuation of the original are exactly reproduced in this extract.

l'autre & que cette seconde visite n'étoit qu'une civilité qu'ils rendoient à la personne de *Monsieur Servien,* mais ils ne furent pas écoutez & *Monsieur Servien* étant depuis allé à *Osnabruk* d'autres Députez des mêmes Villes reparerent la faute de leurs Collegues en rendant à *Monsieur Servien* ce qui lui estoit dû."

It was justly alleged that the French Ambassadors principally made difficulties about ceremonial. The envoys of Princes claimed to be addressed as " Excellency," like those of the Electors. Next, when the full-powers of most of the delegates had been delivered to the two mediators, a lengthy discussion followed about their form and contents. It took more than fifteen months from the date previously fixed for the opening of the Congress, before all these points were disposed of, and even then the amended full-powers from the different courts had not all arrived. It was consequently decided to begin the principal negotiations on November 20, 1644, without waiting for the documents, but still no progress was made. On February 16, 1645, the amended full-powers were at last delivered to the mediators, and on April 10 the formal opening of the Congress took place. On June 11, the proposals of the French and Swedes were presented at Münster and Osnabrück respectively. The negotiations continued to drag on slowly, because the French negotiators raised one difficulty after another, and many of the full-powers, especially those of the Emperor's representatives, were found to be insufficient. The arrival of the Imperial First Delegate, Count Trautmannsdorf, in December 1645, put an end to all this dilatoriness. He stimulated the action of the Congress so vigorously that it continued from that time without a break, even after his recall, up to the end of the negotiations, as the Emperor and the Duke of Bavaria, who had borne the whole burden of the war for the past three years, were now longing for a speedy peace.

Negotiators were sent to Münster by the Emperor

Ferdinand III, Louis XIV, King of France, and other foreign Powers, including Spain, Portugal, Holland, Savoy, Florence, Mantua (these three allies of France against Spain) and the Swiss Confederation ; to Osnabrück by the Emperor, Queen Christina of Sweden and the members of the Empire. On the side of the Emperor were ranged the Catholic members, the Protestant members on that of Sweden. Spain was found among the Allies of the Emperor, Portugal, which had thrown over the yoke of Spain in 1640, and the Catalonian insurgents were *protégés* of France. The States-General sent their representatives to Münster. The only European sovereigns not represented at either gathering were the Kings of England, Poland and Denmark, and the Grand-Duke of Muscovy. Nevertheless, these three Kings and the Grand-Duke of Muscovy were included in the treaties,[1] also the Duke of Lorraine, the King of Spain, the Electors and Princes, including the Duke of Savoy and other states, the Free and Immediate nobles of the Holy Roman Empire, the Hanse Towns, the Princes and Republics of Italy, the Confederated Provinces (Ordines Foederati Belgii), Switzerland, Rhitia (Grisons), and the Prince of Transylvania. The Pope and the Republic of Venice took part only as mediating Powers. At Münster no joint sittings of the plenipotentiaries were held, but each party delivered Notes or memoranda to the Mediators and the Mediators transmitted them to the other side. As there were no Mediators at Osnabrück, the first Swedish proposal, framed in Latin, was solemnly carried to the Emperor's Ambassador by a secretary and two mounted men-at-arms of the Swedish embassy ; copies were also delivered to each electoral representative and to the representative of the Bishop of Madgeburg, others being sent to the colleges of Princes and Imperial Free Cities. The French proposals had to be translated into Latin, which language was often used in the oral discussions.

---

[1] Instrumentum Pacis Caesareo-Suecicum, Art. xvii. § 10.

Direct negotiations proceeded only between the Ambassadors of the Emperor, the King of France and the Queen of Sweden, but sometimes those of other Protestant states were called in. The Catholics and Protestants consulted together separately, but when necessary the representatives of the two religions communicated their ideas to each other in writing, and sometimes general meetings of the members of the Empire were held, who either combined in a joint statement of opinion or stated their respective views separately in the same document. The Ambassadors of the Emperor negotiated solely with those of foreign countries, but the Envoys of the Protestant members of the Empire were sometimes summoned to confer with the Swedish embassy.

The *Nuncio's* efforts at mediation were confined to reconciling the views of the Catholic Powers, *i.e.* the Emperor, the Kings of France and Spain, the Dukes of Savoy, Lorraine, Bavaria and Neuburg, and certain lesser potentates. Those of Contarini comprehended the interests of Holland, Sweden and the Protestant German States. But as the Swedish plenipotentiaries were at Osnabrück, it was found on the whole more convenient that they should treat directly with the Imperial representatives there, and in writing, as was the usual practice in Germany. At Münster, the *Nuncio* appears to have arrogated to himself the sole right of receiving the documents exchanged between the parties, which he showed to his Venetian colleague when he thought it necessary

The Treaty of Osnabrück, concluded by the Emperor and his allies on the one part with the Queen of Sweden and her allies on the other, as also by the Emperor with the Estates of the Empire, and by the Catholic party with the Evangelical Protestants, was signed August 8, 1648. By Article VI, the Emperor recognized the independence of the city of Basel and the other Swiss Cantons. The Treaty of Múnster negotiated by the Emperor and the Germanic Body with the King of

France was not signed till September 17. § 85 provides for " Libertas Commerciis et Navigationi Rheni," which was renewed and extended at the Congress of Vienna in 1815. By the previous agreement it had been settled that the two treaties were to be regarded as a whole, and for this reason the general provisions were inserted in both, so that the two documents are to a great extent identical. The sovereigns named in the preambles naturally differ, while certain articles inserted in the one treaty are absent from the other. The formal re-signature of both took place October 14/24, 1648, at Münster.

The language often used by historians would lead to the supposition that the peace of January 30, 1648, by which Spain recognized the independence of the United Provinces, formed part of the Peace of Westphalia, but this is not so. It was directly negotiated between the Spanish and Netherlands plenipotentiaries, the United Provinces having thrown over their ally the King of France in order to conclude an entirely separate treaty on their own account. The Dutch plenipotentiaries seem to have quitted Münster in August 1648. By Article 53, the Emperor and the Empire were to ratify the treaty. The former did, the latter never. At the exchange of the signed copies and ratifications on May 15, 1648, both parties took an oath to observe the treaty faithfully, in accordance with the ancient custom. There were four copies, two in Spanish and two in Dutch.

§ 442. It is worth while to reproduce here a passage common to both preambles which illustrates the origin of the term " Congress."

" Tandem Divina bonitate factum esse ut . . . utrinque de Pace universali suscepta sit cogitatio, in eumque finem ex mutua partium conventione Hamburgi die vigesimo quinto stylo novo. . . . Decembris Anno Domini millesimo sexcentesimo quadragesimo primo inita, constituta sit dies undecima stylo novo. . . . Mensis Julii, Anno Domini Millesimo sexcentesimo quadragesimo tertio, *Congressui* Plenipotentiari-

orum Monasterii et Osnabrugis Westphalorum instituendo " ;
or, in English, " At length by Divine goodness it came to
pass that on both sides the thought of an universal peace was
adopted, and to that end by a mutual agreement of the parties
entered into at Hamburg on December 25, n.s. A.D. 1641. . . .
for holding a *meeting* of Plenipotentiaries at Münster and
Osnabrück in Westphalia on July 11, n.s., A.D. 1643."

From the word in italics in the Latin and rendered
in English by " meeting," we get the word congress, at
first a term of general application, afterwards restricted
to meetings of plenipotentiaries deputed *ad hoc*, for the
purpose of negotiating a treaty, and at the present day
held to be still further restricted to meetings of superior
importance, as distinguished from mere " conferences,"
which are often carried on by diplomatists already
possessing the character of resident ambassadors.

As will be seen from the treaties concluded in 1648,
the result of the Congress of Westphalia was two-fold :
(1) to put an end to the war which since 1618 up to the
very last moment had devastated Germany, and (2) to
adjust the respective possessions of the Powers concerned.

Conferences respecting the mutual release of prisoners
and other matters connected with the execution of the
treaty were begun in September 1649 at Nüremberg and
completed in 1650.   This gathering, which was attended
by a delegation of thirteen states nominated by the
Diet of the Empire, and by the Prince of Deux-Ponts,
commander-in-chief of the French and allied forces, is
sometimes classed as a congress.

Callières, who possessed unrivalled means of knowing
how negotiations were carried on by the French Court,
says[1]—

" La paix de Munster l'une des plus difficiles & des plus
universelles qui ait été traitée n'a pas été le seul ouvrage de
tant d'Ambassadeurs qui y ont travaillé, un confident du Duc
Maximilien de Baviere envoyé secrètement à Paris en regla les
principales conditions avec le Cardinal Mazarin ; le Duc de

---

[1] *La manière de négocier*, etc., 373.

Bavière étoit alors étroitement lié avec l'Empereur ; cependant cet habile Prince connût qu'il étoit de l'intérest de sa Maison de ne la pas laisser livrer à la discretion de la Maison d'Autriche, & qu'il avoit besoin de l'amitié & de la protection de la France, pour conserver à ses successeurs la dignité Electorale et le haut Palatinat qu'il avoit conquis durant la guerre ; & lorsqu'il fut convaincu de cet intérest, il entraîna l'Empereur & tout l'Empire, & les détermina à conclure la paix avec la France, la Suede et leurs Alliez, suivant le projet qui en fut fait à Paris.

The attempts made at Münster to establish peace between France and Spain by direct negotiation, half-heartedly aided by Dutch endeavours to mediate, ended in failure. The war had broken out in May, 1635, and was carried on chiefly in the Milanais and in the Spanish Netherlands. It continued until the peace of the Pyrenees in 1659, an account of which is given in the next section.

Authorities : Garden, *Histoire des Traités de Paix*, i. cxxxvi ; i. 90, 93, 94 ; *Die Urkunden der Friedenschlüsse zu Osnabrück und Münster nach authentischen Quellen*. Zürich, 1848, p. 98 ; Vast, *Les Grands Traités du Règne de Louis XIV*, i. 1–64 ; Koch and Schoell, *Histoire Abrégée des Traités de Paix*, of which a convenient edition in 4 octavo vols. was published at Brussels, 1837–8. A. Waddington, *La Rép ubl. des Prov.-Unies*, etc., *Modern Europe*, by T. H. Dyer, vol. iii. 1877. Blok, P. J., *Geschiedenis van het Nederlandsche Volk*, vol. ii. 2nd edit. Leiden, 1913.

§ 443. *Congress of the Pyrenees* (so-called), 1659.

It is not quite clear why the conferences held in 1659 between Cardinal Mazarin and Don Luis de Haro, on the part of France and Spain respectively, have been classed as a Congress. The negotiations had been preceded by preliminaries agreed upon in Paris by Antonio Pimentel for Spain and Hugues de Lionne for France, and signed on June 4. Spain, in 1658, had asked for a suspension of hostilities, which Mazarin had at first refused, but finally granted on May 8, 1659. England, one of the allies of France, agreed to the suspension of arms, but was not represented at either set of negotiations, though her envoy, Lockhart, was in the neighbourhood of the Pyrenees during Mazarin's stay there. Mazarin arrived at Bayonne on July 24. Don Luis was expected at San Sebastian four days earlier. Some time was spent over questions of etiquette. Finally, it was agreed to hold the conferences on a tiny island, the Isle des Faisans, 120 paces long by 40 wide, in the river Bidassoa. Here were constructed three temporary buildings, one for each plenipotentiary, and a third at the end of the island, with two doors, one towards Spain, the other towards France, and the island was joined to the banks of the river by bridges of boats. Mazarin stayed at St. Jean de Luz, Don Luis at Hendaye. These arrangements were completed by August 13, when the first meeting took place. In all there were twenty-five of these, including the last but one of November 7, when the treaty was signed. Mazarin and Don Luis fought out the conditions of peace, in conferences *tête-à-tête*, as well as those of the marriage contract between Louis XIV and the Infanta Marie-Thérèse. To Lionne and Pedro Coloma, a Spanish Secretary of State, was entrusted the task of drafting the two instruments. If there were protocols or procès-verbaux of the discussions, they are not easily accessible, but the present writer has found no mention of such papers.[1] Of the treaty there were two texts, French and Spanish ; of the marriage contract only one, in Spanish ; all three were signed and sealed by the two plenipotentiaries. The French copy of the former is signed " le Card. Mazarin, D. Luis Mendez de Haro." The ratification of the King of France was signed November 24, that of the King of Spain December 10. When they were exchanged, the originals of the prelimi-

---

[1] Much information concerning the course of the negotiations is to be found in " *Lettres du Cardinal Mazarin, où l'on voit le Secret de la Négociation de la Paix des Pyrénées, etc., nouv. édit.* Amsterdam, 1745.

naries of June 4 were burnt, at the request of Spain.

The *traité patent* consists of 124 articles. Arts. 1–4 relate to the re-establishment and maintenance of peace ; Arts. 5–27 contain commercial stipulations of which Art 12 defines contraband of war, Art. 13 enumerates articles which shall not be contraband, except when carried to Portugal [regarded as in a state of rebellion against Spain] or to towns or places besieged, blockaded or invested ; and Art. 19 adopts the principle " free ship, free goods," and its converse " enemy ship, enemy goods " as between the parties. Art. 24 grants to the subjects of the respective high contracting parties six months' grace in case of war for withdrawing their property, and exempts them from seizure of their property or persons during that period. Arts. 28–32 stipulate the re-establishment of the respective subjects in the property, honours, dignities and benefices enjoyed by them before the war [which had been proceeding since 1635]. Art. 33 mentions the marriage, for which a separate agreement was to be entered into. Arts. 34–43 enumerate the territories which the King of France is to retain ; Arts. 44–48 those which he is to restore to the King of Spain ; Arts. 49–54 lay down the conditions of the delivery of the places specified in Arts. 34–43. Arts. 55–59 are concerned with the insurgent Catalans, and Art. 60 prepares the way for the abandonment by France of her ally, Portugal. By Art. 61 the King of Spain renounces any rights he might have to the territories ceded to the King of France by the Treaty of Westphalia. Arts. 62–78 concern the Duke of Lorraine, Arts. 79–87 the Prince of Condé. Art. 88 provides for the delivery of Juliers to the Duke of Neuburg. Arts. 89 and 90 confirm the reservation of rights made by Arts. 21 and 22 of the Treaty of Vervins, while Arts. 91–100 refer to Italian princes. Arts. 101 to 123 contain miscellaneous provisions ; Art. 124 the exchange of ratifications and the oaths to be taken on that occasion by the two sovereigns, each in the presence of persons to be deputed by the other party, for the faithful execution of the treaty.

There were also eight secret articles, of which the only ones necessary to mention are Art. 1, by which the King of France undertakes that if the existing differences between Spain and England are not arranged, he will give to the latter no sort of assistance whatever, and Art. 3. The latter, after referring to Art. 60 of the *traité patent* which gives France three months in which she may endeavour to bring about between Spain and Portugal such a state of affairs as may completely satisfy His Catholic Majesty, agrees that if the three months elapse without this result being attained, His Most Christian Majesty will give up the relations he has maintained with Portugal and persons of that country, and will afford them no assistance, either directly or indirectly, and will prevent the export thither of provisions or munitions.

It is thus evident that the parties to the Peace of the Pyrenees were only two in number, and that the interests of two of the belligerent allies of France were practically ignored.

In the course of conversations between Pimentel and Mazarin at Lyon, in December 1658, the latter had hinted that if the desired marriage of the King of France with the Infanta did not take place, peace might be negotiated at a Congress or in any other manner, but in accordance with the principles of the Peace of Westphalia. This, however, is not sufficient to convert the negotiations *à deux* into a Congress, nor does the fact that peace was signed elsewhere than in the capital of one of the parties justify that term being applied to the meeting of Mazarin and Don Luis at the common frontier.

Authorities: Valfrey, *Hugues de Lionne, ses ambassades,* etc. Paris, 1881 ; Vast, *Les grands traités du règne de Louis XIV.* Paris, 1893 ; Koch and Schoell.

§ 444. *Congress of Oliva,* 1660.

The success of the Congress of Westphalia, in 1648, brought about a general opinion that such meetings of plenipotentiaries of belligerents, engaged in a war involving more than two Powers, afforded the best means of arriving at a solution of the questions over which they had fought. Sweden under the impetuous and warlike Charles X, Brandenburg ruled by the Elector Frederick William (who was also Duke of East Prussia, a Polish fief), Jean Casimir King of Poland, Frederick III of Denmark, and the States-General had all taken a hand in the Northern War which broke out in 1655. In May 1659, France, England and Holland agreed together on a course of action dependent on naval co-operation on the part of England, directed towards the reconciliation of Sweden and Denmark. After the abdication of Richard Cromwell the English fleet was withdrawn, but the conclusion of the Peace of the Pyrenees set Mazarin's hands free. Frederick William was especially active in promoting the conclusion of peace by means of a Congress. Much preliminary discussion respecting a suitable meeting-place was followed by the Swedish acceptance of the monastery of Oliva, near the coast, a few miles north of Dantzig, where the members assembled early in January 1660. France, as the mediating Power, was represented by de Lumbres, formerly Envoy to Brandenburg and after 1656 at Warsaw ; Sweden by de la Gardie (general and minister), Benoit Oxenstierna, Schlippenbach and Güldenclau (the last three were diplomatists) ; Poland by the grand Chancellor Prazmowski, Jean Lesczinski, *voiévode* of Posen, and Christopher Paç, Grand Chancellor of Lithuania ; the Emperor by Kolowrat, a diplomatist, and Lisola, Ambassador at Berlin ; the Elector of Brandenburg by Hoverbeck, *geheimrath* and diplomatist, Somnitz agent at Copenhagen, and Albert d'Ostau, a magistrate often employed on diplomatic missions. Denmark, bent on a separate negotiation with Sweden (which was terminated by the Peace of Copenhagen, signed June 6, 1660), held aloof, but sent Parsbierg, a diplomatist, to be present *en observation*. From Holland came Honart, a diplomatist, and from Courland the Chancellor Fölkesahm. Questions of etiquette and procedure occupied a large portion of attention, as was natural to such a comparatively novel method of negotiating peace; other points requiring preliminary settlement were, whether negotiation should be carried on by means of written *pro-memoriâ* or *vivâ voce*; whether certain Powers should be admitted or not; the wording of safe-conducts and full-powers; the use of the distinction " Excellency," and the recognition of the titles assumed by certain sovereigns.[1] Towards the end of January the proceedings were opened by the delivery of written proposals by the different Powers, and nearly a month was spent in exchanging Notes and counter-Notes. At last the mediator succeeded in bringing about the adoption of *vivâ voce* conferences, but these lasted several weeks more. Progress was facilitated by the death of Charles X on February 22, and the labours of the Congress were brought to an end early in May by the conclusion of treaties between Poland, Sweden, the Emperor and Brandenburg.

The result of the Congress was the conclusion of peace between the Northern Powers, and a redistribution of territory in favour of Sweden and Brandenburg.

Authorities: A. Waddington, *Le Grand Electeur Frédéric Guillaume de Brandenbourg*, tome I. Paris, 1905 ; Koch and Schoell, Brussels edit., iv. 105. The text of the treaty in Dumont, vi, part 2, 303 *et seq.*

§ 445. *Congress of Aix-la-Chapelle, 1668.*

The marriage contract of Louis XIV with the Infanta provided that, on condition of the payment of a dowry

[1] Such as " King of Sweden," by Jean Casimir, and " King of the Vandals," by Charles X.

of 500,000 crowns, she renounced all her rights to the Spanish succession. The money was not paid. The French Ambassador at Madrid, Archbishop of Embrun, was instructed in the autumn of 1661 to claim by way of "advance of the heritage for the Queen's dowry (*à titre d'avancement d'hoirie pour la dot de la reine*) the annexation of the Spanish Netherlands, but he was to announce the King's willingness to be contented with the immediate cession of Franche-Comté, Luxemburg, Hainault and Cambrésis, with Aire and St. Omer. He also put forward a claim on behalf of the Queen, founded on an alleged law of inheritance in some provinces of the Netherlands, by which the immovable property of parents descended to the children of a first marriage exclusively. As soon as the surviving parent married again, the parent from that moment retained only a life-interest. The Queen was the sole surviving offspring of Philip IV's first marriage. Her father having died in 1665, Louis XIV put forth a manifesto in 1667, stating the alleged rights of the Queen to various portions of the Spanish monarchy, and specifically Brabant, Limburg, Malines, Antwerp, Upper Gueldres, Namur, Hainault, Artois and Cambrésis. On March 24, 1667, French troops were marched into the Netherlands, without a declaration of war. Holland took the alarm and, in the hope of avoiding hostilities, signed a treaty at the Hague with England for the purpose of compelling the King of Spain to accept the terms offered by France, to which the King of Sweden afterwards acceded.[1] The allies prepared to support their policy by an armed mediation, and Louis XIV, unwilling to face the coalition, offered to negotiate. A treaty was concluded at Saint-Germain-en-Laye, on April 15 (O.S.), with van Beuningen and Trevor, delegates of Holland and England, by which the two latter Powers guaranteed to France the cessions of territory agreed to on behalf of Spain

---

[1] January 23, 1668. Jenkinson, i. 188. Garden, *Hist. gén.* ii. 11., Dumont vii. pt. ii, 92 gives the instrument of accession.

by the Governor of the Spanish Netherlands. A draft treaty between France and Spain was drawn up at the same time to be sent to Aix-la-Chapelle and signed there by the plenipotentiaries of the Powers, without modification (*ne varietur*). After some resistance on the part of both the Spaniards and the Dutch, this draft was converted into a treaty by its signature on May 2, 1668.

The preamble states that the high contracting parties had agreed to choose the imperial town of Aix-la-Chapelle to treat of peace, by the intervention (*entremise*) of His Holiness, as well as of the ministers of several other Kings, Potentates, Electors and Princes of the Holy Empire. Article III stipulates that the King of France shall retain Charleroy, Binch, Athe, Douay with the Fort of Scarpe, Tournay, Oudenarde, Lille, Armentières, Courtray, Bergue and Furnes. Article V stipulates for the restoration of Franche-Comté to the King of Spain.

The copy intended for France was signed by Charles Colbert de Croissy the French plenipotentiary, by Sir William Temple and Beverningk as mediators for England and Holland, and countersigned by the plenipotentiaries of the Pope, of the Electors of Cologne and Mayence, and of the Bishop of Münster. It was signed also on behalf of Spain, but Bergeyck, to whom the Governor of the Netherlands had delegated his powers as plenipotentiary, made difficulties about the insertion of his full powers. It was ratified by the Queen-Regent of Spain on May 16.

Obviously the meeting of plenipotentiaries at Aix-la-Chapelle to append their signatures to a treaty of which the draft had been prepared elsewhere, without further discussion or modification, can only be styled a Congress by a stretch of meaning of the term.

Result : Peace between France and Spain, and acquisition of territory by France.

Authorities : Vast, *Les grands traités du regne de Louis XIV*, ii : Koch and Schoell, Brussels edit., i. 137. Lefèvre-Pontalis, Jean de Witt, i. chap. vii.

§ 446. *Congress of Nijmegen*, 1676–9.

The conclusion, in January 1668, by Holland, of an alliance with England, to which Sweden acceded (see preceding § 445), excited the resentment of Louis XIV. Skilful diplomacy enabled him to isolate Holland (Koch and Schoell, i. 141) and declarations of war having been put forth by England and France in April 1672, the United Provinces were invaded in May. In December the governor of the Spanish Netherlands sent succours to Prince William of Orange, and the invasion of Belgium followed in May 1673. The Elector of Brandenburg had taken up arms on the side of the Dutch, but was compelled to make peace at Vossem, June 6 (O.S.), 1673. The Emperor, the Duke of Lorraine and the King of Spain successively joined the coalition against France, September 22, 1672, July 1 and August 30, 1673. Sweden had already offered her mediation. Negotiations were opened at Cologne, but were unsuccessful. The King of Sweden ranged himself on the side of France in December 1674, but England, in February of the same year, had signed peace with Holland, by the treaty of Westminster, under the mediation of Spain, whose minister signed as plenipotentiary of the States-General. The Duke of Brunswick-Lüneburg and the King of Denmark allied themselves with Holland in June and July respectively, thus completing what is known as the *Grand Alliance of the Hague*, or the Second Coalition. In June, however, Charles II of England offered his mediation, which was accepted by Louis XIV, who proposed Breda as the meeting-place of a congress, for which Nijmegen was ultimately substituted. The Pope and the Republic of Venice also offered their " *bons offices* " as mediators. The French plenipotentiaries, Maréchal d'Estrades, Colbert de Croissy and the Comte d'Avaux, arrived at Nijmegen in June 1676, where they found the English Mediator Jenkins and the Dutch Ambassadors Beverningk and Haren. The town of Nijmegen, with a circle of one league in diameter, was neutralized for the purpose of the negotiations. After long discussions respecting ceremonial and the security of couriers, full-powers were exchanged November 17, 1676. Count Kinski, representing the Emperor, Don Antonio Ronquillo for Spain, and the *nuncio* Bevilacqua (November 1676 and June 1677) also took part in the negotiations. Disputes also arose respecting the empty assumption by the Emperor of the title of Duke of Burgundy, by Charles II of that of King of France, by the Duke of Lorraine of that of Count of Provence. These were terminated by the Congress declaring that titles assumed or omitted by either party should not prejudice the rights of any one. The Elector of Brandenburg sought in vain to be recognized as *Sérénissime* and Duke of Prussia. The ministers of the Electors were admitted as Ambassadors, but it was settled that the French plenipotentiaries should give the post of honour (*la main*) only to the First Ambassadors of Electors. The Dukes of Neuburg, Mecklenburg, Brunswick and Lorraine failed to secure the recognition of their representatives as Ambassadors, but the French plenipotentiaries obtained precedence over all other except the Pope's legate, the representatives of the Emperor and of the King of England ; the title of the latter rested on his position as Mediator. Somnitz, first plenipotentiary of Brandenburg, called by himself on d'Estrades, but refused to visit the other two French plenipotentiaries, and his visit was not returned.

The proceedings began May 3, 1677, by the exchange of written proposals through Jenkins, with whom Sir William Temple had been joined. Charles II of Spain deputed the Marques de los Balbasès and J.-B. Christini in addition to Ronquillo, and Rodick was appointed third Dutch representative. All this time hostilities

were continuing.   At last the Dutch accepted the offers
made to them by France on April 15, 1678, and the
governor of the Spanish Netherlands was also brought
to consent to the terms proposed by the French plenipotentiaries.   In spite of the secret opposition of Temple
and the Prince of Orange, peace between Holland and
France was signed August 10, 1678 ; the signature of the
Spanish treaty followed September 17, after various
difficulties had been smoothed over.   Two copies of the
treaty were prepared, one in French, the other in
Spanish, and laid on a table at which were seated the
two English mediators.   The three French plenipotentiaries entered by one door at the same moment as the
three Spanish ones[1] by the other.   They sat down
simultaneously in exactly similar armchairs, and signed
both copies respectively at the same instant.   The
treaty with the Emperor (in Latin), the Empire and
Sweden was not signed till February 5, 1679.[2]   On
June 29, 1679, a treaty of peace was concluded between
the King of France and the Elector of Brandenburg,
followed by a secret treaty on October 25.

Various disputes arose with respect to the execution
of the treaty with Spain, of which an account is given
by Vast (ii. 43).

Main results : Peace between France and Holland,
and restoration of Maastricht to the latter ; peace
between France and Spain, and a redistribution of the
former's acquisitions in Flanders ; peace between France
and the Emperor, and an exchange of territories.
France retained Franche-Comté, also Valenciennes,
Cambray, St. Omer, Ypres and Maubeuge. (Blok,
Geschied. v. h. Nederland. Volk, iii. 226).

Article XV of the treaty with Holland provides for
six months' grace being accorded to the subjects of the
respective high contracting parties, in case of a rupture,
in the same terms as those of the corresponding article

---

[1] The Conde de la Fuente had been substituted for Ronquillo.
[2] Koch and Schoell, i. 152.

in the Peace of the Pyrenees. In the commercial treaty between the same two Powers of even date Article XV defines absolute contraband, and Article XVI conditional contraband, while Article XXII stipulates for " enemy ship, enemy goods " and " free ship, free goods," with the exception of contraband of war.

Authorities: Vast, *Les grands traités du règne de Louis XIV*, ii. 23 ; Koch and Schoell, Brussels edit., i. 148. Garden, *Hist. gén.*, ii. 110.

§ 447. *Congress of Frankfort,*[1] 1681.

The Peace of Westphalia had transferred the Habsburg rights in Alsace to the King of France, but had left in a state of uncertainty the sovereign rights of France over those portions of territory in Alsace which did not belong to the House of Austria. Various German princes were established, or possessed lands, there. The Peace of Nijmegen, in 1679, left these disputes still unsettled, and in 1681 the Electors of Trier, Maintz and Heidelberg presented a formal complaint to the Diet at Ratisbonne. The Diet having addressed Louis XIV on this subject, he consented in August 1681 to a Conference at Frankfort, to which he deputed Saint-Romain and Harlay as his plenipotentiaries. Delay in the arrival of the Imperial representatives, of whom Stratmann[2] was one, and their pretension to exclude those of the Electors, were the causes of the meeting being postponed till December. Meanwhile, on September 30, French troops occupied Strassburg. The terms offered by the French King on December 14 were coupled with the condition that they should be promptly accepted, and in September 1682, no settlement having been arrived at, he finally instructed his plenipotentiaries to declare that his offer would not remain open beyond November 30. When

[1] De Martens-Geffcken, i. 179, places this among Congresses, also Calvo, iii. 409, probably merely copying his predecessor.
[2] He had been at Nijmegen ; see *Recueil des Instructions*, etc. *Austria*, 120.

this date had expired they handed in a memorial withdrawing the offer, and quitted Frankfort, after intimating that proposals for the maintenance of peace might still be made, up to February 1 following, to Verjus, the French plenipotentiary at Frankfort. Disputes of form and as to the language to be employed in the negotiation took up a whole year. (Koch and Schoell, i. 155).

If this attempt at negotiation is to be included in the list of Congresses, it must be ranged with those that failed.

Authorities : Recueil des Instructions, etc., Autriche, p. 4 ; Cambridge Modern History, v. 48.

§ 448. *Congress of Rijswijk, 1697.*

Already, in 1694, assurances had been received in Paris from Holland that the Dutch desired to abandon the coalition against France, and an informal conference was held at Maastricht between Dykveld on the one side, and Harlay de Bonneuil and Callières [1] on the other. The negotiations were unsuccessful. In March of the following year Callières was authorized to renew them, and he started for Utrecht with a draft treaty embodying the conditions on which Louis XIV was willing to conclude peace. A suspension of arms for six months was proposed, to allow of time for the States-General to bring their allies to accept these terms, which included a secret article recognizing the Prince of Orange as King of England. This time Holland was represented by Jacob Boreel, acting under instructions from Heinsius and Dykveld. The winter passed without the attainment of an agreement. Fresh instructions having reached Callières, he had a meeting, May 1, 1696, with Boreel, who handed to him a series of written proposals, in which a Congress was suggested, and also the appointment of a Mediator or Mediators. Louis XIV, however,

[1] Author of *De la manière de négocier avec les souverains.*

was antagonistic to the idea of a Congress, on the ground
that it would merely prolong the negotiations. He
insisted on peace being signed with Holland alone, as a
preliminary *sine quâ non* to his recognition of William
as King of England. The latter then wrote to the
Emperor Leopold that he thought it was high time to
make peace, and Kaunitz, the Imperial Minister at the
Hague, was informed of the progress already made. The
latter replied that the Emperor would, among other
things, insist on the restoration of Strassburg to the
Empire. In September, Callières still maintained that
he would not meet Kaunitz nor the English Envoy until
after conditions of peace had been arranged with the
Dutch. By the end of the year he appears to have
accepted the idea of a Congress, but simply in the shape
of a formal meeting for the signature of treaties with the
allies modelled on that with Holland. Progress was still
impeded by the Strassburg question, while the Dutch
were endeavouring to obtain a renunciation by Louis
XIV and his son of their claims to the Spanish succession.
It was for them indispensable that Flanders should
continue Spanish, or be conferred on a cadet of Austria
or Spain as an independent sovereignty, with a provision
that it should never be united with either crown.

At last, in February 1697, the mediation of Sweden
was accepted by all the belligerents, and Rijswijk, a
country house of the stadhouder, halfway between
Delft and the Hague, was fixed on as the place of
meeting.

The Congress was opened May 9. Lilienrot, representative of Charles XI of Sweden, acted as Mediator.
Holland was represented by Jacob Boreel,[1] burgomaster
of Amsterdam, Dykveld and van Haren, England by
Lord Pembroke, Viscount Villiers and Sir Joseph Williamson. The Spanish plenipotentiaries were Don Francisco
Bernardo de Quiros and Count Tirimont, those of the

---

[1] He died before the signature of the treaty and was replaced by the
Grand Pensionary Heinsius.

Emperor the Vice-Chancellor Kaunitz, Count Stratmann and Baron Seilern, aulic councillors. The French ambassadors were Harlay de Bonneuil, Verjus de Crécy and Callières. Certain princes of the Empire sent plenipotentiaries, Schmettau and Danckelmann were delegated by the Elector of Brandenburg, and Leopold Duke of Lorraine was also represented ; but these delegates of mere princes had neither officially recognized title nor rank. The allies lodged at the Hague, the French plenipotentiaries at Delft. At Rijswijk one large room was assigned to the allies, another to the French, and the Mediator had an apartment to himself.

The proceedings opened with a speech from the Mediator exhorting the delegates to harmony and union. Kaunitz replied on behalf of the allies, Harlay for France. The full-powers were then produced, and exhibited by the Mediator to the respective parties. He also announced that the assumption or omission of disputed titles of sovereigns should have no effect. It was decided to hold meetings twice a week, on Wednesdays and Saturdays. On Mondays and Thursdays the allies conferred together privately at the Hague. The Mediator kept a protocol of all the proceedings. It was through him that the written demands of the respective parties were transmitted to each other. From time to time there were also private discussions between the various plenipotentiaries. As usual, a dispute arose as to the title of Excellency, claimed by the plenipotentiaries of the Electors and denied to them by those of the Emperor. But no real progress was made towards an agreement on points of real importance, and it looked as if the Congress would end in failure.[1] The delays really arose in connexion with the demand for the recognition of William as King of England, and from the numerous demands of Leopold. The month of June was wasted in discussions which

[1] Macaulay, iv. 788, paints a lively picture of the discussions on matters of etiquette before the real business could be entered upon.

produced no result. Then William[1] intervened to prevent a breakdown, by sending Portland to talk matters over confidentially with Maréchal Boufflers, at his headquarters near Brussels. In the course of five interviews, from July 8 to August 2, they came to an understanding on the principal points of the controversy between the two monarchs. From that moment the negotiations proceeded rapidly, and on September 20 the plenipotentiaries of Holland, England and Spain signed their treaties. That with the Emperor was not concluded till October 30.[2] The war went on, though in a languid fashion during the negotiations. (Blok. *Gesch*, iii. 269).

The following extracts from the correspondence of Matthew Prior.[3] and from his *Journal*, etc., memoirs relating to the Treaty of Rijswijk,[4] are of interest, as depicting the formalities attendant on the signature of an important treaty—

p. 166. " 1697, Sept. 20 [n.s.] Ryswick. Minutes of the treaty (original) as signed by their Excellencies " *and* " the Separate Article also signed by their Excellencies " at the same time. *Latin. Seals and Signatures of the Earl of Pembroke, Lord Villiers and Sir Joseph Williamson. Also: Duplicate* of the treaty (original). *Latin. Seals and signatures of the same persons, and of N. A. Harlay-Bonneuil, Verjus de Créssy, F. de Callières, N. Lillieroot.*

p. 167. Matthew Prior to Sir William Trumbull,[5] 1697, Oct. 1 [n.s.] Hague. . . . " In some discourse I had the honour to hold with you at Whitehall I told you that the French drew up their part of the treaty (*i.e.* that instrument or part which they retain signed by both parties) in French, as the part or instrument which we retain is in Latin : they allege custom for this, and give us for precedent, that the same

[1] See *Notes et documents sur la Paix de Ryswyk*, A. Legrelle, Lille 1894. Macaulay got his account of this secret negotiation from Grimblot, *Letters of William III and Louis XIV*, etc., 2 vols, 1848.

[2] Callières, 375, remarks : " Et la paix de Rysvick a été traitée et resolüe par des negociations secretes, avant que d'être conclüe en Hollande en l'année 1697.

[3] Secretary to the English plenipotentiaries.

[4] Hist. MSS. Com., 1908 ; Calendar of MSS. of the Marq. of Bath, vol. iii.

[5] One of the principal Secretaries of State, appointed in May, 1695.

thing was done at Breda ; [1] they have declared, however, to the Mediator that if it be not found to be as they aver, they will withdraw the instrument already signed, and furnish another in Latin before the ratification."

p. 534. " About ten at night the French sent us another model [of the preamble], which their Excellencies accepted, and Mr. Prior translated as it stands before the Treaty. About eleven the Dutch signed their Treaty [Treaties] of Peace and Commerce ; the Spaniards signed theirs about an hour after ; and about twelve the English went in order to the signing theirs. The place thought fit by the Mediator instead of the great room was a little chamber in the inner part of his own apartment ; the three French Ambassadors sat on one side of an oval table, and the three English did on the other ; the Mediator sat at the end of the table ; the Dutch were present ; the Pensioner and Mons. Dyckvelt sat on the English side, and Mons. Haren on the French side between them and the Mediator. The Earl of Pembroke delivered the Treaty in Latin to Mons. Harlay, who delivered it to my Lord in French. Mons. Harlay read the Latin aloud, my Lord Pembroke collationing it [the French] with the Latin; the same was done with the Secret Article, and they proceeded to the signing, we our part as it was in Latin, and they their part as it was in French, till, the copies being taken fair, both parties might sign the same instrument ; this was done about three in the morning.

" As soon as the Treaty was signed, Mons. Harlay made a compliment of the joy the French Embassy had to acknowledge his Majesty's title in the manner they had done, and added, addressing himself to the English Embassy, that there was all the hope imaginable that the friendship between the Ambassadors themselves would be lasting, since it began on so happy an occasion as that of their signing a peace together. Lord Pembroke answered the compliment, and the Mediator, after having wished both parties joy, read the Dictature by which his Majesty promises that the Queen in France shall have whatever she can have any legal pretension to by the Act of Parliament, or under the Great Seal, the whole of which might amount, it was thought, to 50,000*l* sterling per annum. The French desired that the Dictature might be inserted into the Mediator's protocol, and that they might likewise have a copy of it. Then Mons. de Callières penned, read and delivered to the Mediator a declaration that in case that part of the Treaty of Breda which the French took with

---

[1] In 1667.

them should be found to be in Latin, and not in French, as they allege it was, they would withdraw this, which they had signed in French, and change it for one in Latin before the ratification.

" They parted, the English retaining the part of the Treaty which the French had signed minuted in their own language, and the French retaining the part of the Treaty which the English had signed minuted in Latin ; the like reciprocation was observed as to the Separate Article.

.   .   .   .

".Saturday the 21st [n.s. Sept.]. At Ryswick. The English, Spaniards and Dutch were there with the French and the Mediator in order to the signing of the Treaty in form, of which they had signed the minutes the night before. Whilst the French were busy writing their part of the Treaty fair, Mr. Swinford[1] by my Lord Pembroke's order drew up a *mémoire* by which the French promised to give their part of the Treaty in Latin at the ratification, provided it was so practised at Breda, and promised likewise to release the French Protestants taken upon English ships, and the four ministers of Orange ; this *mémoire* was entered into the protocol of the Mediator, and an authentic copy of it, signed by the Mediator, was given to their Excellencies. Mr. Swinford likewise drew up another *mémoire* on our part, that we should release the Irish taken on board French ships, which the Mediator entered into his protocol and gave the French an authentic copy of it. (N.B. The Mediator gave these copies the Wednesday following, *i.e.* the 25th). The Secretaries of both parties having collationed the Treaties in the presence of the Secretary of the Mediation, the Spaniards, the Dutch and the English signed separately, one after another in the same apartment in which they had signed the minutes the night before, the English about one in the morning, the Dutch being present. The Mediator signed first, and then gave the Latin Treaty to the English Ambassadors, who signed it in the second column, and gave it to the French, who signed it in the third ; this order was observed *vice versa* with the French copy on our side ; the Secretaries of both parties put the seals to the Treaties. The French Ambassadors in the meantime looked over the English *plein-pouvoirs*.

" The Mediator read the Dictature concerning Mary d'Este in France, and gave a copy of it to Mons. de Callière[s], after which they parted.

---

[1] Properly Schweinfurt, one of Prior's assistant-secretaries.

" N.B.—The English and French signed the Separate Article likewise, but only alternatively, as they had done the night before, each party taking one part of the instrument. That, therefore, which the French signed and delivered to us was in the French language, and that which we signed and delivered to them was in the Latin, but this Article was not signed on either side by the Mediator."

The Dutch treaty of peace named Charles XII of Sweden as mediator in place of his father, who had died suddenly on April 15. Articles 3 to 7 simply reproduced Articles 2 to 6 of the political treaty of Nijmegen. By Article 8 all conquests were mutually restored. In Article 14, in place of the six months of the Treaty of Nijmegen, nine months' grace was accorded to the subjects of the high contracting parties to withdraw with their property in case of a rupture. The Dutch also concluded a commercial treaty for twenty-five years, containing some concessions over and above those of the treaty of 1678, of which it was mainly a reproduction.

By Article 4 of the treaty with England, the King of France undertook not to disturb William III in the present possession of the Crown of England or its dependencies, and not to favour any plots or insurrections against his authority, in any manner whatsoever, by land or sea, a reciprocal undertaking being given on the part of the King of England, with the substitution of the words " de son obéissance " for those corresponding to " dont Sa Majesté Britannique jouit présentement," as Louis did not admit that identical language could be employed to describe the power possessed by the two kings over their respective subjects. All places captured were to be mutually restored.

The treaty with Spain provided for trifling exchanges of territory and for delimitation of frontiers. Luxemburg was restored to her. By Article 26, six months' grace only was accorded in case of rupture. Lilienrot signed this treaty also as Mediator.

The treaty with the Emperor confirmed to France the sovereign possession of Strassburg, which had been occupied by the French forces in 1681, but otherwise the peace of Westphalia and that of Nijmegen were to be executed in their entirety. All other places and territories occupied by France during the war were to be restored, including Lorraine, which had been in almost continuous French military occupation since 1634 excepting from 1661 to 1670. The Swedish mediator's signature is wanting to this treaty, but there were twenty-three attached by representatives of Electors, ecclesiastical princes and Free Towns.

On a passage in the preamble to the treaty between William III and Louis XIV, which speaks of " les conférences qui se sont à cet éfet [*i.e.* l'avancement de la paix] au Château de Riswick," Vast observes very pertinently—

" Les conférences de Ryswick n'ont été qu'un fantôme [1] de congrès, où les plénipotentiaires ont été mis à une diète presque absolue de négociations, tandis que les conditions de la paix avec le roi d'Angleterre étaient discutées et arrêtées dans les quatre [cinq] conférences qui eurent lieu à Hall, près Bruxelles, entre le maréchal de Boufflers et lord Bentinck, comte de Portland, du 8 juillet au 2 août 1697."

Authorities: Vast; Legrelle; Grimblot, Koch and Schoell.

449. *Congress of Carlowitz,* 1699.

Ever since 1691, William III had taken an infinity of trouble to mediate a peace between the Porte and the Holy League consisting of the Emperor, John Sobieski, King of Poland, and the Republic of Venice. His efforts had been defeated by the exaggerated demands of the allies, especially of the Emperor, and the intractability of the Turks. Two of his envoys to Constantinople, Sir William Hussey and William Harbord, died in succession during that year. The negotiations were then entrusted to Baron van Heemskerke, Dutch Envoy to the Emperor, and subsequently to the sixth Lord Paget and Jakob Colyer, respectively English and Dutch

[1] Vast, ii. 203 *n.* ; Legrelle, 77, uses exactly the same language.

Envoys at Constantinople. They were opposed by Châteauneuf, French Ambassador to the Porte, and other agents of that Power. But after the capture of Azov by the Russians in 1696 and the victory of Prince Eugene at Zenta in 1697, and the conclusion of the Peace of Rijswijk, by which the Emperor was enabled to apply his undivided attention to the war against Turkey, these diplomatists redoubled their exertions, and under instructions from William III, which were approved by the other Powers concerned, offered to undertake the office of Mediators. A Congress was now agreed to. Preliminary negotiations at Vienna ended in the acceptation of the *uti possidetis* as a basis, to be worked out with the aid of the Mediators, and a patch of territory eight miles long by four wide, about half a mile south of the ruined castle of Carlowitz on the Danube, was fixed upon as the place of meeting. Engineers were at once dispatched thither to prepare the necessary buildings. In order to avoid disputes respecting precedence and ceremonial, the conference hall was constructed with four doors on opposite sides, one each for the Imperial and Ottoman Ambassadors, and the other two for the remaining members of the Congress and the Mediators, so that all could make their entry at the same moment. Nevertheless, disputes did arise, especially between the Venetians, Poles and Russians, but they were happily removed by an agreement that place should not involve any distinction of rank. It was important to avoid delay, for Charles II of Spain was not expected to live much longer, and it was expected that his death would be followed by fresh international complications.

In the course of October 1698, the plenipotentiaries of the different Powers arrived in the neighbourhood of Carlowitz. The Emperor was represented by Count Oettingen, president of the Aulic Council, and Count Leopold von Schlick, commander-in-chief on the Theiss, with Colonel Count Luigi Marsigli as boundary commissioner, and Till, a member of the imperial council-of-war, as secretary and protocollist. Venice sent Cavalier Carlo Ruzini, with Giovanni Battista Nicolesi, as secretary, and Doctor Lorenzo Fondra, as commissioner for the boundary of Dalmatia. Poland was represented by the Palatin Count Stanislas Michelowsky, Russia by privy councillor Procopios Bogdanowitch Wosnizin, and the Porte by the Reis-Effendi Mohammed Rami, who was assisted by Alessandro Maurocordato, interpreter at the Porte, who was fully initiated into all the secrets of European diplomacy. Lord Paget and Jakob Colyer were present as representatives of the mediating Powers.

As soon as news was brought that the Ottoman Ambassador had reached his camp at Carlowitz, the other embassies moved from their halting-places at and near Peterwardein. Guards of honour for the Congress were furnished by three hundred men of an Imperial regiment of Cuirassiers, and by·a brilliant corps of janissaries and sipahis. After the usual petty difficulties as to camping-places, diplomatic etiquette, the exchange of full-powers and official visits, had been disposed of, a first formal sitting took place on November 13. On the next occasion, in order to expedite the transaction of business, strict diplomatic ceremony was laid aside, and was only observed at the signature of the treaties on January 26, 1699. It may be imagined that the ground was earnestly contested by both sides during the two and a half months that the Congress lasted. In order not to delay the conclusion of a general peace, a provisional truce for two years was signed between Russia and Turkey on December 25, o.s. This agreement was drawn up in two copies, of which one in Russian was signed by Bogdanowitch and the other in Turkish was signed by the Reis-Effendi, which were then exchanged.[1] A month later it was found feasible to proceed to the signature of peace between Turkey and the other three Powers. That with the Emperor was signed first. By Article XVI it was

---

[1] Koch and Schoell, xiv. 282 (iv. 259, Brussels edit.).

provided that the parties should send to each other solemn embassies for the confirmation of the peace and the re-establishment of friendly relations, with an exchange of presents suitable to the dignity of both monarchs, which were to cross each other at the frontier at latest by June of the following year. The peace was denominated *armisticium*, to last for twenty-five years, renewable at the desire of either party. The Emperor acquired by this treaty the whole of Hungary except the Banat of Temesvar, with Transylvania and the greater part of Slavonia, and Croatia as far as the river Unna.

Poland agreed to evacuate Moldavia, but obtained, on the other hand, the cession of Kaminiec with Podolia and the Ukraine. The remaining articles of her treaty closely followed those of the treaty with the Emperor. No limit was fixed for the duration of the treaty, and it was renewed by another signed at Constantinople, April 22, 1714.[1]

The treaty with Venice was signed provisionally on the part of the allies by the Imperial and Polish ambassadors alone, as the Venetian was not yet provided with full-powers covering every point. The Morea was ceded to the Venetian Republic, together with the islands of Santa Maura and Egina, and certain fortresses in Dalmatia. Although the signature of the Venetian plenipotentiary was not affixed to the treaty, the Signoria made no difficulty about its ratification. The definitive treaty of peace was signed at Constantinople April 15, 1701. No term of years was fixed, but it was stipulated that the peace should last as long as there was no failure to observe any of its provisions, practically a perpetual truce.[2]

Peter the Great, although on his travels, did not delay the despatch of plenipotentiaries to Constantinople to proceed with the negotiations left incomplete at

[1] *Ibid.*, 278 (iv. 355, Brussels edit.).
[2] Koch and Schoell, xiv. 281.

Carlowitz. In the summer of 1699, the first of his agents arrived at the Turkish capital on board a 36-gun ship built at Azov. The peace negotiators Oukraintzow and Czeredejow arrived some months later, and the Grand Vizier, in order to enforce his demand that the Russian claims should be abated, proceeded to place them under arrest. Lord Paget and Colyer, however, exerted their influence as mediators, and finally, after nearly two year's negotiations, a truce for thirty years was signed July 25, 1702. The town of Azov with all its fortifications, the port and the surrounding district were ceded to the Tsar, together with a strip of coast on the east side towards the Kuban eighty miles in length. Russian merchant ships were to be allowed to pass the straits, and the navigation of the Black Sea to be free to Russian men-of-war. The same rights and privileges were to be accorded to Russian diplomatic agents as to those of other European sovereigns. [1]

Authorities : Zinkeisen, *Geschichte des Osmanischen Reiches in Europa,* 5ter Th. Gotha, 1857 ; Koch and Schoell, Brussels edit., iv. 349.

§ 450. *Congress of Utrecht,* 1712–13.

This congress had for its most important objects to put an end to the war of the Spanish succession, and in connexion therewith to decide on certain territorial readjustments ; the recognition of the Protestant Succession in England, of the titles of the King in Prussia and the Elector of Hanover, the establishment of a strategical Barrier between France and the United Provinces, finally the transfer of the Spanish Netherlands to the House of Austria.

Preliminaries had been signed in London, October 8, 1711, as the result of negotiations between Mesnager, despatched thither on a special mission, and Oxford, Shrewsbury, St. John, Dartmouth and Jersey. Utrecht

[1] The text has never been published, according to Koch and Schoell, xiv. 283.

was proposed as the meeting-place by Louis XIV. The invitations were sent out in the name of the Queen of England, in agreement with the States-General, the date fixed being January 12, 1712, n.s. The plenipotentiaries were to have the rank of ministers durng the negotiations, assuming the title of ambassador only for the purpose of signing the treaty.

The plenipotentiaries were—

England : the Bishop of Bristol, Keeper of the Privy Seal, and the Earl of Strafford, envoy extraordinary and minister plenipotentiary at the Hague.

France : Maréchal d'Huxelles, the Abbé de Polignac,[1] and Mesnager.

The Emperor ; Count Sinzendorf and Baron Consbruch.[2]

States-General : eight in number, one for each of the Seven United Provinces, except the province of Holland, which appointed two : J. van Randwijck, Judge of Nijmegen ; Willem Buys, Pensionary of Amsterdam ; B. van der Dussen, Pensionary of Gouda ; C. van Gheel van Spanbroek ; F. A. Baron de Rheede de Renswoude, President of the Nobility of Utrecht ; S. van Goslinga, Curator of the University of Francquier ; Graef van Knyphausen, Deputy ; and Graef van Rechteren.[3]

Portugal : Conde de Tarouca, ambassador at the Hague, and Dom Luis d'Acunha, special ambassador in London since 1696.

Prussia : O. M. C. de Dönhoff and J. A. Marschall von Biberstein.

Duke of Savoy : Comte de Maffei, envoy extraordinary and minister plenipotentiary in England ; Marquis Solar du Bourg, envoy extraordinary at the Hague ; and Mellarede, conseiller d'Etat.

---

[1] Recalled January 31, 1713, and sent on a mission to Rome.
[2] After the death of the latter, in December 1712, replaced by Baron von Kirchner.
[3] Recalled, and did not sign.

Federated Circles of the Empire : Stadion.
Elector of Treves : Keyserfeldt.
Elector Palatine : Hunheim.
Bishop of Münster and Paderborn : Ducker.
Landgrave of Hesse : Baron von Dalwigk.
Duke of Württemberg and Teck : A. G. v. Heespen.
Poland : Gersdorf.
Sweden : Palamquist.
Duke of Lorraine : Baron Le Bègue.

The gathering was not complete by the date previously announced. Meanwhile, rules of procedure, mainly for the purpose of avoiding controversy about precedence, and especially quarrels between the servants of plenipotentiaries, were framed.

It was not till January 29 that the opening meeting was held. The Bishop of Bristol delivered a short address, to which the first French delegate replied. Strafford and Polignac followed. A large round table had been provided, at which the members seated themselves as they arrived, without regard to questions of precedence, i.e. *pêle-mêle.* Several meetings having taken place, on February 11 the French plenipotentiaries read a document explanatory of their proposals for a peace,[1] and it was agreed to produce the answers of the allies on March 5. No secretary was appointed to act as protocollist, but the Pensionary Buys was chosen as archivist. To him were entrusted copies of the full-powers, after these had been exchanged. There was no president. Sinzendorf, the Imperial first plenipotentiary, whose claim to the presidency had been opposed, especially by the French, seems to have arrogated to himself the right of speaking first on every occasion. He had to be contented with a prominent seat opposite to a large mirror, and the privilege of entering the conference-room before the

---

[1] Weber, 204, who states that these had been settled in secret conferences between French and English plenipotentiaries.

delegates of other Powers. No sort of order was observed, and one report states that the preliminary formality at the first meeting, of asking for the production of the full-powers, was forgotten, the plenipotentiaries being already personally acquainted with each other.

On March 5, accordingly, a general conference was held with the French, at which the allies presented their demands separately.[1] Those of the Emperor, the Germanic Body, Portugal, the Elector of Treves, the Elector Palatine, the Bishop of Múnster, the Landgrave of Hesse and the Duke of Württemberg were in Latin. The English, Dutch and Prussians had framed theirs in French.

At the eighth conference, held on March 9, in reply to the Bishop of Bristol, the French announced that they must have till the 30th to present their observations. When that day arrived, another general conference took place, when the French announced that they were now prepared to enter on oral negotiations in accordance with the forms observed at previous congresses. The allies responded that, having communicated their demands in writing, as had been asked of them, they expected written answers. The French view that the usual proceeding was to hold verbal discussions, at least when there was no mediator, was probably justified by precedent. At Rijswijk there had been a mediator, through whose hands the demands and replies were transmitted. But at Utrecht, as there was no president, everything was done irregularly. A private conference among the allies led to a decision to insist on the French producing written replies. After that no more general meetings took place. Various were the disputes respecting priority in paying or receiving visits of ceremony.

The Empire and the Dutch were still carrying on hostilities, but on July 17 the Duke of Ormond, English commander-in-chief, gave notice that he had agreed

[1] Weber, p. 208.

with the French to a suspension of arms. Immediately afterwards a detached body of the allies under Albemarle suffered defeat at Denain, and when the news was brought to Utrecht, it led to a *fracas* between the servants of Mesnager and Count van Rechteren, one of the Dutch delegates. The French took occasion to announce that by instructions from Paris they were to suspend all peace negotiations until they received satisfaction for the insult offered to a member of their mission.[1] In spite of attempts to overcome this difficulty, the deadlock continued.[2] However, by the secret treaty between the States-General and England of January 19/30, 1712/13, providing for the Barrier in return for a guarantee of the Protestant succession, the Dutch had obtained most of what they had contended for. England and France had in the meanwhile agreed to the contents of their two treaties of peace and of commerce, and were anxious to sign. On March 13 accordingly, the English plenipotentiaries addressed a statement to those of the allies, pointing out that the Congress had now lasted for nearly fourteen months, without any justification. The Queen of England, finding it impossible to remedy this state of affairs, had come to the resolution of completing her own treaty without delay. She advised her allies to follow her example.

In pursuance of this announcement, the two English treaties with France were signed March 31/April 11, 1713, and French treaties with Portugal, Prussia, the Duke of Savoy, and the States-General were concluded simultaneously. By Article IX of the last of these, the King of France undertook that the Spanish Netherlands, ceded to Max Emanuel, Duke of Bavaria, in 1702,

[1] No. 481 of the *Spectator*, of September 12, 1712, is an amusing imaginary discussion of this incident in a coffee-house. I am indebted to Mr. J. W. Foster's *Practice of Diplomacy* for the reminder of this reference.

[2] The fact was that all this time a separate negotiation was being carried on between France and England. A very full narrative in Weber.

should be transferred to the House of Austria. No general meeting took place for the signature of the treaties. Those in which the Duke of Savoy and England were signatories with France were signed at the lodgings of the Bishop of Bristol, the rest at Strafford's apartments. The *asiento*[1] convention of March 26, 1713, was signed at Madrid, and the treaty of peace between England and Spain on March 27, also at the same place. But in order to impart to it a greater degree of solemnity, the latter was signed over again at Utrecht on July 2/13, by the Bishop of Bristol and Strafford for England, and by the Duque de Ossuna and Marques de Monteleone for Spain.

The Emperor continued the war for another nine months, but without success. A conference opened at Rastadt, November 26, 1713, led to the conclusion of peace between France and the Emperor and the Empire on March 6, 1714. The delegates of the German princes met at Baden in Aargau, and signed peace there on September 7 of the same year.

Authorities: Vast, *Les grands traités*, etc., iii. ; Lamberty, *Mémoires pour servir*, vii and viii; O. Weber, *Der Friede von Utrecht.* See also Koch and Schoell, Brussels edit. i. 194.

§ 451. *Congress of Cambray* (1721–5).

In August 1717, Spain, under the ambitious leadership of Alberoni, suddenly made war on the Emperor by seizing Sardinia. England and France were allied with Holland by a treaty of January 4, 1717, and on August 2, 1718, they signed at London a treaty with the Emperor, to which Holland acceded February 16, 1719. The object of the *Quadruple Alliance* thus formed was to force Philip V of Spain and the Duke of Savoy to come to terms with the Emperor Charles VI. The conditions proposed were that the Emperor should renounce his

[1] Asiento de Negros, Contrato que hacían los estranjeros para llevar negros á nuestras colonias. Nuevo Dic. de la Lengua Castellana, s.v.

claims to the throne of Spain, while Philip should give up his rights in the Low Countries, to the Spanish possessions in Italy, and his reversionary claim to Sicily. In return for these concessions the Emperor was to grant to Don Carlos, elder son of Philip by his second wife, Elisabeth Farnese, the eventual investiture of Tuscany, Parma and Piacenza, on the failure of the male line in these dukedoms. Sicily was to be ceded to Charles VI by Victor-Amadeus of Savoy in exchange for Sardinia. In November 1718, Victor-Amadeus acceded to these terms, but Spain refused. The conspiracy of Cellamare against the Regent Orleans led to a declaration of war by France against Spain, and the latter Power, being defeated, accepted the terms offered by the Quadruple Alliance on January 26, 1720, and the agreement was certified by the ministers plenipotentiary of the Emperor, France and England, at the Hague.[1]

It had been stipulated by the treaty of August 2, 1718,[2] that a Congress should be held at a place to be hereafter agreed on, to settle and determine all the " other points of their particular peace, under the mediation of the three contracting Powers," and it was now agreed that the Congress should be held at Cambray in 1721. The Powers represented were the Emperor (Count Windisch-graetz, diplomatic representative at the Hague, and Baron Penterrieder), Spain (Sant Estevan de Gormes and Marques Beretti-Landi), France (Comte de Morville and M. de St. Contest),[3] England and the Italian States. Earl Stanhope, Lord Carteret and Sir Robert Sutton were appointed British plenipotentiaries in September 1720, Lords Polwarth and Whitworth in 1722,[4] with the rank of Ambassadors. The first thing to do was to frame a *règlement* for ceremonial, police and conduct of

---

[1] See Rousset, t. 1 (A), 305. The respective forms of renunciation by the Emperor and Philip V are to be found in Rousset, t. 3 (c), 458, dated September 16, 1718, and 464, dated June 22, 1720. Here also the *grands titres* of the two sovereigns are set out in full.
[2] Jenkinson, ii. 206.   [3] Rousset, t. 1 (A), 306.
[4] Wickham Legg.

servants of the plenipotentiaries, a usual and indeed indispensable step on these occasions. But these do not appear to have been finally approved till April 7, 1725, just as the congress was on the point of being broken up.[1] The Emperor's agent raised objections to the mediation of the kings of France and England. It was December 1723 before these points could be settled. Then the demands of the parties were delivered in writing to the ambassadors of the mediators.[2] The Emperor claimed the grand-mastery of the Order of the Golden Fleece, and to retain the title of " Catholic King " while demanding that Philip V should abandon those derived from territories which he no longer possessed.[3] He also urged that Philip should undertake to restore their ancient privileges (*fueros*) to the Aragonese and Catalans. On the other hand, the mediators were of opinion that the King of Spain could not give up the grand-mastery of the Golden Fleece, which belonged to him as the successor of Charles II of Spain, nor did they consider the Emperor's claim respecting titles to be equitable, nor could the King of Spain listen to proposals regarding the privileges of the Aragonese and Catalans. That was a domestic matter for their own sovereign to decide, all the more that he had granted to these unfaithful provinces the privileges enjoyed by the two Castiles. They also insisted on the suppression of the Ostend East India Company. Neither were the demands of Philip comfortable to a spirit of equity. Efforts were made to reconcile the opposing views by a compromise, but without success. Then there were certain interests of the reigning Duke of Parma, who protested against

---

[1] Rousset, t. 3 (E), 422 ; Koch and Schoell, Brussels edit. i. 239. A. Vandal, *Une Ambassade française*, etc., 128, speaks, incidentally of " *la médiation de France* " alone, but this appears to be inexact.

[2] Rousset, t. 4, 119, *et infra.*

[3] The *grand titre* of the King of Spain attributed to him, among others, the titles of *Archduke of Austria*, Duke of Burgundy, of Brabant and Milan, *Count of Hapsburg and Tirol*, of Flanders (Jenkinson, ii. 399). The titles printed in italics are specifically mentioned in the demands of the Emperor, Art. VI., Rousset, t. 4, 122.

the suzerainty of the Empire,[1] which the mediating Powers and Spain had undertaken to support by a treaty of alliance of June 13, 1721. The Imperial ambassadors advanced a pretension to treat Tuscany and Parma as being already male fiefs, whereas Article V of the Treaty of London merely stipulated that this should follow on Don Carlos' coming into possession. They also objected to the establishment of Swiss garrisons, to be paid by the mediating Powers, at Leghorn, Porto-Ferraio, Parma and Piacenza, which was one of the stipulations of the treaty in question. For a whole year they continued to make difficulties about delivering the " eventual " investiture (*i.e.* the reversion) to Tuscany, Parma and Piacenza. And they furthermore endeavoured to make the guarantee of the Pragmatic Sanction a condition *sine quâ non* of any arrangement, to which the mediators replied that this was outside the scope of the Congress. Finally, when the French Government, early in 1725, decided to send home the Spanish Infanta, destined bride of Louis XV, as she was not of marriageable age, and to espouse him to Marie Leczinska, daughter of the ex-King of Poland, Spain broke up the Congress by withdrawing her plenipotentiaries. The few meetings of the Congress that were ever held, passed in disputes that led to no conclusion, or in framing conventions to grant reciprocal delays. A principal event was the delivery of protests on the part of the Pope against anything that might be done contrary to the interests of the Holy See, September 15, 1722, February 16, 1723, and April 1, 1723. The rest of the time was given up to festivities and petty disputes.[2]

Authorities : See the footnotes to this section ; a detailed account in Koch and Schoell, Brussels edit. i. 239.

§ 452. *Congress of Soissons, 1728-9.*[3]
After the dissolution of the Congress of Cambray,

---

[1] Jenkinson, ii. 271. [2] Rousset, t. i (A), 309, 326.
[3] Dyer, iv. 55, 56, 58 ; Rousset, t. v. 184.

Philip V of Spain, finding it impossible to come to terms
with the French Court, concluded on April 30, 1725, a
peace with Austria, which was negotiated by the notor-
ious Ripperda (§ 338). (Dumont, viii, pt. ii, 113.)
Philip guaranteed the Pragmatic Sanction by which
the succession to the dominions of the House of Austria
was to be assured to Charles' daughter, in return for an
undertaking to use good offices to procure the restoration
of Gibraltar and Minorca to the Spanish Crown, and the
recognition of the Infante Don Carlos as heir to Parma
and Tuscany. By Article 10 of this treaty it was
mutually agreed that the two sovereigns should retain
during their lifetime the titles claimed by them, but
that their successors should bear those only of the
kingdoms and dignities actually possessed by them.
A secret treaty had been signed simultaneously (April
30, 1725), by which the marriage of the two daughters
of the Emperor to the two sons of Philip by his Queen,
Elisabeth Farnese, the restoration of the House of
Stuart to the throne of England, and the recovery of
Gibraltar and Minorca *by force* were stipulated.[1] France,
England and Prussia combined to counteract this move
by signing, September 3, 1725, a treaty known as the
Alliance of Hanover,[2] by which they mutually guaranteed the Treaty of Utrecht, besides the treaties of
Westphalia, and all others which bore reference to the
rights, privileges and immunities of the Germanic Body.[3]
When this became known, extensive warlike preparations were made, and the Spaniards laid siege to Gibraltar
in January 1727. But there was no general desire for
war, and Cardinal Fleury, the more than septuagenarian
minister of Louis XV. was eminently pacific. The
preliminaries of a general peace were signed at Paris,

[1] Dyer, iv. 57.   But there is no proof of the existence of this secret
treaty.
[2] Rousset, t. 2 (B), 189 ; Jenkinson, ii. 274.   There is no mention in
Dumont, nor in Jenkinson's text, of the Treaty of Utrecht.
[3] The States-General acceded Aug. 9, 1726, by a very cautiously
worded instrument (Dumont, viii. pt. ii. 138), and Sweden, Mar. 14,
1727 (*ibid.* 141).

May 31, 1727[1] to which the Emperor, the Kings of France and Great Britain and the States-General were parties, and it was provided that a Congress should assemble at Aix-la-Chapelle, within four months, to arrange a definitive peace. Spain at first held aloof, but finally accepted the preliminaries March 6, 1728.

A Congress was accordingly opened at Soissons, to which place the meeting had been altered to suite the convenience of Fleury. William Stanhope (afterwards Lord Harrington), Lord Walpole (ambassador at Paris) and Stephen Poyntz (minister to Sweden) were appointed British Ambassadors extraordinary and plenipotentiary, May 1728. Thomas Pelham, M.P., was appointed secretary to the embassy in January 1728.[2] For the Emperor, Count Sinzendorf, Grand Chancellor, Count Windischgrätz and Baron Penterrieder[3] (who had been at Cambray) ; for France, Cardinal Fleury,[4] Count Brancas-Cherest (ambassador in Sweden) and the Marquis de Fénélon (ambassador at the Hague) ; for Spain the Duque de Beurnonville (ambassador at Vienna), Marques de Santa Cruz, and Señor Barnachea ; for the States-General, Baron Hop, Baron Goslinga (ambassador at Paris) and Heer Hurgonje.[5] They all arrived between June 10 and 16, 1728. Representatives of Sweden, Russia, Denmark, Poland, Bavaria, Lorraine, Modena, Holstein, the Elector Palatine and the Ostend Company also made their appearance.

The first meeting, of a merely formal character, was held on June 14. The plenipotentiaries having taken their places at a round table *pêle-mêle*, Sinzendorf

---

[1] Rousset, iv. 5.
[2] Wickham Legg, 23.
[3] Died August 10, and Baron Fonseca appointed in his place.
[4] Miruss says : " der Kaiserliche Staatsminister Graf. v. Sinzendorf und der französische Staatsminister, Cardinal Fleury, um Ceremoniel- streitigkeitzen zu vermeiden, waren nur als bevollmächtige Minister accreditirt und wurden doch als Gesandte erster Classe behandelt."
[5] Rousset, v. 43. Blok, *Geschied.* iii. 362, who says the congress met in July.

opened the proceedings with a speech, to which Fleury made a suitable reply. The second assembly was on June 17, at which copies of the full-powers were compared, and it was agreed to meet on Mondays and Thursdays. A *règlement* respecting ceremonial and police had been promulgated, modelled on that of Cambray. No more meetings were held till June 28, 29 and 30. At the last of these the Dutch presented a *mémoire* of their demands, in the name of the allies of Hanover. After this, the Congress passed into a condition of inactivity from which it was unable to extricate itself, and Fleury returned to Paris. Conferences were held from time to time, at which no business of importance was transacted. It was not till July 30 that the Imperial and Spanish plenipotentiaries delivered their replies to the Dutch demands, and the English Ambassadors' preliminary demands for a separate peace with Spain. To this the Spaniards gave in a reply. The only other *mémoire* laid before the Congress was from the Duke of Holstein. Some further meetings took place, but merely for the look of the thing. The Emperor, in order to obtain the consent of all the Powers to the Pragmatic Sanction, interposed every possible obstacle to the proceedings. Thus the negotiations became a mere farce, and the various plenipotentiaries gradually withdrew. Subsequently Spain concluded separate treaties at Seville (November 9, 1729) with Great Britain[1] and France, to which the States-General acceded shortly afterwards. In 1731 (March 16) the Emperor was induced to accept the same provisions by what is known as the *Second Treaty of Vienna*,[2] Article 2 of which recognized the Pragmatic Sanction as far as Great Britain and the States-General were concerned.

The failure of this Congress and of the preceding is to be attributed to the ground not having been properly prepared beforehand.

---

[1] Jenkinson, ii, 304.   [2] Ibid., 318.

Authorities : Besides those mentioned in the footnotes, see Koch and Schoell (Brussels edit.), i. 245.

§ 453. *Congress of Aix-la-Chapelle,* 1748 (and Breda, so-called, in 1746).

At this Congress was concluded the peace which put a final termination to the War of the Austrian Succession, begun in December 1740 by Frederick the Great's invasion of Silesia, and to the war between Great Britain and Spain which had broken out in 1739. By the treaty with Maria-Theresa of Dresden of December 25, 1745, Frederick had secured a separate peace for himself, and thenceforth maintained an attitude of neutrality, but the war was still carried on between France and Spain on the one side, Austria, England and the States-General on the other. Holland, indeed, while furnishing troops, was not officially at war with France until April 1747,[1] when the latter Power declared her intention of invading the territory of the United Provinces, but previously to this, in February 1746, the States-General had taken the step of sending Wassenaer on a mission to Versailles to offer the good offices of the Republic for the re-establishment of peace. He proposed conditions which were eventually converted into the treaty of peace signed at Aix-la-Chapelle, October 18, 1748, but long and intricate negotiations preceded that event.

To Wassenaer had subsequently been added the Pensionary Gilles, and the Dutch permanent diplomatic representative de Hoey was still at Versailles. In concert with the Abbé de la Ville, formerly French minister at the Hague and now employed in the French Foreign Office, a draft in twenty-two articles was prepared on the basis of the *status quo ante bellum.* But

[1] See Rousset, xx. 4, for the letter from the Abbé de la Ville, Versailles April 13, 1747, delivered by his secretary left at the Hague as *chargé des affaires de France à sa place,* enclosing a declaration communicated by the King's order to the Lords the States-General of the United Provinces (see p. 50).

this found no favour at either London, Vienna or Madrid, and the war continued. In June 1746, d'Argenson, the French Minister for Foreign Affairs, sent the Marquis de Puysieulx on a secret mission to the Hague to ascertain what were the real intentions of the Dutch. On his return with a favourable report, the Dutch envoys at Versailles, feeling that they had been ignored on this occasion, resolved that a further development of the negotiations was advisable, and by dint of urgent representations they induced the British ministry to accept a conference at some neutral town, and to the appointment of a British plenipotentiary. Lord Sandwich was selected for this appointment, Puysieulx being chosen to represent France, and it was agreed that Breda should be the place of meeting. The French proposed to themselves to hold merely informal conversations for the purpose of ascertaining what might be offered to the allies of both parties respectively, and though a Congress at Breda is often spoken of, the proceedings had not really that character. When Harrach and Chavanne, the Austrian and Sardinian plenipotentiaries, arrived on the spot, the French ministry instructed their negotiator to refuse direct discussion with them. According to this arrangement the terms were to be debated between the French, British and Dutch, and then communicated to their allies for formal acceptance ; and the Spanish Court was induced to agree that its plenipotentiary, on his arrival, should be placed in a similar position. The so-called Congress of Breda, however, produced no result. Sandwich went away for a time to the Hague, and Puysieulx was recalled to Paris in January 1747, to take the place of d'Argenson, dismissed from office. La Porte-Dutheil, one of the two chief clerks of the French Foreign Office, was sent to Breda as his substitute, and an old lawyer, Melchior Macanaz, was appointed on the part of Spain. This pragmatical person insisted on his right to take a direct part in the discussion of the terms, and put forward absurd pretensions to dispose of the Austrian possessions in Italy in accordance with Spanish convenience. Dutheil refused to admit his claims, while the other plenipotentiaries gave him underhand encouragement to press them. When he was eventually asked to put his proposals on paper and to produce his full-powers, it was found that he was not provided with any. Everybody was in a false position, from which they were only extricated by the opening of the campaign coincident with the French notice to Holland in April 1747 already mentioned.

On July 2, the French won the battle of Lawfeldt,[1] in which Sir John Ligonier was taken prisoner. Maréchal Saxe then conceived the idea of sending him on parole to the Duke of Cumberland, bearing a proposal that peace should be arranged by negotiation between the two commanders-in-chief. But this scheme did not meet with the approval of the governments. Sandwich, who had gone over to London, returned in haste to Cumberland's headquarters, and Puysieulx asked him for a meeting. This was arranged to take place at Liège on September 11. All they were able to agree upon was that a Congress, at which representatives of all the Powers interested might appear, should be convoked at Aix-la-Chapelle at the end of the campaigning season. Both Great Britain and Austria were ready to make peace; the first because the Dutch declared their inability to provide their share of the subsidy for the 30,000 Russian auxiliaries then on the march towards the Rhine in support of the allies, the second because Maria-Theresa feared the possibility of Great Britain concluding peace without her participation. She despatched to Paris draft proposals through the Saxon Envoy there, in which she inserted a condition that the treaty should contain no guarantee of Silesia to Frederick the Great. Kaunitz, Austrian minister at the Hague, and Sandwich were appointed to represent their res-

[1] Lafeld in Dutch.

pective sovereigns, and Saint Severin for Louis XV.
It was not, however, intended that a real Congress
should be held.   The term was employed merely to cover
and facilitate discussion between Saint Severin and the
plenipotentiaries of the two great Powers, whose interests
had by this time diverged.   Chavanne was to represent
Sardinia, Bentinck, the confidential adviser of the
Stadhouder, with Wassenaar, van Borsselen and Onno
Zwier van Haren (Blok. *Geschied*, iii, 440), Holland,
Sotomayor Spain, and Doria Genoa.   Saint Severin left
Paris at the end of March, carrying with him a counter-
draft for the Austrians, from which the promise not to
give a guarantee of Silesia to the King of Prussia was
eliminated.   As soon as he reached Aix-la-Chapelle,
Sandwich and Kaunitz hastened to call on him regardless
of etiquette.   He performed his part skilfully, playing
off one against the other, not without resorting to a
certain amount of deception.   As Kaunitz still opposed
the guarantee of Silesia, while Sandwich was, of course,
ready to renew what had already been given by George
II to Frederick, and it was a part of the French policy
to favour Frederick the Great, Saint Severin finally made
up his mind to close with the British negotiator.   He
confided to him (what was not true, though not in-
credible) that Austria and Spain were on the point of
anticipating the Anglo-French negotiations by the
conclusion of a separate treaty at the expense
of Sardinia, the most cherished ally of England.   A set
of preliminaries in twenty and odd paragraphs was
drawn up on the spot, with the addition of a separate
article undertaking that if any of the Powers interested
should refuse or delay its assent, the Kings of France
and Great Britain and the States-General should agree
on the best means of enforcing the preliminaries.   These
were then shown to Bentinck, whose instructions were
to accept whatever was agreed to by his British colleague.
Kaunitz, when Sandwich read the document to him,
could not believe his ears, but, going off at once to

Saint Severin, inquired whether it was genuine, and received for reply the excuse that he had only signed because of an intrigue between the British and Spaniards for a separate treaty (which, though quite likely, was equally untrue). The Spanish and Sardinian plenipotentiaries were likewise dissatisfied, but in May Chavanne received instructions to accede to the preliminaries. Maria-Theresa also instructed Kaunitz that she would admit the clause relative to Silesia,[1] if it were balanced by a provision renewing the Pragmatic Sanction ; and her adhesion was given on this condition.

Saint Severin then returned to France to report in person to the king, from whom he received orders to sign the definitive treaty without delay, and La Porte-Dutheil, who was a skilled draftsman, was attached to him for that part of the work. The English ministry likewise gave Sandwich a colleague in the person of Sir Thomas Robinson, minister at Vienna. These four, with the addition of Bentinck and Saint Severin, formed a Congress in miniature, and progress was accelerated. The treaty was signed October 18 by the plenipotentiaries of Great Britain, France and Holland (four for the latter Power). It contained twenty-four[2] articles, and two " Separate Articles " were added, one of which declares

---

[1] The copy of the preliminaries does this in paragraph 19, but the narrative by the Duc de Broglie seems to show that it was not there originally. Possibly it was inserted after the signature. Of these preliminaries, dated April 30, four counterparts were executed. In two of them, signed by Saint-Severin, the King of France was named first, and in the two signed by Sandwich the King of England occupied the place of honour. Each of them then received a counterpart signed by the other and by the Dutch plenipotentiaries, while the Dutch plenipotentiaries received the two remaining. Whenever another Power acceded to the preliminaries, four counterparts were prepared, to each of which the instrument of accession was attached. The plenipotentiaries of the two Kings each received a copy in which his sovereign was named first, and the Dutch plenipotentiaries received the other two. They also provided two copies of their acceptation of the accession, while the plenipotentiaries of England and France furnished only one each (Koch and Schoell, Brussels edit. i. 311). This is perhaps what Klüber's statement referred to in § 39 was intended for.

[2] Koch and Schoell enumerate only twenty-three. They also give slightly different dates for the accession of Modena and Genoa.

that none of the titles assumed by the contracting parties, either in the full-powers and in other documents during the course of the negotiations or in the preamble, should prejudice the rights of other Powers, and that the use of the French language in all the copies was not to be regarded as a precedent.

The Austrian accession was given on October 23, that of Spain on October 20, of Modena on October 25, of Genoa on October 28, and of Sardinia on November 20. Frederick the Great, on October 26, despatched to Ammon, his minister at the Hague, full-powers to add his acceptation, but it is not clear that they were utilized. At least, no official trace of it is to be found in the Berlin archives.[1]

The main results were that all the conquests made since the commencement of the war or since the conclusion of the preliminary articles of April 30, either in Europe or the East or West Indies, or in any other part of the world, should be restored. The King of England also undertook to send to the King of France two persons of rank and consideration, to remain as hostages, until a certain and authentic account should be received of the restitution of Cape Breton and of all the conquests made by his arms or subjects in the East and West Indies. The Duchy of Silesia, and the county of Glatz, were guaranteed to the King of Prussia by all the contracting Powers.[2]

Authorities : Duc de Broglie, *Maurice de Saxe et le Marquis d'Argenson ; la Paix d'Aix-la-Chapelle.* Droysen : *Friedrich der Grosse,* 3er Band. Koch and Schoell, as quoted in the footnote.

ANNEX (see p. 45 *n.*)

Rousset, *Recueil,* etc., xx. 4, gives the letter from the Abbé de la Ville, Versailles, April 13, 1747, delivered by

---

[1] De Broglie, 270 *n.*
[2] Jenkinson, ii. 370 ; Koch and Schoell (Brussels edit.), i. 313.

his secretary left at the Hague as *chargé des affaires de France à sa place*, enclosing a declaration communicated by the King's order to the Lords the States-General of the United Provinces.

It states that in July 1741 the States-General had been acquainted with the conditions on which H.M. was willing to put an end to the troubles by which Europe was disturbed. The King even offered to place Dunkirk under the protection of Dutch troops. Since then he had always professed the same desire of conciliation. On September 9, 1745, he proposed to them the calling of a Congress through his minister (text given at foot of the page) to proceed without delay to labour in concert with them at the great work of peace. (The Dutch reply of the same date was an extract from a resolution that they must first ascertain the opinions of the King of Great Britain and the Queen of Hungary as principal parties to the war. At foot of the page.) As the States-General had given asylum to his enemies and furnished them with all sorts of supplies, he could no longer treat the States-General with the same consideration as heretofore. But he was led to suspect that, under the specious veil of a negotiation, their real intention was to put off the danger that threatened them and prepare for greater efforts to continue the war. These suspicions were confirmed by the difficulties that had been purposely raised since the opening of the conferences at Breda. Dutch troops had entered French territory in 1744, without the States-General pretending to carry on a direct war against H.M. He also, in adopting the measure forced on him of entering the territory of the Republic, has no design of breaking with them, but merely to put a stop to the dangerous effects of the protection they accord to the troops of the Queen of Hungary and the King of England, and so forth and so forth.

§ 454. *Fokchany and Bukharest,* 1772–3.

From 1766 onwards, Russia had endeavoured to stir up revolt in Greece, Crete and Montenegro, and at last Turkey declared war against the Empress Catherine II on October 6, 1768, the ostensible ground being her refusal to withdraw her troops from Poland. In August 1769, England and Prussia had endeavoured to mediate between the belligerents, but without success. After the meeting of Frederick the Great and Joseph II at Neustadt, in September 1770, a fresh combination of effort was initiated ; Thugut, the Austrian Resident at Constantinople, and Zegelin, the Prussian Minister, were instructed to urge the Porte to make peace, a step for which the impending partition of Poland between Russia, Austria and Prussia furnished the impelling motive. Catherine declined mediation, but accepted the *bons offices* of Austria and Prussia,[1] while the grand vizier wrote direct to Rumiantzoff, the Russian commander-in-chief, asking for an armistice. It was concluded at Giurgevo, May 30/June 10.[2] It was agreed to hold a congress at Fokchany in the north of Moldavia. The plenipotentiaries of Russia were Gregor Orloff and Obreskoff (the latter was Russian Resident at Constantinople) ; for Turkey, Osman Effendi and the Sheikh Jasintchi Zadé. Thugut and Zegelin accompanied the latter to the place of meeting, and the Congress opened August 19, 1772. The Russian plenipotentiaries refused to admit the Austrian and Prussian diplomatists to the conferences, on the ground that their own full-powers did not make any mention of mediators, and that their admission would consequently be contrary to public law. The Russians and Turks, therefore, remained *tête-à-tête*, but were unable to come to an agreement respecting the independence of the Crimean

---

[1] In a letter of October 9 she wrote to Frederick the Great : " Il faut éviter le mot et la forme de la médiation. Je suis prête à accepter les bons offices de la Cour de Vienne ; Je réclame ceux de Votre Majesté" (A. Sorel, *La Question d'Orient*, etc., 112).

[2] Hammer-Purgstall gives the year as 1771, which is apparently a misprint for 1772. Koch and Schoell, iv. 402, give the date as 1772.

Tartars, which was one of the conditions insisted on by Russia. The conferences were broken off, but at Turkish request the armistice was prolonged, and at the same time Bukharest was indicated as the place where negotiations might be renewed, Obreskoff having in the meantime received fresh powers to act.

The Turks then appointed other plenipotentiaries, three in number, with a suite of secretaries, who set out for Bukharest. On this occasion Thugut and Zegelin were left behind at Constantinople. The conferences began November 20, 1772, and after the exchange of full-powers the further prolongation of the armistice was discussed. The Russians agreed to extend it to March 21, o.s., 1773. Then they put forward their demands, which proved to be more extensive than those previously presented at Fokchány, and to include in particular the cession of Kertsch and Jenikalé in the Crimea, also freedom of navigation of the Black Sea (Koch and Schoell, iv. 403). Time was granted to the Turkish plenipotentiaries to consult their Government, and a twenty-seventh conference took place February 4/15, 1773. After a violent discussion, instructions were again sought from Constantinople, where all the new demands were rejected. On the return of the messenger a further meeting took place, at which Obreskoff announced that if the Russian conditions were not accepted, he was not empowered to meet the Turkish plenipotentiaries any more. Nevertheless, they met again next day and on the following day, but with no better result, and on March 22, the day after the expiration of the armistice, the Turkish delegates quitted Bukharest.

Hostilities were renewed, with disastrous results for the Turks, who at Kutchuk-Kainardji, July 17, 1774, were forced to accept still harder conditions of peace than they had previously rejected.

Authorities: Joseph v. Hammer, *Geschichte des Osman-*

ischen Reiches, 1832, Bd. viii. 371–444 ; Zinkeisen, *Geschichte des Osmanischen Reiches in Europa ;* A. Sorel, *La question d'Orient au* 18ᵉᵐᵉ *siècle ;* Koch and Schoell, Brussels edit. iv. 402.

§ 455. *Congress of Teschen,* 1779.

On December 30th, 1777, the Wilhelmine branch of the Wittelsbach family, who were Electors of Bavaria, became extinct in the male line. The rightful successor was the Elector Palatine. Various claims to portions of the inheritance were set up by Joseph II and his mother, the Empress-Queen Maria-Theresa, by the Elector of Saxony in virtue of a cession of her rights by the Electress-Dowager (sister of the deceased Elector), the Duke of Deux-Ponts and the Duke of Mecklenburg-Schwerin. Immediately after the death of the Elector, Austrian troops took possession of all the territory claimed by Joseph II and Maria-Theresa, with whom the Elector Palatine concluded a convention on January 3, 1778, by which more than one-third of Bavaria was handed over to the House of Austria. Frederick the Great had hoped that France would resist the weakening of a German state in the maintenance of which she had always manifested her interest, but Vergennes persuaded Louis XVI to confine himself to an offer of mediation. Austria thereupon offered to Frederick to admit his right of succession to Anspach and Bayreuth, whenever that branch of the Hohenzollern family should die out, on condition of his withdrawing his opposition. In return he expressed his willingness that she should acquire two districts of Bavaria between the Danube, the Inn and the Salza. As regarding Anspach and Bayreuth, he maintained that his right was incontrovertible. His offer having been rejected on June 26, 1778, he declared the negotiations broken off on July 3.[1] War ensued, but there were no engagements of importance. Negotiations were resumed almost immediately, and after some preliminary sparring, conferences were

---

[1] Koch and Schoell, i. 434, give the date as August 13.

begun at Braunau between the representatives of the belligerents, to be broken off a second time by Prussia on August 16. After the short campaign of 1778, Catherine II of Russia, on September 21, o.s., instructed Golitzin, her ambassador at Vienna, to present a protest against the proceedings of Austria in regard to the Bavarian succession, on the ground that they endangered the constitution of the Empire. The subversion of that constitution would entail a violent shock to all neighbouring states, a derangement of the order and equilibrium of Europe, and a possible danger to Russia herself. The Empress was induced by these considerations to make a fresh effort to persuade the Empress-Queen and the Emperor to bring the troubles to an end by agreeing definitely with the King of Prussia and the other interested parties on a legal and friendly settlement of the Bavarian succession in conformity with the laws and constitutions of the Empire. It cost infinitely, she said, to her friendship for their Majesties to be obliged to declare that she could not, with indifference, see war kindled in Germany, both on account of its object and its possible effects ; and she must seriously consider what was reconcilable with the interests of her Empire, those of the princes her allies who had claimed her support, and, above all, her obligations to her ally the King of Prussia.[1]

Copies of this protest were also forwarded to the Russian diplomatic representatives at Versailles, St. James', Ratisbon, Copenhagen and Stockholm, with instructions to present them to the respective Governments.

Before, however, the document could be delivered in Vienna, Maria-Theresa had herself addressed to Catherine II and Louis XVI a request for their conjoint mediation or good offices in order to arrive at a settlement of the matters in dispute between herself and Frederick. Catherine thereupon appointed Prince

[1] Sbornik, etc., Collection of the Russian Imp. Hist. Soc., lxv. 15.

Repnin to be her plenipotentiary for the purpose of
mediation, and inquired of Louis what form he would
desire the negotiation to take, as well as to the place
and date of the meeting. The French reply to this was
received at Petersburg early in December.

Catherine also added to the effect of her intervention
by despatching troops to the frontier of Galicia, and
investing Repnin with the command-in-chief. The
conclusion of a military convention between the two
allies (Russia and Prussia) was also contemplated, and
would undoubtedly have taken effect if the peace
negotiations had ended in failure.

Frederick had forwarded to Versailles a scheme of
pacification which, being transmitted to Vienna, was
accepted there. Repnin, indeed, states[1] that it was
devised by Louis who, after consulting Vienna, despatched it to Petersburg and Berlin. This was no doubt
the official account of the matter, and Frederick's action
in proposing it to the King of France was merely
confidential and private. After some discussion respecting the meeting place, it was agreed towards the
end of February 1779, to assemble a congress at Teschen
in Austrian-Silesia, and to neutralize that place for the
purpose. This required an *acte de neutralité* signed
and exchanged by the two belligerents.

Maria-Theresa appointed Count Johann-Philip Cobenzl
as her representative, Frederick's plenipotentiary was
Baron Riedesel, France deputed her ambassador at
Vienna, Baron de Breteuil, Russia Prince Repnin. The
Elector Palatine sent Count Anton von Terring-Seefeld,
the Duke of Deux-Ponts delegated Baron von Hohenfels,
and the Elector of Saxony Count Frederick-Augustus
Zinzendorf.

By February 18, 1779, the substance of the treaty of
peace between Austria and Prussia and of the new convention to be substituted for that of January 3, 1778, had
been agreed upon. The troops being in winter quarters,

---

[1] *Sbornik*, etc., 435.

active operations had been suspended, and proposals for an armistice were put forward. It was at first agreed that it should begin on March 10, the day on which the Congress was to assemble, and terminate on April 15. This was subsequently extended to April 28, and finally, when the negotiations were so far advanced as to offer a prospect of their being concluded without much further delay, to the date on which peace should eventually be signed.

The main points of the ultimate agreement had been previously settled, chiefly through the exertions of Repnin, but during the next two months he was busily engaged in smoothing over minor difficulties between the various parties concerned. The papers containing his correspondence for that period afford a good idea of the manner in which a mediator has to discharge his duties if he is to be successful in his task.

Frederick's so-called *ultimatum*, conceding to Austria the cession of the district of Burghausen in Bavaria, concluded with a threat that if it was not accepted he would continue the war. The reply of Maria-Theresa, accepting these terms, stated that she flattered herself that the contingency he had hinted at would not occur.

The instructions to the plenipotentiaries of the belligerent Powers, as well as those of the mediating Ministers, were : to treat for peace without any formality or etiquette whatever, and merely to observe the ordinary proceedings and usages of good society. This was in accordance with a suggestion made by Catherine at the outset. Repnin remained at Breslau, where he arrived December 6/7, o.s., in close touch with Frederick, who was at Reichenbach, near the frontier of Silesia and Bohemia, while Breteuil stayed at Vienna, and carried on an exchange of views with the Chancellor Kaunitz. Zinzendorf reached Breslau January 17, 1779, Hohenfels was there by January 23, but Seefeld did not arrive there until March 1. Consequently they were all ready to leave for Teschen by March 5, which they reached by the 10th. Seefeld did not, however, receive his full-powers for the new convention with Austria until March 17. At the first meeting the plenipotentiaries and Mediators exhibited their full-powers to each other. The plenipotentiaries then delivered their proposals in the shape of drafts of a treaty and of conventions, which were intended to be in agreement with the terms previously accepted in the *ultimata* of the King of Prussia and the Empress-Queen. These were received and transmitted by the Mediators, accompanied by their recommendations to the belligerent Powers and other parties. No general meetings were held, though all the plenipotentiaries met each other daily in social intercourse. Riedesel was admitted to conferences in which the representatives of Munich and Dresden took part. There was one such conference on April 12. At another Cobenzl was present, when the drafts of the various agreements were discussed, and a last conference was held on April 24. The final texts were despatched to Vienna and Munich on April 27. All this time an active correspondence was carried on between Kaunitz and Breteuil, as only a French *Chargé d'affaires* had been left at Vienna, and between Golitzin and Repnin, who was also in constant communication with Frederick's minister Finckenstein at Breslau. It was only on the day of signature that a general sitting of all the plenipotentiaries and the two Mediators took place, in order to exchange the signed documents.

Peace was signed May 13, 1779, the papers having been despatched from Breslau on the 7th and from Vienna on the 8th, ready for signature. There were three principal agreements : a treaty of peace between the Empress-Queen and the King of Prussia, to which were annexed a convention between the Empress-Queen and the Elector Palatine, a convention between the Elector Palatine and the Elector of Saxony, and an *acte* between the Elector Palatine and the Duke of Deux-Ponts. By a separate Article the Elector of Saxony was recognized as a contracting party to the treaty of peace. All these were guaranteed by the mediating Powers. Maria-Theresa also undertook by Article X of the treaty of peace not to oppose the eventual reunion of Anspach and Bayreuth to the Crown of Prussia. The treaties of Westphalia, Breslau of 1742, Berlin of 1742, Dresden of 1745, and of Hubertusburg of February 15, 1763, were confirmed by Article XII. The Emperor and the Empire were to be invited by all the contracting parties to accede to the treaty, and to the other instruments and conventions. The guarantee of France and Russia was stipulated by a separate instrument, signed simultaneously by the French and Russian Mediators.

The territorial rearrangement consisted in the cession by the Elector Palatine to the Empress-Queen of Wildshut, Braunau and other places, situated between the Danube, the Inn and the Salza, constituting the " regency " of Burghausen. This was expressed to be in exchange for Windelheim (to which Austria had no right whatever). Saxony was to receive a sum of 6,000,000 florins in twelve equal annual instalments, besides feudal rights hitherto belonging to the Crown of Bohemia over certain lordships in Saxony. The accession of the Emperor Joseph II was given May 16, 1779, and the approval of the Germanic Body was obtained in February 1780. The only advantage gained by the Duke of Mecklenburg, who had claimed the landgraviate of Leuchtenberg, was the privilege, under certain conditions, of *non appellando*, but the estates of the Duchy, and particularly the town of Rostock, protested, and that, too, with almost entire success.

§ 456. Some trouble was taken to ensure that in the instrument of guarantee signed on behalf of the two mediating Powers the " alternat " should be accorded by Russia to France and *vice versâ*, in the following manner—

" Nous soussignés Plénipotentiaires de Sa Majesté Impériale et Royale Apostolique et de Sa Majesté Prussienne attestons, que la présente copie est parfaitement conforme à l'original fait en double,[1] et que dans l'un des deux Exemplaires Sa Majesté Impériale de toutes les Russies étant nommée la première ainsi que son Plénipotentiaire, il a signé cet Exemplaire le premier, et dans l'autre Exemplaire Sa Majesté Très Chrétienne étant nommée la première, ainsi que Son Plénipotentiaire, c'est lui qui a signé le premier cet autre Exemplaire.

En foi de quoi nous avons signé la présente, etc.

Fait à Teschen le 13 mai 1779.

(L. S.)   JEAN PHILIPPE, Comte Cobenzl.
(L. S.)   JEAN HERMANN, Baron de Riedesel.[2]

Besides this statement, the Austrian and Prussian plenipotentiaries signed the following—

" Comme MM. les Plénipotentiaires Médiateurs ont requis les soussignés Plénipotentiaires de Sa Majesté l'Impératrice-Reine et de Sa Majesté le Roi de Prusse de produire en double les actes tant celui d'Accession de Sa Majesté l'Empereur en qualité de Corégent, que celui d'Acceptation de Sa Majesté Prussienne, afin que l'alternative soit observée de part et d'autre entre les deux Couronnes Médiatrices ;

Les dits soussignés connoissant les intentions de Leurs Cours respectives à cet égard, déclarent qu'il sera satisfait pleinement et sans delai à cette requisition.

En foi de quoi Ils ont signé la présente et y ont fait apposer les cachets de Leurs armes.

Fait à Teschen le 13 mai 1779.

(L. S.)   JEAN PHILIPPE, Comte Coblenz.
(L. S.)   JEAN HERMANN, Baron de Riedesel.

The treaties of Teschen have always been regarded as possessing a very important international significance, since by accepting the guarantee of Russia, in Article XII of the principal treaty, to the Treaties of Westphalia, they admitted that Power to what was, long after indeed, styled the Concert of Europe, and accorded to it the right of intervention in all cases where it could be

[1] *i.e.* the *acte de garantie* given by Russia and France.
[2] F. de Martens, ii. 75 and 96.

alleged that the treaties in question were being infringed. The admission of Russia into the comity of European nations has often been deplored by German political writers.

Authorities : *Sbornik Imperatorskago Russkago Istoriches-kago Obshchestvo*, lxv. *Papiers du Prince Repnin;* Harold Temperley, *Frederick the Great and Kaiser Joseph;* Garden, *Histoire des Traités de Paix*, iv. 235 ; the text of the treaty, conventions, etc., in F. de Martens, *Recueil des Traités et Conventions*, etc., *Autriche*, ii. 65–96 ; d'Angeberg, *Le Congrès de Vienne*, etc., p. 27 ; Koch and Schoell (Brussels edit.), i. 426, give a more detailed account than Garden.

§ 457. *Congress of Rastadt, 1797–9.*

The preliminaries of peace between Austria and the French Republic signed on April 18, 1797, after the suspension of arms on April 8, provided that a Congress should assemble at Berne to negotiate and conclude within three months the definitive peace,[1] on the basis of the integrity of the Empire. But by secret articles it was provided that the Emperor should cede that part of his Italian possessions which lay to the west of the Oglio, receiving in return the mainland territories of Venice east of that river, besides Dalmatia and Istria. Venice was to cede to France her territories west of the Oglio, receiving the three legations of Romagna, Ferrara and Bologna. It is interesting to note that on this occasion Napoleon demanded the *alternat* for the French Republic with the Emperor.

On August 31, conferences for the definitive treaty of peace opened at Udine. Louis Cobenzl superseded the Austrian negotiators Marquis de Fallo and General Count Merveldt on September 26. The treaty was signed at Passariano (where Napoleon was residing) on October 17, though dated from Campo-Formio, a village half-way between Passariano and Udine. By Article XX[2] of the patent treaty a congress was to be held at

[1] G. F. de Martens, vi. 385, Art. 4. [2] *Ibid.*, vi. 420.

Rastadt, at which the plenipotentiaries of France and the Germanic Empire were to arrange a pacification between these two Powers. By secret articles it was agreed that France should acquire the city of Maintz, and that the Emperor should use his good offices to obtain for France a frontier extending along the Rhine from Basel to the Nette, a small stream falling into that river on the left bank below Coblentz, and from there to Venloo in Holland. If the Empire refused to consent, the Emperor was to withdraw his troops, excepting the contingent that he was bound to furnish to the forces of the Empire.

The Directory appointed as its representatives, not professional diplomatists, but two politicians, Treilhard and Bonnier. Bonaparte was to be president of the delegation.

In 1795, a deputation of the Empire had been designated for the purpose of negotiating peace. It consisted of Maintz, Saxony, Austria, Bavaria, Würzburg, Hanover, Hesse-Darmstadt, Baden, Augsburg and Frankfort, under the presidency of Maintz, represented by Baron Albini. It was to negotiate in writing, discuss *mémoires* submitted to it, and vote in writing. It was not to communicate with the proposed French delegation, except through the Imperial commissioner. These arrangements were calculated to multiply obstacles and lengthen out any proceedings on which it might enter. It was now summoned to meet in November 1797 for the Congress of Rastadt.

On the 17th the members began to arrive, as well as representatives of the other States of the Empire. Fersen, the friend of the murdered Queen Marie-Antoinette, appeared for Sweden, but difficulties having been raised by France respecting his recognition, he was replaced by M. de Bildt. Other delegates were Canon Count Stadion for Würzburg, Lehrbach and Cobenzl for the Archduke of Austria and the King of Hungary and Bohemia, as separate entities. Metternich the elder, attended by his son Clement, afterwards the celebrated chancellor, arrived on December 2 as Imperial Commissioner. Others were, for the Elector of Saxony, Count Löben, minister, and after February 27, 1799, Count Hohenthal; for the Duke of Bavaria, Count Preysing, after February 16, 1798, Count Morawitzky, and again, from March 11, 1799, Baron Rechberg u. Rothenloewen; for the Elector of Brunswick as Duke of Bremen, Herr von Reden; for the Landgrave of Hesse-Darmstadt, Baron von Gatzert, minister; for the Margrave of Baden, Baron Edelsheim, minister, and the Geheimrath Meyer; for Augsburg, Herren Pflummern and Schmidt; for Frankfort, Herren Günderode and Schweizer.[1] Professor de Martens of Göttingen came as councillor of the Hanoverian legation.

Bonaparte, without waiting for Metternich, had already, on December 1, come to a preliminary agreement with the other two Austrians respecting the delivery of the city of Maintz to the French troops and the simultaneous evacuation of Venice by the latter. The same day he suddenly gave out that he had been summoned to Paris, and quitted Rastadt, not to return.

Later on in December Count Goertz, a Prussian diplomatist, made his appearance, accompanied by Baron Jacobi-Kloest and Herr von Dohm. Denmark was represented by M. de Rosencranz; and many other deputies of members of the Germanic Body presented themselves. The position of the Emperor was curious, being of a threefold character: Head of the Empire, member of the Deputation and Sovereign Prince. His representatives were far from acting in unison. The deputies of the Empire, having held a preliminary conference among themselves on December 9, offered to exchange their full-powers with the French on the 15th. But these being objected to as insufficient, they had to procure fresh ones from the Diet, which they received on January 15. The principal negotiations were pur-

[1] Garden, *Hist. gén. des Traités de Paix*, vi. 9.

sued by Treilhard with Cobenzl. Much time was wasted in the exchange of written Notes instead of holding *vivâ voce* conferences. In January 1798 the French had advanced their claim to the whole left bank of the Rhine, and invited the deputation of the Empire to consider how the States which possessed territory in that region could be compensated. At Metternich's suggestion the deputation at first returned an absolute refusal, but eventually gave way on March 9. On April 4 they delivered a Note accepting the principle that compensation should be obtained by secularizing ecclesiastical territories on the right bank, but neither the cession of the left bank nor the vote in favour of secularization received the sanction of the Emperor's Delegate. Cobenzl was recalled to Vienna on April 8, and the Congress degenerated into an empty farce. Treilhard, elected a member of the Directory, quitted Rastadt for Paris on May 15, being replaced by Jean de Bry and Roberjot. Affairs, however, made no speedier progress than before. " The deputation of the Empire was obstinate, the Austrians haughty, the Prussians at first cold, then insolent."[1] The French Delegates addressed a series of haughty Notes to the Delegation of the Empire, to which the latter replied submissively, finally on December 9 accepting an *ultimatum* addressed to them by the former. No progress was made however with the preparation of a draft of articles, and the Congress may be said to have come to an end with the year 1798, though it continued in form to exist some months longer. Peace was not sincerely desired by either the French Republic or the House of Austria. On April 7, 1799, the Emperor's representative was recalled, and announced to the Delegation of the Empire that the Emperor had resolved to annul everything that had been agreed to by the Congress. War had already begun again, by the passage of French troops across the Rhine at the end of February, on the

[1] Garden, 365.

pretext of the transit of 25,000 Russian troops through Galicia and Moravia to the Danube. On April 8, Metternich also informed the French Delegates that the war having broken out again *de facto*, and the safety of the Congress being consequently threatened, he had received orders to take no further part in the negotiations, but to quit Rastadt. The French Delegates, ordered by the Directory to hold out at Rastadt as long as possible, did not venture to leave the place, although the Austrian generals had declared it to be no longer neutral. But one of their messengers having been arrested and deprived of the papers he was carrying, they gave notice that the negotiations were suspended, and announced their intended departure. With difficulty they managed to make a start on the 28th April, but before they could get clear of the suburbs they were treacherously attacked by Austrian hussars. Bonnier and Roberjot were killed on the spot, but de Bry, though wounded, succeeded in making his escape. That was the end of the Congress of Rastadt.

Authorities: Sorel, *l'Europe et la Révolution française*, v. ; Garden, *Hist. gén. des traités de paix*, vi. ; G. F. de Martens, *Recueil*, etc., 2ᵐᵉ édit. vi. ; J. Holland Rose, *Life of Napoleon*, i. 142. Koch and Schoell (Brussels edit.), ii. 15.

§ 458. *Congress of Amiens* (so-called) 1801–2.

A good account of the negotiations which preceded this meeting is given by Koch and Schoell.[1] It contains an interesting discussion of the rules of International Law relating to the treatment of coast fishing-boats in time of war.

Preliminary articles of peace between the First Consul and the King of Great Britain and Ireland were signed in London, October 1, 1801, by Otto, commissioner in England for the exchange of prisoners, and Lord Hawkesbury, principal Secretary of State for Foreign Affairs.[2] A summary of these preliminaries may be

---

[1] Brussels edit., ii. 149.   [2] G. F. de Martens, vii. 377.

found in the same work.[1] By Article 15 it was provided that the ratifications should be exchanged within fifteen days, and that, immediately after the completion of this formality, *il sera nommé, de part et d'autre, des pléni-potentiaires, qui se rendront à Amiens pour procéder à la rédaction du traité définitif de concert avec les alliés des puissances contractantes.*[2]

There is no trace here of the word " congress," nor is there in the definite treaty of peace signed at Amiens in French the 25th and in English the 27th of March, 1802. The plenipotentiaries for the parties were the Marquis of Cornwallis, Joseph Bonaparte, Don José Nicolas de Azara, Ambassador to the French Republic, and Roger Jean Schimmelpenninck, Dutch Ambassador to the French Republic, for Great Britain, France, Spain and the Batavian Republic respectively, and the treaty bears the signatures of all four.[3] But in the correspondence of Joseph Bonaparte with Talleyrand and Cornwallis the term " congress " is constantly applied to the negotiation that was being carried on between the English and French plenipotentiaries. In writing to Joseph, December 12, 1801, Talleyrand made use of the following language : " Ce n'est point un congrès général qui vient d'être formé à Amiens et auquel toutes les puissances l'Europe aient le droit d'intervenir par leurs plénipotentiaires ; c'est un congrès de pacification entre la France et ses alliés non pacifiés d'une part ; l'Angleterre et ses alliés non pacifiés de l'autre ; c'est sous ce rapport qu'il ne peut pas même être question au Congrès d'Amiens, de ce qui concerne le Portugal, puisque sa pacification est com-plète."[4] And again, on January 23, he wrote : " Le Congrès d'Amiens n'est pas un congrès général entre quatre puissances distinctes ayant à traiter chacune avec l'autre ; c'est un congrès où la France, l'Espagne

---

[1] Koch and Schoell, Brussels edit., ii. 156. [2] G. F. de Martens, vii. 381.
[3] G. F. de Martens, vii. 404. [4] Du Casse, 47.

et la Hollande réunies, négocient simultanément avec l'Angleterre."

Possibly the reason for giving to this negotiation the name of " congress," as had been done previously in the case of the proposed meeting at Berne (which never took place) and that which was begun at Rastadt between the plenipotentiaries of the French Republic and those of the Germanic Empire, was that in those two instances the locality was a neutral or neutralized city, and, on this occasion, another than the capital of one of the parties.

Joseph and Cornwallis exchanged certified copies of their full-powers, and agreed to defer the exchange of the originals until the end of the negotiation. Although frequent conversations ensued, it was not till December 28 that a protocol of the conferences began to be kept. Who was charged with the drafting of the protocols does not appear, but they were signed by both plenipotentiaries. At the third formal conference the Dutch plenipotentiary was introduced by Joseph. He communicated his full-powers, a copy of which was exchanged with a copy of those of Cornwallis, and he declared that his Government acceded to the bases laid down in the preliminaries of London. At the conference of February 1, Azara was introduced as Spanish plenipotentiary, and the same formalities were observed in his case as in that of Schimmelpenninck. It does not appear from the protocols that either the Dutchman or the Spaniard ever opened his mouth to discuss the provisions of the treaty. The only subsequent occasion on which either was present was the conference of January 22, when Schimmelpenninck asked for a copy of all drafts put forward on either side which might be of interest to Holland. All the other protocols mention only Joseph and Cornwallis. It was finally agreed that the treaty should be drawn up in English as well as French, the Spanish and Dutch plenipotentiaries having apparently been persuaded to renounce their right to have a copy signed in their respective languages. The draft, when finally agreed upon by the two principal contracting parties, was signed by the four plenipotentiaries March 25, and the formal signature of the four copies of the treaty took place the following day.[1]

Authorities : Du Casse, *Hist. des Négoc. diplomat. . . . du Roi Joseph,* t. iii. ; G. F. de Martens, *Recueil,* etc., 2me édit. t. vii. Koch and Schoell (Brussels edit.), ii. 157, where a summary of the Articles is given, followed by a criticism of the treaty itself.

§ 459. *Congress of Prague,* 1813.

After the battle of Lützen Napoleon on May 17 declared himself ready to negotiate for an armistice and to send plenipotentiaries to a peace congress.[2] The armistice was signed on June 4, and was to terminate July 20. On June 26, Metternich had his famous interview with Napoleon at Dresden, nominally to arrange the forms of the congress,[3] and on the 30th he signed with the Duc de Bassano (Maret) a convention in five articles—

" Art. 1. S. M. l'Empereur d'Autriche offre sa médiation pour la paix générale ou continentale. Art. 2. S. M. l'Empereur des Français accepte ladite médiation. Art. 3. Les plénipotentiaires français, russes et prussiens se réuniront, avant le 5 juillet, dans la ville de Prague. Art. 4. Vu l'insuffisance du temps qui reste à courir jusqu'au 20 juillet, terme fixé pour l'expiration par la convention de l'armistice signée à Pleiswitz, le 4 juin, S. M. l'Empereur des Français s'engage à ne pas dénoncer ledit armistice avant le 10 août et S. M. l'Empereur d'Autriche se réserve de faire agréer le même engagement à la Russie et la Prusse. Art. 5. La présente convention ne sera pas rendue publique.
" Elle sera ratifiée, et les ratifications en seront échangées à Dresde dans le terme de quatre jours." [4]

---

[1] Du Casse, 340.　　　　　　　　　[2] Oncken, ii. 308, 315.
[3] Fain, ii. 36 (who gives a wrong date) ; Oncken, ii. 389 ; *Mém. de Metternich,* i. 147 ; ii. 461.
[4] Fain, 45 ; *Mém. de Metternich,* i. 157, where Metternich has inserted the word *armée* after *médiation,* but what he gives is evidently a mere summary of what he proposed (Cf. Fain, 144).

On July 3, Metternich wrote to Bassano postponing the meeting of the plenipotentiaries till July 8, and again, on that date, he put it off till the 12th (Fain, 147, 8).

On July 12, Anstett (a native of Alsace) for Russia, C. W. von Humboldt for Prussia, and Metternich all arrived at Prague. Napoleon delayed sending his plenipotentiaries, and it was not till the 18th that he signed the decree appointing Narbonne and Caulaincourt. The latter did not get to Prague until July 28.

Metternich at once wrote to the French plenipotentiaries proposing to follow the procedure adopted at the Congress of Teschen (q.v.), according to which the parties exchanged written proposals through the mediator, and did not hold conferences, as more expeditious than the method of holding regular sittings and recording them in protocols. The Prussian and Russian plenipotentiaries at once acceded ; but the French, while professing to accept, insisted on oral conferences being combined with the written negotiations, as in accordance with the precedents of Múnster, Nijmegen and Rijswijk. Metternich in reply, transmitted copies of the Prussian and Russian Notes accepting the Austrian proposal, which in the meanwhile Caulaincourt had referred to Napoleon for instructions. To save time, Metternich proposed to proceed at once to the exchange of full-powers, but this was not accepted. After a week's further delay, Narbonne and Caulaincourt wrote, persisting in their proposal of combining the two methods of proceeding. This was declined by Anstett and Humboldt, who adhered to their view that the two ways could not possible be combined, as they were radically different and opposite. Another exchange of Notes followed, August 9 and 10, in which each party insisted on their own plan. Finally, on August 10, Anstett and Humboldt declared that their full-powers had expired. Metternich transmitted copies of their declarations to the French plenipotentiaries on the 11th, expressing the regret with which he found that his functions as mediator had terminated.

On the following day Austria declared war against the Emperor of the French.

Authorities : Fain, Oncken, Metternich. The correspondence relative to the Congress of Prague, given in Fain, 171–205, is also printed in d'Angeberg, *Le Congrès de Vienne,* 1ere partie, 26–44.

§ 460. *Congress of Châtillon,* 1814.

After his defeat at Leipzig, Napoleon made proposals, through the Austrian General Merveldt, whom he released on parole for the purpose, to negotiate for peace. To this overture Metternich responded by despatching to him Saint-Aignan, French minister at Weimar, who had been captured there, with a Note of what the allies were willing to adopt as bases. He also wrote a letter to Caulaincourt, stating that Saint-Aignan would be able to give information as to the views of the allies, but he carefully abstained from attaching his signature to the paper carried by Saint-Aignan. Napoleon, after an interview with the latter, announced his intention of appointing a plenipotentiary, and entrusted the defence of his interests to Caulaincourt, whom he also nominated Minister for Foreign Affairs. The correspondence which ensued led to the Congress of Châtillon, which opened February 5,[1] 1814.

The plenipotentiaries were : for *France,* Caulaincourt ; for *Austria,* Stadion ; for *Russia,* Razoumowski, to whom Anstett was afterwards added ; for *Great Britain,* Aberdeen and Sir Charles Stewart and Cathcart, with Castlereagh in the background ; for *Prussia,* Humboldt. They met at a private house, took their places *pêle-mêle* at a round table, and produced their full-powers in original and in certified copies, which were mutually

---

[1] There is a protocol of Feb. 4, which merely states that the plenipotentiaries made their visits on that day. (Garden, *Hist. gén. des Traités de Paix,* xv. 130).

accepted. The plenipotentiaries of the allies declared that they not only represented the four Powers, but were also ready to treat for peace with France in the name of Europe as a whole, and that the four Powers would be responsible for the acceptation by their allies of whatever arrangements might be agreed upon. They announced that they would carry on a joint negotiation, by sittings for oral discussions to be recorded in the form of protocols. As no secretaries were present, the plenipotentiaries made their own notes, which were afterwards put into shape and approved. To this Caulaincourt agreed. These protocols were prepared in duplicate, and were signed alternately by the French plenipotentiary and by those of the Four Powers, the latter appending their signatures *pêle-mêle*. Every afternoon the plenipotentiaries, including Caulaincourt, dined together at the lodgings of one or other of them informally and in amicable fashion.

The first meeting was held on February 5, and was presided over by Stadion, who took the chair on all other occasions.[1] A declaration was handed to Caulaincourt to the effect that questions of maritime law were to be excluded from discussion. With this exception the proceedings were of a merely formal character and were over in twenty minutes. Razoumowski announced that he had not received his instructions.

After dinner on February 6 a discussion arose respecting the protocol of the first meeting. Caulaincourt had prepared a long memorandum on Razoumowski's statement that he had not received his instructions, and he desired that the protocol should mention the surprise he had expressed at this delay. Stadion answered that it would be sufficient to merely note the fact, without entering upon a long argument, since the allies would otherwise be compelled to reply to the memorandum. On this, Caulaincourt consented to Stadion's proposed wording of the protocol.

[1] Compare F. de Martens, *Recueil* xiv. 197.

On February 7, there was a meeting at noon ; after signing the protocol of the 5th in duplicate, Caulaincourt on one side, the others opposite in no fixed order, the plenipotentiaries of the allies presented their basis of peace—namely, the ancient limits of France, with such minor modifications of the frontier as might be adopted by mutual consent, and the restitution of nearly all the French colonies by England. Caulaincourt having demanded an interval for reflection, the conference separated. At the second meeting, after dinner, he gave in his answer for insertion in the protocol, and the others replied that they received it *ad réferendum*.

After dinner on the 8th, a discussion ensued respecting the protocol. Caulaincourt was asked to omit certain phrases in the preamble to his answer, for, if he maintained them, the allies would have to reply, and that would lead to a written discussion which they would gladly avoid. On their part, the allied plenipotentiaries were ready to excise the preamble of their own proposals, and pass at once to the main question. As Caulaincourt appeared to consent to the proposed alteration, a secretary was sent in the evening to arrange the wording of the protocol with Rayneval, one of his secretaries. However, although willing to cut out a phrase respecting the " natural limits," Caulaincourt said he would demand the insertion of the whole paper rather than consent to its abridgement, and then leave it to them to reply if they wished.

The course of military events interrupted the negotiations, and the next meeting did not take place till the evening of the 17th. On that occasion Stadion read a draft of the treaty proposed by the allies.[1] Caulaincourt said that he must have time to reflect before replying.

Eleven days more elapsed without a meeting of the plenipotentiaries. A sitting was held at 2.30 p.m. on the 28th, at which Caulaincourt asked for a postponement until March 10. On the evening of that day they met at

---

[1] Text in Talleyrand's *Mémoires*, ii. 265.

nine o'clock, when Caulaincourt read a note complaining of the difficulties encountered by his couriers, followed by a declaration fourteen pages long, containing an argument founded on the conditions previously offered at Frankfort, on those announced in the draft communicated on the 7th (17th) and the insufficiency of the concessions to be made by England. When he had finished, Stadion inquired whether this was his answer to the declaration of the allies. He explained that what he had read were simple observations. Stadion thereupon put the document into his portfolio, and was about to break up the meeting when Caulaincourt produced a paper containing what he called a verbal declaration, of which he promised to transmit a copy.

On March 12, the allied plenipotentiaries met during the forenoon, and invited Caulaincourt to a meeting at 8 p.m. He said he had no objections, but regarded as necessary the previous completion and signature of the protocol, in which his declaration had to be included. As there was not time sufficient the meeting was postponed until 1 p.m. on the following day. On that occasion Caulaincourt entered upon a discussion of the observations already presented by him, while the allies insisted upon a direct answer to their proposals. At his suggestion it was finally agreed to meet again at nine o'clock. Stadion, however, sent him a message that if he did not fall in with the ideas of the plenipotentiaries, who had strict orders to demand a clear and precise answer, the negotiations would be broken off.

When they came together in the evening, Caulaincourt repeated what he had already said respecting the answer contained in his written and verbal declarations, which he regarded as sufficiently explicit to afford matter for discussion, and he offered to despatch a courier to Napoleon. Stadion, seeing that there was no intention to present a definite counter-draft, retired for a few minutes to consult with his colleagues. They then returned to the room, and a Note was read stating that, the demand addressed to the French plenipotentiary not having been complied with, the negotiation was at an end. Caulaincourt at once interrupted him, stating that he had a counter-draft, which he was prepared to produce within twenty-four hours ; but as Besnardière, his principal secretary, was unwell, and time was required for putting it into shape, he was ready to present it on the morning of the 15th. The 14th was occupied in drawing up the protocol, which necessitated, as usual, much going to and fro. Caulaincourt desired to insert various phrases respecting the conditions of Frankfort, to which the allies felt bound to reply ; but at last it was agreed to omit them, and to state merely the general results of the meeting : namely, that the allies, having demanded a categorical reply to their three alternatives —viz. that France should either accept the draft treaty offered by them, or reject it, or present a counter-draft corresponding in substance to their draft—an answer must be forthcoming within twenty-four hours.

On March 15, the plenipotentiaries having assembled at ten o'clock, Caulaincourt read his counter-draft. When he had finished, the allies said they must have time to look into it, and demanded that the sitting should be closed. Caulaincourt objected, on the ground that hitherto the protocols had regarded that proposals were taken either *ad referendum* or *ad deliberandum*. Nevertheless, they adhered to their decision.

Accordingly, on March 18, the plenipotentiaries met at one o'clock, to deliver to Caulaincourt a declaration rejecting his counter-draft, and stating that they regarded the negotiation as terminated by the French Government.[1] It was agreed to meet again at 9 p.m. to decide upon the wording of the final protocol. The attempted insertion of two passages which had been accidentally omitted led to the exchange of several messages between the plenipotentiaries of the allies and Caulaincourt in order to determine the text. As it was

[1] Garden, *Hist. gén.* xv. 174 (footnote.)

found impossible for the secretaries to complete this task in time, the final meeting was postponed to 1 p.m. on the 19th.

On that morning Caulaincourt sent Rayneval to de Wacken, one of the Austrian secretaries, to say that he could not consent to the insertion of these new passages in the final protocol, as he had already despatched a copy to Napoleon. The meeting took place at one o'clock, and the protocol was so arranged that the declaration of the allies was left as it had been originally framed, but mention was to be made of the addition which it had been desired to insert. Caulaincourt refused to admit a passage respecting the restoration of the Papal States to the Pope, but he agreed to receive a Note on the subject and to acknowledge its receipt. The day was passed in drawing up and signing the final protocol.

No farewell visits were paid, but the plenipotentiaries of the respective parties left their cards on each other.

Authorities: Sorel, *l'Europe et la Révolution Française,* viii. 191, 203, 209, 221, 223 ; d'Angeberg, *Le Congrès de Vienne et les traités de* 1815 ; A. Fournier, *Der Congress von Châtillon,* and especially the diary of Floret, an Austrian secretary, in the Appendix; Garden, *Hist. générale des Traités de Paix,* xv.

§ 461. *Congress of Vienna,* 1814–15.

This Congress differed from its predecessors in that it was not called together to negotiate a peace, but simply to make arrangements for carrying out the stipulations of a treaty of peace already concluded.

The Treaty of Paris of May 30, 1814,[1] provided by its 32nd Article that—

" Dans le délai de deux mois, toutes les puissances qui ont été engagées de part et d'autre dans la présente guerre enverront des plénipotentiaires à Vienne, pour régler, dans un congrès général, les arrangements qui doivent compléter les dispositions du présent traité."

[1] Duc de Broglie, *Mém. du Prince de Talleyrand,* ii. 182.

There were, in fact, seven separate treaties of peace :
(1) France and Austria ; (2) France and Great Britain ;
(3) France and Prussia ; (4) France and Sweden ; (5)
France and Portugal ; (6) France and Russia ; (7)
France and Spain (20th July). Some of these had
" additional articles," differing in each case. With
Austria were signed a series of " separate and secret
articles," of which Article I provided that

" La disposition à faire des territoires auxquels S. M. Très-
Chrétienne renonce par l'Article III du Traité patent, et les
rapports desquels doit résulter un système d'équilibre réel et
durable en Europe, seront réglés au congrès, sur les bases
arrétées par les Puissances Alliées entre elles, et d'après les
dispositions générales contenues dans les articles suivants."

This " article separé et secret " was also signed with
Prussia.

Various causes led to the postponement of the assemblage of the Congress, and the formal opening was
deferred until November 1.

When Talleyrand arrived at Vienna, on September 24,
he found that the plenipotentiaries of the Allies, *i.e.*
Austria, Great Britain, Russia and Prussia, had already
arranged among themselves that the distribution of the
territories alluded to in the above " separate and secret
article " should be carried out without the intervention
of the other signatories of the Peace of Paris, but by
skilful diplomacy he succeeded in upsetting the scheme,
and eventually the distribution was effected by the
Five Powers in a series of forty-seven conferences.

The following is a list of the plenipotentiaries or
envoys to the Congress between October 3, 1814, and
June 9, 1815.

Plenipotentiaries of the Powers who were parties to
the Peace of Paris of May 30, 1814—

Austria, Metternich [Minister for Foreign Affairs] and
Wessenberg.

Spain, Pedro Gomez-Labrador.

France, Talleyrand [Minister Secretary of State at the Department of Foreign Affairs], Duc de Dalberg, Latour du Pin, A. de Noailles.

Great Britain, Castlereagh [Secretary of State for Foreign Affairs], Wellington, Clancarty, Lord Stewart. (Stratford Canning, British minister in Switzerland, was a member of the committee on Swiss affairs.)

Portugal, Palmella, Saldanha de Gama, Lobo da Silveyra.

Prussia, Hardenberg [Chancellor], Karl Wilhelm von Humboldt.

Russia, Razoumowsky, Stackelberg and Nesselrode [Secretary of State for Foreign Affairs]. (Stein and Anstett represented Russia on the committee on Swiss affairs, and Capo d'Istrias was Russian member of the statistical committee.)

Sweden, Loewenhielm.

Seven other sovereign states, not parties to the Treaty of Paris—namely, Denmark, Genoa, Modena-Massa-Carrara, Orange-Nassau and Holland, Sardinia, Sicily and Switzerland also sent plenipotentiaries. Thirty-six sovereign princes and states of Germany were represented, there were representatives of mediatized German princes and counts, besides those of thirty-three ex-sovereigns, communities, private persons and pretenders. Altogether there were two hundred and sixteen *chefs de mission.*[1]

The plenipotentiaries of the Eight Powers who were parties to the Treaty of Paris undertook to direct the proceedings of the Congress. They set up committees to deal with : (1) the free navigation of rivers passing through the territory of more than one Power, consisting of plenipotentiaries of France, Prussia, Great Britain and Austria, with those of Holland, Bavaria, Baden, Hesse-Darmstadt and Nassau as invited members ; (2) precedence among sovereigns and their

[1] Sorel, *l'Europe et la Révol. franç.,* viii. 382.

diplomatic representatives, consisting of one representative of each of the Eight Powers ; (3) affairs of
Switzerland, one for Prussia, two for Great Britain,
two for Austria, two for Russia, one for France ; (4)
a statistical committee formed of representatives of the
Five Powers, for the purpose of estimating the relative
value of the territories conquered from Napoleon and
his allies, from the point of view of population, not only
as regards number, but also kind and quality. The
report of this committee was destined to aid the plenipotentiaries of the Five Powers engaged in the redistribution of these territories ; (5) a special committee
on the organization of the German Confederation,
composed of representatives of Austria, Prussia, Bavaria,
Hanover and Württemberg. This was afterwards enlarged, so that the Constitution adopted June 8, 1815,
was signed by plenipotentiaries of Denmark, Saxony,
Holland, Brunswick, Electoral Hesse, Saxe-Weimar,
Saxe-Gotha, Saxe-Meiningen, Nassau, Lichtenstein,
Reuss, Schwartzburg-Sonderhausen, Schwartzburg-
Rudolstadt, Waldeck, Schaumburg-Lippe, Lippe,
Lübeck, Frankfort, Bremen, Hamburg, Saxe-Hildburg-
hausen, Saxe-Coburg-Saalfeld, Holstein-Oldenburg,
Mecklenburg-Schwerin, Mecklenburg-Strelitz, Anhalt-
Dessau, Anhalt-Coethen, Anhalt-Bernburg, Hohen-
zollern-Hechingen, Hohenzollern-Sigmarigen, besides
those of the original Five. Baden acceded July 26 and
Württemberg September 1, 1815.

The plenipotentiaries of the Eight Powers also discussed the annexation of Genoa to Piedmont, the prohibition of the slave trade, the arrangements for the
maintenance of Antwerp as a commercial port and the
measures adopted against Napoleon after his escape
from Elba. They appointed a drafting committee to
frame the general treaty or *Acte Final*,[1] formed of plenipotentiaries, one for each of the Eight Powers, with la
Besnardière and Gentz as principal draftsmen.

[1] Treaty is the expression used in the instrument itself.

It had been originally proposed by the Five Powers that the *Acte Final* should be signed by the plenipotentiaries, (1) of the Crowned Heads, (2) of Electoral-Hesse and Grand-Dukes bearing the title of Royal Highness, (3) of other princes and free cities, but it was finally decided to limit signature to the plenipotentiaries of the Eight Powers who were parties to the Treaty of Paris.

At their first conference, on October 30, 1814, they decided to form a committee of three plenipotentiaries to verify the full-powers of the representatives of the Eight Powers, and to invite the plenipotentiaries of other Powers to deposit theirs at a bureau to be opened at the Imperial chancery. On lots being drawn, Russia, Great Britain and France were chosen for this purpose.

Talleyrand proposed that, pending a settlement of questions of precedence among Crowned Heads, the order of places occupied at the sittings should prejudice no one, and that the Austrian First Plenipotentiary, Prince Metternich, should be President. The signatures to the protocol of this sitting were affixed *pêle-mêle*. It was only when the *Acte Final* came to be signed, on June 9, 1815, that the alphabetical order of the Powers according to the French language was definitively adopted.

Article 118 enumerates the treaties, conventions, declarations, regulations and other documents, seventeen in number, which form annexes to the *Acte Final*. One original, signed by those of the plenipotentiaries who had not already departed, was to be deposited in the Imperial Archives at Vienna, each of the other six[1] signatory Powers receiving an original counter part. Each Power had to furnish seven ratifications.[2]

Authorities: d'Angeberg, *le Congrès de Vienne et les Traités de 1815* ; *Cambridge Modern History*, ix. chaps. 19 and 21 ; *British and Foreign State Papers*, ii, iii, vi, xxii.

[1] Spain did not sign, but acceded in 1817.
[2] Garden, *Traité complet*, iii. 196. The Treaty of Vienna was ratified Nov. 4, 1815.

§ 462. *The so-called Congresses of Aix-la-Chapelle*, 1818, *Troppau*, 1820, *Laybach*, 1821, *and Verona*, 1822.

A circular of May 1818, signed by the ministers of Austria, Great Britain, Prussia and Russia at Paris to the Ministers of their Courts accredited to various foreign Powers states that the allied sovereigns who had signed with France the treaty of November 20, 1815, having agreed to meet during the following autumn, in order to take into consideration, in concert with His Most Christian Majesty, the internal condition of France, and to decide whether the military occupation may cease or be continued, Their Imperial and Royal Majesties desire to avoid any unfounded interpretations which might tend to give to their meeting the character of a Congress, and to set aside (*écarter*) at the same time the intervention of other princes and cabinets in the discussions of which the decision is expressly reserved to themselves (*i.e.* by Article 5 of the said treaty).[1]

The Emperors of Austria and Russia, the King of Prussia, the plenipotentiaries of France and Great Britain met at Aix-la-Chapelle for the purpose of expediting the evacuation of French territory occupied by the allied forces. Four treaties of the same tenor and date were signed on October 9, 1818, by the French plenipotentiary with those of the Four other Powers, for the evacuation of French territory by the allied troops.[2] On this occasion the Five Powers also agreed to the creation of an intermediate class of diplomatic agents between Ministers of the second class and *Chargés*

---

[1] d'Angeberg, 1742 ; *Brit. and For. State Papers*, v. 1216.

[2] *Brit. and For. State Papers*, vi. 6. Protocols of Conferences of November 3 and 9, providing for payment by France of the War Indemnity, *ibid.*, ii. 12. Protocol of Conference of Nov. 15, *ibid.*, 14. Declaration of the Five Courts addressed to all the other Courts of Europe dated Nov. 15, announcing their intention to regulate their international relations by the principles of the Law of Nations, *ibid.*, 18. Protocols of Conferences of Nov. 7, 11, 14, 15 (2), 19, 21, *ibid.*, v. 1081. Protocols of Conferences of Oct. 24, Nov. 4, 11, 19, respecting abolition of the Slave Trade, *ibid*, vi. 58, 64, 86. The original protocols at the Public Record Office, F.O., 92, 35–40. For a general account of the proceedings, see F. de Martens, *Traités et Conventions de la Russie*, vii 291–327. Alison Phillips, *Modern Europe*, 5th, edit. 61.

d'affaires, to be denominated Ministers-resident.[1] It was agreed to refer the question of uniform practice with regard to salutes at sea to the diplomatic conference at London.

Meetings of the plenipotentiaries of the Four Powers took place sometimes with the Duc de Richelieu, sometimes without. The former were: for Austria, Metternich; for Great Britain, Castlereagh and Wellington; for Prussia, Hardenberg and Bernstorff ; for Russia, Nesselrode and Capo d'Istrias. The records are styled " Protocole des Conférences d'Aix-la-Chapelle," and the first was dated 29 September. It was signed by all the plenipotentiaries, . including the Duc de Richelieu. The second is of 30 September, without him, as is also the third, of 1 October. On the latter occasion the protocols of that date and of 30 September were approved and signed by all the plenipotentiaries of the four allied Cabinets. At the meeting of 2 October, the Duc de Richelieu was present, and signed the protocol.

The fifth protocol, dated 3 October, records the meeting of the 3 October, which was attended by the plenipotentiaries of the five Courts. The Duc de Richelieu read out a memorandum drawn up in the form of a Note verbale. In this document the Procès Verbal of the Conference of 13 October, 1815, between the plenipotentiaries of the four Allied Courts is spoken of indifferently as a *procès verbal* and as a protocol, which shows that even in France, of which the language employed in drafts is authoritative for the use of diplomatic terms, the two expressions were regarded as denoting the same thing.

The bases of arrangements for the discharge of French liabilities proposed by the Duc de Richelieu were referred to Wellington, as an expert in financial matters, and his report was adopted by the 6th protocol, of 8 October, which was signed only by Metternich, Castlereagh, Wellington and Hardenberg, though the preamble

[1] Text in § 272.   [2] See *Brit. and For. State Papers*, III, 229.

states that it was accepted by the " Ministres des quatre Cours." Protocol No. 7, of October 9, records that the " Ministres des cinq cours " agreed to the draft of a convention relative to the evacuation of French territory, and initialed it. They met again in the evening and proceeded to sign the convention. At the meeting of October 11 it was agreed to address a circular to the ministers of the Four Powers accredited to the Courts which had acceded to the treaty of Paris of November 20, 1815, instructing them to communicate the fact of the signature of the convention. On the same occasion letters were read that the Elector of Hesse had addressed to the sovereigns of the Four Powers asking their consent to his proposed assumption of the title of King, and the plenipotentiaries were unanimously of opinion that such a step would present no advantage, but on the contrary would produce numerous inconveniences. On October 14 the protocols of the previous three meetings were read and approved. A discussion took place on the principles which should be adopted for regulating the relations of the Four Courts and the character of their future meetings as regarded France and other European Powers. The plenipotentiaries of the Five Powers signed a separate protocol declining to consent to the request of the Elector of Hesse.[1]

Besides the main question for the decision of which this meeting of plenipotentiaries had been convoked, many other matters were discussed, such as—the objection of Baden to the transit of the Bavarian contingent of the army of occupation on its withdrawal from French territory ; mediation between Spain and Portugal relative to the occupation of Uruguay by Brazil, which was entrusted to the ministers of the Four Powers at Paris in conjunction with the French government ; the application of the treaties of 1815 to the altered state of things ; the territorial boundaries of Baden ; certain claims of French subjects against foreign governments ;

---

[1] See § 63.

the question of mediation between Spain and her revolted colonies ; the slave trade ; the ownership of the Duchy of Bouillon ; the dispute between Sweden and Denmark respecting the assumption of the Norwegian debt by the former Power ; the Barbary pirates, draft treaty prepared by the diplomatic conference in London, and proposed *démarche* of the British and French Governments ; other territorial questions between certain minor German potentates ; pirates on the coasts of South America sailing under unrecognised flags ; Napoleon's detention at St. Helena ; criminal intrigues in the Low Countries ;. demands of the mediatised Princes and Courts of Germany ; Prince Windischgrätz's claim against the King of Württemberg ; claims of Hesse-Homburg against the Grand-Duke of Hesse-Darmstadt ; invitation to France to join the concert of the Four Powers ; a complaint of the inhabitants of Monaco respecting the system of government introduced by the Prince ; Jews and the legislation affecting them in different countries, which was brought on the tapis by the Russian plenipotentiary Capo d'Istrias.[1]

The Congress was wound up on November 22 by protocol No. 47, by which it was agreed that, the conferences of Paris relating to the occupation of French territory and the execution of the treaty of November 20, 1815, having no longer any object, in view of the Convention of October 9 and subsequent declarations (*Actes*) of Aix-la-Chapelle, the conferences should terminate, and that the ministers accredited at Paris should be instructed " to close the protocol."

§ 463. The same observation—namely, that they were not properly described by the use of the term " congress " is applicable also to the meetings at Troppau on October 20, 1820, adjourned to Laybach in 1821, and at Verona in 1822, which had for their object the repression of

---

[1] F. de Martens, *Traités et Conventions de la Russie*, vii., 298.

revolutionary movements in Naples, Piedmont and Spain.

At the first of these were present the Emperors of Austria and Russia and the Crown Prince of Prussia.[1] Austria was represented at the conferences by Metternich, Russia by Capo d'Istrias,[2] Prussia by Hardenberg. Great Britain deputed Lord Stewart (Castlereagh's brother), her Ambassador at Vienna, while France sent de la Ferronays and Caraman, her Ambassadors at Petersburg and Vienna. The first meeting took place on October 23. The French Government had prepared a memorandum containing a series of questions to Austria as to the objects contemplated by the Congress. As Pasquier states (v. 27) that the idea of holding a Congress had come from France, it is difficult to understand why they did not take the precaution of defining and limiting those objects simultaneously with their proposal for its convocation. The French plenipotentiaries were instructed to attend the meetings, to take part in the discussions and to agree to all resolutions which might be adopted in conformity with the bases laid down in the memorandum referred to, provided these resolutions were accepted by the four other Powers. Should the two plenipotentiaries find themselves in mutual disagreement, they were to refer to Paris for further instructions. This particular order wounded the *amour propre* of Caraman, who claimed that, as the senior, he should have the right of overruling his colleague. Stewart had been authorized to attend the meetings, but to refer to his Government every point that might be raised ; and this attitude on the part of England naturally had the effect of delaying the settlement of any question laid before the Congress. The French plenipotentiaries were instructed to profit by a suitable

---

[1] Pasquier (v. 24) states that the King of Prussia attended in person. According to Gentz (*Briefe an Pilat*, 423, 435) the Crown Prince represented Prussia from Oct. 20 till the King's arrival on Nov. 7.

[2] Shilder, *Alexander I, etc.*, iv. 182, adds Nesselrode and Golovkin for Russia and Bernstorff for Prussia.

occasion to put forward the points contained in the French memorandum, but la Ferronays was told to sound the Emperor Alexander before taking this step. Caraman, however, very imprudently communicated to Metternich the whole of the instructions they had received, in defiance of the directions of the French minister for Foreign Affairs.

At the first meeting, October 23, Metternich took up the whole time by reading a memorandum on the general state of Europe, the remedies to be applied to the evils which threatened the entire social fabric, and the particular measures to be recommended with respect to the constitutional (or, revolutionary) movement at Naples. The right of one State to intervene in the affairs of another, when the political changes that take place in it are of a nature to threaten the interests of the first State and to imperil the very foundations of its existence, was the doctrine which inspired the whole.

The effect of this memorandum was to delay proceedings, in order that the French and English plenipotentiaries might have time to obtain instructions, and an opportunity was thus furnished for frequent conversations between the three Sovereigns.

At the second meeting were read Russian and Prussian memoranda. The former made certain reservations as to the right of intervention, the latter proved to be in entire accordance with Metternich's views.

The French and English Governments were of opinion that it would be a waste of time to discuss general principles of a highly disputable character, and that the Powers would do well to limit themselves to the consideration of the particular case of Naples. The necessary reference to Paris and London for the answers of the two constitutional Powers, caused a delay which enabled the three autocracies to draw still closer together, and Metternich found no difficulty in inducing them to join in a declaration of reciprocal guarantee against all attempts at revolution. Accordingly, on November 19, they signed a *protocole préliminaire*, with two annexes. One was an agreement between the three Powers to invite the King of Naples to meet them at Laybach in order to concert with them the means of re-establishing order in his dominions, the other was the draft of a letter to be addressed to him by each of the three sovereigns conveying to him this invitation. A meeting was then held with the French and English plenipotentiaries, at which the documents were laid before them, with a request to communicate them to their governments and ask for their *bons offices* in unison with those of the three sovereigns.

Both England and France refused to accept the *protocole préliminaire*. The French Government drew up a carefully worded Note explanatory of their views, and instructed their representatives not to deliver it unless they found that verbal statements were insufficient ; and also that if, after finding it indispensable to present this Note, they were invited to fresh conferences at which the doctrine laid down in the protocol came to be discussed, to combat it energetically. Pasquier sent, in addition, a refutation of the protocol clause by clause for their guidance, but they were never to let it go out of their hands nor to allow any one to see it. Caraman, whose personal opinion was identical with Metternich's, had, as already mentioned, taken the extraordinary step of communicating to him not only the official Note, which he had agreed with la Ferronays to suppress, but also the refutation, which he had been prohibited in the most formal manner from showing to any one. Metternich then contrived that the latter document should be seen by the Emperor Alexander, and that it should be suggested to have emanated from Pasquier alone, unknown to the Duc de Richelieu, the Prime Minister. It reached Alexander, either from Caraman directly, or more probably through Nesselrode. Alexander was by this manœuvre thrown entirely into the arms of Metternich. He caused a counter-refutation to be prepared by Capo d'Istrias, and delivered to la Ferronays for transmission to the French Government, who were deeply offended with Caraman when they came to know of his proceedings. It was, however, not judged convenient to recall him.

The Congress lasted a little more than two months. There were only eight meetings of the *plenum*. On December 28, the two Emperors left for Laybach. Before their departure a circular of December 8 was issued to the Austrian, Prussian and Russian ministers at foreign Courts, enclosing a statement of the results of the conferences that had been held (*Brit. and For. State Papers*, viii. 1149). To this Castlereagh replied in a circular of January 19, 1821, to the British ministers at foreign Courts (*ibid.*, 1160) stating the reasons why Great Britain had declined to become a party to the measures adopted by the Three Powers : namely, the establishment of certain general principles for the regulation of the future political conduct of the Allies, and the proposed mode of dealing with the affairs of Naples.[1]

§ 464. At Laybach were present the Emperors of Austria and Russia, the King of Naples, the French, English and Prussian delegates as before, to the French being added Blacas, as chief plenipotentiary, and Sir Robert Gordon, first secretary of the British embassy at Paris, being joined with his chief. The Pope, the King of Sardinia, the Grand Duke of Tuscany and the Duke of Modena were invited by the three Powers to send plenipotentiaries, and the gathering thus assumed more of the character of a general congress.

Of documents emanating from the assemblage[2] there are : a declaration of the sovereigns dated February 13, which was evidently inspired by Metternich, and a

[1] Pasquier, vol. v. chap. i. Alison Phillips, *Modern Europe*, 5th edit. 94.
[2] d'Angeberg, 1804 and 1811 ; *Brit. and Foreign State Papers*, vii. 1175, 1199.

second dated May 12 on behalf of Austria, Prussia and Russia in connexion with the close of the conference,[1] together with a circular of the same date, drafted by Gentz, and issued by the Three Powers to their diplomatic agents at foreign Courts. Towards the end of this circular an intimation was given that, " La réunion qui va finir doit se renouveler dans le courant de l'année prochaine. On y prendra en considération le terme à fixer aux mesures qui, de l'aveu de toutes les Cours d'Italie, et particulièrement de celles de Naples et de Turin, ont été jugées nécessaires pour raffermir la tranquillité de la Péninsule."[2]

§ 465. This further meeting, which is also styled a Congress by historians, took place at Verona. France was represented by her minister for Foreign Affairs, Montmorency, by Caraman ambassador at Vienna, by de la Ferronays ambassador at Petersburg, de Rayneval minister at Berlin, de Serre ambassador at Naples, Blacas, and finally Chateaubriand ambassador in London, and the Duke of Wellington attended for Great Britain. The Emperors of Austria and Russia and the King of Prussia also betook themselves thither, likewise the King of Sardinia and a crowd of Italian princes. The conferences began September 20 and lasted for over two months and a half. France undertook to put down the revolutionary movement in Spain by which Ferdinand VII had been compelled to accept the constitution of 1812. Great Britain was steadily opposed to any kind of intervention in Spanish affairs. A circular signed by Metternich, Bernstorff and Nesselrode, December 14, 1822, to the diplomatic agents of the Three Powers,[3] stated that the withdrawal of the Austrian

---

[1] Pasquier (v. 152) states that the conferences at Laybach ended February 26, after fifteen sittings had been held ; but (p. 194) that the two Emperors did not take their departure until May 12 and 13 respectively.
[2] d'Angeberg, 1713, 1716 ; *Brit. and For. State Papers*, viii. 1204. Alison Philips, *Modern Europe*, 5th edit. 97.
[3] *Brit. and For. State Papers*, x. 921.

troops occupying Piedmont would begin on December 31 and be terminated September 30, 1823, while the Austrian forces in occupation of the two Sicilies would be diminished to the extent of 17,000 men as speedily as possible. The same circular announced the intention of the Three Powers to break off diplomatic relations with Spain. The convention for the cessation of the temporary military line of occupation in Piedmont, signed by the plenipotentiaries of the Three Powers with the Sardinian representatives, was signed the same day as the circular.[1] (For the negotiations at Verona, and the policy adopted by France and the three Northern Powers, see Pasquier, *Mémoires*, v. 451, 454; F. de Martens, *Recueil des Traités et Conventions conclus par la Russie*, etc., iv. pt. i. 322; Chateaubriand, *le Congrès de Verone;* Alison Phillips, *Modern Europe*, 5th edition, 122).

§ 466. *Congress of Paris*, 1856.
Plenipotentiaries—

France : Count Walewski, Minister for Foreign Affairs, and Baron Bourqueney, Envoy Extraordinary at Vienna.

Austria : Count Buol, Minister for Foreign Affairs and President of the Council, and Baron Hübner, Envoy Extraordinary and Minister Plenipotentiary at Paris.

Great Britain : Lord Clarendon, Secretary of State for Foreign Affairs, and Lord Cowley, Ambassador Extraordinary and Plenipotentiary at Paris.

Russia : Count Orloff, Aide-de-Camp of the Emperor, and Baron Brunnow, Envoy Extraordinary and Minister Plenipotentiary to the German Confederation.

Sardinia : Count Cavour, President of the Council and Minister of State for Finance, Marchese de Villamarina, Envoy Extraordinary and Minister Plenipotentiary at Paris.

Turkey : Aali Pasha, Grand Vizier, and Djemil-Bey,

---

[1] *Brit. and For. State Papers*, x. 731.

Envoy Extraordinary and Minister Plenipotentiary at Paris.

The first meeting was held February 25. Count Buol proposed that Count Walewski should be chosen to occupy " la présidence des travaux de la Conférence." and the proposal was unanimously accepted. He then proposed to entrust the drafting of the Protocols to M. Benedetti, directeur des affaires politiques at the ministry for foreign affairs.

The plenipotentiaries then proceeded to produce their full-powers, which were found to be in good and due form and were deposited among the official documents (*actes*) of the Conference.

It was agreed that the plenipotentiaries should undertake mutually to observe strict secrecy with regard to what passed at the " conference."

The Sardinian plenipotentiaries declared that they gave their entire adhesion to the Protocol signed at Vienna, February 1.

It was agreed that the said protocol, with its annex, of which a copy initialled by the plenipotentiaries was annexed to the protocol of this sitting, should be taken as having the character of formal Preliminaries of Peace. The protocol in question stated that a draft of preliminaries annexed thereto having been accepted by the Governments of France, Austria, Great Britain, Russia and Turkey, their representatives agreed that plenipotentiaries provided with full-powers to proceed to the signature of formal preliminaries of peace should meet at Paris within three weeks. The draft preliminaries consisted of five paragraphs, respecting the Danubian Principalities, the Danube; the Black Sea, the Christian populations subject to the Porte, and the right of the belligerents to present conditions additional to the above four.

It was agreed that an armistice should be concluded by the Commanders-in-Chief of the opposing forces, to terminate on March 31, unless it was previously renewed by common agreement. The armistice was not to affect blockades already established or to be established, but the naval commanders were to be ordered to abstain, during its continuance, from all hostilities against the territories of the belligerents.

At the seventh sitting the Congress [1] decided that a committee consisting of Count Buol, Baron Bourqueney and Aali Pasha should be formed for drafting the text of the treaty of peace as far as concerned the Principalities. For the drafting of all the stipulations of the Treaty of Peace, Aali Pasha and the second plenipotentiaries of Austria, France, Great Britain, Russia and Sardinia (see 9th Protocol). Lord Cowley and the Marchese de Villamarina were afterwards added, and Baron Hübner was substituted for Count Buol (ninth protocol).

Also, the Congress decided that the Prussian Government should be invited to send plenipotentiaries to Paris. Accordingly at the eleventh sitting the Prussian plenipotentiaries, Baron Manteuffel, President of the Council and Minister for Foreign Affairs, and Count Hatzfeldt, Envoy Extraordinary and Minister Plenipotentiary at Paris, were introduced, and presented their full-powers, which having been found in good and due form were deposited among the official documents of the Congress.

At the twenty-second sitting, April 8, the first French plenipotentiary proposed the adoption of the four principles forming the basis of what is known as the Declaration of Paris. At the twenty-third sitting a draft of the declaration was adopted, and it was signed at the twenty-fourth sitting by the Plenipotentiaries, *dûment autorisés*, on which occasion, as recorded in the protocol of that sitting, it was further agreed, on the motion of the president, that

" les Puissances qui l'auront signée ou qui y auront accédé,

[1] It will be observed that the assemblage began by styling itself a " Conference," and, then, apparently without discussion of its title, assumed the name of " Congress."

ne pourront entrer, à l'avenir, sur l'application du droit des neutres en temps de guerre, en aucun arrangement qui ne repose à la fois sur les quatres principes objet de la dite déclaration."

The Treaty of Peace was signed at the nineteenth sitting, March 30, together with a Convention respecting the Straits of the Dardanelles and Bosphorus, a Convention between Russia and Turkey, limiting their naval forces in the Black Sea, and a Convention between Great Britain, France and Russia respecting the Aland Islands.

At the twenty-fourth sitting, which was the last, Count Orloff proposed to offer to Count Walewski the thanks of the Congress for the manner in which he had guided its labours. Lord Clarendon supported the motion, which was accepted by all the plenipotentiaries, who determined to make special mention of it in the protocol.

Count Walewski made the usual reply, expressing his gratitude for the indulgence of which he had not ceased to receive proofs during the conferences.

By Article 1 it is stipulated that peace and amity shall from the date of the exchange of ratifications exist between the high contracting parties, their heirs and successors, their states and subjects in perpetuity.

And by Article 20, in return for the towns, ports and territories enumerated in Article 4, to be restored to the Emperor of Russia, the latter consented to a rectification of his frontier in Bessarabia.

Thus the Congress fulfilled the conditions forming part of the definition attempted in § 439.

Authorities : *Parliamentary Papers* 1856 (reprinted in *British and Foreign State Papers*, vol. 46) ; Emile Ollivier, *L'Empire Libéral*, t. iii. ; Comte de Hübner, *Souvenirs d un Ambassadeur*, t. i.

§ 467. *Congress of Berlin*, 1878.

Turkey having refused to accept the suggestions for the future government of her Balkan possessions made by the Six Powers at the Constantinople Conference (§ 487), Russia declared war. On January 19/31, 1878, a protocol defining the bases of peace between the two Powers was signed at Adrianople, and also an armistice This Protocol was followed by Preliminaries of Peace signed at San Stefano,[1] Feb. 19/March 3, 1878, and the ratifications were exchanged at Petersburg, March 5/17, 1878.

On the initiative of Austria-Hungary, invitations to a Congress to be held at Berlin were issued by the German Government.

The objects to be attained were—

1. The establishment of the autonomous and tributary principality of Bulgaria.

2. The formation of the province of Eastern Roumelia, with administrative autonomy.

3. The occupation and administration of Bosnia and Herzegovina by Austria-Hungary.

4. The recognition of the independence of Montenegro, with an accession of territory.

5. The recognition of the independence of Serbia, with an accession of territory.

6. The recognition of the independence of Rumania, and the cession of a portion of Bessarabia to Russia, by Rumania, which received other territory in compensation

7. The cession of Turkish territory in Asia to Russia.

Peace had already been signed by the belligerents.

The plenipotentiaries were—

For *Germany*, Prince Bismarck, Chancellor ; Herr von Bülow, Secretary of State in the Department of Foreign Affairs ; Prince Hohenlohe-Schillingfurst, Ambassador Extraordinary and Plenipotentiary at Paris.

For *Austria*, Count Andrassy, Minister of the Imperial Household and for Foreign Affairs ; Count Karolyi, Ambassador Extraordinary and Plenipotentiary at

[1] On the Sea of Marmora, west of Constantinople.

Berlin ; Baron Haymerle, Ambassador Extraordinary and Plenipotentiary at Rome.

For *France*, M. Waddington, Secretary of State in the Department of Foreign Affairs ; Count de Saint-Vallier, Ambassador Extraordinary and Plenipotentiary at Berlin ; Mons. Desprez, Director of Political Affairs at the French Foreign Office.

For *Great Britain*, Lord Beaconsfield, Prime Minister ; Marquis of Salisbury, Secretary of State for Foreign Affairs ; Lord Odo Russell, Ambassador Extraordinary and Plenipotentiary at Berlin.

For *Italy*, Count Corti, Minister for Foreign Affairs ; Count de Launay, Ambassador Extraordinary and Plenipotentiary at Berlin.

For *Russia*, Prince Gortchakow, Chancellor ; Count Peter Schuvaloff, Ambassador Extraordinary and Plenipotentiary in London ; Mons. d'Oubril, Ambassador Extraordinary and Plenipotentiary at Berlin.

For *Turkey*, Carathéodory Pasha, Minister of Public Works ; Mehemed Ali, General ; Sadoullah Bey, Ambassador Extraordinary and Plenipotentiary at Berlin.

At the first sitting, June 13, 1878, on the proposal of Count Andrassy, Prince Bismarck was elected President.

After accepting in a few words the task of presiding, Prince Bismarck proposed as secretary M. de Radowitz, German minister at Athens, and as his assistants the Count de Moüy, first secretary of the French Embassy at Berlin, Herr Busch, Legations-rath, Baron von Holstein, Conseiller de Légation, and Count Bismarck, Secretary of Legation.

These gentlemen were then introduced and presented to the Congress.

The President then announced that to the Bureau thus formed would be entrusted the documents and full-powers, which the members of the Congress would be so good as to deposit for this purpose with the Bureau. Thereupon the plenipotentiaries handed over their full-powers, except the Turk Sadoullah Bey, the two other Turks not having yet arrived.

The President then delivered a speech defining the scope of the Congress, and proposed the order in which the various questions should be taken. He suggested the confidential exchange of views between plenipotentiaries between the sittings of the Congress.

At the second meeting it was agreed to take the protocol of the previous sitting as read, unless a member had made an amendment to it, or asked to have it read.[1] The President expressed the expectation that the plenipotentiaries would be unanimous in keeping their deliberations secret. He proposed also that all proposals and documents destined to appear in the protocol, should be put in writing and read by the member who introduced them.

At the third sitting it was agreed that Greek representatives could be invited to attend, whenever it should be thought necessary, although the Greeks were not signatories of the treaty of 1856 and Convention of 1871.

At the eighth sitting it was announced that Mons. Delyannis, Greek minister for Foreign Affairs, and Mons. Rangabé, Minister at Berlin, had been designated to represent Greece. They were accordingly heard at the ninth sitting. On the latter occasion it was also decided to hear the Rumanian delegates under the same conditions as those of Greece. Permission to attend had been refused to the Serbians.

At the tenth sitting the Rumanian delegates, Messieurs Bratiano and Cogalniceano were heard.

At the fourteenth sitting it was decided to admit a representative of Persia with respect to the town of Khotour, and he was accordingly heard at the fifteenth sitting.

A Drafting Committee was formed at the eighth sitting, consisting of Prince Hohenlohe, Baron Haymerle, Mons. Desprez, Lord Odo Russell, Count de Launay, M.

---

[1] *Brit. and For. State Papers*, lxix. 893.

d'Oubril and Carathéodory Pasha—that is, one for each Power.

At the ninth sitting a Boundary Committee was appointed, consisting of Prince Hohenlohe, Baron Haymerle, Count de Saint-Vallier, Lord Odo Russell, Count de Launay, Count Peter Schuvaloff and Mehemed Ali Pasha.

At the seventeenth sitting the Drafting Committee presented a report, and certain of the articles destined to form part of the treaty were read, discussed and agreed to.

At the eighteenth sitting the remainder of the draft articles were read, and the draft preamble agreed to.

At the nineteenth sitting the Congress laid down the principle " que se sont les ratifications, et non pas seulement la signature, qui donnent aux Traités leur valeur définitive."

The Congress closed with the twentieth sitting, on July 13.

The President invited the plenipotentiaries to proceed to the signature of the treaty, whereupon Count Andrassy, in the name of his colleagues, expressed their warm gratitude to His Serene Highness Prince Bismarck for the wisdom and indefatigable energy with which he had directed their labours ; and also their respectful acknowledgment of the goodwill and hospitality experienced from H.M. the Emperor of Germany and the august imperial family.

Prince Bismarck made a suitable acknowledgement of the compliment.

The seven copies of the treaty were then signed, all in the French language.

The President then declared the labours of the Congress to be terminated. He expressed the thanks of the Congress to those of the plenipotentiaries who had served on committees, and particularly to Mons. Desprez and Prince Hohenlohe. Also to the members of the secretariat and all functionaries and officers who had taken part in the consideration of special questions. Finally he thanked his colleagues once more for their goodwill towards himself, and closed the sitting.

The ratifications were exchanged August 3, and a *procès-verbal* drawn up signed by representatives of the signatory Powers, viz. Odo Russell, Radowitz, E. Mayr,[1] Moüy,[1] Arapoff,[1] and Sadoullah Bey. The Turkish ratification did not arrive in time, but Sadoullah Bey undertook to exchange it a fortnight later.

[1] *Chargés d'affaires.*

CONFERENCES

§ 468. THE practice of holding Conferences of the diplomatic representatives of the Great Powers for the settlement of international questions was a natural development from the Congress of Vienna and the so-called Congresses held at Aix-la-Chapelle in 1818, and at Troppau, Laybach and Verona in 1820, 1821 and 1822, where the leading Powers, then considered to be only five in number, had taken upon themselves the general direction of the affairs of the Continent as a whole. This gradually developed into what has been known as the Concert of Europe.

" Conference," so-called, became the adopted procedure for the regulation of international affairs earlier than is usually supposed.

In 1814 after the armies of Austria, Prussia and Russia crossed the Rhine, the principal ministers of the Four Allied Powers began to consult together on the terms of peace to be offered. On January 29 there was a meeting at Langres which Castlereagh[1] in his despatch

[1] Webster, 141.

of that date terms a " Council." It was composed of Metternich and Stadion for Austria, Nesselrode and Razoumowksy for Russia, Hardenberg for Prussia and Castlereagh for Great Britain, with the Russian Pozzo di Borgo and the Austrian Binder as Secretaries.[1] It was agreed to enter on negotiations at Châtillon with Caulaincourt, that the Four Great Powers should treat for peace with France in the name of Europe, reserving to themselves the right to make suitable communications to their allies, that a proposal should be made to France for the limitation of her territory to what it had formerly been, subject to a suitable rearrangement of the frontier, that France should be made acquainted with the general arrangements to be entered into among the other European Powers, but not to make these a subject of negotiation, to give identical instructions to the delegates of the Four Great Powers, and finally, in case the negotiation was broken off, to make the conditions offered to the French Government known to the French nation.

The congress of Châtillon opened on February 5, 1814 (§ 460). Military operations continued to be carried on during the congress.

On February 13 a conference was held at Troyes between the principal ministers of the Allies to decide on the reply to be given to Caulaincourt's request of the 9th for an armistice and other points of policy, and on Metternich's proposal a draft treaty of peace was agreed to, which was delivered to the French negotiator on February 17.

This was followed on February 25 by a conference at Bar-sur-Aube, to settle a modification of the plan of campaign, which was attended by the three monarchs, their ministers and chiefs of staff. The Emperor Alexander himself drew up the protocol.[2]

The military operations ended with the capitulation

---

[1] Sbornik, xxxi, 360, where the text of the protocol is to be found.
[2] Sbornik, xxxi, 364.

of Paris on March 31, and the entry of the Allies the same day.

After the ministers of the allies came together in Paris they no doubt held frequent meetings, but the only extant protocol is that of a meeting of April 10[1] of the plenipotentiaries of Austria, Prussia and Russia with those of Napoleon Buonaparte, to agree on the articles of a treaty fixing the arrangements relating to the Emperor Napoleon and his family. Castlereagh who had reached Paris that day, and signed the protocol, together with Metternich, Nesselrode and Hardenberg was present ; on behalf of Napoleon the signatories were Caulaincourt, Ney and Macdonald.

The draft handed to Caulaincourt at Châtillon on February 17 was taken as the basis of the treaty of peace agreed to with the ministers of Louis XVIII and signed on May 30.

On May 31 the ministers of the Four Powers had a conference at Paris at which it was agreed to defer to the proposed meeting in London and the Congress at Vienna provided for by the treaty of peace the final destination of the territories which had fallen into the hands of the allies.[2]

The Emperor Alexander, the King of Prussia and Metternich then proceeded to London, where certain conferences were held, of which there are records.[3] The first of these is an " Apostille " to the Paris protocol of May 31, signed by Münster and Hardenberg[4], providing for temporary occupation of certain territories in North Germany by Hanoverian troops.

On June 16 the protocol provides for the issue of a circular to all the participating Powers, inviting them to send their plenipotentiaries to Vienna by August 1. It was also agreed to convene the plenipotentiaries of Austria, Russia, France, Great Britain, Prussia, Spain

---

[1] *Brit. and For. State Papers*, i, 132.
[2] F. de Martens, *Traités et Conventions*, etc. iii. 168.
[3] P.R.O. F.O., $\frac{29}{5}$
[4] Cousin of the Prussian Chancellor.

and Sweden in committee, to present a draft of [territorial] arrangements for Europe, in accordance with a plan to be settled beforehand by the Courts of Austria, Russia, Great Britain and Prussia, for which purpose their ministers were to meet in Vienna not later than the first days of August.

But Alexander having formed the intention of proceeding straight to St. Petersburg, a conference met on June 20 to consider the postponement of the Congress to the month of September. The ministers of Austria, Great Britain and Prussia were evidently under the apprehension that Alexander might resolve to stay away from Vienna and they urged him to give assurances that he would abandon any such intention. In that case the plenipotentiaries to the Congress should meet there on September 1, that the Four Great Powers should formally undertake not to allow anything to be prejudged in the meantime, and that the occupation of the territories of which the destiny was not definitely fixed by the treaty of peace or by previous treaties between the four Courts should continue to be only provisional. The record was signed by Metternich, Castlereagh and Hardenberg.

Next comes a *procès-verbal* of the Conference of June 22, of which the object was to decide on the measures to be taken for collecting the arrears of revenue from the Belgian provinces.

A protocol of June 24 lays down the measures for carrying out the union of Belgium with Holland and the transfer of the provisional government to the Prince of Orange. The final arrangements to be negotiated at Vienna. This was signed " Castlereagh," and " seen and approved " by Nesselrode, Metternich and Hardenberg.

For the Congress of Vienna see § 461.

In 1815, shortly after the battle of Waterloo, the plenipotentiaries of the Allied Powers arrived in Paris, and it was arranged that they should meet regularly every forenoon at the British Embassy to discuss current business, and to frame the conditions of a peace with France. When military questions were involved the respective commanders-in-chief were present besides the civil plenipotentiaries. A secretary was appointed to draw up the protocols, which were simply to express the result of discussions and the decisions arrived at. These protocols were signed by the four principal plenipotentiaries, namely Metternich for Austria, Castlereagh for Great Britain, Hardenberg for Prussia and Nesselrode for Russia. The whole body was designated a Conference, which term was also applied to the daily sittings. The communications of the conference to the French Government were to be in the form of Notes signed by the principal representatives of the Four Powers. Sometimes *procès-verbaux* and even protocols were signed by other members of the conference, both civil and military. Early in October the following committees were set up :—1. Drafting Committee of the treaty, with Gentz and de la Besnardière as draftsmen, under the supervision of Wessenberg, Capo d'Istrias and Humboldt ; 2. Finance Committee, charged with business relative to the payment of the war contribution, composed of the French Minister of Finance, Balduin for Austria, Bulow for Prussia and Rosenhagen for Great Britain. Of these the second and fourth were merely what are now styled technical delegates ; 3. Military Committee, for the evacuation of France by the armies of the Allies and the temporary occupation of the north-eastern territory, consisting of Wellington for Great Britain, Anstett for Russia, Prohaska for Austria, Boyen and Gneisenau for Prussia ; 4. Committee for the execution of the treaty of 1814, Wessenberg for Austria, Sir Charles Stuart (ambassador) for Great Britain, Anstett for Russia, Alstenstein for Prussia, Lowenhielm for Sweden, Palmela for Portugal and Labrador for Spain. At the sitting of July 16, at which military questions dealt with, the commanders-in-chief were present, but the protocol was signed by Metternich, Castlereagh, Hardenberg and Nesselrode alone. It is curious to observe that the volumes containing all the despatches and other papers connected with the Peace Conference of Paris are nevertheless labelled " Congress of Paris " by the binder employed by the Foreign Office. The number of sittings held by the plenipotentiaries was seventy-eight. The records of their meetings with the French plenipotentiaries, of which there were two only, are styled *procès-verbaux*. They were signed by the plenipotentiaries of all the parties. Some of the final arrangements between the plenipotentiaries of the allies are called *procès-verbaux*, and these number twenty-one out of the seventy-eight. The protocol of November 3 is described as being *sur les arrangements territoriaux et le Systême Défensif de la Confédération Germanique ; et qui tiendra lieu d'une Convention particulière à ce sujet.*

After the signature of the Second Treaty of Paris, the diplomatic representatives of the Allied Powers were constituted a permanent Conference for the purpose of superintending the execution of the treaty and its subsidiary conventions, to supervise the work of the commissions appointed to examine the private claims against the French Government, to see to the regular payment of the instalments of the war indemnity and the furnishing of supplies to the army of occupation. They met once a week, and the results of their deliberations were recorded in protocols. As time went on other subjects were referred to the Conference, such as the diminution of the army of occupation, the intrigues of French political refugees in the Netherlands, the dispute between Spain and Portugal over the occupation of the Banda Oriental by Brazil, mediation between Spain and her insurgent colonies in South America, and lastly the question of reducing the period of occupation of French territory from five years to three. They also made the final arrangements for the meeting of the sovereigns at Aix-la-Chapelle, acting in all these matters in accordance with instructions received from their respective governments. This Conference was finally closed by protocol No. 47 of Aix-la-Chapelle, of November 22, 1818, and its own final protocol was numbered 307, which affords an index of the amount of work accomplished.

Another Conference was constituted at Frankfort, consisting of the Allied diplomatic representatives accredited to the German Diet. They were occupied with the exact definition of the frontiers of the component states of the German Confederation. They were :— For Austria Wessenberg, for Great Britain Clancarty, for Prussia C. W. v. Humboldt, and for Russia, Anstett. The Conference held numerous meetings, of which the results were recorded in forty-one protocols. They elaborated ten or eleven treaties defining the frontiers which were made annexes to a Recèz Général of July 20, 1819, summarizing their contents.

The diplomatists of the Allies accredited to Great Britain formed a third Conference in London, for the discussion of measures tending towards the general abolition of the slave trade, and for the repression of the Barbary pirates.

Conferences have a less formal character than Congresses,[1] and at first the number of Powers which took part in them was much less than, for instance, at the earliest Congress, that of Westphalia. It was easier, therefore, to arrive at a settlement of matters in controversy.

The first international gathering to which the name has been usually given was the Conference on the affairs of Greece, held in London in 1827–32. Conferences being usually held at the capital of one of the Powers taking part, the presidency is almost always offered to the Secretary of State or Minister for Foreign Affairs,

---

[1] The sittings of the delegates to a Congress were often spoken of as *conférences*.

the other members being ordinarily the local diplomatic representatives of the other Powers. The president designates the secretaries, whose principal function is to draw up the protocols[1] or *procès-verbaux* of the sittings. It is the custom to include among these at least one French official, as French is the universally recognized language of international documents. Sometimes, but not always, the members are furnished with special full-powers.

Exceptions to the usual composition of Conferences are those held for the discussion of military and naval questions, the care of the wounded in warfare (*e.g.* Nos. 11, 13, 14, 17, 21, 23, 24 and 25 of the list given below). At these it is the practice to appoint special delegates qualified by technical knowledge in addition to diplomatists.

§ 469. The principal international Conferences held during the nineteenth and twentieth centuries are comprised in the following list—

1. Affairs of Greece, London, 1827–32.
2. Affairs of Belgium, London, 1830–3.
3. Vienna, peace proposals for terminating the Crimean War, 1855.
4. Sound dues, abolition of, Copenhagen, 1857.
5. Danubian Principalities, Paris, 1858.
6. Syria, pacification of, Paris, 1860–1.
7. Stade toll, redemption of, Hanover, 1861.
8. Affairs of Mexico, Orizaba, 1862.
9. Scheldt dues, redemption of, Brussels, 1863.
10. Denmark, London, 1864.
11. Amelioration of the condition of wounded soldiers, Geneva, 1864.
12. Luxemburg, London, 1867.
13. Declaration respecting the use of explosive projectiles of less than 400 *grammes*, Petersburg, 1868.

---

[1] Koch and Schoell (xiii. 269 *n.*) says that the use of " protocole " for " procès-verbal " dates from the Congress of Vienna, as does also the use of " annexe " in place of " pièce annexée."

14. Treatment of sick and wounded soldiers, Geneva, 1868.

15. Cretan affairs, Paris, 1869.

16. Black Sea question ; Inviolability of Treaties, London, 1871.

17. Rules of warfare on land, Brussels, 1874.

18. Turkish affairs, Constantinople, 1876–7.

19. Navigation of the Danube, London, 1883.

20. Affairs of Africa (Slave Trade, Rivers Congo and Niger, Rules for future Occupation on the coast of Africa), Berlin, 1884–5.

21. First Pan-American Conference, Washington, 1889–90.

22. First Peace Conference, The Hague, 1899.

23. Chinese affairs, Peking, 1900–1.

24. Second Pan-American Conference, Mexico, 1901–2.

25. Revision of the Geneva Convention of 1864, Geneva, 1906.

26. Algeciras, Affairs of Morocco, 1906.

27. Third Pan-American Conference, Rio de Janeiro, 1906.

28. Second Peace Conference, The Hague, 1907.

29. International Naval Conference, London, 1908–9.

30. Fourth Pan-American Conference Buenos Ayres, 1910.[1]

31. Balkan Affairs, London, 1913.

32. Bucarest, July 30–August 10, 1913.

33. Paris, Peace Conference, 1919.

34. Washington, November 12, 1921.

Of these conferences Nos. 20, 22, 26, and 28, both by their form and the importance of the subjects discussed at them, were perhaps worthy to be called Congresses, but the Governments concerned preferred to give them the more modest title of conferences.

A brief account of the proceedings at each of these is appended, except No. 31. No record of that has as yet seen the light. It resulted in a treaty between Turkey and

---

[1] For these Pan-American Conferences, see Ch. Dupuis, *Le Droit des gens*, etc. Paris, 1920, p. 394.

the four allied Balkan States which had waged war against her : Bulgaria, Servia, Greece and Montenegro. It was never ratified.

§ 470. *Conference relative to the Affairs of Greece, London*, 1827–32.

In 1826 the British Government took advantage of the mission of the Duke of Wellington to Petersburg to congratulate the Emperor Nicholas I on his accession to the throne, in order to make proposals to Russia for dealing with the affairs of Greece, in revolt against Turkey. The result was a Protocol, signed March 23, April 4, 1826.[1]

The preamble states that His Britannic Majesty having been invited by the Greeks to interpose his good offices in order to bring about a reconciliation between them and the Porte, and having offered his mediation to the latter Power, and His Imperial Majesty being desirous of bringing about, by an arrangement in conformity with the wishes of religion, justice and humanity, a cessation of the struggle of which Greece and the Archipelago are the scene, the Undersigned have agreed—

1. That the arrangement to be proposed to the Porte, if it accepted the mediation offered to it, would place Greece under the Ottoman Empire, paying an annual tribute, of which the amount would be fixed by agreement. That the Greeks should be governed by authorities chosen and named by themselves, in whose nomination the Porte should take part, so that they would enjoy complete liberty of conscience and commerce, and have the exclusive conduct of their domestic administration, and that the Greeks should acquire Turkish properties situated on the Greek continent or islands.

2. That if the proposed mediation be accepted, Russia will use her influence in support of the mediation, the mode and time at which Russia should take part in the

[1] *Brit. and For. State Papers*, xiv. 629 ; xl. 1206, Martens *Nouveau Recueil*, vii. 40.

negotiations which would follow on this mediation to be determined later on by agreement between the two Cabinets.

3. In case Turkey declines to accept the mediation of Great Britain, the two Powers will nevertheless regard the terms of the arrangement mentioned in Article 1 as the basis of the reconciliation which they will endeavour to effect by their interposition, whether in common or separately.

4. Great Britain and Russia reserve to themselves the measures necessary for determining the details of the arrangements in question, the limits of the territory and the names of the islands which they will propose to the Porte to comprise under the term Greece.

5. Neither His Britannic Majesty nor His Imperial Majesty will seek for any increase of territory, exclusive influence, or commercial advantage for their subjects, other than what every other nation can obtain.[1]

6. His Britannic Majesty and His Imperial Majesty will bring this protocol confidentially to the knowledge of their Allies, and will propose to them to guarantee, in concert with Russia, the final compromise which shall reconcile Turkey and Greece, His Britannic Majesty not being able to guarantee it.

The protocol was signed by Wellington, Nesselrode and Lieven, the latter of whom, Russian Ambassador in London, had hastened to return to Petersburg, in order to assist in its negotiation. He had been actively concerned in the steps taken by his Government which had led to this plan of action in common being adopted.

Russia proceeded to communicate the protocol to the diplomatic agents of Austria, France and Prussia at Petersburg, and also instructed her representatives at the Courts of these three Powers to read it to the respective ministers for Foreign Affairs. France alone accepted its principles. Metternich protested against

[1] This sort of stipulation is known as an *article de désintéressement*.

both coercion and mediation, the latter being, in his view, inapplicable to disputes between a sovereign Power and its rebellious subjects.

The French Government having then proposed to convert the protocol into a treaty, discussion of a draft presented by Russia was initiated in London in May 1827, and the Treaty was signed in July.[1] It followed in the main the provisions of the protocol, and a secret article was added, stipulating that in case Turkey declined the offered mediation, or in case either party refused to accept the conditions laid down, the representatives of the Three Powers in London should be authorized to discuss and decide on the ulterior measures which might become necessary.

The treaty bore the signatures of Lord Dudley, Secretary of State for Foreign Affairs, Prince Polignac, French Ambassador, and Prince Lieven, Russian Ambassador Extraordinary and Plenipotentiary.

The first meeting of the Conference was held July 12. From the bare record contained in the protocols drawn up on that and subsequent occasions, it does not appear that any formalities, such as the interchange of full-powers or the appointment of a secretary to take the minutes, were considered necessary.

On October 20 took place the Battle of Navarino, in which the Turko-Egyptian fleets were destroyed by the united naval squadrons of the Three Powers.

At the fifth sitting, on December 12, a *protocole de désintéressement* was adopted.[2]

Russia declared war on Turkey April 14/26, 1828.

On July 19, 1828, at the ninth meeting, French intervention in the Morea was authorized,[3] and on November 16, at the fifteenth meeting, the Morea and certain of the islands of the Cyclades, as forming the territory of the

[1] *Brit. and For. State Papers*, xiv. 632 ; Marten's *Recueil*, 2nd edit., vii. 282 ; a more correct copy at 446.

[2] *Ibid.*, xvii. 220. [3] *Ibid.*, 371

proposed Greek State, were placed under the guarantee of the Three Powers.[1]

At the sixteenth sitting, March 22, 1829, the Arta-Volo line was adopted as the future frontier between Greece and Turkey.[2]

Peace was signed between Russia and Turkey at Adrianople, September 14. By Art. X, Turkey declared her adhesion to the treaty of July 6, 1827, and the *acte* of 10/22 March 1829 (Martens, *Nouv. Recueil* viii. 149). The treaty of Adrianople obtained the Arta-Volo for Greece, and independence was irrevocably decided (Prokesch-Osten, *Geschichte des Abfalls der Griechen*, ii. 361).

At the twenty-second sitting, February 3, 1830,[3] Greece was declared to be an independent State, but with a restricted area. However, on September 26, 1831, after the refusal of the throne by Prince Leopold (afterwards first King of the Belgians) the Arta-Volo line was reverted to, and the throne was offered to Prince Otho, second son of the King of Bavaria, and his acceptance was recorded in the Treaty of May 7, 1832,[4] between the Three Powers and the King of Bavaria. It was signed on behalf of France by Prince Talleyrand, on that of Great Britain by Lord Palmerston, on that of Russia by Prince Lieven and Baron Matuszewic, and on that of Bavaria by Baron de Cetto.

It will be observed that each sitting is termed a conference in the protocols, and at the same time the whole negotiation is denominated a Conference. After the settlement of the main question and the choice of the future king of Greece by the above-mentioned treaty, further meetings, Nos. 52 to 67 were held between July 21 and August 17, 1837, both inclusive, for the determination of questions relating to the boundary line finally adopted, the levy of a body of troops in Bavaria for the service of the King of Greece, and the conditions

---

[1] *Brit. and For. State Papers*, xvii. 405.

[2] *Ibid.*, xvi. 1083. [3] *Ibid.*, xvii. 3. [4] *Ibid.*, xix. 33.

on which the Three Powers undertook to guarantee the service of a loan to the new kingdom.[1]

Authorities: Parliamentary Papers; F. de Martens, *Recueil des Traités et Conventions,* etc., t. xi; *Cambridge Modern History,* vol. x. The Parliamentary papers have been reprinted in the *British and Foreign State Papers* (see references in footnotes), and in the *Recueil des Traités* known under the name of G. F. de Martens, tt. xii. and xiii.

§ 471. *Conference on Belgian Affairs.*

While the Conference on the Affairs of Greece was proceeding in London, another international question of equal importance came to be discussed. It arose out of the insurrection of the Belgians against the King of Holland, and the necessity of devising other arrangements than those made by the Congress of Vienna for the union of the former Austrian Netherlands with Holland under one sovereign. The success which had attended the Conference of the three Powers respecting the Greek difficulty probably induced statesmen to believe that London would suit equally well as the meeting-place for the endeavour to find a solution for this new problem.

The first sitting was held November 4, 1830, the plenipotentiaries being: for

Austria, Prince Paul Esterhazy, Ambassador;

France, Prince Talleyrand, Ambassador;

Great Britain, Lord Aberdeen, Secretary of State for Foreign Affairs;

Prussia, Baron v. Bülow, Envoy Extraordinary and Minister Plenipotentiary;

Russia, Count Matuszewic, Envoy Extraordinary and Minister Plenipotentiary.

The protocol says: " S. M. le Roi des Pays-Bas ayant invité les Cours d'Autriche, de France, de la Grande Bretagne, de Prusse, et de Russie, en leur qualité de Puissances signataires des Traités de Paris et de Vienne, qui ont constitué le Royaume des Pays-

Bas, à déliberer, de concert avec S. M. sur les meilleurs moyens de mettre un terme aux troubles qui ont éclaté dans ses États ; et les Cours ci-dessus nommées ayant eprouvé, avant même d'avoir reçu cette invitation, un vif désir d'arrêter, dans le plus bref délai possible, le désordre et l'effusion du sang ; ont concerti, par l'organe de leurs Ambassadeurs et Ministres accrédités à la Cour de Londres, les déterminations suivantes '' (Martens, *Nouveau Recueil*, x. 77).

There is no mention in the protocol of the exchange of full-powers,[1] of the selection of a chairman, of the appointment of secretaries, nor of procedure. Lord Aberdeen presided as a matter of course. The Dutch Ambassador Extraordinary and Plenipotentiary was invited to join the deliberations, but did not sign the protocol of the sitting. An armistice was decided on.

At the fourth meeting, *Nouv. Recueil*, x. 93, Lord Palmerston replaced Aberdeen and additional plenipotentiaries were added : Prince Lieven, the Russian Ambassador, Baron Wessenberg, *geheimrath*, for Austria, and Falck for Holland. Subsequently Baron de Zuylen de Nyevelt (Dutch Ambassador at Constantinople) was appointed second plenipotentiary for the King of Holland.

At the seventh meeting, December 20, it was recognized that the independence of Belgium was a necessity, and it was further decided to invite the provisional Government to send commissioners to London, armed with full-powers. (*Nouv. Recueil*, x. 124). Blok says Falck was not allowed to be present (iv. 307). A copy of the protocol was sent to him, to which he returned a strong protest against the decision contained in it, and to the manner in which it was expressed (*Nouv. Recueil*, x. 17). On January 11, 1831, the Conference offered the crown of Belgium to Prince Leopold of

[1] The protocol states that " The Powers who signed the Treaties of Paris and Vienna have agreed, through the instrumentality of their Ambassadors and Ministers accredited to the Court of London, on the following resolutions." Hence, special full-powers were unnecessary .

Saxe-Coburg. The offer was made by Palmerston, next by the Austrian and Russian representatives. (Blok, iv. 308).

On January 20, 1831, at the eleventh sitting, the limits of Dutch and Belgian territory were fixed. It was decided that Belgium should form a State perpetually neutral, and that she on her part should observe neutrality towards all the Powers, who would guarantee the integrity and inviolability of her territory.[1] On the next occasion, January 27, articles were framed regarding the shares of the public debt to be borne by Holland and Belgium respectively, and laying down that Antwerp should be only a commercial port.

At the fourteenth sitting, February 1, Great Britain proposed that no member of either of the five reigning families of the negotiating States should be King of Belgium. All agreed, excepting the French plenipotentiary, who took the proposal *ad rèferendum;* but at another sitting, held later in the day, he announced that France also consented.

At the twentieth meeting, March 17, a French communication regarding the boundaries of Luxemburg was considered.

Leopold was elected on June 4 (Blok. iv, 319).

On June 26, at the twenty-sixth sitting, a draft of eighteen articles was discussed, which, if approved, were to be converted into a definitive treaty. The draft was accepted by the Belgian commissioners.

July 25, the twenty-eighth meeting was held. A long protest against the eighteen articles was received from Holland. At the following sitting, August 4, the Dutch produced their full-powers, which were deposited in the archives of the conference.

On the following day, at a further sitting, warning was given to Holland not to attack the city of Antwerp from the citadel, which was still held by Dutch troops. On

---

[1] This was no new idea. It seems to have originated in the mind of John de Witt about 1657.

July 27, the assemblage of a British fleet in the Downs, and the despatch of a French army to the assistance of the Belgians, were announced. But on August 18 the French plenipotentiary notified the withdrawal of the French forces.

At the thirty-fourth meeting, held August 23, the retirement of the Dutch troops into Dutch territory was announced, and a suspension of arms for six weeks was proposed, which was accepted by the plenipotentiaries of Holland and Belgium on August 31 (thirty-seventh sitting). The production of his full-power by Mons. Sylvain van de Weyer, the Belgian plenipotentiary, had already taken place, and a copy was deposited in the archives of the Conference, at the thirty-fifth sitting (August 30).

At the thirty-ninth sitting (September 3) the parties were called on to state their views as to, (1) the frontier ; (2) Luxemburg ; (3) the partition of the public debt.

A draft of articles for the separation of Belgium from Holland, twenty-four in number, was submitted for consideration on October 14 (forty-ninth sitting), and on November 15, 1831, a treaty embodying them was signed by the plenipotentiaries of the Five Great Powers and Mons. van de Weyer.[1] The ratifications were exchanged January 31, 1832, between France, Great Britain and Belgium at the fifty-fifth sitting, but it was not until April 18 that the Austrian and Prussian plenipotentiaries were able to exchange theirs, and that of Russia was not produced till May 4. At a subsequent meeting, the fifty-ninth, held on that day, the fact was communicated to the Belgian and Dutch plenipotentiaries. The King of Holland refused to sign the treaty, and a good deal of desultory discussion ensued. At last, on September 30 (sixty-ninth sitting), Palmerston brought forward a slightly amended draft of the twenty-four articles (which he had communicated to the Dutch plenipotentiary on the 6th), and accompanied it with a

---

[1] Protocols 1–53 in *Brit. and For. State Papers*, xviii. 723.

statement, explaining the nature and purpose of the alterations.[1] On the following day the seventieth and, as it proved, last sitting was held. The French plenipotentiary moved the adoption of a resolution that, in view of the persistent refusal of Holland to accept the twenty-four articles, the Conference must seek for the means of placing Belgium in possession of the citadel of Antwerp. This motion was supported by Palmerston, but the remaining three plenipotentiaries of the Great Powers opposed it, declaring that they could not associate themselves with any measures of coercion which might be adopted by the French and British Governments, and offering to refer the questions at issue to the decision of the Prussian Government. This was refused by the British and French plenipotentiaries, who expressed their regret at finding their colleagues unprepared to join in efficacious measures for executing a treaty which had been ratified by their Courts several months previously.[2]

This was practically the end of the Conference.

Great Britain and France thereupon concluded, on October 22, 1832,[3] a convention for the fulfilment of the obligations undertaken by the two Powers under the treaty of November 15, 1831. On its being communicated to the representatives of the other three Powers, the Prussian plenipotentiaries formally retired from the Conference, and the further proceedings were conducted by the two first-named Powers.

November 9, Baron de Zuylen submitted drafts of a treaty between Holland and Belgium in twenty-three articles, and of a treaty between Holland and the Five Powers. Two days later, Earl Grey (Prime Minister) addressed a Note to the Dutch plenipotentiaries rejecting these documents, and declaring that the surrender of the citadel must precede any further negotiations with

---

[1] G. F. de Martens, *Nouveau Recueil*, etc., xii. 484.
[2] Protocols 53–70 in *Brit. and For. State Papers*, xix. 55.
[3] *Brit. and For. State Papers*, xix. 258.

them. They replied to him next day, and on November 13 he requested them to send any further communications to the Foreign Office.

The Dutch garrison of Antwerp capitulated on December 23[1] to the French Expeditionary Force under Maréchal Gérard.

December 30, Palmerston forwarded to Jerningham, the British representative at the Hague, the draft of a convention between Holland, France and Great Britain in nine articles.

1833, January 9, the Dutch plenipotentiaries delivered to Palmerston and Talleyrand drafts of conventions in four and five articles respectively.

February 14, Palmerston and Talleyrand communicated to them drafts of three conventions, to which they replied on the 26th.

In March, the Dutch Government despatched M. Dedel to London as their special plenipotentiary, and on the 23rd he presented another draft convention with the two Western Powers in seven articles. On April 2, Palmerston and Talleyrand again replied, objecting to the draft, and after more correspondence had passed, they transmitted a fresh one.

In addition to the French military expedition under Maréchal Gérard, Great Britain and France had blockaded the coast of Holland in November 1832.[2] The blockade was continued until Holland made overtures for peace, and a Convention was signed in London, May 21, 1833, providing that there should be no renewal of hostilities against Belgium, and that the navigation of the Scheldt and Meuse should be free and open.

Matters remained *in statu quo* until 1839, when the twenty-four articles of November 15, 1831, were converted into the Annex to a treaty signed in London by the plenipotentiaries of the Five Powers with the

---

[1] *Brit. and For. State Papers*, xix. 1418.
[2] *Camb. Mod. Hist.*, x. 543 ; *Nouv. Recueil*, nouv. série, t. iv. 97 ; *Brit. and For. State Papers*, xix. 1420, 1438.

plenipotentiaries of the King of Holland, dated April 7/19,[1] Article 1 of which declared the annexed articles, forming the tenor of a treaty concluded the same day between the King of the Belgians and the King of Holland,[2] to have the same force as if they were textually inserted in the treaty itself, and that consequently they were placed under the guarantee of the High Contracting Parties.

The neutrality of Belgium is defined in Article 7 of the latter treaty, as follows—

" La Belgique, dans les limites indiquées aux articles I, II et IV formera un État indépendant et perpétuellement neutre. Elle sera tenue d'observer cette même neutralité envers tous les autres Etats."

And the whole of this treaty is embodied in the Treaty between the Five Great Powers, with Belgium, in virtue of Article 1 by which the five Sovereigns

" *déclarent que les articles ci annexés et 'formant la teneur du Traité conclu en ce jour entre S. M. le Roi des Belges et S. M. le Roi des Pays-Bas, grand-duc de Luxembourg, sont considérés comme ayant la même'force et valeur, que s'ils étaient textuellement insérés dans le présent Acte, et qu'ils se trouvent ainsi placés sous la garantie de Leurs dites Majestés.*"

Thus there were three treaties, one between the Five Powers and Holland, one between the Five Powers and Belgium, and one between Holland and Belgium, all of the same tenor. Also on the same day one signed by Austria and Prussia, being an Acte d'accession on the part of the German Confederation. It contains the first seven articles of the twenty-four annexed to the treaties signed by the Five Powers with Belgium and Holland, and the ratifications were exchanged on June 8 (*Brit. and For. State Papers*, xxvii. 1002). Article V of the treaties of 1839 is :—" Sa Majésté le Roi des Pays Bas, Grand Duc

---

[1] *Brit. and For. State Papers*, xxvii. 990.
[2] *Ibid.*, xxxvii. 1320.

de Luxembourg, s'entendra avec la Confédération Germanique et les Agnats de la Maison de Nassau, sur l'application des stipulations renfermées dans les Articles III et IV, ainsi que sur tous les arrangements que les dits Articles pourraient rendre nécessaires, soit avec les Agnats ci-dessus nommés de la Maison de Nassau, soit avec la Confédération Germanique."

Authorities: Parliamentary Papers, *British and Foreign State Papers* (see references in footnotes) ; G. F. de Martens et Frédéric Murhard, *Nouveau Recueil des Traités*, vols. x. xi. xii., and ditto, *nouvelle série*, vol. iv. ; F. de Martens, *Recueil des Traités et Conventions de la Russie*, vols. xi. xii. ; Lecomte et Lévi, *Neutralité Belge et Invasion Allemande.*

§ 472. *Conference of Vienna,* 1855.

The object of this conference was to arrive at a basis for the negotiation of peace between France, Great Britain, and Turkey on the one side, and Russia on the other.

A first meeting was held March 15, 1855. The plenipotentiaries were : for

Austria, Count Buol, Minister for Foreign Affairs, and Baron Prokesch-Osten ;

France, Baron Bourqueney, Envoy Extraordinary and Minister Plenipotentiary at Vienna ;

Great Britain, Lord John Russell, ex-cabinet Minister, and Lord Westmorland, Envoy Extraordinary and Minister Plenipotentiary at Vienna

Russia, Prince Alexander Gortchakoff, Minister Plenipotentiary at Vienna, and M. Titoff.

Turkey, Aariffi Effendi.

At this meeting it was agreed to record the proceedings of the sittings in the form of protocols, Count Buol to be president, the protocols to be drawn up by Baron de Meysenberg, Aulic Councillor at the Ministry for Foreign Affairs. Full-powers were produced, examined and accepted.

Count Buol opened with a speech. Baron Bourqueney spoke next, then Lord John Russell, followed by Lord

Westmorland, who merely assented to what his chief had said.

Prince A. Gortchakoff replied and M. Titoff assented to what he said. Aariffi Effendi wound up.

It was agreed to form committees for the consideration of the Four Points, but this does not seem to have been acted on, and each point was discussed in turn in full conference, on a memorandum presented by the second Austrian plenipotentiary. At the ninth sitting were added Mons. Drouyn de Lhuys and Aali Pasha, French and Turkish Ministers for Foreign Affairs.

The Four Points were—

1. The Protectòrate of Russia over Moldavia and Wallachia to cease, and the privileges conferred by successive Sultans on those principalities as well as on Serbia to be henceforward placed under the collective guarantee of the Contracting Powers.

2. The freedom of navigation of the Danube to be secured by effectual means, and to be controlled by a permanent syndical authority.

3. The Treaty of July 13, 1841, to be revised, with the double object of connecting the existence of the Ottoman Empire with the European equilibrium, and of putting an end to the preponderance of Russia in the Black Sea.

4. Russia to abandon the principle of covering with an official Protectorate the Christian subjects of the Sultan of the Eastern Church, but the Christian Powers would lend each other their mutual assistance in order to obtain from the initiative of the Ottoman Government the confirmation and observance of the religious rights of the Christian communities subject to the Porte, without distinction of ritual.[1]

The second part of the third point became a stone of stumbling to the Russian negotiators, and after thirteen meetings had been held, the Conference met for the

---

[1] A. Kinglake, vii. 317.

last time on June 4, when it was finally established that the objects aimed at had not been attained.

Hostilities, therefore, proceeded.

Authority: Parliamentary Papers, reprinted in *Brit. and For. State Papers*, xlv. 54.

§ 473. *Conference for the Abolition of the Sound Dues,* 1857.

Protocol of February 3, 1857.   Present, for

Denmark, Mons. Bluhme, Director of the Ore Sound Customs and Privy Councillor ;

Austria, Mons. Jaeger, Chargé d'Affaires ;

Belgium, Mons. Beaulieu, Envoy Extraordinary and Minister Plenipotentiary ;

Spain, Señor Teran, Minister Resident ;

France, Mons. Dotezac, Envoy Extraordinary and Minister Plenipotentiary ;

Great Britain, Sir Andrew Buchanan, Envoy Extraordinary and Minister Plenipotentiary ;

Hanover, Herr Hanbury, Minister Resident ;

Mecklenburg-Schwerin, Herr Prosch,* Geheimer Legations-rath ;

Holland, den Heer du Bors, Minister Resident ;

Oldenburg, Herr Erdmann,* Conseiller de Régence ;

Prussia, Count Oriolla, Envoy Extraordinary and Minister Plenipotentiary ;

Russia, Mons. Tegoborski,* Conseiller de Collège ;

Sweden and Norway, Baron de Welterstedt, Chargé d'Affaires ;

Free Towns and Hanse Towns, Herr Krüger, Minister Resident.

These were mostly diplomatic representatives of the Powers concerned.   Those whose names are marked with an asterisk were apparently deputed *ad hoc.*

The first Conference was held January 4, 1856, and the proceedings were opened by the Danish Commissioner. It appears that an exchange of views had previously taken place between the Governments concerned.

On May 9, 1856, the delegates of Oldenburg, Russia, and Sweden and Norway had signed a protocol with the Danish Commissioner, accepting on behalf of their Governments the proposals of Denmark.

After further negotiation outside the Conference, a meeting was held, as above stated, and a draft approved by the French, British and Prussian Governments was proposed to the Danish Commissioner. It had been previously communicated to several other Governments, whose delegates on this occasion intimated their readiness to accord their acceptance. The delegates from Hanover, Mecklenburg and the Hanse Towns were present at this meeting, in addition to those of the States represented at the conferences of 1856.

After further meetings, at which the draft underwent amendment, the Treaty was finally signed on the night of March 14, 1857, one counterpart for each Power represented.

Other States acceded afterwards. The United States concluded a separate treaty, April 11, 1857.

Authorities : *Brit. and For. State Papers*, xlvii. 35, xlix. 902 ; Calvo, §§ 370–1 ; G. F. de Martens and Ch. Samwer, *Nouv. Rec. Gén.*, xvi. partie ii. 336–66.

§ 474. *Conference concerning the Danubian Principalities*, 1858.

This took place at Paris. The plenipotentiaries were, for

Austria, Baron Hübner, Ambassador Extraordinary and Plenipotentiary ;

France, Count Walewski, minister of Foreign Affairs ;

Great Britain, Lord Cowley, Ambassador Extraordinary and Plenipotentiary ;

Prussia, Count Hatzfeldt, Envoy Extraordinary and Minister Plenipotentiary ;

Russia, Count Kisseleff, Ambassador Extraordinary and Plenipotentiary ;

Sardinia, Marchese di Villamarina, Envoy Extraordinary and Minister Plenipotentiary ;

Turkey, Fuad Pasha, minister of Foreign Affairs ;

Object : To frame a constitution for Moldavia and Wallachia, in accordance with the stipulations of Articles 22–26 of the Treaty of Paris of March 30, 1856, and on the basis of the report made by the commission set up by Article 23.

The Conference opened in May, and on August 19 concluded a convention[1] embodying a constitution for the " United Provinces of Moldavia and Wallachia." In January 1859, the two assemblies chose the same person as Hospodar, which eventually led to the union of the two provinces under the name of Roumania.

The only plenipotentiary who produced full-powers was Fuad Pasha, appointed *ad hoc*.

Authorities : Parliamentary Papers, reprinted in *Brit. and For. State Papers*, xlviii. 81 ; *Cambridge Modern History*, xi. 644.

§ 475. *Conference for the Pacification of Syria*, 1860–61. Held in Paris. The plenipotentiaries were, for

France, Mons. Thouvenel, minister and Secretary of State for Foreign Affairs ;

Austria, Prince Metternich-Winneberg, Ambassador Extraordinary ;

Great Britain, Lord Cowley, Ambassador Extraordinary and Plenipotentiary ;

Russia, Count Paul Kisseleff, Ambassador Extraordinary and Plenipotentiary ;

Prussia, Prince Henry VII of Reuss-Schleitz-Köstritz, Chargé d'Affaires par interim ;

Turkey, Ahmed Vefik Effendi, Ambassador Extraordinary.

The first meeting was held August 3, 1860.[2] This was followed by a convention signed on September 5, by

[1] *Brit. and For. State Papers*, xlviii. 70.
[2] See Debidour, *Hist. diplom. de l'Europe*, ii. 237.

which France undertook to despatch a force of 6000 men, being one-half of what might eventually be employed in the way of European troops, to contribute to the re-establishment of tranquillity. Great Britain, Austria, France, Prussia and Russia undertook to maintain sufficient naval forces on the coast of Syria.

A further Conference was held in Paris, at the invitation of the French Government, on February 19, 1861, followed by another on March 15.[1]

On June 9, 1861,[2] a Conference was held at Constantinople between the diplomatic representatives of Great Britain, Austria, France, Prussia and Russia, with a Turkish representative : namely, Sir Henry Bulwer, Prokesch-Osten, Marquis de Lavalette, Baron v. der Goltz, Prince Lobanow, and Aali Pasha. On this occasion was signed the Règlement Organique by which the administration of the Lebanon has since been regulated.

Authority: Parliamentary Papers, and see also footnotes.

§ 476. *Conference respecting the Redemption of the Stade Toll, Hanover, 1861.*

The Delegates of the States represented were, for

Great Britain, Henry Francis Howard, Envoy Extraordinary and Minister Plenipotentiary to Hanover ;

Austria, Count von Ingelheim, ditto ;

Belgium, Baron Nothomb, ditto ;

Brazil, Chevalier d'Araujo, ditto ;

Denmark, C. E. J. de Bülow, envoyé en mission extraordinaire à Hanovre ;

Spain, Chevalier de Teran, Minister Resident at Copenhagen ;

France, Baron de Malaret, Minister Plenipotentiary to Hanover ;

Hanover, Count Platen-Hallermund, minister for Foreign Affairs ;

[1] *Brit. and For. State Papers,* li. 278.　　[2] *Ibid.,* 287.

Mecklenburg-Schwerin. H. J. de Wickede, Councillor of the Ministry of Finance ;

Holland, Baron Stratenus, Envoy Extraordinary and Minister Plenipotentiary to Hanover ;

Portugal, Count de Lavradio, ditto to Great Britain ;

Prussia, Prince G. d'Ysenburg u. Budwingen, ditto to Hanover ;

Russia, J. Persiany, ditto ;

Sweden and Norway, Sterky, Minister-resident and Consul General to Lübeck, Bremen and Hamburg ;

Lübeck, Theodor Curtius, Senator ;

Bremen, O. Gildemeister, Senator ;

Hamburg, C. H. Merck, Syndic.

The first meeting was held June 17, at the Ministry for Foreign Affairs at Hanover.

The Hanoverian minister for Foreign Affairs nominated Herr v. Witzendorff, Secretary-General of the Ministry for Foreign Affairs, as protocollist.

The delegates who were present exhibited their full-powers, which, being found in good and due form, were deposited with the archives of the Conference.

The Prussian delegate, being unable to attend, owing to his not having received his instructions, the meeting was adjourned to the following day.

At the second meeting, June 18, the Hanoverian delegate explained the object of the Conference, and stated that the High Contracting Parties having already given their adherence to the proposals of Hanover, all that remained to do was to draw up the treaty and a protocol regulating the provisional state of things to last until all the formalities requisite in order to bring the treaty into force were completed. He accordingly laid two drafts before the delegates, the former of which was then discussed and disposed of.

The Portuguese Delegate asked that his Sovereign should be described as King of Portugal and the Algarves, and the Russian delegate claimed that to the title of His

Majesty the Emperor of All the Russias the title of King of Poland and Grand Duke of Finland should be added.

At the third meeting, June 19, the draft protocol was taken into consideration and adopted.

A copy of the treaty having been read, was initialled by the delegates, and the same process was performed with respect to a copy of the protocol.

At the fourth meeting, June 22, a copy of the treaty, having been compared with the text initialled on the last occasion, was signed and sealed by the plenipotentiaries. The same proceeding was observed with the protocol.

The Hanoverian plenipotentiary delivered a speech expressing his thanks for the confidence shown to him by the Delegates during the Conference.

The Portuguese Delegate proposed a resolution thanking the Hanoverian Delegate, president of the Conference, and it was carried unanimously.

On each occasion the protocol of the previous sitting was read, approved and signed.

Authorities : *Brit. and For. State Papers*, li. 32 ; G. F. de Martens and Ch. Samwer, *Nouv. Rec. Gén.*, xvii. partie i. 406–24.

§ 477. *Conference of Orizaba on the Affairs of Mexico, April 11, 1862.*

This conference was held between the plenipotentiaries and commanders-in-chief of the Allied Powers, consisting of the diplomatic representatives of Great Britain, France and Spain, *i.e.* Sir C. Lennox Wyke, the Count de Saligny, the Conde de Reus, Admiral Jurien de la Gravière, and Commodore Dunlop. It was held at the residence of the Conde de Reus, and the secretaries of the three missions, Sir John Walsham, Comte de la Londe and Señor Juan Antonio Lotez de Ceballos, were present to draw up the *procès-verbal* of the discussion.

On this occasion the British and Spanish representatives announced that their troops would be withdrawn.

Authority : *Brit. and For. State Papers*, liii. 532.

§ 478. *Conference for the Redemption of the Scheldt Dues, Brussels,* July 1863.

The representatives of the Powers were, for

Great Britain, Lord Howard de Walden, Envoy Extraordinary and Minister Plenipotentiary ;

Austria, Baron v. Hügel, ditto ;

Belgium, Mons. Ch. Rogier, minister for Foreign Affairs ;

Brazil, Senhor J. T. do Amaral, Minister Resident ;

Chile, Don. M. Cavallo, Envoy Extraordinary and Minister Plenipotentiary ;

Denmark, Baron de Bille-Brahe, Minister Resident ;

Spain, Don D. C. de Portugal y Quesada, Envoy Extraordinary and Minister Plenipotentiary ;

France, Baron de Malaret, ditto ;

Hanover, Baron de Hodenberg, Minister Resident ;

Holland, Baron Gericke d'Herwynen, Minister ;

Italy, Conte de Montalto, Envoy Extraordinary and Minister Plenipotentiary ;

Oldenburg, Herr Geffcken, ditto ;

Peru, Don M. Irigoyen, Chargé d'Affaires ;

Portugal, Vizconde de Seisal, Envoy Extraordinary and Minister Plenipotentiary ;

Prussia, Herr v. Savigny, ditto ;

Russia, Prince Nicolas Orlow, ditto ;

United States, Mr. Sanford ;

Sweden and Norway, Mons. A. de Mansbach, Minister Resident ;

Turkey, Musurus Bey, Ambassador Extraordinary and Plenipotentiary ;

Lubeck, Bremen and Hamburg, Herr Geffcken (see above for Oldenburg).

The first meeting was held July 15, at the ministry for Foreign Affairs.

The Turkish plenipotentiary, in a complimentary

speech, proposed that the Belgian minister for Foreign Affairs should be asked to preside.

The minister, having accepted, stated that Baron Lambermont, who was provided with full-powers to take part in the deliberations of the Conference, was willing to undertake the task of drawing up the protocols, in which he would be assisted by Mons. Léopold Orban, of the Belgian diplomatic service.

The plenipotentiaries then exhibited their full-powers, which were deposited with the archives of the Conference.

The president then explained that the different governments had successively entered into separate conventions for the redemption of the Scheldt tolls, which Belgium alone had discharged since 1839, and that it was now proposed to convert these into a general treaty.

A draft of the proposed treaty was read, and after some slight discussion was adopted. It was then initialled by the plenipotentiaries. The United States representative declared that he gave his *adhésion* to the draft treaty. After its signature by the plenipotentiaries present, he would accede to it by a special *Acte* with Belgium, in accordance with the diplomatic practice of his Government and in conformity with the precedents observed in analogous circumstances.

At the meeting of July 16, the protocol of the previous sitting was read.

The French plenipotentiary expressed the opinion that the participation of the United States plenipotentiary at the negotiation in conference of a treaty which he did not propose to sign, did not appear to be exactly in conformity with diplomatic conditions. He consequently insisted that the intervention of the United States minister in the *Actes* of the Conference should not be invoked as a precedent on other occasions.

The protocol was thereupon approved.

The plenipotentiaries compared the treaty with the copy initialled at the preceding meeting, and apposed

K

their signatures thereto. Herr Geffcken, as representing a Grand Duke and the three Hanse towns, signed last, out of the alphabetical order.

Mons. Rogier thanked the plenipotentiaries for their benevolent attitude and the assistance they had afforded to him.

The Conference unanimously adopted a vote of thanks to him for presiding. The protocol of the sitting, which had been prepared on the spot, was read and approved.

Authorities: G. F. de Martens and Ch. Samwer, *Nouv. Rec. Gén.,* xvii. partie ii. 223–43 ; *Brit. and For. State Papers,* .iii. 16.

§ 479. *Conference on the Affairs of Denmark, London,*[1] 1864.

The invitations were sent out by Great Britain, and the first sitting was held April 20. There were present, for

Denmark, G. Guaade, Mons. de Bille and Krieger ;

France, Prince de la Tour d'Auvergne, Ambassador Extraordinary ;

Great Britain, Earl Russell, Secretary of State for Foreign Affairs, and Earl Clarendon, Chancellor of the Duchy ;

Russia, Baron Brunnow, Ambassador Extraordinary and Plenipotentiary ;

Sweden and Norway, Comte Wachtmeister.

Protocol No. 1, sitting of April 25, records that in addition to the above there were present, for

Austria, Count Apponyi, Ambassador Extraordinary, and Mons. Biegeleben ;

German Confederation, Baron de Beust ;

Prussia, Count Bernstorff, Ambassador Extraordinary and Plenipotentiary, and M. de Balan.

[1] For the events which preceded this Conference, see *Cambridge Modern History,* xi. 436

Count Apponyi proposed that Earl Russell should preside.

The Hon. William Stuart, a secretary of legation in the British diplomatic service, was appointed to draw up the protocols, on the nomination of the president.

Earl Russell proposed a suspension of hostilities, to which the Danish First plenipotentiary replied that Denmark would perhaps agree to cease hostilities, excepting blockades already established, provided Austria and Prussia desisted from levying war contributions.

The protocol was signed in the order of the English alphabet. Thus the Germanic Confederation signed after France, whereas, according to the usual order observed, namely, that of the French alphabet, Baron de Beust would have signed before Denmark, as for the Confédération Germanique.

At the opening of each sitting the protocol of the previous one was read and approved.

On June 25, at the twenty-fifth full meeting, Earl Russell read a declaration that, in view of the fact that the suspension of hostilities, which on June 9 had been prolonged to the 26th, would expire on the following day, the object of the Conference had not been attained.

Authority: Parliamentary Papers, reprinted in *Brit. and For. State Papers*, liv. 173.

§ 480. *Conference of Geneva*, for the amelioration of the condition of soldiers wounded in armies in the field, 1864.

The Conference was called together by the Swiss Confederation, and was attended by delegates from the following Powers—

Baden,* Belgium,* Spain,* France,* Great Britain, Grand - ducal Hesse,* Italy,* Holland,* Portugal,* Prussia,* Saxony, Sweden and Norway,* Switzerland,* and Württemberg.*

* Powers whose delegates signed the Convention.

The delegates were mostly professional men, but Spain was represented by her *Chargé d'Affaires* to the Swiss Confederation, Holland by the secretary of her legation at Frankfort, Sweden and Norway by the military attaché at Paris ; France, besides two military men, sent a *sous-directeur* from the ministry for Foreign Affairs ; Prussia, in addition to a military surgeon and an *employé* from the Ministry of War, deputed her Envoy Extraordinary and Minister Plenipotentiary at Berne, and the Swiss delegation was headed by the Commander-in-Chief of the Swiss Army, General Dufour.

At the beginning of the first sitting the Prussian First delegate proposed that the presidency should be offered to General Dufour. Having taken the chair, General Dufour asked the Conference to accept Dr. Brière, divisional surgeon of the Federal army, as secretary.

General Dufour then welcomed the representatives of the various Governments, and explained that the object before them was the conclusion of a treaty for the neutralization of the military sanitary service and wounded soldiers.

The full-powers were next verified. Those of the French and Swiss representatives alone were found to be in good and due form. The representatives of Baden, Belgium, Great Britain, Hesse, Italy, Prussia, Saxony and Sweden were authorized solely to take part in the discussions, but had no power to sign. Those of Spain, Holland, Portugal and Württemberg were authorized to negotiate and sign the proposed convention, but the Spanish delegate declared that he would telegraph to his Government to inquire whether a special power would be sent to him for the signature. All announced, however, that they were ready to apply to their Governments for the necessary powers.

It was agreed that all were entitled to take part in the discussion of the general subject, and a diplomatic committee was appointed, composed of the first delegate of Prussia, the Spanish delegate, the first French delegate, one of the British delegates (deputy-inspector of hospitals) and the president of the International Committee, Mons. Gustave Moynier, the second Swiss delegate. Their function would be, when the substance of the treaty had been voted, to put it into shape.

General Dufour then delivered a discourse, setting forth the purpose of the Conference, after which a draft treaty was read. A discussion took place as to whether the voting should be individual or by delegations, but the first French delegate pointed out that no vote could be taken, as the majority could not bind even an insignificant minority.[1] The president alone signed the protocol of the sitting.

At the second meeting, the United States minister at Berne and the European agent in Paris of the United States sanitary commission exhibited their full-powers, which authorized them solely to be present at the negotiations, but not to sign.

It was decided that the members of the International Committee of Geneva might attend the sittings, but neither speak nor vote. The Dutch delegate obtained the same favour for Captain Van de Velde, but it was resolved that no more admissions of this nature should be granted.

Some of the articles of the draft Convention were discussed, and some were referred to the diplomatic committee to be re-drafted.

At the third sitting the *procès-verbaux* of the first and second were read and adopted, after some modifications had been introduced.

Dr. Fenger* presented himself as delegate for Denmark, and read out his full-powers, which authorized him to negotiate and sign the convention.

The delegates of Baden deposited the full-powers received from their Government, authorizing them to sign the convention.

The discussion was continued. At the fifth sitting

---

[1] Without doubt this is the correct international doctrine.

four more delegates announced that they were empowered to sign the convention. At the end of this sitting the Convention was approved. The representatives of Saxony and Hesse made reserve of the consent of the German Diet.

At the seventh sitting the convention was signed by the delegates of States whose names are marked with a asterisk on p. 131, and also Fenger.

By Article 9 it was provided that the Governments which had not been able to depute plenipotentiaries to the Conference should be invited to accede to the Convention.

Authorities: G. F. de Martens, *Nouv. Rec. des Traités*, xx. 375–99 ; Text of the Convention, p. 607 ; Pearce Higgins, *The Hague Peace Conferences*, p. 8, gives in a note the long list of Powers which subsequently acceded.

§ 481. *Conference respecting Luxemburg, London, 1867.* Invitations were sent out by the King of Holland, Grand-Duke of Luxemburg.

Protocol No. 1, sitting of May 7.

The plenipotentiaries were, for

Austria, Count Apponyi, Ambassador Extraordinary ;

Belgium, Mons. Van de Weyer, Envoy Extraordinary and Minister Plenipotentiary ;

France, Prince de la Tour d'Auvergne, Ambassador Extraordinary and Plenipotentiary ;

Great Britain, Lord Stanley, Secretary of State for Foreign Affairs ;

Italy, Marquis d'Azeglio, Envoy Extraordinary and Minister Plenipotentiary ;

Holland and Luxemburg, Baron Bentinck, Envoy Extraordinary and Minister Plenipotentiary ; Baron de Tornaco, President of the Government of the Grand Duchy ; Mons. Servais, Vice-President of the Council of State and of the Superior Court of Justice ;

Prussia, Count Bernstorff, Ambassador Extraordinary and Plenipotentiary ;

Russia, Baron Brunnow, Ambassador Extraordinary and Plenipotentiary.

The sitting was held at the official residence of the First Lord of the Treasury.

Count Apponyi proposed that Lord Stanley should be president, who, having accepted, nominated the Hon. Julian Fane, secretary of the British Embassy in Paris, as protocollist.

Lord Stanley proposed to invite the Italian minister to join the Conference, although Italy was not a party to the treaty of 1839, and on this being agreed to, the Marquis d'Azeglio was introduced and took his place.

The plenipotentiaries then proceeded to the verification of their full-powers, which were deposited in the archives of the Conference.

It was agreed (as usual) that the proceedings should be kept secret.

Lord Stanley having stated that the Conference had met at the invitation of the King of Holland, Grand Duke of Luxemburg, proposed that his representatives should be invited to present the considerations which had prompted this step. He laid before the Conference a draft treaty, which was read out. It had already been communicated by him to the Plenipotentiaries.

The Prussian plenipotentiary pointed out an omission in the said draft, of part of the programme of the Conference : namely, the European guarantee of the neutrality of the Grand Duchy ; he hoped it would be remedied when Article 2 came to be discussed.[1] The plenipotentiaries of Austria, France, the Netherlands and Russia confirmed the statement of the Prussian plenipotentiary that the Powers had accepted as the basis of negotiation the neutrality of Luxemburg under a collective guarantee.

Protocol No. 2, sitting of May 9.

[1] The discussion which ensued, and especially Count Bernstorff's observations, are important, in view of the violation of the neutrality of Luxemburg and Belgium by Germany in 1914.

Lord Stanley accepted the addition proposed by Count Bernstorff at the previous sitting, by which the neutrality of Luxemburg would be placed under the collective guarantee of the Powers.

The Belgian plenipotentiary repeated his previous observation that the neutrality of Belgium is placed under the guarantee of *each* of the Powers which signed the treaties of 1839.

The text of the treaty was agreed to, with the exception of Article 4, and was initialled by the plenipotentiaries.

Protocol No. 3, sitting of May 10.

The protocol of the first sitting was read and approved.[1]

The addition of Article 6 respecting the relations between Luxemburg and Limburg, proposed the day before by Baron Bentinck, was adopted and initialled.

Protocol No. 4, sitting of May 11.

The protocols of the second and third sittings were read and approved.

Lord Stanley proposed a wording of Article 4, which was accepted and initialled.

Then a copy of the treaty (the counterpart destined to be retained by Great Britain) was signed.

Baron Brunnow, as *doyen d'âge*, proposed a vote of thanks to Lord Stanley, who returned a suitable acknowledgment of the compliment.

Protocol No. 5, sitting of May 13.

The protocol of the fourth sitting was read and approved.

Signature took place of the other counterparts of the treaty.

Baron Brunnow asked the other plenipotentiaries to thank Mr. Fane for the zeal and talent with which he had discharged the functions entrusted to him by the president.

The protocol of the present sitting was read, and approved, and signed.

[1] It should be noted that, in accordance with the usual custom, this and the other protocols were signed by *all* the plenipotentiaries.

A *procès-verbal* of the exchange of ratifications, dated May 31, was drawn up and signed by all the plenipotentiaries, the signature of Lord Stanley coming first, then the rest in the alphabetical order of the French names of the States represented.

Authorities: Parliamentary Papers, reprinted in *Brit. and For. State Papers*, lvii. 32 ; G. F. de Martens, *Nouv. Rec.*, etc., continued by Ch. Samwer and Jules Hopf, xviii. 432 ; text of the treaty, 445. For Bismarck's views see Busch's *Bismarck: Some Secret Pages of his History*, i. 500–1. For the previous history of this affair, see Ollivier, *Empire Libéral*, ix. 166 and 261, 5, 7, 311–339.

§ 482. *Conference relative to the employment of explosive bullets in time of war*, held at Petersburg in 1868, at the invitation of the Emperor of Russia.

It was attended by commissioners (*commissaires*) from the following States—

Austria,* Bavaria, Belgium, Denmark, France,* Great Britain,* Greece, Italy,* Holland, Portugal, Prussia,* Russia,* Sweden and Norway, Switzerland,* Turkey and Württemberg. The commissioners sent by the States whose names are marked with an asterisk were military officers, the rest being diplomatic representatives at Petersburg. But Russia had among her delegates Baron Jomini, deputed by the Ministry for Foreign Affairs, and the diplomatic representative of Sweden and Norway was a professional soldier. The *Chargé d'affaires* of Persia joined the Conference at the second sitting.

The Russian First delegate opened the proceedings as president of the first sitting, Oct. 28/Nov. 9. No mention is made in the protocol of the appointment of a protocollist, nor of the verification of full-powers.

At each meeting the protocol of the previous one was read and approved, and was signed by the members present.

At the third meeting, November 4/16, the president

announced that the task of the military commission being now terminated, it remained for the plenipotentiaries to meet at the ministry for Foreign Affairs to give to the declaration its international form and value. He thanked the commissioners for the help they had given to the humane work undertaken in common.

The French commissioner proposed that the gratitude of the delegates should be expressed to the president for the courtesy he had shown to them all in directing their discussions.

The delegates also passed a vote of thanks to the delegate of the Ministry for Foreign Affairs in recognition of the exactness with which he had drawn up the protocols.

The declaration, dated Nov. 29/Dec. 11, 1868, was signed by the diplomatic representatives, authorized thereto by their Governments.

Authorities: De Martens, *Nouv. Rec.* etc., xviii. 450-74 *Brit. and For. State Papers*, lviii. 16.

§ 483. *Conference held at Geneva in October* 1868, for the revision of the Convention of Geneva of August 22, 1864, respecting the treatment of soldiers wounded on the field of battle and of ambulances.

The Conference was summoned by the Swiss Government.

The following States were represented at the first sitting, October 5 :—

North Germany, Austria, Baden, Bavaria, Belgium, Denmark, France, Great Britain, Italy, Holland, Sweden, and Norway, Switzerland and Württemberg. To these were added at the sixth sitting, October 13, a Turkish delegate. The delegates were military and naval officers and surgeons, with the exception of the German First delegate, minister of the North German Confederation at Berne ; the Danish delegate, consul in Switzerland ; the Dutch Second delegate, who was in the diplomatic service, and the Swiss Second delegate, president of the International Committee for the Succour of Wounded Soldiers.

The Swiss First Delegate, General Dufour, opened the proceedings.

The object of the Conference was twofold : (1) to extend the principles of the Convention of August 22, 1864, to the navy (*à la marine*) ; (2) to add to the text of the Convention certain explanations and developments asked for, in particular by the international conference held in Paris the preceding year, during the Universal Exhibition.

After explaining the object of the Conference, the president proposed Captain Philippe Plau of Geneva as secretary.

The Dutch First Delegate then proposed that the Swiss First Delegate should be called on to preside. It was also agreed that, in case he should on any occasion be prevented from presiding, a vice-president should be appointed.

With respect to voting, it was decided that each State should have one vote. A majority to be sufficient to discuss a particular subject, but that unanimity would be required for its final adoption.

A special committee, consisting of German, French, British, Italian and Dutch naval officers was appointed to frame a draft relating to the naval portion of the subject.

At the second sitting, October 6, the *procès-verbal* of the preceding one was read and adopted, after amendment.

A discussion arose respecting the extent of the powers of the different delegates, and each delegation having stated in turn what was the nature of its powers, it was found that only eight out of thirteen were empowered to sign an additional *Acte*.

In consequence, it was decided to confine the present proceedings to the preparation of a draft.

At the fourth sitting, October 9, a draft was read and discussed ; it contained only general principles, by way of elucidation of the Convention of 1864.

At the fifth sitting it was announced that the French First Delegate, Admiral Coupvent de Bois, had been nominated *rapporteur*[1] of the maritime committee. The report framed by him was read, and then the draft, article by article. The whole draft of additional articles was then read through and adopted. It was intended to sign this draft at the next meeting, October 13, but on that occasion a discussion took place which necessitated its being referred back to the naval committee (*commission de marine*).

At the seventh sitting, October 19, it was proposed to insert in the protocol an expression of satisfaction with the *bons offices* of the secretary of the Conference.

The *rapporteur* of the naval committee presented a new draft, which was read article by article, and adopted.

It was decided to sign the draft on the following day, which was accordingly done. On that occasion the British Minister at Berne, duly provided with full-powers, also signed on behalf of his Government. The *Acte* was compared with the draft, signed and sealed. There was only one original, which it was provided should be deposited in the archives of the Swiss Confederation.

The First Delegate for Holland made a speech expressing the high admiration, veneration and gratitude of the Conference for the manner in which the president had conducted and directed the discussions.

The " additional article " states that the Commissioners appointed by the respective Governments " dûment autorisés à cet effet, sont convenus, sous

[1] This is a French parliamentary institution, which puts great power into the hands of the person who discharges the function. Imagine the advantage such a position would confer on an advocate of " immunity of private property at sea in time of war " who was named *rapporteur* to a committee on the law of maritime warfare.

réserve d'approbation de leurs gouvernements, des dispositions suivantes."[1]

A footnote on p. 612 of the collection referred to states that : " Ces articles ont été approuvés par tous les Etats signataires de la Convention de 1864, à l'exception des anciens Etats pontificaux " ; but Dr. Pearce Higgins, in *The Hague Peace Conferences*, p. 13, informs us that they were never ratified, but that, with some modifications, these provisions have been acted on since 1868. Articles 6–15, he adds, were embodied in the Convention adopted by the Hague Conference of 1899 for the adaptation to maritime warfare of the principles of the Geneva Convention of 1864.

Authority for the protocols : *Nouv. Rec.* etc., xx. 400-35.

§ 484. *Conference on Cretan Affairs, Paris, 1869.*

The Government of the North German Confederation proposed, on December 18, 1868, that the Powers who were parties to the Treaty of Paris of March 30, 1856, should endeavour to find the means of appeasing the differences that had arisen between Turkey and Greece, and suggested that the Powers should furnish their ambassadors in either London or Paris with full powers.

It was decided that France should send out invitations for a conference to be held in Paris.

The first sitting was held January 9, 1869. There were present, for

Austria-Hungary, Prince Metternich, Ambassador ;

France, the Marquis de Lavalette, minister for Foreign Affairs ;

Great Britain, Lord Lyons, Ambassador Extraordinary and Plenipotentiary ;

Italy, the Chevalier Nigra, Envoy Extraordinary and Minister Plenipotentiary ;

Prussia and the *North German Confederation*, Count Sohms, Minister Plenipotentiary ;

[1] De Martens, *Nouv. Rec.*, xviii. 615 ; *Brit. and For. State Papers.* lxxiii. 1113.

Russia, Count Stackelberg, Ambassador Extra-ordinary ;

Turkey, Mehemmed Djemil Pasha, Ambassador Extra-ordinary and Plenipotentiary, and

Mons. Desprez, directeur des affaires politiques at the Ministry for Foreign Affairs, secretary of the Conference.

The plenipotentiaries met at the office of the minister for Foreign Affairs, and entrusted the presidency to the Marquis de Lavalette, on whose nomination Mons. Desprez was nominated secretary.

The full-powers were verified and found in good and due form.

The president then opened the discussion in a short speech.

The Greek minister, Mons. Rangabé, who was introduced at the request of the Russian plenipotentiary, read a note announcing that he was not authorized to be present at the discussions unless he were admitted on a footing of entire equality with the Turkish ambassador. The plenipotentiaries were of opinion that they could not recognize this claim, seeing that the Conference consisted of the representatives of Powers who were parties to the Treaty of Paris of March 30, 1856, acting in accordance with the spirit of the protocol of April 14, 1856.[1] Their view was that Greece, not having been a party to the important transactions of that period, should be admitted simply *à titre consultatif*. The protocols were signed by all the plenipotentiaries.

Second sitting, January 12. The president announced that the declaration in favour of the postponement of measures of a hostile character,[2] initialled at the previous sitting, had been sent to Constantinople and Athens, but that no reply had as yet been received.

[1] In which the plenipotentiaries, in the name of their Governments, expressed a recommendation (*vœu*) that States between which a serious disagreement arose should, before appealing to arms, have recourse, as far as circumstances might permit, to the good offices of a friendly Power.

[2] Turkey had sent an *ultimatum* to Greece on December 11, 1868.

Third sitting, January 14. The president announced that Turkey accepted the declaration, but that no answer had arrived from Greece.

It was agreed that the Conference should proceed, even if Greece declined to take part *à titre consultatif*.

Fourth sitting, January 15. The president submitted the draft of a declaration, to be communicated to the Greek Government, on international law respecting the duties of neutrals in such a case as the present.[1] This was agreed to, but its initialling was postponed in order to give time for the consideration of a document transmitted from Athens, entitled *Mémoire sur le conflit Greco-Turc*.

Fifth sitting, January 16. It was held that the Greek *mémoire* made no difference to the views expressed in the draft declaration of the previous meeting, and after some slight modification it was adopted and initialled definitely (*ne varietur*).

Sixth sitting, January 20. The Greek Government still refused to take part in the Conference unless on a footing of equality with Turkey, but agreed to maintain the *statu quo* pending the result of the Conference. The Turkish plenipotentiary announced that if Greece accepted the declaration, Turkey would abstain from executing the measures foreshadowed as the consequence of her *ultimatum*.

The plenipotentiaries, with the exception of the Turkish, appended their signatures to the declaration, a copy of which was inserted in the protocol.

Seventh sitting, February 18. The president opened the proceedings by reading a letter from Mons. Deliyanni, Minister for Foreign Affairs at Athens, dated Jan. 25/Feb. 6, and addressed to Mons. Rangabé, announcing the acceptance of the declaration. The Conference, on the motion of the Chevalier Nigra, took note of this acceptation (*adhésion*), and held that diplo-

[1] An insurrection of the Greek inhabitants of Crete against Turkey had been encouraged and assisted by Greece.

matic relations were thereby re-established *ipso jure* between Turkey and Greece.

The Austro-Hungarian plenipotentiary proposed a vote of thanks to the president of the Conference, and the others concurred. Thanks were also accorded to Mons. Desprez.

The Marquis de Lavalette, in reply, expressed the hope that the work accomplished in the spirit of the protocol of April 14, 1856, would be a precedent for the future.

The plenipotentiaries joined unanimously in giving utterance to this hope (*vœu*), and the Conference, having attained the object of its mission, declared itself dissolved.

Authorities: G. F. de Martens, *Nouveau Recueil Général*, continued by Ch. Samwer and J. Hopf, xviii. 80–109 ; Parliamentary Papers, reprinted in *Brit. and For. State Papers*, lix. 813 ; E. Ollivier, *L'Empire Libéral*, xi. 177.

§ 485. *Conference relative to the Inviolability of Treaties, and the Revision of the Treaty of March* 30, 1856, so far as regards the Neutralization of the Black Sea, the Straits of the Dardanelles and Bosphorus, and the Navigation of the Danube, London, January to March 1871. For the despatch of Prince Gortschakow which was the occasion of this Conference, see Strupp, *Urkunden zur Geschichte des Volkerrechts*, i. 16.n.

This Conference was, as a matter of form, called together at the instance of the King of Prussia.

At the sitting of January 17 there were present, for
North Germany, Count Bernstorff ;
Austria-Hungary, Count Apponyi ;
Great Britain, Earl Granville ;
Italy, the Chevalier Count Cadorna ;
Russia, Baron Brunnow ;
Turkey, Musurus Pacha.
The meeting took place at the Foreign Office.
Musurus Pacha proposed that Lord Granville be

appointed president. The motion was adopted unanimously.

Lord Granville replied, proposing that the Hon. Wm. Stuart should be entrusted with the drafting of the protocols. In his opening speech he stated that Mons. Jules Favre, appointed French plenipotentiary, was not able to be present, and then moved that the following Annexe to the *procès-verbal* should be signed (which was done)—

Les Plénipotentiaires de l'Allemagne du Nord, de l'Autriche-Hongrie, de la Grande-Bretagne, de l'Italie, de la Russie, et de la Turquie, réunis aujourd'hui en Conférence, reconnaissent que c'est un principe essentiel du droit des gens qu'aucune Puissance ne peut se délier des engagements d'un Traité, ni en modifier les stipulations, qu'à la suite de l'assentiment des Parties Contractantes, au moyen d'une entente amicale.

En foi de quoi . . . les dits Plénipotentiaires ont signé le présent Protocole.

Full-powers were verified at the first sitting.

It was signed by all the plenipotentiaries present in the French alphabetical order of the States represented, and on March 13 also by the Duc de Broglie, French plenipotentiary. For Bismarck's views, see Busch, *Bismarck, Some Secret Pages of his History*, i. 304, 440, 467, 512. Saying attributed to Bismarck, " L'observation des traités entre les grands États n'est que conditionnelle, des que la lutte pour la vie les met à l'épreuve " (Welschinger, *La Guerre de* 1871, i. 202).

At the second sitting, January 24, after the signature of the protocol of the first sitting, Count Bernstorff, announced that his sovereign had changed his title, and asked that he might in future be designated as the plenipotentiary of Germany.

The Russian ambassador stated that he had received instructions to recognize the imperial title of His Majesty the King of Prussia.

The request of the plenipotentiary of Germany was agreed to by the other plenipotentiaries.

At the third sitting, February 3, a draft treaty was considered, which had been discussed unofficially after the last sitting. It was amended and added to, and further discussion was deferred to February 7.

At the fourth sitting the plenipotentiaries initialled the draft of the *procès-verbal* of the third sitting.

At the fifth sitting, March 13, the Duc de Broglie was introduced by the president to the Conference as French plenipotentiary, who then presented his full-powers, which were found to be in good and due form. The draft of the treaty was discussed, and, various amendments having been adopted, one original of the final text (that for Great Britain) having been prepared during the sitting, was thereupon signed and sealed.

At the sixth sitting, March 14, the other originals of the treaty were signed and sealed. The usual votes of thanks were adopted.

At each sitting of the Conference the *procès-verbal* of the previous meeting was read and approved.

Authorities : *British and Foreign State Papers*, lxi. 1193 ; G. F. de Martens, *Nouveau Recueil Général*, cont. par Ch. Samwer et J. Hopf. xviii, 273.

§ 486. *Conference of Brussels on the Rules of Military Warfare*, 1874.

It was proposed by the Russian Government.

First sitting, July 27. There were present, for

Germany, 5 members ;
Austria-Hungary, 2 ;
Belgium, 3 ; [1]
Denmark, 2 ;
Spain, 3 ;
France, 2 ;
Great Britain, 1 ;
Greece, 1 ;
Italy, 2 ;
Holland, 2 ; [1]

[1] One diplomatist.

Russia, 2 ;
Sweden and Norway, 1 ;
Switzerland, 1.

The delegates were received by the minister for Foreign Affairs at his office, and welcomed by him.   He proposed his own *chef de cabinet* as protocollist.

The Russian First delegate offered the presidency to the Belgian First delegate, Baron Lambermont, of the ministry of Foreign Affairs, who declined it.   He in turn proposed for that office the Russian delegate, Baron Jomini, of the Russian ministry for Foreign Affairs, who was thereupon unanimously requested to undertake it.

A draft was submitted by the Russian delegation, and a committee was appointed to study it.

At the second *séance plenière*, July 29, the president asked for the verification of the full-powers of the delegates.   This having been performed, they were found to be in good and due form.

The committee held eighteen meetings, from July 30 to August 24, both inclusive, the protocols of which were signed by the president and the secretary.

The third *séance plenière* was held August 5, the fourth and fifth on August 26 and 27.

On the latter occasion it was proposed to close the discussions and to sign the final protocol, but not to declare the Conference closed.

Thereupon the final protocol was signed.   It stated that the delegates would lay the results of their labours before their respective Governments as a conscientious study, apt to serve as the basis of an ulterior exchange of ideas and of a development of the provisions of the Geneva Convention of 1864, and the Declaration of Petersburg of 1868.   It would be for the Governments to decide what part of the draft could be accepted as it stood, and what part would require more mature consideration.

At p. 133 of the British Blue Book there is a despatch from the Foreign Office expressly stating that the British delegate, Sir A. Horsford, had no authority to act in a plenipotentiary capacity. If he signed the final protocol, it must be done in his individual capacity, and not be taken to pledge H.M. Government in any manner.

The text of the Declaration is at p. 151 of the Blue Book. It was never ratified.

Authorities : *Parliamentary Papers*, reprinted in *Brit. and For. State Papers*, lxv. 1110 ; Dr. Pearce Higgins, *The Hague Peace Conferences*, p. 257.

§ 487. *Conference of Constantinople*, 1876–7.

Between the plenipotentiaries of the Great Powers, of which the objects were : (1) to obtain administrative autonomy for Bosnia and Herzegovina ; (2) to settle terms of peace between Serbia and Montenegro and the Porte ; and (3) an increase of territory, if possible, for Montenegro.

The plenipotentiaries were, for

Germany, Baron Werther, Ambassador ;

Austria-Hungary, Count Zichy, Ambassador, and Baron Calice, Envoy Extraordinary and Minister Plenipotentiary ;

France, Count Bourgoing, Ambassador, and Count Chaudordy (sent from Paris) ;

Great Britain, Marquis of Salisbury, Secretary of State for India, as Special Ambassador, and Sir Henry Elliott, Ambassador ;

Italy, Count Corti, Envoy Extraordinary and Minister Plenipotentiary ;

Russia, Count Ignatiew, Ambassador ;

Turkey, Safvet Pasha, Minister for Foreign Affairs, and Edhem Pasha.

The First Secretary of the Austro-Hungarian embassy drew up the *comptes-rendus* of the sittings. At the opening of each sitting the *compte-rendu* of the previous one was read and approved.

Nine preliminary *conférences*, consisting only of the foreign plenipotentiaries, were held from December 11 to 22, both inclusive, at the Russian Embassy. Probably Ignatiew was the senior Ambassador. After that there were meetings of the full Conference, including the Turkish representatives. Safvet Pasha was appointed president. Caratéodory Pasha was secretary, with another Turkish official and Mons. Moüy of the French embassy as assistant secretaries.

Full-powers were produced by Edhem Pasha, the Marquis of Salisbury, Mons. Chaudordy and Baron Calice. The other plenipotentiaries, being resident diplomatic representatives of the respective Powers, were not required to produce special full-powers.

Nine full meetings of the Conference were held, beginning with December 23, n.s., and ending with January 20, n.s.

On the last of these occasions the Turkish representatives refused to accept the propositions of the Six Powers, and they were thereupon informed that the Conference was at an end, and that all the plenipotentiaries would return home.

A final meeting was held on the following day, at the Austro-Hungarian embassy, at which the protocol of the ninth sitting was signed, but the Ottoman plenipotentiaries did not present themselves.

Authority: *Parliamentary Papers*, reprinted in *Brit. and For. State Papers*, lxviii. 1114.

§ 488. *Conference on the Navigation of the Danube, London*, 1883.

The invitations were sent out by the British Government.

The objects of the Conference were : to take into consideration the execution of Articles 54 and 55 of the Treaty of Berlin of July 13, 1878, concerning the navigation of the Danube, namely : (1) Extension of the powers of the Commission as far as Braila ; (2) Confirmation of the regulations drawn up in accordance with Article 55 of the said Treaty ; (3) Prolongation of the powers of the European Commission.

The plenipotentiaries were, for

Germany, Count Münster, Ambassador ;

Austria-Hungary, Count Károlyi, Ambassador ;

France, Mons. Tissot, Ambassador, and Mons. Barère, Minister Plenipotentiary ;

Great Britain, Earl Granville, Secretary of State for Foreign Affairs, and Lord Edmond Fitzmaurice, parliamentary Under-Secretary of State ;

Italy, Count Nigra, Ambassador ;

Russia, Baron Mohrenheim, Ambassador ;

Turkey, Musurus Pasha, Ambassador.

At the first sitting, February 8, 1883, Count Münster proposed Earl Granville as president, who, having accepted, nominated Mr. J. A. Crowe[1] as secretary.

The president announced that the Turkish Ambassador had not yet received his full-powers.

At the second meeting the Turkish plenipotentiary took his seat.

The president proposed that the deliberations of the Conference should be kept secret.

After some discussion it was agreed to invite Rumania and Serbia to attend the sittings in order that they might be consulted and heard. The observations of Bulgaria (being a vassal State) were to be presented textually through the Turkish ambassador.

The Rumanian and Serbian delegates being introduced, stated that their instructions were to take part with a deliberative voice. They would refer the point to their Governments, but in the meantime they would refrain from attending. [Prince Ghica was Envoy Extraordinary and Minister Plenipotentiary in London for Rumania. Mons. Marinovitch had been specially delegated from Serbia for the Conference.]

At the third meeting, the Serbian Minister, having

---

[1] Afterwards Sir Joseph Crowe.

been authorized to accept the conditions laid down, took his seat. [The ground of the position assigned to these representatives was that the Conference was, as it were, the sequel of the Treaty of Berlin, to which their Governments were not parties.]

A declaration was adopted approving of the Regulations above mentioned under (2).

At the fourth meeting, February 20, the Serbian Minister attended, but did not sign the protocol.

The question of the permanent prolongation of the powers of the European Commission was discussed, but not settled.

At the fifth meeting, February 24, proposals defining the power of the Commission were adopted, with reserves on the part of the Russian plenipotentiary.

A drafting committee was set up, consisting of six plenipotentiaries.

At the sixth sitting, March 1, prolongation for twenty-one years, subject to the Russian reserve, and continuation after that period for successive periods of three years, unless notice of modification were given, was agreed to.

At the seventh sitting, March 7, the text of the treaty was agreed to, after certain verbal modifications had been made in the draft at the suggestion of the Russian plenipotentiary.

At the eighth meeting, March 10, the Turkish plenipotentiary proposed the usual vote of thanks to the president, and the Italian plenipotentiary proposed the vote of thanks to the secretary.

Counterparts of the treaty as approved by the plenipotentiaries were compared, and found to be correct, whereupon they were signed and sealed.[1]

Authority : *Parliamentary Papers*, reprinted in *Brit. and For. State Papers*, lxxiv. 1231. [They do not include the *procès-verbal* of the exchange of ratifications.]

[1] *Brit. and For. State Papers*, lxxiv. 20, 23.

§ 489. *Conference respecting the Affairs of Africa* (Slave Trade ; Rivers Congo and Niger ; Rules for future Occupation on the Coast of Africa), Berlin, November–December, 1884.

Convoked by Germany, in consequence of an idea which had suggested itself to the German and French Governments, in order to establish an agreement on the following principles—

1. Freedom of commerce in the basin and mouths of the Congo.

2. Application to the Congo and Niger of the principles adopted by the Congress of Vienna with a view to consecrating freedom of navigation on several international rivers, principles which were later applied to the Danube.

3. Definition of the formalities to be observed so that new occupations on the coast of Africa may be regarded as effective.

The following were the plenipotentiaries who attended the first sitting, November 15, 1884—

Germany, His Serene Highness Prince Bismarck, Chancellor ; H.E. Count Hatzfeldt, Secretary of State for Foreign Affairs ; Herr Busch, Under-secretary of State for Foreign Affairs ; Herr v. Kusserow, Geheimer Legationsrath ;

Austria-Hungary, H.E. Count Széchényi, Ambassador;

Belgium, Count van der Straten-Ponthoz, Minister at Berlin ; Baron Lambermont, Envoy Extraordinary and Minister Plenipotentiary, Secrétaire-général du Ministère des Affaires Etrangères at Brussels.

Denmark, Mons. de Vind, Minister at Berlin ;

Spain, Conde de Benomar, Minister at Berlin ;

United States of America, Mr. Kasson, Minister at Berlin ;

France, H.E. Baron de Courcel, Ambassador at Berlin ;

Great Britain, H.E. Sir Edward Malet, Ambassador at Berlin ;

Italy, H.E. Conte de Launay, Ambassador at Berlin ;
Holland, Jonkheer van der Hoeven, Minister at Berlin ;
Portugal, Marquis de Penafiel, Minister at Berlin, Councillor Serpa Pimentel, a peer of the kingdom ;
Russia, Count Kapnist, Minister Plenipotentiary at Berlin ;
Sweden and Norway, General Baron Bildt, Minister at Berlin ;
Turkey, H.E. Said Pasha, Ambassador at Berlin.

Prince Bismarck opened the sitting with a short address of welcome, and proposed to constitute the Conference by nominating the president and the members of the secretariat.

Count de Launay, representative of Italy and *doyen* of the diplomatic body, proposed to confide the presidency to Count Bismarck, in accordance with precedent.

Count Széchényi declared that the proposal was acceded to.

Prince Bismarck accepted, and asked leave to be replaced by one of his colleagues in case other business or the state of his health should require it.

He proposed Mons. Raindre, French conseiller d'ambassade, Count William Bismarck, councillor at the Ministry of State, and Dr. Schmidt, vice-consul attached to the German ministry for Foreign Affairs, as secretaries.

These suggestions being approved, the members of the secretariat were introduced and presented to the Conference.

Prince Bismarck announced that the powers of the plenipotentiaries had been deposited at the secretariat for examination as far as might be necessary. Diplomatic agents accredited at Berlin were, however, considered to possess the necessary powers for representing their Governments at the Conference.

He then delivered a discourse describing the objects of the Conference, and announced that drafts would be presented dealing with freedom of commerce in the basin of the Congo and its mouths, with the freedom of navigation on the Congo and the Niger, and with the formalities to be observed in order that new occupation of the coasts of Africa should be considered to be effective.

Sir Edward Malet read a declaration expressing the views of his Government.

The *procès-verbal* was signed by the plenipotentiaries in the French alphabetical order of their Governments, except that the German plenipotentiaries signed last.

Annex. Draft declaration respecting freedom of commerce in the basin of the Congo and its mouths.

Second sitting, November 19. Count Hatzfeldt presided in place of Prince Bismarck, who was indisposed.

Proposed that communication beforehand of the printed protocol of the preceding sitting should take the place of the traditional reading at the commencement of each sitting. In case no change was made by any member, the text would be regarded as approved, the signature should take place at the beginning of the sitting, and the original would then be deposited with the archives. Agreed.

He announced that the Russian representative was unable to be present, by reason of his health.

Also, that Mr. Sanford, plenipotentiary of the United States, had been admitted to the Conference, in pursuance of a communication from the United States minister at Berlin, defining the character of his mission.

Mr. Kasson read a declaration in the English language, of which a translation was inserted in the protocol.

On the motion of the president, a commission was set up, consisting of the representatives of Germany, Belgium, Spain, the United States, France, Great Britain, Holland and Portugal, to report on the meaning of the expression " territories constituting the basin of the Congo and of its affluents " in the draft presented by the German Government, and distributed at the first and second sittings.

The members of the Conference offered the services

of their *délégués-adjoints* for the purposes of the said commission.

The third sitting was held November 27, under the presidency of Count Hatzfeldt.

The report of the commission had previously been printed, circulated and was now discussed. Certain amendments were adopted, and referred to the drafting committee for insertion in their proper place, and on its being resolved to refer back a portion of the report to the commission, it was agreed that every member of the Conference should be entitled to sit on the commission or be represented on it.

It was also agreed that the said commission should nominate the drafting committee.

Fourth sitting, December 1.

A commission had been appointed to prepare the definitive draft of the Declaration relating to commercial freedom, and to study the definition of the Congo area, and next that of the Niger. It was also decided to publish the protocols of sittings, as incorrect reports had found their way into the press.

Annexes : 1. Declaration respecting freedom of commerce in the basin of the Congo, its mouths and neighvouring territories.

2. Report of the commission entrusted with the examination of the foregoing subject. There were *procès-verbaux* of the commissions.

Fifth sitting, December 18. Count Hatzfeldt being indisposed, Herr Busch presided, by nomination of Prince Bismarck.

Discussion took place of a declaration respecting the navigation of the Congo, which was adopted, after each article had been passed under review.

The *Acte* respecting the Niger was discussed, and, after reviewing each article, the Conference adopted it as a whole.

A recommendation (*vœu*) of the commission respecting the liquor trade was adopted.

A motion respecting the suppression of the slave trade was submitted by the British plenipotentiary.

Annex. Report of the commission appointed to examine the draft *Actes* of Navigation for the Congo and Niger.

Sixth sitting, December 22. Herr Busch presided.

A proposal respecting the liquor trade was read and adopted.

The British proposal respecting the slave trade was discussed and referred to the commission.

Annexes : 1. Proposal of the drafting committee for an additional article to the Declaration respecting the freedom of commerce in the conventional basin of the Congo (*i.e.* neutralizing the free zone—proposal No. 33).

2. Proposal of the British plenipotentiary to add at the end of paragraph 4 of proposal No. 33 the words : *et il ne pourra, après avoir pris du charbon sous ces conditions, le prendre dans les mêmes eaux qu'après un intervalle de trois mois.*

3. Italian proposal, to renounce the extension of military action to the basin of the Congo, etc. Subsidiary proposal to substitute an engagement first to have recourse to the mediation of a friendly Power.

Seventh sitting, January 7, 1885. Presidency of Herr Busch.

Discussion of a draft Declaration respecting the slave trade, which was adopted with a slight, merely verbal, amendment.

A draft Declaration respecting formalities to be observed in the case of new occupations on the coasts of Africa was referred back to the commission. This draft formed an *annex* to the protocol.

Eighth sitting, January 31. Presidency of Herr Busch.

The *annex* to protocol No. 7 was discussed and adopted.

The form to be given to the Final Act was discussed, and the question was referred to the commission.

Annexes : 1. A report of the commission charged with the examination of the draft Declaration respecting new occupations on the coasts of Africa.

2. Observations submitted to the commission, at its sitting of January 5, by Count Benomar, on the subject of the right of visit on the west coast of Africa.

Ninth sitting, February 23. Presidency of Herr Busch.

A letter was read from the president of the International Association of the Congo, notifying the conclusion of treaties by which its flag is recognized as that of a friendly State or Government. It was proposed that this letter, as well as the observations of various plenipotentiaries thereon, and copies of the said treaties, be annexed to the protocol.

On the motion of the president the Final Act was discussed, and two amendments were adopted. The draft Declaration respecting neutrality of the conventional basin of the Congo was discussed, and the " subsidiary proposal " annexed to the sixth protocol was adopted. The Final Act was passed under review and adopted.

The Italian plenipotentiary moved a vote of thanks to Herr Busch for the tact and conciliatory spirit with which he had conducted the work of the Conference.

Annexes : 1. Copies of treaties by which the International Association of the Congo had obtained recognition from various Governments.

2. Draft General Act of the Conference of Berlin.

3. Report on certain fresh modifications of the text, respecting neutrality and general dispositions, as well as the definitive form of the decisions emanating from the Conference.

Tenth sitting, February 26, 1885. Presidency of Prince Bismarck.

Discourse of the president, reviewing the course of the Conference.

The Italian plenipotentiary's reply. The Final Act, having previously been printed and distributed, was taken as read.

Before proceeding to its signature, the president communicated the Act of Adhesion of the International Association of the Congo, a letter from its president, Colonel Strauch, and his full-powers.

After which, the plenipotentiaries proceeded to the signature of the Final Act.

The signature of the plenipotentiary of the Power for which each copy was destined was first appended, then of those of the remaining Powers in the French alphabetical order of the States which they represented, beginning with Germany.

It was not ratified by the United States, but the German plenipotentiaries and the diplomatic representatives of the other Powers assembled, and signed a protocol recording the deposit of the respective ratifications in the German Imperial Archives. The ratifications were produced, and after examination were found to be in good and due form, after which the protocol, dated April 19, 1885, was signed by those present, in the French alphabetical order of the States represented, except that Germany signed last.

Authority : *British and Foreign State Papers*, lxxv. 1178, and lxxvi. 1021.

§ 490. *First Hague Peace Conference*, 1899.

The initiative came from the Emperor of Russia, who proposed to the Governments who were represented on this occasion that a Conference should meet at the Hague for the purpose of seeking for the means of putting an end to the incessant increase of armaments and to forestall the calamities which threatened the entire world.[1]

[1] See M. de Beaufort's speech in *Conf. Intern. de la Paix*, nouv. édit., 1907, p. 10.

The invitations were issued by the Queen of Holland.

The topics suggested for discussion in Count Moura-vieff's Circular on Dec. 30, 1898/Jan. 11, 1899, were : (1) the limitation of armed forces ; (2) the limitation of new firearms and explosives; (3) the restriction of already existing explosives and prohibition of the discharge of projectiles from air-craft ; (4) the prohibition of submarines and eventually of rams ; (5) application of the Geneva Convention of 1864 and additional articles of 1868 to naval warfare ; (6) neutralization of ships and boats employed in saving the shipwrecked during or after an engagement ; (7) revision of the unratified Brussels Declaration of 1874 respecting the laws and customs of war on land ; (8) good offices, mediation and arbitration.

The following twenty-six States were represented—

Germany, Austria-Hungary,* Belgium,* China, Denmark, Spain,* United States,* Mexico, France,* Great Britain,* Greece, Italy,* Japan, Luxemburg, Montenegro (represented by Russia), Holland, Persia, Portugal,* Rumania,* Russia, Servia, Siam, Sweden and Norway, Switzerland, Turkey, and Bulgaria. In every case the First Delegate was appointed *ad hoc*, and was of the rank of either minister of State, Ambassador, or Envoy Extraordinary and Minister Plenipotentiary at some other Court, but the States whose names are marked with an asterisk had also appointed their diplomatic representatives at the Hague. The delegates were assisted by naval and military officers of distinction, and in many instances by professors of International Law.

The first sitting, May 18, was opened by the Netherlands minister for Foreign Affairs, who moved that the presidency should be conferred on the Russian First delegate, Ambassador in London, who in turn proposed that the Netherlands First delegate, formerly minister for Foreign Affairs, should be honorary president.

The president then nominated a Netherlands diplomatist as secretary-general, and one of the Russian delegates as *secrétaire-général-adjoint*. The other secretaries were members of the French, Belgian and Netherlands diplomatic service. Two Netherlands naval and military officers were also appointed technical secretaries.

At the second sitting, May 20, after delivering an address on the scope of the Conference, the president proposed that the subjects mentioned in the circular of December 30, o.s.,[1] should be shared among three committees, with power to set up sub-committees. The Conference, he added, did not hold itself competent to discuss any question but those already indicated by him. Each State was entitled to be represented on all three committees. It was agreed that each State should have only one vote, whether at the full meetings of the Conference, or in the committees. The technical and scientific delegates were empowered to be present at the full meetings, and all delegates to take part in the work of the committees. The committees were to appoint their officers and to regulate their own procedure.

Finally, he asked the delegates who had not already done it to send their full-powers to the secretariat. Remarking that the Conference had undertaken to observe the secrecy of the discussions, he proposed that the secretariat should be authorized to organize a service of communications to the press.

A *rapporteur* was appointed to draw up a report on the work of each committee, which was afterwards discussed at a full meeting of the Conference.

A drafting committee was appointed, which, among other things, prepared the Final Act, which was signed by the plenipotentiaries only. It contained an enumeration of the Conventions embodying the definite results obtained, certain Declarations, one Resolution in favour of the limitation of military expenditure, and six Recommendations (*vœux*). Only one original of the

[1] January 11, 1899, n.s. J. B. Scott, i. 44-6.

Final Act was signed, and it was deposited at the Netherlands ministry for Foreign Affairs.

The closing meeting took place on July 29. At the morning sitting the Final Act, the Conventions and the Declarations were signed.

At the afternoon sitting there were read a letter from the Queen of Holland to the Pope, of May 7, announcing the convocation of the Conference, and the reply of His Holiness to Her Majesty, dated May 29.

The president delivered a discourse, in which he asked the Conference to thank the Queen of Holland for her hospitality, the eminent statesmen and jurists who had presided in the committees and sub-committees, the *rapporteurs* and the secretariat, and also thanked the members for the consideration they had shown to himself as president, concluding with some general remarks on the work accomplished.

The German First Delegate, Count Münster, as *doyen d'âge*, proposed a vote of thanks to the president, Mons. de Staal, and to the honorary president, Mons. van Karnebeck, to which they responded.

The Netherlands Minister for Foreign Affairs then addressed the assembly in a speech which he concluded in these words : " Pour nous, le souvenir de votre séjour ici restera à jamais un point lumineux dans les annales de notre pays parce que nous avons la ferme conviction que ce séjour a ouvert une nouvelle ère dans l'histoire des relations internationales entre les peuples civilisés."

The president then declared the meetings of the Conference to be at an end.

Authorities : *Conférence Internationale de la Paix La Haye, 18 Mai—29 Juillet 1899, nouv. édit.* La Haye, 1907 ; Dr. J. B. Scott, *The Hague Peace Conferences of 1899 and 1907* (2 vols.) ; Dr. Pearce Higgins, *The Hague Peace Conferences;* *Brit. and For. State Papers,* xci. 963–1017, has the Acte Final, Conventions and Declarations.

§ 491. *Conference of Peking*, 1900–1.

Object. An agreement with China for the re-establishment of normal international relations with the Treaty Powers, for satisfaction for the attacks on the foreign legations at Peking in the summer of 1900 and the destruction of life and property, and for material guarantees against the possibility of such attacks in the future.

Plenipotentiaries. The diplomatic representatives of the following Powers : Germany, Austria-Hungary, Belgium, Spain, the United States, France, Great Britain, Italy, Japan, the Netherlands and Russia : namely, Baron v. Mumm, Baron Czikann, Mons. Joostens, Señor B. J. de Cologan, Mr. E. H. Conger and afterwards Mr. W. W. Rockhill,[1] Mons. Pichon and afterwards Mons. Beau, Sir E. Satow, Marchese Salvago Raggi, Baron T. Nishi and afterwards Mr. J. Komura, Heer F. M. Knobel (Minister Resident), Mons. Michel de Giers. For China, Prince Ch'ing and Li Hung-chang. There were four secretaries, of the French, Russian, British and German legations. No protocols have been published, but the Blue Books, China, Nos. 5 and 6 (1901) and China, No. 1 (1902), contain fairly full reports of the meetings of the Conference and of the discussions in the various committees that were set up. The Chinese plenipotentiaries were invited to attend on the few occasions when their presence was required. The sittings of the *plenum*, about sixty in number, were presided over by the *doyen* of the Diplomatic Body, and were held at his house, except for a short time, when the British representative was recovering from an illness, and they were temporarily transferred to the British legation. Very full *procès-verbaux* of the sittings were drawn up, and after being circulated among the foreign members, were signed by them. There was no

---

[1] The latter was only plenipotentiary for the Conference, the diplomatic relations being entrusted to the Secretary of Legation as *Chargé d'affaires*.

presentation of full-powers, the credentials of the respective diplomatists being held to be sufficient. The two Chinese representatives, however, were provided with full-powers, of which a separate *exemplaire* was delivered to each foreign diplomatist.

The arrangements agreed upon were recorded in a Final Protocol, signed by all the plenipotentiaries, foreign and Chinese, September 7, 1901.

Authorities : *Parliamentary Papers* as above. [The *procès-verbaux* have not been published.]

§ 492. *Conference for the Revision of the Geneva Convention of 1864, Geneva, 1906.*

The Swiss Federal Council issued circulars on February 17, 1903, January 22, 1904, and March 10, 1906, inviting the various Governments to send delegates to a Conference to be held at Geneva, and framed a list of questions to be examined by the International Conference.

The Conference assembled on June 11. The plenipotentiaries for the thirty-seven different Powers represented consisted of twenty-eight diplomatists and consuls, three naval officers, sixteen combatant military officers, nineteen military medical officers, eight international jurists, and three members of Red Cross societies. A complete list of the names and qualifications of the plenipotentiaries is given at the beginning of the Convention which was signed at the conclusion of the proceedings, and also in the Final Protocol.

The opening session was under the presidency of the President of the Swiss Confederation. The Swiss First delegate, Minister at Petersburg, was elected president of the Conference, and one of the Swiss delegates to the Conference of 1864, who was then president of the Société génevoise d'utilité publique, was elected honorary president.

At the first session of the Conference, June 12, the secretariat was nominated.

The roll of delegates was called over, and they were requested to state the extent of their full-powers.

Rules for the conduct of the proceedings were agreed to. French was adopted as the language of the Conference, each delegation had only one vote on a division, all propositions had to be put in writing, printed and distributed before discussion, the *procès-verbaux* were to give a succinct, but not *verbatim*, account of the proceedings. Every delegate had the right of having his declarations printed *in extenso*.

Four committees to deal with separate portions of the Swiss list of questions were formed. Each had a chairman, vice-chairman, *rapporteur* and secretary.

At the second session the results of the election of officers of the committees were made known, and it was agreed to print summaries of the proceedings in committee.

At the third session, June 27, a drafting committee was nominated, to consist of the four *rapporteurs*, four international jurists, and seven delegates whose nationalities had not been represented on the *bureaux* of the committees.

At the fourth session, June 28, reports of the committees were considered, and the drafts of certain articles were agreed to.

At the sixth session, July 5, the report of the drafting committee and the draft of the Convention were presented, and accepted without discussion.

A recommendation (*vœu*) respecting arbitration by the Hague Tribunal of differences which, in time of peace, might arise between the contracting Powers regarding the interpretation of the Convention, was agreed to for insertion in the Final Protocol.

The proceedings terminated with the usual expression of thanks to the officers of the Conference.

At the closing session, June 6, the Convention and Final Protocol were signed, each in one original, to be deposited in the archives of the Swiss Confederation.

There is a *procès-verbal* of the deposit of the British ratification, dated April 16, 1907, and signed by the British minister at Berne and the President of the Swiss Confederation. It is to be assumed that similar certificates were signed on the occasion of the deposit of the ratifications of other contracting States.

Up to 1909, the following additional States had ratified the Convention : Austria-Hungary, Belgium, Brazil, the Congo, Denmark, Germany, Italy, Japan and Corea, Luxemburg, Mexico, Russia, Siam, Spain, Switzerland, and the United States of America. Colombia, Cuba, Nicaragua, Turkey and Venezuela have acceded.

Authorities : *Papers relating to the Geneva Convention* [Cd. 3933] ; *Brit. and For. State Papers*, xcix. ; *Actes de la Conférence*, edited by Prof. Röthlisberger, published by the Imprimerie Henri Jarrys ; Dr. Pearce Higgins, *The Hague Peace Conferences*, p. 35.

§ 493. *International Conference at Algeciras relating to the affairs of Morocco*, 1906.

The Conference was held in consequence of an invitation addressed to the Powers by the Sultan of Morocco. The plenipotentiary delegates were, for

Germany, Herr von Radowitz, Ambassador Extraordinary and Plenipotentiary at Madrid, and Count Tattenbach, Envoy Extraordinary and Minister Plenipotentiary at Lisbon ;

Austria-Hungary, Count von Welsersheimb, Ambassador Extraordinary and Plenipotentiary at Madrid, and Count Bolesla-Koziebrodzki, Envoy Extraordinary and Minister Plenipotentiary in Morocco ;

Belgium, Baron Joostens, Envoy Extraordinary and Minister Plenipotentiary at Madrid, and Count Buisseret-Steenbecque de Blarenghien, Envoy Extraordinary and Minister Plenipotentiary in Morocco ;

Spain, Duque de Almovodar y Rio, Minister of State,

and Don Juan Pérez-Caballero y Ferrer, Envoy Extraordinary and Minister Plenipotentiary at Brussels ;

United States of America, Mr. Henry White, Ambassador Extraordinary and Plenipotentiary at Rome, and Mr. S. R. Gummeré, Envoy Extraordinary and Minister Plenipotentiary in Morocco ;

France, Mons. Paul Revoil, Ambassador Extraordinary and Plenipotentiary to the Swiss Confederation, Mons. Eugène Regnault, Minister Plenipotentiary ; the French edition describes him as *délégué technique*.

Great Britain, Sir Arthur Nicolson, Ambassador Extraordinary and Plenipotentiary at Petersburg ;

Italy, Marchese Visconti-Venosta, and Signor G. Malmusi, Envoy Extraordinary and Minister Plenipotentiary in Morocco ;

Morocco, Hadj Mohammed Ben-el Arbi Et-torrés, Delegate at Tangier and Ambassador Extraordinary, Hadj Mohammed Ben Abdesselam El Mokri, ministre des dépenses, Hadj Mohammed Es-seffar and Sid Abderrhaman Benins ;

Holland, Jonkheer H. Testa, Envoy Extraordinary and Minister Plenipotentiary at Madrid ;

Portugal, Conde de Tovar, Envoy Extraordinary and Minister Plenipotentiary at Madrid, and Conde de Martens Ferrão, Envoy Extraordinary and Minister Plenipotentiary in Morocco ;

Russia, Count Cassini, Ambassador Extraordinary and Plenipotentiary at Madrid, Mons. B. Bacheracht, Minister in Morocco ;

Sweden, Mons. R. Sager, Envoy Extraordinary and Minister Plenipotentiary at Madrid and Lisbon.

The opening meeting took place January 16, 1906, in the rooms of the Casa Consistorial at Algeciras.

The Spanish plenipotentiary delegate welcomed the other delegates in the name of the King and of his Government.

The German First delegate, on the ground of his priority in alphabetical order, proposed that the Spanish representative should be president.

The president then nominated as secretaries a chief of section in the Ministry of State, the French councillor of embassy at Madrid, and two Spanish secretaries of embassy as assistants.

The delegates then proceeded to the apartment destined for the sittings, and took their seats in the alphabetical order of the French names of the States they represented, beginning from the right of the president, the Moorish delegates being placed at his left.

The president delivered a speech, explaining the scope and aim of the Conference. He mentioned the programme, to the preparation of which certain Powers had contributed, while others had accepted it.

The French and German delegates expressed their concurrence in the remarks of the president.

The order in which the different questions on the programme should be taken was agreed to on the motion of the president.

The *procès-verbal* of each meeting was signed by the president only, and countersigned by the two principal secretaries.

At the second sitting, January 22, it was decided to admit to the sittings the secretaries of the different delegations.

Telegrams from the Spanish Senate and Chamber of Deputies, expressing their hopes for the successful issue of the Conference, were read.

The First Italian delegate, on the ground of his age, claimed the privilege of giving expression to the sentiments of the Conference in reply.

The Second Moorish delegate then delivered an address in Arabic. It was agreed that a French translation should be prepared by the interpreters present at the Conference, for the delegates to express their opinion on it at the ensuing meeting.

A draft *règlement* respecting contraband trade in arms and munitions, prepared by the drafting committee,[1] was laid before the Conference and discussed.

At the end of the sitting, the German First delegate, on the ground of the privilege conferred by the alphabetical order, proposed to send a respectful message of congratulation to the King on the occasion of his *fête*-day.

At the third meeting, January 24, the president observed that the *procès-verbal* of the previous sitting having only been just then distributed, it would be convenient, before having it read, to give the delegates time to make themselves acquainted with its contents.

A telegram of thanks from the King in reply to the message of congratulation was read.

The translation of the Moorish delegate's address was read by one of the interpreters, and it was ordered to be annexed to the *procès-verbal* of this sitting.

The discussion of the draft *règlement* presented on January 22 was continued.

January 25, second sitting in Committee, on taxation.

At the fourth meeting the text of the *règlement* was adopted.

At the fifth meeting, February 7, the *procès-verbaux* of the third and fourth meetings were approved.

At the end of the sixth meeting, February 10, the Conference resolved to go into Committee.

At the fifteenth meeting, March 29, it was decided to print and distribute the *comptes-rendus* of the sittings in committee.

---

[1] The *procès-verbal* states that the drafting committee had been designated at the first meeting, but there is no mention of it in the *procès-verbal* of that meeting, unless it be assumed to be identical with the secretariat.

At the seventeenth meeting, April 2, the president decided that it was not in order to discuss any subjects but those included in the programme or which immediately flowed from them.

A draft *Acte Général*, framed by a special committee, was submitted and adopted. The date for signature was fixed.

A draft additional protocol prepared by a special committee was adopted.

A recommendation (*vœu*) in favour of religious toleration towards Jews and other Moorish subjects was proposed by the United States First delegate and unanimously accepted by the Conference.

Another recommendation (*vœu*) that the Sultan of Morocco should adopt measures for the limitation and gradual abolition of the practice of slavery, and, above all, for the prohibition of the public sale of slaves, proposed by the British delegate, was unanimously approved.

A third recommendation (*vœu*) in favour of the increase and improvement of coastal lighting was proposed by the German First delegate, and unanimously accepted.

A fourth recommendation (*vœu*) that the statistics of importation should be framed in such a manner as to show the country of origin of goods, proposed by the First delegate for Austria-Hungary, was also adopted.

Thanks were addressed to the committee which had revised the text of the *Acte Général*.

The closing meeting was held on April 7.

The president presented the authentic text of the *Acte Général* and also that of the Additional Protocol. He announced that the full-powers deposited at the secretariat had been found in good and due form, and he invited the delegates to proceed to the signature of the above-mentioned documents, which were then read.

The Italian First delegate, in virtue of his age, and precedence having been courteously conceded to him by the German First delegate, moved the usual vote of thanks to the president, and also one of gratitude to the King for the hospitality accorded to the Conference.

After the president's reply, the act of signature was performed.

The president then addressed a speech to the Conference, winding up its proceedings, and especially thanking all those who had assisted in the preparation, framing and translation of the documents forming the *Acte Général*.

Besides the eighteen meetings of the Conference, there were twelve sittings in committee. The *comptes-rendus* of the sittings in committee were not signed.

The *Acte Général* was signed in one original, to be deposited in the Archives of the Spanish Government, certified copies being distributed to the various Governments through the usual diplomatic channel; and the ratifications were to be deposited at Madrid by December 31.

The Moorish delegates declared that they were unable for the moment to sign the *Acte Général*, and the purpose of the Additional Protocol was to empower the Italian Minister at Tangier, who was the *doyen* of the diplomatic body at that city, to join his efforts to those of the Moorish delegates with the view of obtaining the Sultan's entire ratification of the *Acte Général*, and the simultaneous execution of the contemplated reforms.

Authorities: *Conférence Internationale d'Algeciras*, folio, without title-page, date or place. In the *Brit. and For. State Papers*, xcix, there is a copy of the *Acte Général*, in which the British plenipotentiary's name is placed first in the preamble, and at the head of the signatures, but in the original document the strict alphabetical order was followed. Also *Protocoles et Comptes rendus de la Conférence d'Algesiras*, Paris, Imprimerie Nationale, 1906.

§ 494. *Second Hague Peace Conference, 1907.*

The convocation of this Conference was proposed in the first instance by Mr. Roosevelt, President of the United States, but the Emperor of Russia having intimated to him through the Russian ambassador at Washington that he was ready to assume the responsibility of summoning it, Mr. Roosevelt willingly gave way. The programme of subjects to be discussed was given in a Note addressed to each Government by the Russian diplomatic representative accredited to it, but during the Conference other subjects were admitted for consideration.

The invitations were sent out in the name of the Netherlands Government.

On this occasion invitations were addressed to forty-seven States, including those of South America which had not been invited to the Conference of 1899.

The Conference was opened on June 15 by the Netherlands minister for Foreign Affairs, who proposed that the Russian First delegate (Mons. Nelidow, Ambassador at Paris) should be president. The Netherlands minister for Foreign Affairs was chosen as honorary president, and the Netherlands First delegate, Mons. de Beaufort, as effective vice-president.

After the opening discourse of the president, the secretariat was formed, consisting of a Netherlands diplomatist as *secrétaire-général*, and a Russian diplomatist as *secrétaire-général de rédaction*. Other secretaries were members of the diplomatic services of France, the Netherlands, the United States, Belgium, Rumania, Italy, Spain, Russia, Japan, Great Britain, Greece, Germany, and a Netherlands naval officer, twenty-one in number.

At the second full meeting the delegates were requested to produce their full-powers to the secretary-general. A *règlement* for the conduct of business was approved. Four committees were set up to deal with separate classes of questions, each with power to establish sub-committees.   A drafting committee was formed.   Each delegation had only one vote at full meetings and in committees, which was given in the alphabetical order of the French names of the States represented by the delegations voting.

The procedure at this Conference closely followed that of a Congress (*cf.* the Congress of Berlin, § 467), but there was much uncertainty as to the effect of a negative vote.   Sometimes complete unanimity was held to be necessary, on other occasions a majority was regarded as sufficient to entitle a proposal to be recorded as part of the proceedings.   Nevertheless, it was recognized that every State could refuse to sign, or might sign with reserves, any of the conventions or declarations which were produced by the Conference.

As on previous occasions, the chairmen and *rapporteurs* of committees occupied positions of great influence and authority, which could easily be utilized for the promotion of policies in which their own Governments were specially interested.

China, Guatemala, Norway and Switzerland appointed their diplomatic representatives at the Hague to be their First delegates.   The other First delegates were appointed *ad hoc*, and many of the secondary delegates also.   Among the latter, however, were the diplomatic representatives of the United States, Belgium, Brazil, Spain, France, Great Britain, Japan, Mexico, Persia, Portugal, Rumania, Russia and Servia.

The final full sitting took place on October 18.

In his closing speech, the president proposed to address to the Queen of the Netherlands the gratitude of the delegates for the august interest she had taken in their labours and for the gracious hospitality accorded to them by the Netherlands Government, and which Her Majesty had deigned to promise equally for the eventuality of future conferences.   He recalled that at one of the most recent sittings thanks had been expressed to the august initiator of these Conferences, His Majesty the Emperor of Russia, and he hoped that the Conference would render homage to the President of the United States, who had been the first to propose the convocation of the Second Conference, and authorize himself to send to him a telegram gratefully recognizing this fact. Lastly, he proposed an expression of profound gratitude to the Netherlands minister for Foreign Affairs, and to all the departments of the Netherlands Government.

Mons. de Beaufort replied to the compliment, and proposed a vote of sympathy, gratitude and veneration to Mons. de Nelidow, after which he passed to other topics, amongst which he dwelt on the necessity of a fixed set of rules of procedure for the next conference.

Sir Edward Fry, British First delegate, as *doyen d'âge*, proposed that the thanks of the Conference be given to Mons. de Nelidow and to Mons de Beaufort.

Count Tornielli, Italian First delegate, expressed the thanks of the Conference to the Government printing department.

Mons. Saenz Peña, Argentine First delegate, expressed his thanks to the Russian and Netherlands Governments for the invitations to the nations of Latin America to take part in the Conference. Other eloquent speeches were made by the First delegates of Colombia, Japan and Persia, and by the Netherlands minister for Foreign Affairs, the Jonkheer van Tets van Goudriaan.

Authorities : *Deuxième Conférence de la Haye, Actes et Documents*, La Haye, Imprimerie Nationale, 1907. Three vols. folio ; Dr. J. B. Scott and Dr. Pearce Higgins, works cited for the First Hague Conference ; British Blue Books : *Misc.* Nos. 1, 4, and 6 (1908) [Cd. 3857, 4081, 4175] ; official publications of other countries ; a general sketch in John W. Foster's *Diplomatic Memoirs*, vol. ii.

§ 495. *International Naval Conference, London*, December 1908 to February 1909.

This Conference was, in a sense, a continuation of part of the Second Hague Peace Conference of 1907. On that occasion an attempt had been made to define contraband, to lay down rules for blockade, to determine the conditions under which neutral prizes might legitimately be sunk, and merchant vessels be converted into vessels of war on the high seas—but without success.

In February 1908, the British Government, through their representatives at Berlin, Madrid, Paris, Rome, Petersburg, Tokio, Vienna and Washington, invited the Governments of Germany, Spain, France, Italy, Russia, Japan, Austria-Hungary and the United States (to which the Netherlands was afterwards added) to attend a conference in London on the generally recognized principles of International Law within the meaning of Article VII, paragraph 2, of the Convention for the Establishment of an International Court of Appeal in matters of prize, signed at the Second Peace Conference. The subjects proposed for inclusion in the programme were—

(*a*) Contraband, including the circumstances under which particular articles can be considered as contraband ; the penalties for their carriage ; the immunity of a ship from search when under convoy ; and the rules for compensation where vessels have been seized but have been found, in fact, only to be carrying innocent cargo ;

(*b*) Blockade, including the questions as to the locality where seizure can be effected, and the notice that is necessary before a ship can be seized ;

(*c*) The doctrine of continuous voyage in respect both of contraband and blockade ;

(*d*) The legality of the destruction of neutral vessels prior to their condemnation by a Prize Court ;

(*e*) The rules as to neutral ships or persons rendering " unneutral service " (*assistance hostile*) ;

(*f*) The legality of the conversion of a merchant vessel into a war-ship on the high seas ;

(*g*) The rules as to the transfer of merchant vessels

from a belligerent to a neutral flag during or in contemplation of hostilities ;

(*h*) The question whether the nationality or the domicile of the owner should be adopted as the dominant factor in deciding whether property is enemy property.

The invitations having been accepted, the Governments concerned exchanged in the course of the autumn memoranda setting out their views as to the rules of International Law on the various points of the programme.

A document founded on these memoranda was drawn up in advance as a basis of discussion at the Conference.

Lord Desart, Solicitor to the Treasury, Director of Public Prosecutions and King's Proctor, was appointed British Plenipotentiary, assisted by two naval delegates, one Foreign Office official and one legal adviser to the Foreign Office. Each of the other Powers was represented by a plenipotentiary appointed *ad hoc*, with the assistance of technical delegates. Among the Japanese delegates were the councillor and the naval attaché to the Japanese embassy in London, and one of the Russian delegates was the Russian naval agent in London.

At the first meeting, December 4, the British Secretary of State for Foreign Affairs opened the proceedings.

On the proposal of Mons. Renault, *doyen d'âge* of the delegates present, seconded by Herr Kriege, German First Delegate, Lord Desart was elected president.

At the second meeting a secretariat was appointed, consisting of one member for each Power, excepting France and Great Britain, each of which furnished two. A *règlement* of procedure was adopted.

After the fourth meeting, the Conference went into

committee, under the chairmanship of the French plenipotentiary.

An Examining Committee for working out in detail the questions which presented special difficulty, a small Legal Committee, and a Drafting Committee, were set up.

Meetings of the *plenum* were held from time to time. At the eleventh of such meetings the Report, which took the form of a commentary on the proposed Declaration, prepared by the French plenipotentiary, was considered and adopted, and at the twelfth sitting, held February 26, 1909, the Declaration of London and the Closing Protocol were agreed to and signed. Some of the plenipotentiaries had already quitted London, and other delegates signed in their place.

The examination of the full-powers, which was made by the proper department of the Foreign Office, was not mentioned until the final sitting, when it was stated that they had been found in good and due form.

The president wound up the proceedings with a speech reviewing the results accomplished. He paid a tribute of thanks to the French plenipotentiaries and to his colleague, Mons. Fromageot, for his invaluable assistance in the preparation of the document which served as the basis of discussion.

The German and Austro-Hungarian plenipotentiaries followed. The latter offered the thanks of the Conference to the president and other members of the British delegation. The Japanese plenipotentiary also spoke.

The proceedings then closed.

The Declaration has the form of a treaty, but has not been ratified.

Authorities : *Proceedings of the International Naval Conference*, Misc. No. 5 (1909) ; *Correspondence and documents respecting the International Naval Conference*, Misc. No. 4 (1909) [Cd. 4554 and 4555] ; Dr. Pearce Higgins, *The Hague Peace Conferences*.

§ 496. *Conference on Balkan Affairs,* 1912–1913.

Object. To arrange terms of peace between Turkey and the Allied Balkan States, Bulgaria, Greece, Montenegro and Serbia. The Conference was held at the Palace of Saint James in London and was attended by delegates of all the belligerent Powers. The first meeting was held on December 16, 1912, under the presidency of the British Secretary of State for Foreign Affairs, who welcomed the delegates on behalf of his Sovereign, by whom the Palace had been placed at their disposal for the purpose of the Conference. At the tenth meeting, held on January 6, 1913, it was decided by the delegates, as no agreement had been reached, to suspend the work of the Conference. Shortly afterwards hostilities were resumed in the Balkans, and continued until the signature of an armistice on April 20. The belligerents having accepted unconditionally the mediation of the Great Powers, the Conference reassembled in London under the auspices of the latter, and at the first meeting held on May 30th, under the presidency of the British Secretary of State for Foreign Affairs, the plenipotentiaries of the Allied Balkan States and Turkey signed the treaty of peace, known as the Treaty of London, of May 30, 1913. At the final meeting held on June 9, it was decided to dissolve the Conference and to leave to the Governments concerned the task of concluding the separate Acts necessary to complete the treaty of peace. In consequence, however, of the outbreak of the second Balkan war (June, 1913) the treaty remained unratified.

Concurrently with the earlier meetings of the Conference between the Allied Balkan States and Turkey, meetings of the Ambassadors of the Great Powers were held at the British Foreign Office in London to deal with Balkan affairs. The first meeting was held on December 17, 1912, and the meetings continued until August 11, 1913. No official record has been published of the

N

discussions and decisions of the London Conference of Ambassadors on Balkan affairs.

Authority, The Foreign Office Records.

§ 497. *Conference of Bucarest.*

By the Treaty of London of May 30, 1913, Article VI, the division of the territories conquered from Turkey among the Balkan allies was to be arranged by an international commission convoked at Paris. Bulgaria being dissatisfied with the share offered to her, attacked Serbia on June 30, which was supported by Greece, in accordance with the treaty of alliance signed on June 1, 1913. At the same time Turkey re-entered the field and recovered Adrianople, which she had surrendered by the unratified treaty of London, and Rumania put forward a demand for the cession of territory in N. Bulgaria. The latter Power being defeated, a conference of the five Powers concerned was called at Bucarest, which sat from July 30 to August 10, and resulted in the signature of a treaty of peace.

The first sitting took place on July 30, at the Ministry for Foreign Affairs at Bucarest. The delegates of the respective Powers were—

For *Bulgaria :* M. D. Tontcheff, Minister of Finance ; Major-Gen. I. Fitcheff, Chief of the Staff ; M. S. Radeff ; and Lieut.-Col. of the Staff, C. Stancioff.

For *Greece :* M. El. Venizelos, President of the Council and Minister of War ; M. D. Panas, Minister Plenipotentiary ; M. N. Politis, Prof. of International Law at the University of Paris ; Captain C. Pali.

For *Montenegro :* Gen. S. Yanko Voukotitch, President of the Council of Ministers and Minister of War ; M. Y. Matanovitch, former Director-general of Ports and Telegraphs, former Chargé d'Affaires.

For *Rumania :* M. Maïoresco, President of the Council, Minister for Foreign Affairs ; M. A. Marghiloman, Minister of Finance ; M. Take Jonesco, Minister of the Interior; M. C. G. Dissesco, Minister of Public Instruction and Worship; General C. Coanda, Inspector-General of Artillery; Col. C. Christesco, Under-chief of the Grand Staff.

For *Serbia :* M. N. P. Pachitch, President of the Council of Ministers, Minister for Foreign Affairs ; M. M. G. Ristitch, Envoy Extraordinary and Minister Plenipotentiary of Serbia at Bucarest ; Dr. M. Spalaï-kovitch, Minister Plenipotentiary ; Col. K. Smilianitch and Lieut.-Col. D. Kalafatovitch.

The first Serbian delegate proposed to confide the presidency of the work of the Conference to the first delegate of Rumania. The proposal having been received with the hearty assent of all the plenipotentiaries ; M. Maïoresco accepted, adding : " *Gentlemen,* I thank you for the honour you have been so good as to confer on me by choosing me to preside over our meetings. I could only suffice for this important task by appealing to your kind support and entire indulgence."

The president then proceeded to propose that the Secretariat should be composed of MM. Pisoski, minister plenipotentiary and diplomatic agent of Rumania at Cairo, and J. C. Filitti, Director of Political Affairs at the Ministry for Foreign Affairs, with the assistance of M. Lahovary, secretary of legation. The secretaries nominated by the delegations of the other belligerent States would help them in their work, namely, MM. D. Svilokossitch, first secretary of legation, and Dr. M. Gavrilovitch, Secretary at the Ministry for Foreign Affairs of Serbia ; M. Th. Papazoff, legal adviser of the Bulgarian delegation, and M. Tsamados, secretary of the Hellenic delegation.

These proposals having been accepted, the members of the bureau were introduced and presented to the Conference. The president requested his colleagues to deposit their full-powers with the chief of the secretariat, in order that they might be verified by the next sitting.

M. Maïoresco then proceeded to read a speech welcoming the delegates in the name of the King, his August Sovereign, and thanking them for the ready acceptance of the proposal to come to Rumania and endeavour to resolve there the serious questions which would have a decisive influence on the future of the States represented at the Conference.

He was convinced that all were animated by the desire of bringing to a satisfactory conclusion the work for which they were met, and of ensuring to the Christian peoples who were still in the field, either by preliminary conventions, or by a definitive treaty, a durable peace founded on a just equilibrium amongst their States.

It would be of good augury for the fulfilment of their task if they could, at the very first sitting, come to an agreement respecting one of the most urgent and important preliminary measures. He would mention the necessity of a suspension of arms. On the occasion of their meeting to deliberate on the conditions of a peace acceptable to all the belligerents, he felt he was discharging a humane duty in proposing a suspension of arms for at least five days.

M. Venizelos responded in the name of the allies, accepting the proposal of a momentary suspension of hostilities. M. Maïoresco's proposal having been unanimously accepted, the military delegates were requested at once to fix the details necessary for carrying out the decision of the Conference, and to draw up a *procès-verbal*.

M. Tontcheff, first delegate for Bulgaria, said—

" *Monsieur le Président,* I thank you for your welcome and for your good words. The Bulgarian delegation, over which I have the honour of presiding, has arrived here with the fixed and loyal desire of promptly concluding peace. Our goodwill will spontaneously fall in with all initiatives of a character to establish a stable situation in the Balkans. We are fortunate in being called to this task at a capital like Bucarest, where European opinion has always been predominant. I express the hope that we shall all do our best to make it prevail in our discussions as a guarantee of the justice and durability of our decisions."

The sitting was suspended in order to allow the military delegates to draw up the *procès-verbal* concerning the suspension of arms.

When the sitting was resumed, General Coanda read the above-mentioned *procès-verbal*, which was approved by the Conference and was annexed to the protocol of the sitting.

[*Signatures of the delegates.*]

Protocol No. 2. Sitting of July 31.

The protocol of the previous sitting was read and approved.

On the proposal of the president, it was unanimously agreed to adjourn the sitting to the following afternoon, in order that the various delegations might proceed to a preliminary exchange of ideas regarding the partition of territories. This preparatory work would facilitate the task of the Conference by settling points on which there was complete agreement, leaving only those on which a divergence of view had arisen to be brought before the Conference.

[*Signatures.*]

True Copy.
    A. PISOSKI.
    FILITTI.

Protocol No. 3. August 1.

The protocol of the previous sitting was read and approved.

The first delegate of Bulgaria said that he knew the proposals of the allies. The Bulgarian delegation would study them, and hoped to be able to produce their counter-proposals at the next sitting.

At the suggestion of M. Maïoresco, it was agreed to adjourn until the following afternoon, in order that the negotiations amongst the delegates of the various States might continue.

[Signatures.[1]]

True copy.
   A. Pisoski.
   Filitti.

Protocol No. 4. August 2.

The president said : If you are willing, gentlemen, we will employ to-morrow in negotiations, which we all hope will end in an appreciable result. In giving notice of our next meeting for Monday, the day after to-morrow, I calculate that we shall begin the sitting with positive data which will be submitted to the examination of the Conference, but on which, in essence, agreement will have been already established. I am convinced that the peoples whom we represent here, await with anxious impatience the end of our labours.

Protocol No. 5. August 4.

The president announced that the hope he had expressed at the previous sitting had been only partially realized. But an agreement had been arrived at between Rumania and Bulgaria which would be completed by an exchange of Notes. A procès-verbal had been drawn up, which General Coanda would read. The meetings of the other delegations had not yet reached a result which could be laid before a plenary sitting. The negotiations must continue, but yet for not too long a time. Definite results not having been attained during the suspension of arms for five days, he proposed to prolong it for a short period, and for the last time. He proposed for this last period one of three days, to begin at noon, August 5. God grant that their labours might end during the four days which remained to them. This was agreed to unanimously.

---

[1] This form is adhered to throughout.

The *procès-verbal* alluded to having been read by General Coanda, and the first Bulgarian delegate having declared that an understanding had been established with Rumania on the basis of the said *procès-verbal*, it was annexed to the protocol of the sitting.

Protocol No. 6. August 5.

A telegram was read by the first Greek delegate, to the effect that a Bulgarian officer with a flag of truce had presented himself at the outposts, and declared that as the first armistice expired at noon and the second did not begin till one o'clock, the Bulgarian army would attack in the interval. The King of Greece declared that in that case he would order a general attack by his troops.

The opinion was expressed that there had been a misunderstanding.

The president communicated a Note presented to him by Mr. Jackson, U.S. minister at Bucarest, expressing the hope of his Government that a clause ensuring full civil and religious liberty to the inhabitants of any territory which might come under the rule of any of the five Powers might be inserted in any convention concluded at Bucarest.

It was unanimously agreed that the principle was universally recognized, and that it would consequently be superfluous to mention it in the treaty to be concluded.

The president announced that the negotiations between the various delegations had not yet produced results which could be placed before a plenary conference. He hoped they would be concluded very soon, and that the final fate of the Conference would become known at the next sitting, which he fixed for the following afternoon.

Protocol No. 7. August 6.

Telegrams were read showing that the incident mentioned on the previous occasion was due to a misunderstanding on the part of the Bulgarian officer, and it was declared to have been disposed of.

An agreement between Serbia and Bulgaria as to their common frontier was announced. There still remained the agreement between Bulgaria and Greece, which had yet to be reached.

The sitting was suspended for an hour.

When it was renewed, the president announced that peace might be considered certain. He considered that agreement had been arrived at between the plenipotentiaries of Bulgaria and Greece.

A detailed declaration by the Montenegrin delegation was read, and attached to the protocol of this sitting.

It was announced that an agreement had been arrived at between Bulgaria and Greece, the terms of which would be stated in a *procès-verbal* annexed to the protocol of the sitting.

The president advised that information should at once be given to the armies that an armistice without limit of time had been decided on by the plenipotentiaries. It would be for the military delegates to come to an understanding on the clauses and details of the armistice and report to the next sitting.

He then stated that, having happily arrived at the end of its labours, the Conference should turn its attention to the drafting of the treaty of peace, and proposed that each delegation should appoint a member of the drafting committee. The following were designated : for

Bulgaria : M. S. Radeff ;
Greece : M. N. Politis ;
Serbia : M. M. Spalaïkovitch ;
Montenegro : M. Matanovitch ;
Rumania : MM. Pisoski and J. C. Filitti, and General Coanda was added as a military delegate.

Protocol No. 9. August 7.

A *procès-verbal* in two parts, describing the frontier

between Greece and Bulgaria, was read, and another, also in two parts, describing the new frontier between Serbia and Bulgaria. Then a *procès-verbal* agreeing to an unlimited armistice was also read. These five documents were annexed to the protocol of the sitting.

Protocol No. 10. August 8.

The president stated that the Austro-Hungarian and Russian Governments had given notice that they reserved to themselves the right of revising whatever decision might be taken by the Conference with respect to Cavalla.

The draft treaty was partly read and discussed.

Protocol No. 11. August 9.

The remaining articles were discussed and agreed to.

Protocol No. 12. August 10.

The final text of the treaty was read over and accepted unanimously.

The president proposed that it should be signed by both civil and military delegates, but that the seals of the First Delegates alone should be affixed.

The five copies of the treaty were then signed.

The First Greek delegate made a speech thanking M. Maïoresco for the great impartiality and perfect tact with which he had presided over the delicate labours of this illustrious Assembly, and paying him other compliments, to which he made a suitable reply.

M. Spalaïkovitch proposed that at the conclusion of the *Te Deum*, the plenipotentiaries should proceed in a body to the Royal Palace to write their names in the King's visitors' books.

Lastly, M. Maïoresco drew attention to the fact that the Conference had held its first meeting July 17/30, and that on this date, July 28/August 10, its lofty mission of bringing peace to the peoples whom they represented had been accomplished. Evidently such a result could not have been obtained but for the assiduous zeal and high competence of the members. It was his duty to express their particular thanks to the delegates who had accepted special functions, especially their military colleagues and the draftsmen of the treaty. Lastly, he thanked the secretariat for the indefatigable industry with which it had acquitted itself of its difficult task, and not forgetting, either, the officials who had facilitated the formalities required by the work of the Conference.[1]

§ 497A. *Paris Peace Conference* of 1919.

The usual preliminary of a treaty of peace is an Armistice. On October 5, 1918 the German Government transmitted through the Swiss Government their request to the President of the United States to take in hand the restoration of peace.[2] After some correspondence, the President, on October 23, sent the papers to the Governments with which the United States was associated as a belligerent, with a suggestion that the military advisers of the Entente Powers should be asked to submit to the Governments associated against Germany the necessary terms of such an armistice as would ensure to them the unrestricted power to enforce the details of the peace to which the German Government had agreed. Accordingly, on November 5 the President, having received the necessary reply from the Allied Governments informed the German Government that Marshal Foch had been authorized to receive properly accredited representatives of the German Government and to communicate to them the terms of an armistice.

During the days immediately preceding, Marshal Foch had discussed the terms of an armistice with the generals of the Allies, and the naval authorities had added their quota of suggestions. Then a meeting of the Supreme Council of the Allies, together with Colonel E. M. House (United States), Venizelos (Greece), Vesnitch

---

[1] *Nouveau Recueil Général*, t. viii. 19.
[2] *Documents and Statements*, 234

(Bulgaria), Marshal Foch, Admiral Wemyss, Generals Sir Henry Wilson, Bliss (United States) and de Robilant (Italy), was held at Versailles on October 31. On November 2 Clemenceau raised the question of adding the words "reparation of damages." The Belgian, Italian and British representatives objected that this subject was not properly included in an armistice convention, but it was nevertheless agreed to. Then the French minister of Finance proposed to preface those words by the addition of :—" With the reservation of all ulterior claims and reclamations on the part of the Allies and the United States " (*sous réserve de toutes revendications et réclamations ultérieures de la part des Alliés et des Etats-Unis*). This was likewise adopted. On November 4 the consideration of the terms was resumed, and the text of an article respecting surface ships was adopted. Thereupon the Allies replied to the President on November 5 declaring their willingness to make peace on the terms laid down in his address to Congress of January 8, 1918 (the Fourteen Points) and the principles of settlement enunciated in his subsequent addresses. On clause 2, relating to what is usually described as the freedom of the seas, they reserved to themselves complete freedom in the Peace Conference, and they declared that by the restoration of invaded territories they understood compensation made by Germany for all damage done to the civilian population of the Allies and their property by the aggression of Germany by land, by sea, and from the air.

On November 8 the two delegations met at Rethondes station in the forest of Compiègne. Marshal Foch made some slight concessions. The German Government intimated their acceptance on the 10th, and signature of the armistice convention followed at five a.m. on November 11. It came into force at eleven o'clock of that day.[1]

[1] Tardieu, *La Paix*, 66–81. *Geschichte des Waffenstillstands*, published by the German Government, and Mermeix *Les négociations secrètes et les quatre Armistices*, Paris, 1921 ; also *Die deutsche Waffenstillstands-Kommission-Bericht über ihre Tätigkeit vom Abschluss des Waffenstillstandes bis zum Inkrafttreten des Friedens*. Charlottenburg, 1920.

The Peace Conference.

The Five Great Powers assumed the exclusive direction of the proceedings, just as at Vienna in 1815. Up to the time of delivery of the terms of peace to the German Delegates on May 7, 1919, the meetings of the Plenum, *i.e.* the representatives of the Allied and Associated Powers, were eight in number, besides a secret session. At the first of these plenary assemblies the Prime Minister of France was chosen permanent chairman, in accordance with precedent. A principal secretary-general and five others bearing the title of secretary were appointed for the respective Great Powers, besides four vice-presidents. As at Vienna, the Great Powers began their private and confidential conversations before any general meeting of plenipotentiaries.

At the plenary session of January 25, five resolutions were submitted and adopted, appointing committees or commissions.[1]—1. To work out the details and constitution of the proposed League of Nations; 2. To inquire into and report on the responsibility of the authors of the war and the enforcement of penalties; 3. To examine and report on the amount which the enemy countries ought to pay by way of reparation and what they were capable of paying; 4. To inquire into the conditions of employment from the international aspect; 5. To inquire into and report on the international control of ports, waterways and railways. There was a general discussion before these resolutions were adopted, and it was agreed that representatives of minor Powers with special interests should meet to elect members of these commissions in addition to those nominated by the Five Great Powers.[2] There was also a drafting Commission. Minutes of these meetings were kept and printed from stenographic notes.

[1] *66th Congress 1st session, Document No.* 106, *Hearings before the Committee on Foreign Relations of the United States Senate,* 300. The record is headed " Protocol No. 2," 277. This is rather an inaccurate designation for what resembles more nearly a newspaper report.

[2] List of members, *ibid.,* 309.

Although each of the Great Powers was entitled to five plenipotentiaries and each of the minor Powers to two,[1] the Supreme Council which actually carried on the main work of the Conference was a much smaller body. It consisted at first of the President of the United States and the Prime Ministers of France, Great Britain, and Italy, with their ministers for Foreign Affairs, and the Japanese Ambassadors at Paris and London, ten in all. This lasted from January 12 till March 24. From that time onward it was reduced to a Council of four, the President and the three Prime Ministers. During the absence of the Italian delegation from April 24 to May 5 it became a Council of three. Of their very numerous daily conversations it seems that stenographic records[2] were made in French and English, and sometimes, as in matters concerning Austria, they were also translated into Italian.[3] A distinction seems to have been made between stenographic reports and procès-verbaux. Copies of the latter, which were sometimes very detailed, were supplied to the plenipotentiaries. The record of a discussion on January 16 regarding the situation in Russia has been printed, besides one of January 21.[4] On the latter occasion, in addition to the members of the Council of ten, there were present twelve other persons, including three out of the five secretaries of the delegations and the official interpreter. Under such circumstances it was not possible to prevent the leakage of information that the principals wished to keep secret, and this led to the drastic measure of restriction above-mentioned. The memoranda of the debates on the League of Nations were not taken down in shorthand. They were regarded as confidential, and so, it may be presumed, were those of other sittings of the Supreme Council. By January 25 one of the delegates from Japan,

---

[1] See the Preamble to the Treaty of Versailles in *History of the Peace Conference of Paris*, edited by H.W. V. Temperley, v. iii. 105.
[2] *Hearings before the Committee on Foreign Relations of the United States Senate*, 1235.
[3] *Ibid.*, 171.   [4] *Ibid.*, 1240.

besides three ambassadors, had arrived. But the protocol of the plenary sitting of that date was signed by M. Clemenceau and the six secretaries alone. The third plenary meeting, at which a draft Covenant of the League of Nations was read, was held on February 14. The Commission on that subject met on April 10 and 11,[1] and definitely agreed on the text to be presented to the Conference, which was done at the fifth plenary sitting on April 28.

The United States Secretary of State was appointed chairman of the Commission on the Responsibility of the Authors of the War and the Enforcement of Penalties,[2] and its work was divided among three sub-commissions.

The so-called Council of Four, representing the Principal Allied and Associated Powers was in reality a Council of Five, as it included a Japanese member.[3] The matters discussed were summarized, and the conclusions arrived at were recorded in a *procès-verbal*, copies of which were distributed within twenty-four hours, and it was open to the members to correct anything it might contain. Every decision required the unanimous consent[4] of the Peace Conference, which never decided any question by a majority vote. In the *commission* on the League of Nations voting was resorted to, on at least one occasion.

A " protocol " must be regarded as being properly the record of an agreement arrived at, and is probably more condensed than a mere *procès-verbal*. As an instance however of the latter, the deposit of ratifications is recorded in a *procès-verbal*, which obviously is simply a statement of fact, not the account of a discussion.

By the treaty of Versailles the territories renounced by Germany were to be apportioned by the Principal Allied and Associated Powers (Art. 118), just as, by the separate articles of the treaty of Paris of May 30, 1814, the disposition of the territories ceded by France was left to the Four Powers.

[1] *Ibid*, 270.   [2] *Ibid.*, 314.   [3] *Ibid.*, 521.   [4] *Ibid.*, 527.

The Economic Commission was composed of delegates of the Great Powers, representatives of certain of the minor Powers being associated with them from time to time. The work was shared among sub-committees, which considered different branches of the subject.[1] The members met from time to time to compare notes, and the whole of the economic clauses were gone over and subjected to criticism by this group. The sub-commissions sat frequently and towards the end almost continuously, and when they arrived at a conclusion they presented a report to the Commission for approval amendment, or rejection. When finally adopted these reports were put together to form a whole. Then the reports of the Commission were presented to the Supreme Council and were accepted. After that they were handed over to the Drafting Commission,[2] and emerged substantially in the form in which they appear in the text of the Treaty. The decisions of the Commission were taken unanimously.

The records of the Financial Commission were not stenographic, for there was a good deal of discussion not necessary to put on the minutes. The latter were kept in French and English, and contained the substance of the agreements arrived at, were written up and presented to the members. At the subsequent meeting they were approved with whatever alterations were necessary.

In addition to the Committees already mentioned, a Supreme Economic Council was formed, Territorial Commissions were set up for Czecho-Slovakia, for Poland, for Rumania and Jugo-Slavia, for Greece and Albania, for Belgium and Denmark, besides Military, Naval and Air Commissions. Perhaps the most important of all was the Drafting Commission, on which the five principal Powers were represented. Subordinate to this were the Economic and Financial Drafting Commissions. Besides all this machinery, a Council of Five was formed

[1] *Ibid.*, 9.   [2] *Ibid.*, 12.

out of the Ministers for Foreign Affairs, which followed the procedure of the former Council of Ten. This was the organ for the insertion in the Treaty of clauses omitted by oversight, and, while the Four were occupied with the negotiation of the treaty with Germany, it was able to proceed with the discussion of the Austrian treaty.

The whole treaty with Germany having thus been framed, there was in the first place the exchange of credentials on May 1, next the delivery of the terms to the German delegates on May 7. This was followed by discussion between the parties, in the shape of Notes delivered by the Germans and answered by the Allies. As in 1815 Alexander I had intervened to mitigate the terms proposed by the Allied plenipotentiaries, so on this occasion there was a disposition on the part of Great Britain and the United States to make some concessions from the original draft.[1] That document has not been printed in England. Finally, on May 30, the Germans put in a lengthened criticism of the draft, which was answered on June 16 by a Note signed by the president of the Conference, covering the " Reply of the Allied and Associated Powers to the observations of the German delegation on the conditions of peace," the composition of which is ascribed to a member of the British Peace Delegation.[2]

Some minor concessions were made, but, as in 1815, the original text was on the whole maintained, and signature followed on June 28, together with that of a supplementary protocol,[3] indicating precisely the conditions in which certain provisions of the treaty are to be carried out. The deposit in Paris of the required

---

[1] Thompson, *The Peace Conference Day by Day*, 388.

[2] See *Reply of the Allied and Associated Powers*, 1919 [Cmd. 258], also *International Conciliation*, November, 1919, No. 144. For the *Comments by the German Delegation on the Conditions of Peace*, see No. 143 of the same publication. Those comments have not been printed officially in England.

[3] Edit. H. W. V. Temperley, *A History of the Peace Conference of Paris*, iii, 345.

number of instruments of ratification did not take place till January 10, 1920.

The Treaty of Vienna was signed June 9, 1815, but owing to Napoleon's escape from Elba, his few days' campaign in Belgium and the second invasion of France by the Allies, the exchange of ratifications did not take place until January 15, 1816.[1] The deposit of ratifications of the Treaty of Versailles was impeded mainly by the difficulties encountered by the Allies in obtaining satisfaction from Germany for failure to execute the provisions of the Armistice of November 11, 1918, of which the chief violation was the scuttling of the German fleet at Scapa Flow on June 21, 1919, a week before the signature of the treaty of peace. On November 6 the Allies sent a Note to Germany, accompanied by a protocol relating to the unexecuted provisions of the Armistice of which they required the signature before the Peace Treaty could come into operation. It was not till January 10 that the German Government was induced to sign this document, and on the same day the deposit of ratifications was accomplished at the Ministry of Foreign Affairs at Paris in a plenary sitting of the signatories of the Treaty. Thus while four months and thirty six days elapsed between the signature of the Treaty of Vienna and exchange of ratifications, the interval in the case of the treaty of Versailles was six months and twelve days.

After the signature of the Treaty of Peace with Germany the Council of Four was broken up, and its members, except of course the French member, left Paris. The current business in connexion with the execution of its provisions, and the framing of the treaties with the other belligerents, was committed to the five Ministers of Foreign Affairs. In September, Mr. Balfour quitted Paris, and his place on that body was taken by Sir Eyre Crowe. This council also came

[1] French ratification, signed " Louis " and counter-signed " Richelieu," certificate of exchange at Paris signed and sealed " Charles Stuart," and " Richelieu," at the Public Record Office.

o

to an end after the deposit of ratifications, and was succeeded by a Conference of the Ambassadors of the Allies accredited at Paris. This recalls the conference of ministers which existed there from 1815 to 1818, whose function was to watch over the course of domestic political events and keep the Commander-in-Chief of the Army of Occupation informed. They had also to take cognisance of the proceedings of the financial commissioners appointed to see to the execution of the clauses of the second treaty of Paris relating to the payment of the war indemnity, of the cost of the army of occupation, and of the liquidation of the private claims against the French Government.

The Treaty of Versailles embraced a far more extensive series of provisions. The duty of enforcing their execution devolved on various constituted bodies. The boundaries of the new States had to be delimited, in some cases a plebiscite had to be resorted to in order to determine the line of partition. Of a permanent nature are the constitution of the League of Nations and the organisation for the international regulation of Labour conditions. The international commissions for the traffic on the Elbe, Oder, Niemen, Danube, Rhine and Moselle present the same character. The clearing offices and Mixed Arbitral Tribunals set up under the Economic clauses are, of course, only provisional, also the inter-allied Commissions of Control for the execution of the Military, Naval and Air clauses providing for disarmament. The inter-allied Reparation Commission is likely to continue in existence for many years to come. It will also have an eye to the carrying-out of the Financial clauses of the Treaty.

Although the uninterrupted presence of the Prime Ministers in Paris was no longer considered imperative after the signature of the Treaty of Versailles, they still continued to meet from time to time in France, Great Britain and Italy for the discussion of matters of common concern arising out of that Treaty and for the consideration of other treaties with enemy belligerents. No leading representative of the United States was present at these gatherings until President Harding authorized the attendance of the American Ambassador to Paris in August 1921. Germany maintained a Peace Delegation in Paris, the head of which corresponded with the chairman or the secretary-general of the Supreme Council and with the Council of Ambassadors. The decisions arrived at by the Supreme Council on each occasion were made public in the form of official *communiqués*.[1]

Questions somewhat difficult of solution appear likely to arise respecting the relations of governments with the Council of the League of Nations, which consists of representatives of the Principal Allied and Associated Powers, together with representatives of four other members of the League.

According to the Commentary on the Covenant presented to Parliament in 1919 ([Cmd. 151]), p. 13, it would seem to have been intended that the representatives of the Principal Allied and Associated Powers, who are to meet at least once a year, will be the political chiefs of the Great Powers. The commentary goes on to say that " there is nothing in the Covenant to prevent their places being taken, in the intervals between the regular meetings, by representatives permanently resident at the seat of the League."

Up to the moment of writing however, the representatives of the Great Powers have not been the political chiefs of those Powers, but their delegates. Numerous meetings of these political chiefs have, it is true, taken place, but they met, not as members of the Council. Their meetings have been held by them as political chiefs pure and simple.

The delegates, at any rate so far as the practice of Great Britain is concerned, do not receive their instructions directly from the respective Ministers for Foreign Affairs. Questions in which the latter are interested

[1] See 1921, *Misc. No. 15. Protocols and Correspondence* [Cmd. 1325].

are referred to them, by the secretary to the Cabinet, and the Secretary of State's reply is in the shape of a memorandum to the secretary of the Cabinet explaining his views, which is then communicated by him to the British representatives on the Council or Assembly of the League.

By Art. XVIII of the Covenant, every treaty or international agreement entered into after the signature and ratification of the Treaty of Versailles is to be forthwith registered with the Secretariat of the League and to be published as soon as possible. This applies of course to treaties or international agreements signed by the Secretary of State or by one of his representatives abroad and duly ratified by the Sovereign. It seems too that postal conventions, signed by the Postmaster-General and not ratified, are communicated to the League. But there may be other minor agreements of which the communication would be inconvenient, as their publication might defeat the end for which they were concluded, and this point is still unsettled.

Equally difficult is the question of diplomatic immunity under Art. VII of the Covenant. Would it be legally correct, for instance, to extend diplomatic immunities and privileges to a British subject in the position of a representative of a member of the League or in that of an official of the League when engaged on the business of the League, so as to exempt him from the jurisdiction of British courts of law, and if so, what matters would this exemption cover?

Very trenchant and well-merited criticisms of the Treaty of Versailles are to be found in J. M. Keynes' *The Economic Consequences of the Peace, London,* 1920, and *A Revision of The Treaty, London,* 1922, also in Nitti, *L'Europa Senza Pace, Firenze,* 1921. Besides the works mentioned in the footnotes, Baruch's *The Making of the Reparation and Economic Sections of the Treaty* may be consulted with advantage, also Haskins and Lord's *Some Problems of the Peace Conference.*

§ 497b. *Washington Conference on the Limitation of Armament.*

Invitations were sent out by the President of the United States on August 11, 1921, to Great Britain, Japan, France and Italy, for a Conference on the Limitation of Armament, to be held in Washington on November 11, in connection with which Pacific and Far Eastern questions would also be discussed, and on the same day to the Republic of China to participate in the discussion of Pacific and Far Eastern questions in connection with the Conference on the Limitation of Armament. Also on October 4 to Belgium, the Netherlands and Portugal.

Acceptances were received from France, China, Great Britain, Japan, Italy, Portugal, the Netherlands and Belgium, severally dated August 15, 18, 22, 24, September 1, October 12, 17 and 19.

The plenipotentiaries deputed by the several Powers were for

The United States : Charles Evans Hughes, Secretary of State ; Henry Cabot Lodge, Senator ; Oscar W. Underwood, Senator ; Elihu Root, former Secretary of State and Senator. Besides these, there was an Advisory Committee consisting of twenty-one persons, of whom four were women, a Secretariat of sixteen persons, five for ceremonial, protocol, etc. There was a technical staff for the limitation of armament of twenty persons, one on chemical warfare, consisting of a professor of chemistry and officers of the Army and Navy, one on Pacific and Far Eastern questions of sixteen persons, for legal questions of four persons, one on Economic questions and merchant marine of two persons, one on Communications of four civilian officials and officers of the Army and Navy, two cartographers, one of whom was a woman, two for the Press, one for Archives, one Disbursing officer, and two editors.

Belgium : Ambassador to the United States, with three technical advisors, one assistant technical adviser, one secretary general, and two assistant secretaries general.

Great Britain : The Rt. Hon. David Lloyd George, Prime Minister and First Lord of the Treasury (who did not proceed) ; the Rt. Hon. Arthur James Balfour, Lord President of the Privy Council ; the Rt. Hon. Baron Lee of Fareham, First Lord of the Admiralty ; the Rt. Hon. Sir Auckland Campbell Geddes, Ambassador to the United States ;

The Dominion of Canada : The Rt. Hon. Sir Robert Laird Borden, Prime Minister ;

The Commonwealth of Australia : The Rt. Hon. George Foster Pearce, Minister for Defence ;

The Dominion of New Zealand : The Hon. Sir John William Salmond, Judge of the Supreme Court of New Zealand ;

The Union of South Africa : The Rt. Hon. Arthur James Balfour ;

India : The Rt. Hon. Valingman Sankaranarayana Srinivasa Sastri, Member of the Indian Council of State.

The British Delegation included also a Foreign Affairs Section consisting of eight members of the diplomatic service and Foreign Office, a Naval Section of nine officers, a Military Section of seven officers, an Air Section of four officers, an Economic Section of two civilian officials, a Canadian Section of two, an Australian of four, a New Zealand of two, an Indian of three, a Publicity of two, a secretariat of five ; that is one for each, and a Cabinet Secretariat.

France : Mons. Briand, President of the Council and Minister for Foreign Affairs (up to November 24 only) ; Mons. Viviani, former President of the Council (till December 12 only) ; Mons. Albert Sarraut, Minister of the Colonies ; Mons. Jules Jusserand, Ambassador to the United States.

To the French Delegation were attached a secretariat consisting of eight persons, Experts, three for military questions, five for naval, one for legal, two for political, four for financial and economic, four for colonies, one for cables and wireless telegraph, three for the press, and three counsellors.

Italy: Hon. Carlo Schanzer, Senator, President of the Delegation ; Hon. Vittorio Rolandi-Ricci, Ambassador to the United States ; Mr. Filippo Meda, Representative.

The Italian Delegation had a Secretary General, four Diplomatic advisers, four Military, three Naval, two Aviation and six Economic advisers, two for press service, three private Secretaries, four Secretaries and two Assistant Secretaries.

Japan: Baron Tomosaburo Kato, Minister for the Navy ; Baron Kijuro Shidehara, Ambassador to the United States ; Prince Iyesato, President of the House of Peers ; Mr. Masanao Hanihara, Vice-Minister for Foreign Affairs.

The Japanese Delegation had a Secretary-General and eighty-nine other members, discharging various functions.

The Republic of China : Mr. Sao-ke Alfred Sze, Envoy Extraordinary and Minister Plenipotentiary at Washington ; Mr. V. K. Wellington Koo, Envoy Extraordinary and Minister Plenipotentiary at London ; Mr. Chung-Hui Wang, former Minister of Justice ; Mr. Chao-chu Wu.

The Chinese delegation comprised also two Superior Advisers, a Secretary-General and an AssistantSecretary General, twelve Counsellors, seventeen Technical Delegates, three Directors of Departments and one Assistant Director, thirty-nine Secretaries, thirty-three Attachés, six translators, and twelve Clerks.

The Netherlands: Jonkheer H. A. van Karnebeek, Minister for Foreign Affairs ; Jonkheer Franz Beclaerts van Blokland, Envoy Extraordinary and Minister Plenipotentiary ; Dr. E. Moresco, Vice-President of the Council of the Netherlands East Indies ; Alternate Delegates, Dr. J. C. A. Everwijn, Minister to the United

States, and Jonkheer Willem Hendrik de Beaufort, Minister Plenipotentiary at Washington.

To the Netherlands Delegation eight other officials were attached, including a Press Secretary.

The Portuguese Republic: Mr. José Francisco de Horta Machado de Franca Viscount d'Alte, Envoy Extraordinary and Minister Plenipotentiary at Washington; Mr. Ernesto Julio de Carvalho e Vasconcellos, Captain of the Portuguese Navy, Technical Director of the Colonial Office, and they had a Press Secretary.

Besides the Secretary-General of the Conference, there were six other Secretaries and Assistant-secretaries, drawn from the United States service, two Interpreters, one Archivist and a Disbursing Officer.

"AGENDA FOR CONFERENCE ON THE LIMITATION OF ARMAMENT

LIMITATION OF ARMAMENT

One.—Limitation of Naval Armament, under which shall be discussed:

(*a*) Basis of limitation.
(*b*) Extent.
(*c*) Fulfilment.

Two.—Rules for control of new agencies of warfare.

Three.—Limitation of land armament.

PACIFIC AND FAR EASTERN QUESTIONS.

One.—Questions relating to China.

First: Principles to be applied.

Second: Application.

Subjects:

(*a*) Territorial integrity.
(*b*) Administrative integrity.
(*c*) Open door.—Equality of commercial and industrial opportunity.
(*d*) Concessions, monopolies or preferential economic privileges.
(*e*) Development of railways, including plans relating to Chinese Eastern Railway.

(*f*) Preferential railroad rates.

(*g*) Status of existing commitments.

Two.—Siberia. (Similar headings.)

Three.—Mandated islands. (Unless questions earlier settled). Electrical Communications in the Pacific.

Under the heading of " Status of Existing Commitments," it is expected that opportunity will be afforded to consider and to reach an understanding with respect to unsettled questions involving the nature and scope of commitments under which claims of rights may hereafter be asserted."

The places of the plenipotentiaries at the hollow square of tables were arranged according to the diplomatic rule that governs such matters. The American Secretary of State had his seat at the middle of the top table, with the other three American delegates on his right ; at his left were the British delegates ; next on the right came the French delegates ; next on the left came the Italian delegates, and last on the right came the Japanese delegates.

This was the arrangement of seats at the first plenary session on November 12. At the subsequent sessions the seats at the top of the table were moved one place to the left, so that the Secretary of State occupied a seat to the left of the middle, and so, to one of the French delegates a seat was assigned at the right end of the top row.

The Press was admitted on the floor of the room to the plenary sessions, and the audience was accommodated in galleries.

Apart from the public sessions, the main part of the business was transacted in committees. These were the Committee on Limitation of Armament and the Committee on Pacific and Far Eastern questions. The former, composed of the Plenipotentiary delegates of the Five Great Powers, held 21 sittings, the latter, composed of the Plenipotentiary delegates of the nine Powers that took part in the Conference, 31 sittings.

Each had power to appoint such sub-committees as it might from time to time deem advisable.

At the first plenary session, presided over by the Secretary of State of the United States of America, after prayer offered by the Rev. Dr. Abernethy of the Calvary Baptist Church of Washington, an introductory speech was delivered by the President of the United States, printed copies of which in French and English were laid on the desks of the delegates, and, with the consent of the French first delegate, it was not orally translated. At subsequent plenary sessions practically every speech was repeated in French, as being the language of diplomacy. Very rarely was a speech translated into Japanese, and never into Italian or into any of the other languages represented at the table.

Records of the speeches made in the committees were kept, but sometimes these were slightly modified or toned down. Of those meetings official *communiqués* in a highly condensed form were published.

The President having withdrawn after delivering his speech, the British First Delegate proposed that the American Secretary of State should be permanent head of the Conference, in accordance with the usual practice.

The Secretary of State then delivered a speech in which he proposed a scheme for the execution of heading *one* of the section Limitation of Naval Armament of the agenda, and briefly mentioned the second part of the agenda, Pacific and Far Eastern questions. This he followed up with a concrete proposal for the limitation of the American, British and Japanese navies.

The Chairman then proposed as Secretary General the Hon. John W. Garratt, a former minister plenipotentiary, and that the heads of missions of the Five Great Powers, or such representative as each Power might respectively select for the purpose, should con-

stitute a committee on programme and procedure with
respect to the limitation of armament ; further that
the heads of missions of the Five Powers and of the
other Powers invited to take part in the discussion of
Pacific and Far Eastern questions, or such representatives as they might respectively designate, should
form a committee on programme and procedure for
the discussion of those questions. He also suggested
that the credentials of the delegates should be left
with the Secretary-General at the close of the session.
These proposals were agreed to.

On the motion of Senator Lodge it was agreed that
the Conference should adjourn to the following Tuesday.

The second session was held three days later. The
record of the first session had been previously distributed
to the delegates, and such corrections as were found to
be necessary had been given to the Secretary-General.
No objection being raised, it was unanimously approved.
This procedure was followed at each of the subsequent
sessions.

The British and Japanese First delegates intimated
their acceptance of the American plan in principle,
and short speeches followed from the Italian and French
leading delegates. Further discussion was carried on
in the committee, aided by a sub-committee of experts.

The third plenary session was held on November 21.
It was opened by the Chairman, who was followed by
the French Prime Minister, who explained the French
view with regard to land armament (*three* of the chapter
" Limitation of Armament "). After him the British
First Delegate spoke sympathetically with the French
point of view. The Italian Minister for Foreign Affairs,
and also the Secretary of State spoke. It came ultimately to be recognized that an agreement on this
question was impossible. Two days later the committee
which had this matter in hand had a private general
discussion on subjects relating to it and to new agencies
of warfare. These were referred to the sub-committee

consisting of the heads of delegations with instructions to bring in an order of proceeding with regard to these subjects, and with power to appoint sub-committees to deal with the questions relating to poison gas, aircraft, and rules of international law. After this the matter of land armament disappeared from the agenda, and the Conference resumed the discussion of the limitation of Naval Armament. The important point to be settled was the ratio to be fixed between the naval strengths of the United States, Great Britain and Japan, and concurrently those of France and Italy. These were finally, after much discussion, fixed at 5, 5, 3, 1.75 and 1.75 for the Five Powers. The discussion on the tonnage of submarines, carried on in committee led to no agreement, nor was any arrived at on the tonnage of other auxiliary craft.

Of the treaties which were the outcome of the Conference the subject matter of one, namely the Four Power Treaty (No. III) relating to the Insular Possessions and Insular Dominions in the Pacific Ocean, was not included among the *agenda*. It was designed to terminate and supersede the Anglo-Japanese alliance of which the necessity was recognized as no longer existing. The discussion of this compact was carried on by the heads of the delegations concerned as something additional to the other work of the Conference. It was read out at the fourth plenary session on December 10, and was introduced by Senator Lodge. The French Second delegate and the British First delegate followed him. A doubt having arisen with respect to the words " insular possessions and insular dominions,". it was found necessary to conclude a supplementary treaty defining the application of these terms in relation to Japan ; this forms No. V of the treaties signed at Washington. This Treaty is to remain in force for ten years, and after the expiration of that period is to continue to be in force subject to the right of any of the High Contracting Parties to terminate it by giving twelve months' notice. The fact of its conclusion was made the subject of identic communications to the Netherlands and Portuguese Governments by each of the signatory Powers.

An important part of the *agenda* consisted of questions relating to China, some of them interesting Japan in particular. The questions at issue between those two Powers were adjusted by the help of the American Secretary of State and the British First Delegate, in thirty meetings each lasting over three hours. These matters were disposed of by the Treaties numbered VI and VII, and by Resolutions Nos. 3, 4, and the two additions thereto, Nos. 5, 6, 7, 8, 9, 10, 11 and 12, and the annexed declarations. They were adopted at various plenary sessions.

Of all the results achieved by the Conference, the Treaty between the United States, the British Empire, France, Italy and Japan, limiting Naval Armament, signed February 6, 1922, was the most important. It confines the size of battleships to be hereafter constructed to 35,000 tons, and the calibre of guns to 16 inches. It specifies the existing battleships which may be retained by each of the contracting Powers. All other battleships possessed by the United States, Great Britain, or Japan are to be scrapped, in accordance with the rules laid down in the Treaty. There are also rules governing the replacement of ships more than 20 years old. The total tonnage to be retained by the United States will be 525,850 tons, by the British Empire will be 558,950 tons, by France 221,170 tons, by Italy 182,800 tons, by Japan 301,320 tons.

Article XXIII provides for the Treaty remaining in force " until December 31, 1936, and in case none of the contracting Powers shall have given notice two years before that date of its intention to terminate the Treaty, it shall continue in force until the expiration of two years from the date on which notice of termination shall be given by one of the Contracting Powers, whereupon the Treaty shall terminate as regards all the Contracting Powers."

Thus what has been designated as a "naval holiday" has been provided for, to last for nearly ten years.

Article XXIV is the usual ratification clause. A single original of the Treaty was signed, to be deposited in the United States archives, and copies to be transmitted to the other parties.

Treaty No. 2 with a view to rendering more effective the rules adopted by civilized nations for the protection of the lives of neutrals and non-combatants at sea in time of war, and to prevent the use in war of noxious gases and chemicals, lays down that: Article I (1) A merchant vessel must be ordered to submit to visit and search to determine its character before it can be seized. A merchant vessel must not be attacked unless it refuses to submit to visit or search after warning, or to proceed as directed after seizure. A merchant vessel must not be destroyed unless the crew and passengers have been first placed in safety. (2) Belligerent submarines are not under any circumstances exempt from the universal rules above stated ; and if a submarine cannot capture a merchant vessel in conformity with these rules the existing law of nations requires it to desist from attack and from seizure and to permit the merchant vessel to proceed unmolested.

Article III.—The Signatory Powers, desiring to insure the enforcement of the humane rules of existing law declared by them with respect to attacks upon and the seizure and destruction of merchant ships, further declare that any person in the service of any Power who shall violate any of those rules, whether or not such person is under the orders of a government superior, shall be deemed to have violated the laws of war and shall be liable to trial and punishment as if for an act of piracy and may be brought to trial before the civil or military authorities of any Power within the jurisdiction of which he may be found.

Article IV.—The Signatory Powers recognize the practical impossibility of using submarines as commerce destroyers without violating, as they were violated in the recent war of 1914—1918, the requirements universally accepted by civilized nations for the protection of the lives of neutrals and non-combatants, and to the end that the prohibition of the use of submarines as commerce destroyers shall be universally accepted as a part of the law of nations they now accept that prohibition as henceforth binding as between themselves and they invite all other nations to adhere thereto.

Article V.—The use in war of asphyxiating, poisonous or other gases, and all analogous liquids, materials or devices, having been justly condemned by the general opinion of the civilized world and a prohibition of such use having been declared in treaties to which a majority of the civilized Powers are parties,

The Signatory Powers, to the end that this prohibition shall be universally accepted as a part of international law binding alike the conscience and practice of nations, declare their assent to such prohibition, agree to be bound thereby as between themselves and invite all other civilized nations to adhere thereto.

No. 3 being " A Treaty between the United States of America, Belgium, the British Empire, China, France, Italy, Japan, the Netherlands and Portugal (known as the Nine Power Treaty), relating to principles and policies to be followed in matters concerning China, signed February 6, 1922, contains the following important articles :

The contracting Powers other than China undertake by Article I (1) to respect the sovereignty, the independence, and the territorial and administrative integrity of China ; (2) to provide the fullest and most unembarrassed opportunity to China to develope and maintain for herself an effective and stable government ; (3) to use their influence for the purpose of effectually establishing and maintaining the principle of equal opportunity for the commerce and industry of all nations throughout the territory of China [this is " the open door "] ; (4) to refrain from taking advantage of conditions in China in order to seek special rights or privileges which would abridge the rights of subjects or citizens of friendly States, and from countenancing action inimical to the security of such States. Articles II to V are developments of Article I. By Article V the contracting Powers, other than China, agree fully to respect China's rights as a neutral in time of war to which China is not a party ; and China declares that when she is neutral she will observe the obligations of neutrality. Article VIII provides for the adhesion of non-signatory Powers, and Article IX is the usual ratification clause.

Another Treaty was signed on February 6 between the same set of Powers relating to the Chinese Customs Tariff. Article I provides for the revision of the existing tariff, so as to make the customs duties equivalent to an effective 5 per cent. *ad valorem*. By Article II it is agreed to hold a special conference in China, on a day and at a place to be designated by China, in order to take immediate steps to prepare the way for the speedy abolition of *likin* and for the fulfilment of the other conditions laid down in certain treaties which China concluded in 1903 with Great Britain, the United States and Japan respectively. Article VI recognizes the principle of uniformity in the rates of customs duties levied at all the land and maritime frontiers of China. By Article VIII the adhesion by certain non-signatory Powers is provided for. There were two texts, English and French, both authentic.

The so-called Four-Power Treaty between the United States, the British Empire, France and Japan, relating to their insular possessions and insular dominions in the Pacific Ocean, was signed December 13, and the supplementary Treaty, containing a definition of those terms, on February 6.

A number of Resolutions accompanying these Treaties were also adopted. (*i*) For a commission of jurists to consider amendments of laws of war. It had been framed by the Committee on Limitation of Armament and recommended for adoption by the Conference, and was passed at the sixth plenary session, February 4; (*ii*) Excluding from the purview of the Commission to consider and report upon the rules of International Law of rules or declarations relating to submarines or the use of noxious gases and chemicals already adopted by the Powers in this Conference (at sixth plenary session, February 4); (*iii*) Regarding a Board of Reference for Far Eastern Questions (at sixth plenary session, February 4); (*iv*) Regarding Extraterritoriality in China, under which a Commission is to be established to inquire into the present practice of extraterritoriality in China, with a view to reporting to the Governments of the several Powers their findings of fact in regard to re-commendations of the Commission (at fourth plenary session, December 10); (*v*) Regarding foreign Postal Agencies in China, and undertaking that their withdrawal shall be effected not later than January 1, 1923 (at the fifth plenary session, February 1, 1922); (*vi*) Re-garding Armed Forces in China, by which the Powers declare their intention to withdraw their armed forces now on duty in China without the authority of any treaty or agreement, whenever China shall assure the protection of the lives and property of foreigners in China, and to that end the Governments of the Eight Powers will instruct their diplomatic representatives in Peking, whenever China shall so request, to associate themselves with three representatives of the Chinese Government to conduct an inquiry into the issues raised by the foregoing declaration and the corresponding declaration by China of her intention and capacity to assure the protection of the lives and property of foreigners in China, and to report thereon (at fifth plenary session, February 1, 1922); (*vii*) Regarding radio stations in China and accompanying declarations (at fifth plenary session, February 1) ; (*viii*) Regarding Unification of Railways in China and accompanying declaration by China (at fifth plenary session, February 1, 1922) ; (*ix*), Regarding the reduction of Chinese military forces (at fifth plenary session, February 1, 1922) ; (*x*) Regarding existing commitments of China or with respect to China, *i.e.*, the political and other international obligations of China and of the several Powers in relation to China (at fifth plenary session, February 1, 1922) ; (*xi*) Regarding the Chinese Eastern Railway, approved by all the Powers including China (at the sixth plenary session, February 4, 1922) ; and (*xii*) Regarding the Chinese Eastern Railway, approved by all the Powers other than China.

On February 4 there was also signed by China and Japan a Treaty settling outstanding questions relative to Shantung, which had been pending ever since China refused to sign the Treaty of Versailles, Article 156 of which provided that Germany should renounce in favour of Japan all her rights, title and privileges which she acquired in virtue of the treaty concluded by her with China on March 6, 1898, and disposing of all other arrangements relative to the province of Shantung, together with all Japanese rights of whatever kind relating to the Tsingtao-Tsinanfu Railway. The Treaty consists of 28 articles and an annex, besides an Understanding between China and Japan supplementing the Shantung Treaty. Ratifications to be exchanged at Peking, not later than four months from the date of its signature. It was made known at the fifth plenary session, on February 5, and the announcements in Article I that Japan will restore to China the former German leased territory, at Kiaochow, and in section iii with regard to the withdrawal of Japanese troops, were followed by the British First Delegate's declaration of the British Government's intention to hand back Wei-hai-wei to China. This was confirmed by an exchange of letters of February 3 between Mr. Balfour and Mr. Sze. See White Paper [Cmd. 1627], pp. 26–28. France also declared in committee her willingness to restore Kwang-chow-wan to China under certain conditions [Senate Document, p. 540].

The closing session of the Conference was held on February 6, 1922, on which occasion the President of the United States delivered a farewell address to the delegates.

Siberia, Mandated Islands and Electrical Communications in the Pacific, with which subjects the Agenda terminated, do not seem to have been discussed by the whole Conference. But an arrangement between the United States and Japan, which took the form of an Agreement relative to the Island of Yap, described in the instrument itself as a Convention, was arrived at by those Powers outside the Conference, and was signed February 11, 1922. The plenipotentiaries were the United States Secretary of State and the Japanese Ambassador at Washington. The ratifications were to be exchanged at Washington as soon as practicable. The Convention was signed in duplicate. It appears to come under the last two subjects on the Agenda.

Authorities.—Senate Document No. 126, 67th Congress, 2nd Session ; Papers published by the American Association for *International Conciliation*, Nos. 169 of December 1901 and 172 of March 1922 ; Mark Sullivan, *The Great Adventure at Washington*, London, 1922 ; Sir John N. Jordan, Article in the *Quarterly Review* for July 1922 ; White Paper presented to Parliament [Cmd. 1627]. Miscellaneous, No. 1 (1922), entitled *Conference on Limitation of Armament* (*Treaties, Resolutions, etc.*).

CHAPTER XXVII

TREATIES AND OTHER INTERNATIONAL COMPACTS

TREATY, CONVENTION, ADDITIONAL ARTICLES, ACTE FINAL

§ 498. INTERNATIONAL compacts or engagements embrace a great diversity of subjects and are placed on record in a variety of shapes. Consequently they may be classed according to either matter or form.

The principal forms they assume may be enumerated as follows—

1. Treaty.
2. Convention.
3. Additional Articles.
4. Acte Final.
5. Declaration.
6. Agreement.
7. Arrangement.
8. Protocol.
9. Procès-verbal.
10. Exchange of Notes.
11. Réversale.
12. Compromis d'Arbitrage.
13. Modus Vivendi.
14. Ratification.
15. Adhesion and Accession.

Which of these forms shall be adopted in a particular case is partly a matter of convenience and is partly determined by usage. Thus, the treaty form is nearly always employed for preliminaries of peace, and always for the final result of peace negotiations, for marriages between exalted personages, *i.e.* members of Imperial or Royal families. In 1815 the treaty of peace of November 20 was supplemented by various conventions. Agreements respecting commerce and navigation, for the extradition of criminals, for the delimitation of boundaries, for arbitration, are found in the shape of treaties or of conventions, indifferently. Generally speaking, it may be said that the more important the subject matter, the more likely is it that it will be embodied in a treaty or a convention, and that the relative importance decreases as we go down the list. *Lettres réversales* appear to be confined to questions of etiquette between crowned heads, and *réversales* are also employed for the rectification of an error in etiquette or in drafting.[1] But see below, §§ 591, 592.

---

[1] De Castro y Casaleiz i. 379.

§ 499. Originally the expression " treaty " was applied to the negotiation ; the practice has prevailed of applying it also to the final proceeding which closes the negotiation. Hence the complete term would be " traité et appointement " to denote a treaty.[1] The verb *traiter* means " to negotiate."

" Stipulate " and " stipulation " are properly used with reference to the clauses of a compact. As is well known, the etymology is from *stipula*, a straw, which was broken between the parties to a bargain, and the bringing together of the two ends of the fracture symbolized accordance in the terms. It is incorrect to employ these words to denote a demand for a particular condition ; but any one who desires to justify their misuse can quote the passage from Rabelais given in Littré's *Dictionary of the French Language*, s. v. " stipuler."

Treaties and conventions do not differ as regards their structure. According to Garcia de la Vega,[2] it is the length of time for which a compact is concluded that should determine the question whether it is to be styled a treaty or a convention. He adds that this rule is not observed as regards commercial matters ; a commercial instrument is called treaty when it regulates duties on cargo, but takes the name of convention when it is occupied only with the charges on the ship. But this way of putting it does not appear to be quite exact. Commercial agreements are as a rule concluded for a term of years, yet they are frequently denominated treaties, and so also with extradition. The privileges and immunities of consuls are usually defined in a convention, and many other instances where, though there is no limit of time, the convention form has been utilized, will be found among the examples given further on.

The *Guía práctica del diplomático Español* classifies[3] treaties as treaties of peace, alliance, friendship, subsidy,

[1] De Maulde-la-Clavière, i. 193. [2] 250 *n*. [3] i. 386.

guarantee, neutrality, cession of territory, limits, establishment, working of forests, river navigation, easements, repatriation, relief of destitute subjects, jurisdiction, extradition, execution of judgments, judicial assistance. It mentions both treaties and conventions respecting the slave trade, customs union, commerce and navigation, also monetary conventions, postal, telegraph, railway and consular conventions. In recent times many multinational conventions have been concluded, for the protection of literary and industrial property, regarding collisions at sea and salvage ; suppression of the White Slave traffic ; status of naturalized citizens who again take up their residence in their country of origin—to say nothing of the numerous conventions aimed at the definition of rules of international law in time of war negotiated at the Hague Peace Conferences of 1899 and 1907.

§ 500. The principal parts of a treaty are—

1. The preamble, beginning with (*a*) the names and titles of the high contracting parties ; (*b*) a summary of the objects contemplated or, in other words, a statement of the purpose ; (*c*) the names and official designations of the plenipotentiaries appointed by the high contracting parties ; (*d*) a paragraph stating that the plenipotentiaries have produced their full-powers, which were found to be in good and due form, and that they have agreed upon the following articles.

2. The various stipulations or articles, beginning with the most general, next the particular ones, and finally the articles, if any, providing for the means of executing them.

3. An article providing for ratification and for the place and time of exchange of ratifications.

4. A clause stating that : " In witness whereof (*En foi de quoi*) the respective plenipotentiaries have affixed their signatures and seals (or, seals of their arms).

5. Locality, date and signatures and seals.

If the treaty is to endure for a fixed number of years, its duration will be stated at the end of the articles and before No. 3. Sometimes this takes the shape of a stipulation that either party may, twelve months before the term fixed, " denounce " (*i.e.* give notice to terminate) the treaty, and that if neither party makes use of this right, the duration of the treaty shall be prolonged from twelve months to twelve months, or for any other period that may be agreed upon, until one of the parties exercises his right and gives the required notice.

§ 501. Treaties between two parties are drawn up either in the languages of the respective parties—or in that of one of them, the other counterpart being in French—or there may be a single French text in two counterparts. Each party prepares the counterpart which is to be deposited in his national archives, and in it each party names his own country and sovereign first, his own country's plenipotentiaries first, and he signs it first, in the place of honour, which is the left side of the paper.

If there are more than two contracting parties, then there may be one counterpart for each, or a single original signed by all, of which a certified copy is delivered to each party. In either case the rules of the " alternat " are followed, *i.e.* the name of the country to which the document is destined occupying the place of honour in the preamble, wherever the parties are again named in the body of articles, and, lastly, in the subscription, the names of the other contracting parties and their respective plenipotentiaries taking rank afterwards in the alphabetical order of the names of the various countries according to the French language.

In international documents Grande Bretagne, not Angleterre, is official, although the latter designation is the usual one in speech and literature. If the United

States were to insist on being spoken of as Amérique, that Power would rank after Germany (Allemagne).

§ 502. In going through the different classes of compacts included in this and the following chapters, it will be observed that treaties and conventions are usually expressed as concluded between sovereigns of monarchical states, between republics, or between a republic and the head of a monarchical state. The practice may be stated more shortly by saying that they are concluded between sovereigns, seeing that a republic is itself sovereign. There are some exceptions. The treaty of defensive alliance of May 16, 1912, between Greece and Bulgaria (§ 517), was made between *les deux royaumes*, and the agreement for a French protectorate over Morocco (§ 529) was concluded between " *le Gouvernement de la République française et le gouvernement de S. M. Chérifienne.*" When we come to other forms of compact we find this procedure is more common in their case. Thus in the additional protocol to the Convention for the establishment of an International Prize Court, we find it was made between " *l'Allemagne* " and other countries, and to the " Protocole additionnel à l'Arrangement Monétaire " between the French, Belgian, Greek, Italian, and Swiss Governments, those " Governments " are made parties. In the protocol embodying the terms on which peace negotiations were to be undertaken between the United States and Spain, it is stated that authority to conclude the same was derived from the respective Governments. Other cases where the Governments were expressed as parties are certain Declarations (§ 539), Agreements (§ 551) and Arrangements (§§ 555, 556), and as in all these cases ratification was provided for, it becomes evident that some form of ratification by Governments is required, worded differently from that used where Sovereign Powers ratify. A form which may be adapted for this purpose is given in § 612.

Marriage Treaties

§ 503. Treaty for the marriage of H.R.H.[1] the Duke of Connaught and H.R.H. Princess Louise Margaret of Prussia, signed at Berlin, February 26, 1879.[2]

In the name of the Holy and Blessed Trinity.

Preamble stating the purpose, the names of the high contracting parties, the consent of the parties to the marriage, and also of the bride and bridegroom not being high contracting parties, names of the plenipotentiaries.

Who having communicated to each other their respective full-powers, found in good and due form, have agreed upon and concluded the following articles—

[Art. 1. For the marriage.

Art. 2. Annual allowance to the bride by the bridegroom.

Art. 3. In case of widowhood, annual allowance in lieu of dower.

Art. 4. Dowry granted to the bride by the Emperor of Germany, and trousseau, including jewels.

Art. 5. Renunciation on the bride's part to succession to the Prussian throne so long as male heirs are in existence.

Art. 6. Ratifications to be exchanged as soon as possible.]

In witness whereof the respective plenipotentiaries have signed the same, and have affixed thereto the seals of their arms.

Done at Berlin, the 26th day of February, in the year of our Lord 1879.

[*Seals and Signatures.*]

(Text in English and German. Four originals in all.)

---

[1] Wherever abbreviations of this class are used in this book, it is to be understood that the corresponding words are written out in full in the original instrument.

[2] *Brit. and For. State Papers,* lxx. 3.

§ 504. Treaty between Her Majesty and the Prince of Waldeck and Pyrmont, for the marriage of H.R.H. Prince Leopold, Duke of Albany, with H.S.[1]H. (*Durchlaucht*) the Princess Helena Frederica Augusta of Waldeck and Pyrmont.—Signed at Berlin, April 20, 1882.[2]

This closely follows the form of the preceding, except that there is no reservation of ultimate rights of succession in the event of the failure of the male line of Waldeck and Pyrmont. (In English and German likewise, each text signed by the plenipotentiaries of both parties, so there must have been in all four copies, two in each language.)

§ 505. Treaty between Great Britain and Rumania, for the marriage of H.R.H. Princess Marie of Great Britain and Ireland, with H.R.H. Prince Ferdinand of Rumania.—Signed at Bucarest, December 15, 1892.[3]

Preamble—

Her Majesty the Queen of the United Kingdom of Great Britain and Ireland, Empress of India, on the one part, and H.M. the King of Rumania, on the other part, already connected by ties of friendship, having judged it proper that an alliance should be contracted between their respective Royal Houses by a marriage agreed to on both sides, between H.R.H. Marie Alexandra Victoria, Princess of Great Britain and Ireland, Duchess of Saxony, granddaughter of H.M. the Queen of Great Britain and Ireland, Empress of India, and eldest daughter of H.R.H. Alfred Ernest Albert, Duke of Edinburgh, Earl of Kent and Ulster, Duke of Saxony, Duke of Saxe-Coburg and Gotha, etc., and of H.I.[4]H. the Grand Duchess Marie Alexandrowna of Russia ;

And H.R.H. Ferdinand Victor Mainrad, Prince and Heir to the Throne of Rumania, second son of H.R.H. Leopold Stephen Charles Antoine Gustave Edward Thasilo, Prince of Hohenzollern, Burgrave of Nuremberg, Count of Sigmaringen and Veringen, Count of Berg, Lord of Haigerloch and Woehrstein, etc., and of H.R.H. Princess Antonia

---

[1] Serene.　　　[2] *Brit. and For. State Papers*, lxxiii. 33.
[3] *Brit. and For. State Papers*, lxxxiv. 101.　　　[4] Imperial.

of Portugal, Duchess of Saxony, and nephew of H.M. the King
of Rumania ;

And the two High Betrothed Parties, as also H.R.H. the
Prince Leopold of Hohenzollern, and H.R.H. Princess Antonia,
his Consort, having declared their consent to such alliance ;

In order, therefore, to attain so desirable an end, and to
treat upon, conclude, and confirm the Articles of the Treaty
of the said Marriage, H.B.M., on the one part, and H.M. the
King of Rumania, on the other part, have named as their
Plenipotentiaries, that is to say—

[Here follow the names of the plenipotentiaries of the
said two high contracting parties.]

Who, after having, etc. . . . . the following Articles—

Art. 1. [The marriage to be solemnized at Sigmaringen
as soon as the same may conveniently be done.

Immediately after the celebration of the marriage a
formally authenticated Act of the same shall be delivered
by the competent authority in good and due form.]

Art 2. [The marriage settlement to be made on either
side, will be agreed upon and expressed in a separate
marriage contract.]

Art. 3. [By her marriage with H.R.H. Ferdinand,
etc., who professes the Roman Catholic Faith, H.R.H.
the Princess Marie, etc., forfeits for ever all her rights
of succession to the Crown and Government of Great
Britain and Ireland and the dominions thereunto
belonging, or any part of the same.]

Art. 4. [Ratification clause.]

In witness whereof, etc.

Done in duplicate at Bucharest the 3rd/15th day of
December, in the year of our Lord 1892.

[*Seals and signatures.*]

(Also signed in the Rumanian language.)

TREATIES OF PEACE

§ 506. It was formerly usual, and sometimes the
practice is still observed, of prefacing a treaty of peace

by a first article undertaking that it shall be perpetual. Thus Article I of the Treaty of Versailles of September 3, 1783 [1] (headed :—

" Au Nom de la Très Sainte et Indivisible Trinité, Père, Fils, et Saint Esprit.   Ainsi soit-il ")

runs thus :—

Il y aura une paix Chrétienne, universelle et perpetuelle, tant par mer que par terre, et une amitié sincère et constante sera rétablie, entre Leurs Majestés Britannique et très Chrétienne, et entre leurs héritiers et successeurs, royaumes, états, provinces, pays, sujets, et vassaux, de quelque qualité et condition qu'ils soient, sans exception de lieux ni de personnes ; en sorte que les hautes parties contractantes apporteront la plus grande attention à maintenir entre elles, et leurs dits états et sujets, cette amitié et correspondance réciproque, sans permettre dorénavant que, de part ni d'autre, on commette aucunes sortes d'hostilités, par mer ou par terre, pour quelque cause ou sous quelque prétexte que ce puisse être : Et on évitera soigneusement tout ce qui pourroit altérer, à l'avenir, l'union heureusement rétablie, s'attachant au contraire à se procurer réciproquement, en toute occasion, tout ce qui pourroit contribuer à leur gloire, intérêts, et avantages mutuels, sans donner aucun secours ou protection, directement ou indirectement, à ceux qui voudroient porter quelque préjudice à l'une ou à l'autre des dites hautes parties contractantes.   Il y aura un oubli et amnistie générale de tout ce qui a pu être fait ou commis, avant ou depuis le commencement de la guerre qui vient de finir." [2]

Notwithstanding, in 1793 the recently established French Republic declared war against Great Britain, a war which was carried on, with the slight intermission which followed on the Peace of Amiens, between France and Great Britain, the latter often with, sometimes without, allies, until 1815.

A faint echo of this sort of undertaking is presented by Article 1 of a treaty signed January 30, 1881 :—

[1] Text in F. de Martens *Recueil*, etc., xiii. 160.
[2] Jenkinson, iii. 335.

" Habrá total olvido de lo pasado y una paz sólida é inviolable entre Su Majestad el Rey de España y la República de los Estados Unidos de Colombia."

§ 507. *Preliminary Treaty of Peace between Russia and Turkey.*—Signed at San Stefano, February 19/March 3, 1878.[1] [Ratifications exchanged at Petersburg, March 5/17, 1878.]

Preamble.

S. M. l'Empereur de Russie et S.M. l'Empereur des Ottomans, animés du désir de rendre et d'assurer à leurs pays et à leurs peuples les bienfaits de la paix, ainsi que de prévenir toute nouvelle complication qui pourrait la menacer, ont nommé pour leurs Plénipotentiaires à l'effet d'arrêter, conclure et signer les Préliminaires de la Paix.

[Here follow the names of the plenipotentiaries.]

Lesquels, après avoir échangé leurs pleins-pouvoirs, trouvés en bonne et due forme, sont convenus des Articles suivants :—

[Arts. I to XXIX. Article I lays down the frontier between Turkey and Montenegro.]

XXIX. Le présent acte sera ratifié par LL. MM. II. l'Empereur de Russie et l'Empereur des Ottomans, et les ratifications seront échangées dans quinze jours, ou plutôt si faire se peut, à St. Pétersbourg, où l'on conviendra également du lieu et de l'époque à laquelle les stipulations du présent acte seront revêtues des formes solennelles usitées dans les Traités de paix.

Il demeure toutefois bien entendu que les Hautes Parties Contractantes se considèrent comme formellement liées par le présent acte depuis le moment de la ratification.

En foi de quoi les Plénipotentiaires respectifs ont revêtu le présent acte de leurs signatures et y ont apposé leurs cachets. Fait à San Stefano, le 19 février/3 mars, 1878.

[*Seals and signatures.* Followed by the addition of the final paragraph of Article XI, which had been omitted.]

[*Date.* *Signatures.*]

[1] *Brit. and For. State Papers,* lxix. 732.

§ 508. *Treaty between Great Britain, Austria-Hungary, France, Germany, Italy, Russia and Turkey for the Settlement of Affairs in the East*[1] (Bulgaria ; Eastern Rumelia ; Greece ; Bosnia and Herzegovina ; Montenegro ; Danube ; Batoum ; Armenia ; Religion, etc.).— Signed at Berlin, July 13, 1878.[2]

Au nom de Dieu Tout-Puissant. S. M. la Reine du Royaume-Uni de la Grande Bretagne et d'Irlande, Impératrice des Indes ; le Président de la République Française ; S. M. l'Empereur d'Allemagne, Roi de Prusse ; S. M. l'Empereur d'Autriche, Roi de Bohême, &c., Roi Apostolique de Hongrie ; S. M. le Roi d'Italie ; S. M. l'Empereur de Toutes les Russies, et S. M. l'Empereur des Ottomans, désirant régler dans une pensée d'ordre Européen, conformément aux stipulations du Traité de Paris du 30 Mars, 1856, les questions soulevées en Orient par les événements des dernières années et par la guerre dont le Traité Préliminaire de San Stefano a marqué le terme, ont été unanimement d'avis que la réunion d'un Congrès offrirait le meilleur moyen de faciliter leur entente.

Leurs dites Majestés et le Président de la République Française ont en conséquence nommé pour leurs Plénipotentiaires, savoir :—

[Names of the plenipotentiaries appointed by each respective Head of a State, in the strict French alphabetical order of the Powers represented.]

Lesquels, suivant la proposition de la Cour d'Autriche-Hongrie et sur l'invitation de la Cour d'Allemagne, se sont réunis à Berlin munis de pleins-pouvoirs qui ont été trouvés en bonne et due forme.

L'accord s'étant heureusement établi entre eux, ils sont convenus des stipulations suivantes :—

[Follow the articles, some of which were embodied in the Treaty of Peace, between Russia and Turkey, signed at Constantinople, Jan. 27/Feb. 8, 1879.]

[1] There does not seem to be any reason for the position assigned to Germany here, and in the preamble.
[2] This heading forms no part of the instrument.

Le présent traité sera ratifié, et les ratifications en seront échangées à Berlin dans un délai de trois semaines, ou plus tôt si faire se peut.[1]

En foi de quoi, etc.

[*Place, date.*]   [*Signatures.*]

[Taken from the counterpart destined to Great Britain which was signed in the first place by the British plenipotentiaries. After them the signatures come in the following order :—Turkey, Germany, Austria, France, Italy, Russia.[2] Turkey probably signed the original, alone, on the right hand.]

§ 509. *Traité de Paix entre la Russie et la Turquie.*— Signé à Constantinople, le 27 janvier/8 février, 1879.

Au nom de Dieu Tout-Puissant

Preamble

S. M. l'Empereur de Toutes les Russies et S. M. l'Empereur des Ottomans, désirant consacrer le rétablissement de la paix entres les deux Empires et régler définitivement, par un Traité, les clauses du Traité préliminaire de San Stéfano qui doivent faire l'objet d'une entente directe entre les deux Etats, ont nommé pour leurs Plénipotentiaires :

[Names of respective high contracting parties, of the plenipotentiaries, official designations and their decorations.]

Lesquels, après avoir échangé leurs pleins pouvoirs, trouvés en bonne et due forme, sont tombés d'accord sur les Articles suivants—

Art I. Il y aura désormais paix et amitié entre les deux Empires.

Art. XII. Le présent sera ratifié, et les ratifications en seront échangées à St. Pétersbourg, dans l'espace de deux semaines, ou plus tôt si faire se peut.

En foi de quoi les Plénipotentiaires de Russie et de Turquie y ont apposé leurs signatures et le sceau de leurs armes.

---

[1] The *procès-verbal* of the exchange of ratifications is given § 582.

[2] *Brit. and For. State Papers*, lxix. 749. *Nouv. Recueil, 2ème Série,* iii. 449, without cross-headings.

Fait à Constantinople, le 27 janvier/8 février, 1879.

[*Seals and Signatures.*]

(From the Russian counterpart.)[1]

§ 510. *Preliminaries of Peace between Turkey and Greece.*—Signed at Constantinople, September 6/18, 1897.

Preamble.

La Grèce ayant confié aux Grandes Puissances le soin de ses intérêts en vue du rétablissement de la paix avec la Turquie, et la Sublime Porte ayant accepté leur médiation, les conditions suivantes qui doivent servir de base principale et définitive aux relations futures des deux pays ont été arrêtées entre leurs Excellences les Représentants de l'Allemagne, de l'Angleterre, de l'Autriche-Hongrie, de la France, de l'Italie et de la Russie d'une part, et Son Excellence le Ministre des Affaires Etrangères de S. M. Impériale le Sultan de l'autre :—

Art. IX. En cas de divergence dans le cours des négociations entre la Turquie et la Grèce, les points contestés pourront être soumis par l'une ou l'autre des Parties intéressées à l'arbitrage des Représentants des Grandes Puissances à Constantinople, dont les décisions seront obligatoires pour les deux Gouvernements. Cet arbitrage pourra s'exercer collectivement ou par désignation spéciale des intéressés, et soit directement soit par l'entremise de Délégués spéciaux.

En cas de partage égal des voix, les arbitres choisiront un sur-arbitre.

Article Final. Aussitôt que le présent Acte aura reçu l'approbation de S. M. le Sultan, laquelle sera donnée dans un délai de huit jours, les clauses qu'il contient seront portées par les Représentants des Grandes Puissances à la connaissance du Cabinet d'Athènes et deviendront exécutoires.

Fait en double à Constantinople le 6/18 septembre, 1897.

[Follow the signatures, in the order of Turkey, Austria-Hungary, Russia, France, Great Britain, Germany, Italy, which was probably the order of seniority of the Ambassadors.]

There were annexed three declarations and a General Description of the new frontier line between Greece and

---

[1] *Brit. and For. State Papers,* lxx. 551.

Turkey in Thessaly. The first of these will be found among " Declarations " at § 538.

The negotiations for the definitive Treaty of Peace then proceeded at Constantinople between the plenipotentiaries of Turkey and Greece, in the course of which the Greek plenipotentiaries expressed their wish for information as to the proposals which would be made by the Turkish Government respecting the arrangements contemplated by Article III of the Preliminaries. The Turkish plenipotentiaries having given the views of their government, the Greek plenipotentiaries made formal reservations. The respective statements made were recorded in a Protocol of November 7/19, 1897, which has the aspect of an ordinary protocol or *procès-verbal* such as is kept by way of minutes of discussions during a negotiation. Together with the text of the Article in question, this document will be found among Protocols, § 560.[1]

§ 511. *Treaty of Peace between Greece and Turkey.*— Signed at Constantinople, November 22/December 4, 1897.[2]

S. M. le Roi des Hellènes et S. M. le Sultan, Empereur des Ottomans, s'étant mis d'accord pour compléter et convertir en Traité de Paix définitif les Préliminaires de Paix du 6/18 septembre, 1897, signées par Leurs Excellences les Représentants de l'Allemagne, de l'Autriche-Hongrie, de la France, de la Grande Bretagne, de l'Italie, et de la Russie, agissant au nom de la Grèce, d'une part, et par S. E. le Ministre des Affaires Etrangères de S. M. I. le Sultan, d'autre part, ont nommé à cet effet pour leurs Plénipotentiaires, savoir :—

[Names, official designations and decorations.]

Lesquels, etc.

---

[1] *Brit. and For. State Papers*, xc. 546.
[2] *Brit. and For. State Papers*, xc. 422.

XV. En cas de divergence dans le cours des négociations [1] entre la Grèce et la Turquie, les points contestés pourront être soumis, par l'une ou l'autre des Parties intéressées, à l'arbitrage des Représentants des Grandes Puissances à Constantinople, dont les décisions seront obligatoires pour les deux Gouvernements.

Cet arbitrage pourra s'exercer collectivement ou par désignation spéciale des intéressés, et soit directement, soit par l'entremise de Délégués spéciaux.

En cas de partage égal des voix, les Arbitres choisiront un sur-arbitre.

XVI. [Ratifications to be exchanged in fifteen days, or sooner if possible.]

En foi de quoi, etc.

Fait en double à Constantinople, le 22 novembre/4 décembre, 1897.

[*Seals and signatures.*]

§ 512. *Between the United States and Spain* (signed also in the Spanish language).—Paris, December 10, 1898.

Preamble.

The United States of America and H.M. the Queen Regent of Spain, in the name of her august son, Don Alfonso XIII, desiring to end the state of war now existing between the two countries, have for that purpose appointed as Plenipotentiaries :—

The President of the United States [names] ;

And H.M. the Queen-Regent of Spain [names and official designations] ;

Who, having assembled in Paris, and having exchanged their full-powers, which were found to be in due and proper form, have, after discussion of the matters before them, agreed upon the following Articles :—

Article XVII provides for the exchange of ratifications

[1] Apparently for (1) Convention regulating disputed questions of nationality ; (2) A consular convention ; (3) An extradition treaty ; (4) Convention for the repression of brigandage on the common frontier, provided for by Art. 11.

at Washington "within six months from the date whereof, or earlier if possible."

In faith whereof, etc.
Done in duplicate at Paris, the 10th day of December, in the year of our Lord 1898.[1]

§ 513. *Treaty of London*, 17/30 mai, 1913.

Preamble.

S. M. le Roi des Hellènes, S. M. le Roi des Bulgares, S. M. le Roi de Montenegro et S. M. le Roi de Serbie (ci-après désignés par les mots " les Souverains alliés ") d'une part ; et S. M. l'Empereur des Ottomans d'autre part,
Animés du désir de mettre fin au présent état de guerre et de rétablir des relations de paix et d'amitié entre leurs Gouvernements et leurs sujets respectifs, ont résolu de conclure un Traité de paix et ont choisi à cet effet pour leurs Plénipotentiaires—

S. M. le Roi des Hellènes : S. E. M. [names and official designations and so for all the other contracting parties].

Qui, après s'être communiqué leurs pleins-pouvoirs, etc.

Article 1

Il y aura à dater de l'echange des ratifications [2] du présent traité, paix et amitié entre S. M. l'Empereur des Ottomans d'une part, et LL. MM. les Souverains alliés d'autre part, ainsi qu'entre Leurs héritiers et successeurs, Leurs États et sujets respectifs, à perpetuité.

Article 2

S. M. l'Empereur des Ottomans cède à LL. MM. les Souverains alliés tous les territoires de Son Empire sur le continent européen à l'ouest d'une ligne tirée d'Enos sur la mer Egée à Midia sur la mer Noire, à l'exception de l'Albanie.
Le tracé exact de la frontière d'Énos à Midia sera déterminé par une commission internationale.

---

[1] *Brit. and For. State Papers*, xc. 382.
[2] This treaty was never ratified.

Article 3

S. M. l'Empereur des Ottomans et LL. MM. les Souverains alliés déclarent remettre à S. M. l'Empereur d'Allemagne . . . et à S. M. l'Empereur de Toutes les Russies le soin de régler la délimitation des frontières de l'Albanie et toutes autres questions concernant l'Albanie.

Article 4

S. M. l'Empereur des Ottomans déclare céder a LL. MM. les Souverains Alliés l'ile de Créte et renoncer en leur faveur à tous les droits de souveraineté et autres qu'il possédait sur cette île.

Article 5

S. M. l'Empereur des Ottomans et LL. MM. les Souverains alliés déclarent confier à S. M. l'Empereur d'Allemagne . . . et S. M. l'Empereur de toutes les Russies le soin de statuer sur le sort de toutes les îles ottomanes de la mer Egée, l'ile de Crète exceptée, et de la péninsule du Mont-Athos.

Article 6

S. M. l'Empereur des Ottomans et LL. MM. les Souverains alliés déclarent remettre le soin de régler les questions d'ordre financier résultant de l'état de guerre qui prend fin et des cessions territoriales ci-dessus mentionnées à la commission internationale convoquée à Paris, à laquelle ils ont délégué leurs représentants.

Article 7

Les questions concernant les prisonniers de guerre, juridiction, nationalité et commerce seront réglées par des conventions spéciales.

Article Final

Le présent traité séra ratifié et les ratifications seront échangées à Londres dans le plus bref délai possible.

En foi de quoi, etc.

Fait à Londres le 17 (30) mai, 1913, à midi (heure de Greenwich).

[Signatures of Greek plenipotentiaries.   Signatures of plenipotentiaries of Bulgaria, Montenegro, Serbia and Turkey.]

(From the Greek Counterpart.)[1]

[1] *Nouveau Recueil Général*, etc., 3ème série, t. viii. 16.

§ 514, *Treaty of Peace.*—Signed at Bucarest, July 28/ August 10, 1913.[1]

TRAITÉ DE PAIX

Preamble.

LL. MM. le Roi de Roumanie, le Roi des Hellènes, le Roi de Monténégro et le Roi de Serbie, d'une part, et le Roi des Bulgares, d'autre part, animés du désir de mettre fin à l'état de guerre actuellement existant entre Leurs pays respectifs, voulant, dans une pensée d'ordre, établir la paix entre Leurs peuples si longtemps éprouvés, ont résolu de conclure un traité définitif de paix. LL. MM. ont, en conséquence, nommé pour Leurs Plénipotentiaries, savoir :—

S. M. le Roi de Roumanie :
S. E. . . .
S. M. le Roi des Hellènes :
S. E. etcetera. . . .

Lesquels, suivant la proposition du Gouvernement de Roumanie, se sont réunis en Conférence à Bucarest, munis de pleins pouvoirs, qui ont été trouvés en bonne et due forme.

L'accord s'étant heureusement établi entre eux, ils sont convenus des stipulations suivantes :—

Article premier

Il y aura, à dater du jour de l'échange des ratifications du présent traité, paix et amitié entre S. M. le Roi de Roumanie, S. M. le Roi des Hellènes, S. M. le Roi de Monténégro, S. M. le Roi de Serbie et S. M. le Roi des Bulgares, ainsi qu'entre Leurs héritiers et successeurs, Leurs États et sujets respectifs.

Article X

Le présent traité sera ratifié et les ratifications en seront échangées à Bucarest dans le délai de quinze jours ou plus tôt si faire se peut.

En foi de quoi, etc.

Fait à Bucarest le vingt huitième jour du mois de juillet (dixième jour du mois d'août) de l'an mil neuf cent treize.

[Seals of the first plenipotentiaries only, and signatures of the plenipotentiaries of Rumania, Greece, Montenegro,

[1] *Ibid.,* 61.

and Servia to the left, of those of Bulgaria to the right.]

(From the Roumanian counterpart.)

§ 515. *Treaties of Alliance.*

Text of the treaty of alliance of Chaumont, March 1, 1814, is in G. F. de Marten's, *Nouv. Recueil, depuis* 1808 *jusqu' à présent*, i. 683. There were 6 originals, Austria and Russia, Austria and Great Britain, Austria and Prussia, Russia and Great Britain, Russia and Prussia, Great Britain and Prussia.

Traité d'Alliance entre l'Allemagne et l'Autriche-Hongrie.—Signé à Vienne le 7 octobre, 1879.

In Erwägung, dass Ihre Majestäten der Deutsche Kaiser, König von Preussen, und der Kaiser von Oesterreich, König von Ungarn, es als Ihre unabweisliche Monarchenpflicht erachten müssen, für die Sicherheit ihrer Reiche und die Ruhe ihrer Völker unter allen Umständen Sorge zu tragen :

In Erwägung, dass beide Monarchen ähnlich wie in dem früher bestandenen Bundesverhältnisse, durch festes Zusammenhalten beider Reiche, im Stande sein werden, diese Pflicht leichter und wirksamer zu erfüllen ;

In Erwägung schliesslich, dass ein inniges Zusammengehen von Deutschland und Oesterreich-Ungarn Niemanden bedrohen kann, wohl aber geeignet ist, den durch die Berliner Stipulationen geschaffenen europäischen Frieden zu konsolidieren,

haben Ihre Majestäten

der Kaiser von Deutschland und

der Kaiser von Oesterreich, König von Ungarn,

indem Sie Einander feierlich versprechen, dass sie ihrem rein defensiven Abkommen eine agressive Tendenz nach keiner Richtung jemals beilegen wollen, einen Bund des Friedens und der gegenseitigen Vertheidigung zu knüpfen beschlossen.

Zu diesem zwecke haben Allerhöchstdieselben zu Ihren Bevollmächtigten ernannt :

Se. Majestät der Deutsche Kaiser

Allerhöchstihren ausserordentlichen und bevollmächtigten Botschafter General-Lieutenant Prinzen Heinrich VII., Reuss, etc., etc.

Se. Majestät der Kaiser von Oesterreich, König von Ungarn, Allerhöchstihren Wirklichen Geheimen Rath, Minister des Kaiserlichen Hauses und des Aeusseren, Feldmarschall-Lieutenant Julius Grafen Andrassy von Csik-Szent-Kiràly und Krasna Horka, etc., etc.

welche sich zu Wien am heutigen Tage vereinigt haben und nach Austausch ihrer gut und genügend befundenen Vollmachten übereingekommen sind, wie folgt :

Artikel I

Sollte wider Verhoffen und gegen den aufrichtigen Wunsch der beiden Hohen Kontrahenten Eines der beiden Reiche von Seiten Russlands angegriffen werden, so sind die Hohen Kontrahenten verpflichtet, Einander mit der gesammten Kriegsmacht Ihrer Reiche beizustehen und demgemäss den Frieden nur gemeinsam und übereinstimmend zu schliessen.

Artikel II

Würde einer der Hohen Kontrahirenden Theile von einer anderen Macht angegriffen werden, so verpflichtet hiermit der andere Hohe Kontrahent, dem Angreifer gegen seinen Hohen Verbündeten nicht nur nicht beizustehen, sondern mindestens eine wohlwollende neutrale Haltung gegen den Hohen Mitkontrahenten zu beobachten.

Wenn jedoch in solchem Falle die angreifende Macht von Seite Russlands, sei es in Form einer aktiven Kooperation, sei es durch militärische Massnahmen, welche den Angegriffenen bedrohen, unterstützt werden sollte, so tritt die im Artikel I dieses Vertrages stipulirte Verpflichtung des gegenseitigen Beistandes mit voller Heeresmacht auch in diesem Falle sofort in Kraft und die Kriegführung der beiden Hohen Kontrahenten wird auch dann eine gemeinsame bis zum gemeinsamen Friedensschluss.

Artikel III

Dieser Vertrag soll in Gemässheit seines friedlichen Charakters und um jede Missdeutung auszuschliessen von beiden Hohen Kontrahenten geheimgehalten und einer dritten Macht nur im Einverständnisse beider Theile und nach Massgabe spezieller Einigung mitgetheilt werden.

Beide Hohen kontrahenten geben Sich nach der bei der Begegnung in Alexandrowo ausgesprochenen Gesinnungen des Kaisers Alexander der Hoffnung hin, dass die Rüstungen Russlands sich als bedrohlich für Sie in Wirklichkeit nicht

TREATIES 233

erweisen werden, und haben aus diesem Grunde zu einer Mittheilung für jetzt keinen Anlass,—sollte sich aber diese Hoffnung wider Erwarten als eine irrthümliche erweisen, so würden die beiden Hohen Kontrahenten es als eine Pflicht der Loyalität erkennen, den Kaiser Alexander mindestens vertraulich darüber zu verständigen, dass Sie einen Angriff auf einen von Ihnen als gegen Beide gerichtet betrachten müssten.

Urkund dessen haben die Vollmächtigten diesen Vertrag eigenhändig unterschrieben und Ihre Wappen beigedrückt.

Geschehen zu Wien, am 7 October, 1879.[1]

[Seals and signatures.]

ANNEXATION

§ 518. *Treaty between Japan and Corea.*—Signed at Seoul, August 22, 1910.

Preamble : (Translation).

H.M. the Emperor of Japan and H.M. the Emperor of Corea, having in view the special and close relations between their respective countries, desiring to promote the common weal of the two nations and to assure permanent peace in the Extreme East, and being convinced that these objects can be best obtained by the annexation of Corea to the Empire of Japan, have resolved to conclude a Treaty of such annexation and have, for that purpose, appointed as their plenipotentiaries, that is to say :—

[High contracting parties ; names and official description of plenipotentiaries.]

Who upon mutual conference and deliberation have agreed to the following Articles :—

Art. 8. This Treaty, having been approved by H.M. the Emperor of Japan and H.M. the Emperor of Corea, shall take effect from the date of its promulgation.

In witness whereof, etc.[2]

[Date and signatures.]

(Promulgated August 29, 1910.)[3]

[1] *Nouv. Rec. Gén.* 2ème série xv. 471 ; English translation in *Brit. and For. State Papers,* lxxiii. 270.
[2] *Brit. and For. State Papers,* ciii. 992.
[3] Although described as "annexation," this transaction would technically fall under the heading of merger.

BOUNDARY TREATY

§ 519. *Between Great Britain and the United States.*

Preamble.

H.M. the King of Great Britain and Ireland and of the British Dominions beyond the Seas, Emperor of India, and the United States of America, being equally desirous of fixing and defining the location of the international boundary line between the United States and the Dominion of Canada in Passamaquoddy Bay and to the middle of Great Manan Channel, and of removing all causes of dispute in connection therewith, have for that purpose resolved to conclude a Treaty, and to that end have appointed as their Plenipotentiaries : H.B.M. : [name, decoration, and official designation].

The President of the United States of America : [name and official designation].

Who, after having communicated, etc. . . .

This Treaty shall be ratified by H.B.M. and by the President of the United States, by and with the advice and consent of the Senate thereof, and the ratifications shall be exchanged in Washington as soon as practicable.

In faith whereof, etc.

Done at Washington the 21st day of May, in the year of our Lord, 1910.[1]

[*Seals and signatures.*]

§ 520. *La France et les Pays-Bas.*—Courtray, March 28, 1820 (in French).

S.M. le Roi de France et Navarre et S.M. le Roi des Pays-Bas, Prince d'Orange Nassau, Grand-Duc de Luxembourg, &c. voulant régler tout ce qui a rapport à la délimitation de leurs États respectifs, d'après ce qui est stipulé dans les Traités de Paris du 30 mai, 1814, et du 20 novembre, 1815, et conformément au paragraphe 6 de l'Article 1 du dernier Traité, ont à cet effet, nommé des Commissaires, savoir :

S.M. Très-Chrétienne [name, official designation and decorations].

Et S.M. le Roi des Pays-Bas [name, official designation and decorations].

Lesquels, après avoir échangé leurs plein pouvoirs, etc.

---

[1] *Brit. and For. State Papers*, ciii. 319.

LXXIII. Le présent Traité de Limites sera ratifié par les Hautes Parties Contractantes, et l'échange des ratifications se fera[1] dans l'espace de six semaines, à compter du jour de sa signature, ou plus tôt, si faire se peut.

En foi de quoi, nous avons signé le présent Traité et y avons apposé le cachet de nos armes.

Fait à Courtray, le 28 mars, 1820.[2]

[*Seals and signatures.*]

SUPPRESSION OF THE SLAVE TRADE

§ 521. *Between Great Britain, Austria, France, Prussia and Russia.*—Signed at London, December 20, 1841. (In both English and French, in parallel columns.)

Preamble.

Au nom de la Très Sainte et Indivisible Trinité.

LL. MM. l'Empereur d'Autriche, Roi de Hongrie et de Bohême, le Roi de Prusse et l'Empereur de toutes les Russies, voulant donner un plein et entier effet aux principes déjà énoncés dans les déclarations solennelles faites par l'Autriche, la Prusse et la Russie, d'accord avec d'autres Puissances Européennes au Congrès de Vienne, le 8 février, 1815, et au Congrès de Vérone le 28 novembre 1822,—déclarations par lesquelles les dites Puissances ont annoncé qu'elles étaient prêtes à concourir à tout ce qui pourrait assurer et accélérer l'abolition de la Traite des Nègres ; et LL. MM. ayant été invitées par S.M. la Reine du Royaume Uni de la Grande Bretagne et d'Irlande, et par S.M. le Roi des Français, à conclure un Traité pour la suppression plus efficace de la Traite, leurs dites MM. ont résolu de négocier et de conclure ensemble un Traité pour l'abolition finale de ce traffic ; et à cet effet elles ont nommé pour leurs Plénipotentiaires, savoir :

S.M. la Reine etc. [names, titles, decorations and official designations] :

S.M. l'Empereur d'Autriche, etc. etc. . . .

[And the other sovereigns and plenipotentiaries in their proper order.]

Lesquels, après s'être communiqué leurs pleins pouvoirs, trouvés en bonne et due forme, ont arrêté et signé les Articles suivants :—

[No limit of duration.]

---

[1] No mention of place.
[2] *Brit. and For. State Papers,* lv. 395.

XIX. Le présent Traité, consistant en 19 Articles, sera ratifié, et les les ratifications en seront échangées à Londres, à l'expiration de 2 mois, à compter de ce jour, ou plus tôt si faire se peut.

En foi de quoi, les Plénipotentiaires respectifs ont signé le présent Traité, en texte Anglais et Français, et y ont apposé le sceau de leurs armes.

Fait à Londres, le 20 Décembre, l'an de Grace, 1841.[1]

[*Seals and signatures.*]

(Order of signature, Great Britain, Austria, France, Prussia and Russia. The English text also signed in the same order. From the British counterpart.)

EXTRADITION

§ 522. *Between the United States of America and Paraguay.*—Signed at Asuncion, March 26, 1913.

Preamble.

Extradition Treaty between the United States of America and the Republic of Paraguay.

The United States of America and the Republic of Paraguay, desiring to strengthen their friendly relations and to promote the cause of justice, have resolved to conclude a treaty for the extradition of fugitives from justice, between the United States of America and the Republic of Paraguay, and have appointed for that purpose the following Plenipotentiaries :—

The President of the United States of America [name and official designation] ; and

The President of Paraguay [name and official designation] ; Who, etc. . . .

Art. VIII. " Under this Convention, neither of the Contracting Parties shall be bound to deliver up its own citizens."[2]

The instrument is designated " convention " in other articles where it is specifically referred to, except in Article XIV providing for its coming into force on the day of exchange of ratifications, where it is again styled a " treaty." [To expire after six months from the date

[1] *Brit. and For. State Papers,* xxx. 269.
[2] *Nouveau Recueil Général,* 3ème série, viii. 364.

on which either party gives notice to terminate.] (In English and Spanish in parallel columns. Only one set of seals and signatures.)

Out of thirty-one instruments providing for the extradition of criminals, examined by the writer, eighteen are styled convention, thirteen are treaties. The exception, exempting from extradition the subjects or citizens of the respective high contracting parties, is inserted in every one of these. Many of these instruments remain in force till six months after notice to terminate given by either party, others for periods of five years subject to six months' notice given before the end of any such period ; others for ten years and after that continuously with right to give six months' or one year's notice.

COMMERCE AND NAVIGATION

§ 523. *Treaty of Commerce between Great Britain and the Republic of Bolivia.*—Signed at La Paz, August 1911.

(English and Spanish in parallel columns, with only one set of seals and signatures.)

Preamble in the usual form.

Article X

" The High Contracting Parties agree that during the period of existence of this Treaty they mutually abstain from diplomatic intervention in cases of claims or complaints on the part of private individuals affecting civil or criminal matters in respect of which legal remedies are provided.

" They reserve, however, the right to exercise such intervention in any case in which there may be evidence of delay in legal or judicial proceedings, denial of justice, failure to give effect to a sentence obtained in his favour by one of their nationals or violation of the principles of international law."

Article XV

" The stipulations of the present Treaty shall not be applicable to any of H.B.M.'s Colonies or Possessions beyond the seas unless notice to that effect shall have been given, on behalf of any such Colony or Possession by H.B.M.'s Representative in the Republic of Bolivia to the Bolivian

Minister for Foreign Affairs, within one year from the date of the exchange of the ratifications of the present Treaty.

" Nevertheless, subject to the provisions of Article XIV,[1] the goods produced or manufactured in any of H.B.M.'s Colonies, Possessions, and Protectorates shall enjoy in Bolivia complete and unconditional most-favoured-nation treatment so long as such Colony, Possession, or Protectorate shall accord to goods the produce or manufacture of Bolivia treatment as favourable as it gives to the produce or manufacture of any other foreign country."

Art. XIV. [Duration to be ten years from exchange of ratifications, and afterwards for one year from the date on which either party gives notice to terminate.]

[Ratifications to be exchanged in London within one year from the date of signature.]

" Done in duplicate, in English and Spanish, this first day of August in the year one thousand eight hundred and eleven."

The corresponding paragraph in Spanish is fuller :—

" Hecho en dos ejemplares, en inglés y castellano, de un mismo tenor, en la ciudad de La Paz el día 1° de Agosto de mil novecientos once." [2]

§ 524. *Treaty of Commerce and Navigation between Belgium and Norway.*—Signed at Brussels, September 25, 1911. In French. Preamble in the usual form. Article XX provides that in case of a difference of opinion with regard to the interpretation or application of the treaty, recourse shall be had to arbitration by a tribunal composed of three members, two chosen outside the " nationals " and inhabitants of the two countries, who shall choose the third ; if they cannot agree on the choice, the third shall be chosen by a government

---

[1] " The stipulations contained in this Treaty shall not apply to cases in which the Government of the Republic of Bolivia may accord special favours, exemptions, and privileges to the citizens or products of conterminous States in the matter of commerce. Such favours cannot be claimed on behalf of Great Britain on the ground of most-favoured-nation rights, as long as they are not conceded to any other non-conterminous State.

[2] *Nouveau Recueil Général*, 3ème série, viii. 822 ; *Brit. and For. State Papers*, civ. 132.

designated by the two arbitrators, and if they are unable to agree, then by lot. The treaty to come into force ten days after the exchange of ratifications, and to remain in force for ten years. If neither party gives notice to terminate twelve months before the end of the period, it will remain in force until one year after one or other of the contracting parties shall have given notice.[1]

This provision is generally adopted in treaties of commerce and navigation, the original period of duration varying from five to ten or twelve years. The longer period is the more usual.

ARBITRATION

§ 525. Agreements to refer disputed questions to arbitration seldom take the name of " Treaty." Out of ninety such compacts enumerated in the volume entitled *Traités Généraux d'Arbitrage communiqués au Bureau International de la Cour Permanente d'Arbitrage*, Première Série (La Haye, 1911), only seven are so entitled. The remainder are styled " Convention " (but sometimes also " Arrangement "). However designated, they have always been concluded for a term of years, mostly for five, sometimes for ten. When there is no provision for continuance if notice is not given of intention to terminate, renewal is usually effected by an Exchange of Notes.

The seven treaties are : the Argentine Republic and the Oriental Republic of the Uruguay, June 8, 1899 ; Spain and the United States of Mexico, January 11, 1902 ; The Oriental Republic of the Uruguay, Argentina, Bolivia, Guatemala, Salvador, Santo Domingo, Mexico, Paraguay and Peru, January 29, 1902 ; Spain and Bolivia, February 17, 1902 ; Spain and Guatemala, February 28, 1902 ; Bolivia and Brazil, June 25, 1909, and Italy and the Netherlands, November 20, 1909. The Treaty of Friendship, Commerce and Navigation

---

[1] *Brit. and For. State Papers*, ciii. 578.

between Honduras and Mexico of March 24, 1908,[1] contains in Article 1 provisions for the reference of disputes to arbitration.

Strictly speaking, none of these treaties, conventions or arrangements, provide generally for reference of disputes to arbitration, for all but five except matters affecting the vital interests, independence or honour of the contracting parties.

§ 526. An attempt to remove this exception was made in a treaty between Great Britain and the United States signed at Washington, August 3, 1911.

Preamble.

The United States of America and H.M. the King of Great Britain and Ireland, and of the British Dominions beyond the Seas, Emperor of India, being equally desirous of perpetuating the peace, which has happily existed between the two nations as established in 1814 by the Treaty of Ghent, and has never since been interrupted by an appeal to arms, and which has been confirmed and strengthened in recent years by a number of Treaties whereby pending Controversies have been adjusted by agreement or settled by arbitration or otherwise provided for ; so that now, for the first time, there are no important questions of difference outstanding between them, and being resolved that no future differences shall be a cause of hostilities between them or interrupt their good relations and friendship ;

The High Contracting Parties have therefore determined, in furtherance of these ends, to conclude a Treaty extending the scope and obligations of the policy of arbitration adopted in their present Arbitration Treaty [2] of the 4th April, 1908, so as to exclude certain exceptions contained in that Treaty and to provide means for the peaceful solution of all questions of difference which it shall be found impossible in future to settle by diplomacy and for that purpose they have appointed as their respective plenipotentiaries :

The President of the United States of America, the Hon. Philander C. Knox, Secretary of State of the United States, and H.B.M., the Right Honourable James Bryce, O.M., His Ambassador Extraordinary and Plenipotentiary at Washington ; who having, etc. . . .

---

[1] *Nouveau Recueil Général*, 3ème série, viii. 398.
[2] To be exact, the compact in question was a " Convention."

Art. VII. The present Treaty shall be ratified by the President of the United States of America, by and with the advice and consent of the Senate thereof, and by H.B.M. The ratifications shall be exchanged at Washington as soon as possible, and the Treaty shall take effect on the date of the exchange of its ratifications. It shall thereafter continue in force continuously, unless and until terminated by twenty-four months' written notice given by either High Contracting Party to the other,

In faith whereof, etc.[1]

[*Seals and signatures.*]

This treaty did not come into operation.

REPATRIATION

§ 527. The treaties between Switzerland and the Netherlands providing for the repatriation of the subjects or citizens of the one country when expelled from the other, May 7, 1910, and the treaty between the Netherlands and France for the repatriation of persons of unsound mind, of February 11, 1911, have no limit of duration, nor are they subject to notice to terminate. They are in form perpetual.[2]

CONVENTIONS

§ 528. Convention is an adaptation of the Latin word *conventio*, compact, covenant.

As has been stated in the Section concerning Treaties, there are several classes of subjects which are also dealt with in the shape of conventions. Amongst these we find *Arbitration* (Austria-Hungary and Brazil, October 19, 1910, in *Nouveau Recueil Général*, etc., 3ème série, viii. 159; Brazil and Venezuela, April 30, 1909, *ibid.*, vi. 20); *Boundaries* (Germany and Belgium, frontiers of the German Protectorate of East Africa and the Belgian Colony of the Congo, August 11, 1910, *Nouv. Rec. Gén.*, 3ème série, vii. 366, no limit of duration); *Commerce*, (Norway and Rumania, March 18/31, 1910, *Brit. and*

---

[1] *Brit. and For. State Papers*, civ. 308.
[2] *Nouveau Recueil Général*, etc., 3ème série, vii. 284.

For. State Papers, ciii. 398 ; France and Japan, August 19, 1911, *Nouv. Rec. Gén.*, 3ème série, viii. 867) ; *Extradition* (Austria-Hungary and Bulgaria, May 18/31, 1911, *Nouv. Rec. Gén.*, 3ème série, viii. 575) ; *Junction of Railways at Common Frontier* (Austria-Hungary and Italy, November 26, 1910, *Nouv. Rec. Gén.*, 3ème série, 804, no limit of duration), and the *Slave Trade* (Great Britain and Germany, March 29, 1879, *Brit. and For. State Papers*, lxx. 34, without any limit of duration). These are merely examples ; to enumerate all that are now in force would take up an undue amount of space.

Next there are such conventions as the following : *Assistance judiciaire* (Austria-Hungary, Austria, Hungary[1] and Serbia, March 30/17, 1911, *Nouv. Rec. Gén.*, 3ème série, 575) ; *Consular Conventions* (United States and Sweden, June 1910, *Nouv. Rec. Gén.*, vii. 516 ; Austria-Hungary and Bulgaria, May 31/18, 1911 ; *Brit. and For. State Papers*, civ. 695) ; *Diplomatic and Consular Marriages* (Italy and Mexico, December 6, 1910, no limit of duration, *Nouv. Rec. Gén.*, vii. 824) ; *Reciprocal admission of physicians, surgeons, midwives and veterinary surgeons to practice in frontier communes* (France and Belgium, October 25, 1910, *Nouv. Rec. Gén.*, vii. 799) ; *Fisheries in Territorial Waters* (Denmark with Sweden and Norway, July 14, 1899, *Brit. and For. State Papers*, civ. 912) ; *Effect of Naturalization*, i.e. position of the children of French parents naturalized in Switzerland as regards military service (France and Switzerland, July 23, 1879, *Brit. and For. State Papers*, lxx. 879 ; *i.e.* naturalization of emigrants (United States and Nicaragua, December 7, 1908, *Nouv. Rec. Gén.*, 3ème série, vi. 464) ; *Succession to Personal Property* (Germany and Greece, December 1/November 18, 1910, *Nouv. Rec. Gén.*, 3ème série, vii. 814).

Military Conventions (Bulgaria and Serbia, June 19,

---

[1] Austria-Hungary, Austria and Hungary contracting as three separate parties.

1912, *Nouv. Rec. Gén.*, 3ème série, vii. 7 ; Bulgaria and Greece, September 22, 1912, *ibid.*, 14).

There are also a considerable number of conventions between more than two States. Among these may be mentioned the following :—*Concernant les conflits des lois relatifs aux effets du mariage sur les droits et devoirs des époux dans leur rapport personnel et sur les biens des époux* (Germany, Belgium, France, Italy, Netherlands, Portugal, Rumania and Sweden, July 17, 1905, *Nouv. Rec. Gén.*, vi. 480) ; *Status of Naturalized Citizens who again take up their residence in the Country of their Origin* (United States of America and seventeen Republics of Latin America, August 13, 1906, *Brit. and For. State Papers*, ciii. 1010, notice to terminate may be given by any contracting party) ; *Répression de la Traite des Blanches* (entre la Grande Bretagne et 13 autres Puissances, 4 mai, 1910, notice may be given by any contracting party, *ibid.*, 244) ; *l'Unification de certaines Règles en matière d'Abordage* (Grande-Bretagne et 23 autres Puissances, 23 septembre, 1910, faculté de dénoncer pour toute haute partie contractante, *Brit. and For. State Papers*, ciii. 434) ; *l'Unification de certaines Règles en matière d'Assistance et de Sauvetage maritimes* (mêmes Puissances, et même date, *ibid.*, 441) ; *Protection de la Propriété industrielle*, 2 juin, 1911, denonciation facultative pour chaque Puissance, *Brit. and For. State Papers*, civ. 116) ; *Measures for the Preservation and Protection of the Fur Seals in the North Pacific Ocean* (Great Britain, the United States, Japan and Russia, July 7, 1911, for fifteen years, with right to give one year's written notice of termination at the end of fourteen years, and also to request a conference for extension, *Brit. and For. State Papers*, civ. 175).

There are also the conventions signed at the First and Second Hague Peace Conference for the Pacific Settlement of International Disputes, the Recovery of Contract Debts, the Commencement of Hostilities, the Laws and Customs of War on Land, and nine others all relating to operations of war, their conditions and consequences. These latter conventions remain in force and are binding on all the Powers who have ratified them and have not made use of the right to give one year's notice of withdrawal, but are not to be operative in a war between belligerents of whom any is not a party to these conventions.[1]

When international conventions are signed between a considerable number of Powers, it is usual to have one original, of which a certified copy is furnished to each signatory State. It will also be observed that nearly all conventions have a preamble like that of a treaty, and that the concluding articles respecting ratification are similar. They are signed and sealed in the same manner as treaties, with equally strict observation of the rules of the *alternat*.

§ 529. An exception to the usual practice of naming the plenipotentiaries in the preamble is the following Convention for the organization of a French Protectorate in Morocco.

Preamble—

Le Gouvernement de la République française et le gouvernement de S.M. Chérifienne, soucieux d'établir au Maroc un régime régulier, fondé sur l'ordre intérieur et la sécurité générale, qui permette l'introduction des réformes et assure le développement économique du pays, sont convenus des dispositions suivantes :

Article 4. Les mesures que nécessitera le nouveau régime de protectorat seront édictées, sur la proposition du Gouvernement français, par S.M. Chérifienne ou par les autorités auxquelles elle en aura délégué le pouvoir. Il en sera de même des règlements nouveaux et des modifications aux règlements existants.

Article 9. La présente convention sera soumise à la ratification du Gouvernement de la République française et l'instrument de ladite ratification sera remis à S.M. le Sultan dans le plus bref délai possible.

[1] A. Pearce Higgins, *Hague Peace Conferences*.

En foi de quoi, les soussignés ont dressé le présent acte et l'ont revêtu de leurs cachets.

Fait à Fez, le 30 mars 1912.

(L.S.)   REGNAULT.

(L. S.)   MOULAY ABD EL HAFID.[1]

ADDITIONAL ARTICLES

§ 530. Compare the additional articles of May 30, 1814, and November 20, 1815, where the wording is " aura la même force et valeur que s'il était inséré mot-a-mot au Traité de ce jour. Il sera compris dans la Ratification dudit Traité (*Brit. and For. State Papers*, i. 172, and iii. 292).

Articles additionels à la Convention de Commerce franco-danoise du 9 février, 1842.—Signés à Copenhague, le 9 février, 1910.

Les Soussignés [names and official designations] dûment autorisés à cet effet, sont convenus des articles additionels suivants à la Convention de Commerce et de Navigation, signée à Paris, le 9 février, 1842.

[Articles I and II]

III. Les présents articles auront la même force et valeur que s'ils faisaient partie intégrale de la Convention précitée du 9 février, 1842 ; ils seront appliqués dans les mêmes limites géographiques et cesseront leurs effets en même temps que ladite Convention en cas où celle-ci viendrait à être dénoncée.

IV. Les présents articles, expédiés en double, entreront en vigueur un mois après leur signature,[2]

[*Place, date.*]

[*Seals and signatures.*]

It will be observed that here is no provision for ratification.

§ 531. The Acte additional à la Convention sur la péche entre la Suisse et l'Italie, signé à Rome, le 8 février, 1911, may be classed with the foregoing.

---

[1] *Nouveau Recueil Général*, 3ème série, vi. 332.

[2] *Brit. and For. State Papers*, ciii. 417 ; *Nouveau Recueil Général*, 3ème série, vi. 889.

Preamble.

Allo scopo di risolvere alcune questioni sorte nella applicazione della convenzione fra l'Italia e la Svizzera, conclusa a Lugano il 13 giugno 1906 e le cui ratifiche furono scambiate il 27 luglio 1906 in Roma, per l'esercizio della pesca nelle acque comuni ai due Stati,

i sottoscritti, in nome dei loro governi, e debitamente all' uopo autorizzati, hanno convenuto quanto segue :

[*Articles I to VIII*]

IX. Il presente atto addizionale sarà ratificato e le ratifiche saranno scambiate il piú presto possibile.

Fatto a Roma, in doppio esemplare, l'8 febbraio 1911.[1]

[*Official designations and signatures.*]

In this case ratification was considered necessary.

" ACTE FINAL "

§ 532. *Acte Final*, or Final Instrument, is a statement winding up the proceedings of a Congress or Conference and containing a summary of the separate treaties or conventions which have been adopted. It is sometimes called *Acte Général*. Usually an article is inserted declaring that the separate treaties or conventions summarized and annexed thereto have the same force as if they had been textually included. Thus in 1815 the *Acte Final*[2] of the Congress of Vienna states that—

" Les Puissances qui ont signé le traité conclu à Paris le 30 mai 1814, s'étant réunies à Vienne, en conformité de l'article XXXII de cet acte, avec les Princes et États leurs alliés . . . désirant maintenant de comprendre dans une transaction commune les différents résultats de leurs négociations, afin de les revêtir de leurs ratifications réciproques, ont autorisé leurs plénipotentiaires à réunir dans un instrument général les dispositions d'un intérêt majeur et permanent, et à joindre à cet acte, comme parties intégrantes des arrangements du Congrès, les traités, conventions, déclarations, règlements et autres actes particuliers, tels qu'ils se trouvent cités dans le présent traité . . .

[1] *Nouveau Recueil Général*, etc., 3ème série, vii. 867.

[2] Treaty, as it is called in the preamble ; in Art. xcviii, it is described as *Acte*, and as *traité général*.

Art. 117. Les règlements particuliers relatifs à la navigation du Rhin, du Necker, du Mein, de la Moselle, de la Meuse
et de l'Escaut, tels qu'ils se trouvent joints au présent acte,
auront la même force et valeur que s'ils avaient été textuellement insérés.

Art. 118. Les traités, conventions, déclarations, règlements
et autres actes particuliers qui se trouvent annexés au présent
acte, et nommément :

[1 to 17] sont considérés comme parties intégrantes des
arrangements du Congrès, et auront partout la même force
et valeur que s'ils étaient insérés mot à mot dans le traité
général." [1]

§ 533. *Conférence Internationale de la Paix*, 1899. [2]

Preamble relates how the Conference was invited and
where it met.

Then follow the names of the delegates representing
each Power that had taken part.

Enumeration of the Conventions and Declarations
annexed.

But, as the Conventions and Declarations were to
remain open for signature until December 31, 1899, they
could obviously not be declared to form an integral part
of the Acte Final.

Resolution adopted : that the Conference considers
the limitation of the charges which lie heavy on the world
is greatly to be desired for the increase of the material
and moral welfare of humanity.

Six recommendations (*vœux*) En foi de quoi, les Plénipotentiaires ont signé le présent acte et y ont apposé
leurs cachets.

Fait à La Haye le 29 juillet, 1899, en un seul exemplaire qui
sera déposé au Ministère des Affaires Etrangères et dont des
copies, certifiées conformes, seront délivrées à toutes les
Puissances représentées à la Conférence.

[*Signatures.*]

[1] Cited by Pradier-Fodéré, ii. 417n.
[2] See a volume entitled accordingly. La Haye, 18 mai/29 juillet,
1899, Ministère des Affaires Etrangères, nouvelle édition. La Haye,
Martinus Nijhoff, 1907.

The Acte Final of the Second International Peace Conference was drawn up in precisely the same form.

§ 534. Under the heading of Acte Final may properly be included the Acte Général of the Conference of Berlin (*q.v.*) signed in that capital February 26, 1885. It was, in fact, spoken of as the Acte Final, until in the course of the ninth protocol, of February 23, its designation was changed.

This document is headed—

Au nom de Dieu Tout-Puissant.

Then comes the enumeration of the Powers that took part in the conference : the object with which it had been called together ; the names of the plenipotentiaries of the respective Sovereigns and Presidents ; who, furnished with full-powers, found in good and due form, had discussed and adopted in succession, three declarations, which are enumerated and described, an " Acte de Navigation du Congo." " Un Acte de Navigation du Niger," and a declaration " introduisant dans les rapports internationaux des règles uniformes relatives aux occupations qui pourront avoir lieu à l'avenir sur les côtes du Continent Africain, Et ayant jugé que ces différents documents pourront être utilement coordonnés en un seul instrument, les ont réunis en un Acte Général composé des Articles suivants :—of which the first three Declarations form chapters i. to iii., the two Actes de Navigation become chapters iv. and v., and the last-named declaration is converted into chapter vi. Chapter vii. consists of General Provisions, including the faculty of acceding (*adhérer*) to non-signatory Powers, ratification, and transmission of instruments of ratification to the German Government, in whose archives they would be deposited. Finally—

En foi de quoi, etc.

" Fait à Berlin, le 26ᵉ jour du mois de février, 1885." [1]

[*Seals and Signatures.*]

The whole is divided into thirty-eight articles or paragraphs, irrespective of the numbering of the chapters.

As all these agreements were actually embodied in the *Acte Général* it was not necessary to add a statement that they formed an integral part thereof.

[1] *Brit. and For. State Papers*, lxxxvi. 4.

CHAPTER XXVIII

TREATIES AND OTHER INTERNATIONAL COMPACTS (*contd.*)
DECLARATION, AGREEMENT, ARRANGEMENT

DECLARATION

§ 535. THIS term is applied in three different senses : (1)
as " the title of a body of stipulations of a treaty according to which the parties engage themselves to pursue
in future a certain line of conduct. The Declaration of
Paris, 1856, the Declaration of St. Petersburg, 1868,
and the Declaration of London, 1909, are instances of
this. Declarations of this kind differ in no [essential]
respect from Treaties. (2) One speaks of declarations
when States communicate to other States or *urbi et orbi*
an explanation and justification of a line of conduct
pursued by them in the past, or an explanation of views
and intentions concerning certain matters. Declarations of this kind may be very important, but they

hardly comprise transactions out of which rights and duties of other States follow. (3) But there is a third kind of Declaration out of which rights and duties do follow for other States, and it is this kind which comprises a specific international transaction, although the different declarations belonging to this group are by no means of a uniform character. Declarations of this kind are, declarations of war, declarations on the part of belligerents concerning the goods they will condemn as contraband, declarations at the outbreak of war on the part of third States that they will remain neutral, and so forth."

" The attempt to distinguish fundamentally between a ' Declaration ' and a ' Convention ' by maintaining that whereas a ' Convention creates rules of particular International Law between the contracting States only, a " Declaration " contains the recognition, on the part of the best qualified and most interested Powers, of rules of universal International Law,' does not stand the test of scientific criticism." [1]

The term Declaration is here used only in the sense of (1).

International agreements involving matters of the highest importance are also recorded in the form of a Declaration, of which some useful examples are here given :—

§ 536. The so-called " Declaration of Paris " of 1856, in an annex to Protocole No. 23 of the Conferences held at Paris relative to the General Treaty of Peace after the Crimean War. A paragraph by way of supplement to this declaration was inserted in Protocole No. 24, and both are reprinted here, because the text-books of International Law generally omit the second document. [2]

[1] Oppenheim, 2nd edit. §§ 487, 508.
[2] *Parliamentary Papers*, 1856.

Annexe au Protocole No. 23.[1]

Déclaration.

Les Plénipotentiaires qui ont signé le Traité de Paris du trente mars, mil huit cent cinquante-six, réunis en Conférence,
Considérant :—

Que le droit maritime, en temps de guerre, a été pendant longtemps l'objet de contestations regrettables ;

Que l'incertitude du droit et des devoirs en pareille matière, donne lieu, entre les neutres et les belligérants, à des divergences d'opinion qui peuvent faire naître des difficultés sérieuses et même des conflits ;

Qu'il y a avantage, par conséquent, à établir une doctrine uniforme sur un point aussi important ;

Que les Plénipotentiaires assemblés au Congrès de Paris ne sauraient mieux répondre aux intentions dont leurs Gouvernements sont animés, qu'en cherchant à introduire dans les rapports internationaux des principes fixes à cet égard ;

Dûment autorisés, les susdits Plénipotentiaires sont convenus de se concerter sur les moyens d'atteindre ce but ; et étant tombés d'accord ont arrêté la Déclaration solennelle ci-après :—

1. La course est et demeure abolie.

2. Le pavillon couvre la marchandise ennemie, à l'exception de la contrebande de guerre.

3. La marchandise neutre, à l'exception de la contrebande de guerre, n'est pas saisissable sous pavillon ennemi ;

4. Les blocus, pour être obligatoires, doivent être effectifs, c'est à-dire, maintenus par une force suffisante pour interdire réellement l'accès du littoral ennemi.

Les Gouvernements des Plénipotentiaires soussignés s'engagent à porter cette Déclaration à la connaissance des États qui n'ont pas été appelés à participer au Congrès de Paris, et à les inviter à y accéder.

Convaincus que les maximes qu'ils viennent de proclamer ne sauraient être accueillis qu'avec gratitude par le monde entier, les Plénipotentiaires soussignés ne doutent pas que les efforts de leurs Gouvernements pour en généraliser l'adoption ne soient couronnés d'un plein succès.

La présente Déclaration n'est et ne sera obligatoire qu'entre les Puissances qui y ont ou qui y auront accédé.

Fait à Paris, le seize avril, mil huit cent cinquante-six.

[Suivent les signatures].

[1] Proposed by the French Plenipotentiary at the sitting of April 8, 1856.

Extract from Protocole No. 24—
Séance du seize avril, 1856.
" Sur la proposition de M. le Comte Walewski, et reconnaissant qu'il est de l'intérêt commun de maintenir l'indivisibilité
des quatre principes mentionnés à la Déclaration signée en ce
jour, MM. les Plénipotentiaires conviennent que les Puissances
qui l'auront signée ou qui y auront accédé, ne pourront entrer,
à l'avenir, sur l'application du droit des neutres en temps de
guerre, en aucun arrangement qui ne repose à la fois sur les
quatre principes objet de la dite Déclaration."

It should be observed that the plenipotentiaries who
signed the declaration stated themselves to be *dûment
autorisés,* language employed often in protocols, and
considered to be of equal binding force with a statement
that full-powers have been exhibited.

§ 537. Another Declaration of even greater importance
is the " Declaration of London," drawn up with the
forms of a treaty, as the result of the deliberations of the
International Naval Conference held in London, December 1908—February 1909.[1] See § 495 above. It has not
been ratified.

§ 538. A declaration may be annexed to a treaty : for
instance, the following one, signed by the Turkish
minister for Foreign Affairs and the Ambassadors of the
Great Powers at Constantinople who, as mediators, had
negotiated the preliminaries of peace between Turkey and
Greece in 1897, constituting the Ambassadors arbitrators between the two Powers.

Déclaration annexe à l'Acte Préliminaire de Paix du
6/18 septembre, 1897.

En procédant à la signature des Préliminaires de Paix en
date de ce jour, S.E. le Ministre des Affaires Etrangères de
S.M.I. le Sultan déclare que dans la pensée du Gouvernement
Ottoman la médiation qui vient d'être exercée par les Six
Grandes Puissances pour le rétablissement de la paix et pour
la fixation de la base des relations futures entre la Turquie et

---

[1] *Nouveau Recueil Général,* etc., 3ᵗᵐᵉ, série, vii. 39.

la Grèce ne doit en rien influer sur le mandat d'arbitre que les Représentants des dites Puissances peuvent être appelés éventuellement à remplir en vertu de l'Article IX de ces Préliminaires de Paix, et en conséquence les arbitres auront, comme de règle, la plus parfait plénitude d'appréciation des points ou des questions qui leur auront été soumis par les Parties.

LL. EE. les Ambassadeurs prennent acte de cette observation et reconnaissent qu'elle est conforme au sens de l'Article IX [1]

[Signatures, no seals.]

§ 539. Déclaration entre la Belgique et l'Italie concernant l'Article XVI du Traité [Convention] d'Extradition conclu le 15 janvier, 1875 :—signée à Bruxelles, le 10 mars, 1879 (modifying an article of an anterior convention).

Le Gouvernement de S.M. le Roi d'Italie et le Gouvernement de S.M. le Roi des Belges, désirant assurer la pleine exécution de l'Article XVI de la Convention d'Extradition du 15 janvier, 1875, sont convenus de ce qui suit :—

Dans le cas où les frais de voyage et de séjour, alloués en vertu du dit Article XVI et d'après les tarifs ou règlements en vigueur dans le pays où l'audition du témoin aura lieu, ne suffiraient pas pour couvrir des dépenses qui devraient réelement être faites, la différence sera couverte par le Gouvernement requérant.

En foi de quoi les Soussignés ont dressé la présente déclaration, qui aura la même valeur et la même durée que la Convention d'Extradition à laquelle elle se rattache.

Fait en double original à Bruxelles, le 10 mars, 1879.[2]

[Signatures and official designations, no seals.]

§ 540. Substitution of a new article for one of an anterior convention. In this case ratification was held to be necessary.

Déclaration

Les Gouvernements signataires de la Convention conclue à la Haye le 6 mai 1882, pour régler la police de la pêche dans la Mer du Nord, en dehors des eaux territoriales, ayant jugé

[1] *Brit. and For. State Papers*, xc. 549.
[2] Ibid, lxx. 591.

utile de modifier la teneur du paragraphe 5 de l'article 8, sont convenus de ce qui suit :—

Article I

Le paragraphe 5 de l'article 8 de la Convention du 6 mai 1882 est remplacé par la disposition suivante :

.   .   .   .   .   .

Article II

La date de l'entrée en vigueur de la présente déclaration sera fixée lors du dépôt des ratifications, qui aura lieu à la Haye aussitôt que faire se pourra, et de la même manière dont s'est effectué le dépôt des ratifications de la Convention du 6 mai 1882.

En foi de quoi, les Plénipotentiaires respectifs ont signé la présente Déclaration et y ont apposé leur cachets.

Fait à la Haye, le 1er février 1889 en six exemplaires.[1]

[Official designations, seals and signatures. Four of the plenipotentiaries are Envoy and Minister of the Powers they represent, one is a Consul-General, one is the Netherlands minister for Foreign Affairs. It was evidently held that they did not require special full-powers, and they do not even say that they are *dûment autorisés.*]

§ 541. Declaration between the United Kingdom and France respecting Egypt and Morocco, together with the secret articles signed at the same time.—Signed at London, April 8, 1904.[2]

This declaration, of the most far-reaching importance, has no preamble, no full-powers were exhibited, there is no limit of time, except in Article IV, with respect to the trade of both nations with Morocco and Egypt, and no stipulation is made as to ratification. The Secretary of State and the French ambassador simply state that they have been duly authorized to sign.

[1] *Nouveau Recueil Général*, etc., 2ème série, xv. 568.
[2] *Treaty Series*, 1911, No. 24.

[*Article* I–IX]

En foi de quoi S.E. l'Ambassadeur de la République française près S.M. le Roi du Royaume-Uni de la Grande-Bretagne et d'Irlande et des Territoires brittaniques au delà des Mers, Empereur des Indes, et le Principal Secrétaire d'État pour les Affaires Etrangères de S.M.B., dûment autorisés à cet effet, ont signé la présente Déclaration et y ont apposé leurs cachets.

Fait à Londres, en double expédition, le 8 avril, 1904.

[*Seals and signatures.*]

There is an English text, which is printed side by side with the French, the *alternat* being duly observed, in which " British Dominions beyond the Seas " is used where the French has " Territoires," etc. The secret articles have no such concluding clause, but merely the place, date, seals and signatures.

§ 542. *Demarcation of Frontier.*

Articulos declaratorios de la demarcación de fronteras entre la República Argentina y los Estados Unidos del Brasil firmados en Río de Janeiro el 4 de Octobre de 1910.

En la ciudad de Río de Janeiro, á los cuatro dias del mes de Octobre de mil novecientos diez, reunidos en el Palacio Itamaty los Señores [names and official designations], debidamente autorizados, convinieron en los siguientes articulos declaratorios : . . .

En fé de lo cual, los dos Plenipotenciarios, en el día y lugar arriba declarados, firman y sellan con sus respectivos sellos esta Acta en cuatro ejemplares, dos en castellano y dos en portugués, para que en el Ministerio de Relaciones Exteriores de la República y en el del Brasil se conserven dos ejemplares, uno en cada idioma.[1]

[*Seals and signatures.*]

§ 543. Déclaration relative à la délimitation de la frontière entre le Cameroun et l'Afrique équatoriale française ; signée à Paris, le 28 septembre 1912.

---

[1] *Nouveau Recueil Général*, etc., 3ème série, vii. 783.

Consisting of—

(1) Arrangement relatif à la délimitation entre le Cameroun et l'Afrique Equatoriale Française conformément à l'accord du 4 novembre 1911 (37 articles in 4 chapters) ; (2) Arrangement relatif à la remise des territoires à échanger entre le Cameroun en l'Afrique Equatoriale Française (20 articles) (3) Convention relative au régime des concessions (50 articles).

En Foi de quoi les Soussignés ont dressé la présente Déclaration qu'ils ont revêtue de leur sceau.

Fait à Paris, en double exemplaire le 20 septembre 1912.

[*Seals and signatures.*]

The persons signing are not spoken of as plenipotentiaries, nor is it stated even that they are duly authorized by their governments. No full-powers were exhibited, and no provision was made for ratification. This is to be explained by the wording of the preamble :—

" Le Gouvernement de S.M. l'Empereur D'Allemagne, Roi de Prusse [in the German text " Die Kaiserlich Deutsche Regierung "], Et Le Gouvernement De La République Française, désirant, en vue de l'Exécution de la Convention signée à Berlin le 4 novembre 1911,[1] déterminer la frontière entre le Cameroun et l'Afrique Équatoriale Française, préciser les conditions de la remise des territoires échangés et régler certaines questions connexes, ainsi qu'il été prévu par les articles 3 et 5 de la convention du 4 novembre 1911 précitée, sont convenus de ce qui suit : "[2]

§ 544. Another declaration which it was held necessary to ratify is one between Great Britain and Belgium, for the simplification of the procedure for the settlement of differences between British and Belgian fishermen in the North Sea outside territorial waters, and of reducing as much as possible the injuries sustained from the

---

[1] See same collection, v. 651. This was a convention by which the French and German governments, " *Comme suite et complément de la convention du 4 novembre* 1911 *relative au Maroc, et en raison des droits de protection reconnus à la France sur l'Empire chérifien,*" agreed to exchange portions of their territories in Equatorial Africa. In this exchange Germany received, naturally, far more than she gave up. In the German translation *Abkommen* is used to render " *convention.*"

[2] *Nouveau Recueil Général,* 3ème série, vii. 135-88.

fouling of their fishing gear, signed at Brussels May 2, 1891. It is described as being agreed upon by the two governments, and Article VII provides for ratification.

" In witness whereof the undersigned Envoy Extraordinary and Minister Plenipotentiary at Brussels of H.M. the Queen of the United Kingdom of Great Britain and Ireland, and the undersigned Minister for Foreign Affairs of H.M. the King of the Belgians, have drawn up the present declaration in duplicate, and have affixed thereto the seal of their arms." [1]

[*Place, date.*]

[*Seals and signatures.*]

It was signed also in the French language.

§ 544A Declaration between the French, Russian and British Governments of September 5, 1914.

The undersigned duly authorized thereto by their respective Governments, hereby declare as follows :—

The French, Russian, and British Governments mutually engage not to conclude peace separately during the present war.

The three Governments agree that when terms of peace come to be discussed no one of the Allies will demand conditions of peace without the previous agreement of each of the other Allies.

In faith whereof the undersigned have signed this Declaration and have affixed thereto their seals.

Done at London, in triplicate, this 5th day of September, 1914.

PAUL CAMBON [Ambassador].
BENCKENDORFF [Ambassador].
E. GREY [Secretary of State for Foreign Affairs].

Japan adhered to this declaration by an exchange of notes signed October 19, 1915, by K. Inouyé, Japanese Ambassador.

A declaration was signed by the representatives of the above four Powers and of Italy, in quintuplicate, on November 30, 1915, containing the same undertaking.

[1] *Brit. and For. State Papers*, lxxxiii. 23.

AGREEMENT

§ 545. The same absence of strict formality is found in compacts entitled Agreements or Arrangements. No difference is to be discerned between the two, but perhaps the former may seem to indicate a fancied superior degree of binding force. The subject matter with which they deal is of very varying character and importance. What in English is called an Agreement is often styled *"Arrangement"* in French, but also *"Accord."* In German *Vereinbarung* is used for both; so also *Abkommen.* French *" arrangement "* in one document may be rendered *protocolo* in the corresponding Spanish text; *Convenzione* in Italian and *Convenio* in Spanish are found as the equivalents of the English word Agreement, though doubtless a more accurate translation for both would be " convention."

§ 546. *Naval 'force to be maintained by Great Britain and the United States on the American Lakes, made in April* 1817, *and notified by the United States Government April* 28, 1818.

By the President of the United States of America.

A Proclamation.

Whereas an Arrangement [1] was entered into at the City of Washington, in the month of April, in the year of our Lord, 1817, between Richard Rush, Esq., at that time acting as Secretary for the Department of State of the United States, and the Right Honourable Charles Bagot, His Britannic Majesty's Envoy Extraordinary and Minister Plenipotentiary, for and in behalf of His Brittanic Majesty ; which Arrangement is in the words following, to wit :—

" The Naval Force to be maintained upon the American Lakes, by His Majesty and the Government of the United States, shall henceforth be confined to the following Vessels on each side ; that is—

" On Lake Ontario, to 1 Vessel not exceeding 100 tons burden, and armed with 1 eighteen pound cannon.

[1] The arrangement was concluded by an Exchange of Notes, see J. W. Foster, *A Century of American Diplomacy,* 252.

" On the Upper Lakes, to 2 Vessels, not exceeding like burden each, and armed with like force.

" On the Waters of Lake Champlain, to 1 Vessel not exceeding like burden, and armed with like force.

" All other armed Vessels on these Lakes shall be forthwith dismantled, and no other Vessels of War shall be there built or armed.

" If eithei party should hereafter be desirous of annulling this Stipulation, and should give notice to that effect to the other Party, it shall cease to be binding after the expiration of 6 months from the date of such notice.

" The Naval Force so to be limited shall be restricted to such services as will, in no respect, interfere with the proper duties of the Armed Vessels of the other Party."

And whereas, the Senate of the United States have approved of the said Arrangement, and recommended that it should be carried into effect ; and the same having also received the sanction of His Royal Highness the Prince Regent, acting in the name and on the behalf of His Britannic Majesty ;

Now, therefore, I James Monroe, President of the United States, do, by this my Proclamation, make known and declare that the Arrangement aforesaid, and every stipulation thereof, has been duly entered into, concluded, and confirmed, and is of full force and effect.

Given under my hand, at the City of Washington, this 28th day of April, in the year of our Lord, 1818, and of the Independence of the United States the 42nd.

JAMES MONROE.

By the President :
John Quincy Adams, *Secretary of State.*

" A Notice of the intention of the United States to terminate the agreement with Great Britain of 1817, relative to vessels of war on the Great Lakes, was given, pursuant to the reservation of that right, by the Executive on November 23, 1864. A resolution with a view to such termination had during the preceding session of Congress passed the House, but had failed of consideration in the Senate. After the notice had been communicated to the British Government, a joint resolution was passed by Congress, approved February 9, 1865, which " adopted and ratified " the notice " as if the same had been authorized by Congress." Notwithstanding this legislative sanction, the notice was, before the expiration of the required six months, withdrawn by the Executive ; and the arrangement has subsequently been recognized by both Governments as subsisting."

Crandall, *Treaties and their Making and Enforcement*, 1916.

§ 547. *Preliminaries of Peace.*

Preamble.

S.M. le Roi d'Italie et S.M. l'Empereur des Ottomans, animés par un égal désir de faire cesser l'état de guerre existant entre les deux Pays et en vue de la difficulté d'y parvenir, provenant de l'impossibilité pour l'Italie de déroger à la loi du 25 février 1912 qui a proclamé sa souveraineté sur la Tripolitaine et sur la Cyrénaique, et pour l'Empire Ottoman de formellement reconnaître cette souveraineté,

ont nommé Leurs Plénipotentiaires : [1]

lesquels, après avoir échangés leurs pleins pouvoirs respectifs trouvés en bonne et due forme, sont convenus du *modus procedendi* secret suivant—

[I to VII]

" VIII. Les deux Hautes Parties Contractantes s engagent à maintenir secret le présent Accord.

" Toutefois les deux Gouvernements se réservent la faculté de rendre public cet Accord au moment de la présentation du Traité public (Annexe n. 4) aux Parlements respectifs.

" Le présent Accord entrera en vigueur le jour même de sa signature.

" IX. Il est bien entendu que les Annexes mentionnées dans le présent Accord en forment partie intégrante.

" En foi de quoi les Plénipotentiaires ont signé le présent Accord et y ont apposé leurs cachets.

" Fait à Lausanne en deux exemplaires, le 15 octobre 1912." [2]

[Seals and signatures.]

[1] No names given, but evidently the same as in the treaty which bears date three days later.

[2] *Nouveau Recueil Général*, etc., vii. 3.

The foregoing " Accord " has the forms of a treaty, except that it contains no provision for ratification.

§ 549. Political events in the Far East rendered it desirable to extend and develop the provisions of the alliance of 1902, between Great Britain and Japan, in 1905 and 1911 in succession. The Agreement of 1911 was as follows :—

Preamble.

" The Government of Great Britain and the Government of Japan, having in view the important changes which have taken place in the situation since the conclusion of the Anglo-Japanese Agreement of the 12th August, 1905, and believing that a revision of that Agreement responding to such changes would contribute to general stability and repose, have agreed upon the following stipulations to replace the Agreement above mentioned, such stipulations having the same object as the said Agreement, namely :—

" (*a*) The consolidation and maintenance of the general peace in the regions of Eastern Asia and of India ;

" (*b*) The preservation of the common interests of all Powers in China by insuring the independence and integrity of the Chinese Empire and the principle of equal opportunities for the commerce and industry of all nations in China ;

" (*c*) The maintenance of the territorial rights of the High Contracting Parties in the regions of Eastern Asia and India, and the defence of their special interests in the said regions :—

" Art I. It is agreed that whenever, in the opinion of either Great Britain or Japan, any of the rights or interests referred to in the preamble of this Agreement are in jeopardy, the two Governments will communicate with one another fully and frankly, and will consider in common the measures which should be taken to safeguard those menaced rights or interests.

" Art. II.   If by reason of unprovoked attack or aggressive action, whenever arising, on the part of any Power or Powers, either High Contracting Party should be involved in war in defence of its territorial rights or special interests mentioned in the preamble of this Agreement, the other High Contracting Party will at once come to the assistance of its ally, and will conduct the war in common, and make peace in mutual agreement with it.

" Art. III. The High Contracting Parties agree that neither of them will, without consulting the other, enter into separate arrangements with another Power to the prejudice of the objects described in the preamble of this Agreement.

" Art. IV. Should either High Contracting Party conclude a treaty of general arbitration with a third Power, it is agreed that nothing in this Agreement shall entail upon such Contracting Party an obligation to go to war with the Power with whom such treaty of arbitration is in force.[1]

" Art. V. The conditions under which armed assistance shall be afforded by either Power to the other in the circumstances mentioned in the present Agreement, and the means by which such assistance is to be made available, will be arranged by the naval and military authorities of the High Contracting Parties, who will from time to time consult one another fully and freely upon all questions of mutual interest.

" Art. VI. The present Agreement shall come into effect immediately after the date of its signature, and remain in force for ten years from that date.

" In case neither of the High Contracting Parties should have notified twelve months before the expiration of the said ten years the intention of terminating it, it shall remain binding until the expiration of one year from the day on which either of the High Contracting Parties shall have denounced it.[2] But if, when the date fixed for its expiration arrives, either ally is actually engaged in war, the alliance shall, *ipso facto*, continue until peace is concluded.

" In faith whereof the undersigned, duly authorised by their respective Governments, have signed this Agreement, and have affixed thereto their seals.

" Done in duplicate at London, the 13th day of July, 1911.

> " E. GREY, *His Britannic Majesty's Principal Secretary of State for Foreign Affairs.*
>
> ' TAKAAKI KATO, *Ambassador Extraordinary and Plenipotentiary of His Majesty the Emperor of Japan at the Court of St. James.*" [3]

---

[1] Articles III. and IV. of the Agreement of 1905, concerning Japanese interests in Corea and British interests on the frontier of India, were omitted in 1911. So also VI of 1905, respecting a war in which Japan was then engaged. Articles V and VI of 1911 are identical with VII and VIII of 1905.

[2] This is the ordinary form of a clause for automatic renewal.

[3] *Brit. and For. State Papers*, civ. 173 ; compare with xcviii. 136.

Settlement of Claims.

§ 550. *Preamble.*

" Whereas Great Britain and the United States are signatories of the Convention of the 18th October, 1907, for the Pacific Settlement of International Disputes, and are desirous that certain pecuniary claims outstanding between them should be referred to arbitration, as recommended by Article XXXVIII of that Convention :

" Now, therefore, it is agreed that such claims as are contained in the Schedules drawn up as hereinafter provided shall be referred to arbitration under Chapter IV. of the said convention, and subject to the following provisions—

[*Article* I *to* IX]

" X. The present Agreement, and also any Schedules agreed thereunder, shall be binding only when confirmed by the two Governments by an exchange of notes.

" In witness whereof this Agreement has been signed and sealed by [official designation and name] on behalf of [. . .] and by [official designation and name] on behalf of [. . .]

" Done in duplicate at the city of Washington, this 18th day of August, 1910." [1]

[*Seals and signatures.*]

§ 551. *Renewal of Arbitration Convention.*

" Accordo Prorogante la Durata della Convenzione d'Arbitrato del 28 Marzo 1908.

Preamble.

" Il Governo degli Stati Uniti d'America e il Governo di S.M. il Re d'Italia, essendo desiderosi di prorogare il periodo di cinque anni, durante il quale la Convenzione d'Arbitrato conclusa fra essi il 28 Marzo 1908 deve remanere in vigore, il quale periodo sta per spirare, hanno autorizato i sottoscritti, cioè [names, official designations, etc.] a concludere l'accordo seguente :

Articolo I

" La Convenzione d'Arbitrato del 28 Marzo 1908, fra il Governo degli Stati Uniti d'America ed il Governo di S.M. il

[1] *Brit. and For. State Papers*, ciii. 322. The exchange of notes on p. 329 shows that this Agreement and the schedule of Claims were submitted to the Senate for its advice and consent before ratification.

Re d'Italia, la durata della quale a termini dell' Articolo III di essa, era stata fissata ad un periodo di cinque anni dalla data dello scambio delle ratifiche della detta Convenzione, il quale periodo terminerà il 22 Gennaio 1914, viene col presente atto rinnovata e mantenuta in vigore per un nuovo periodo di cinque anni, a datare dal 22 Gennaio 1914.

Articolo II

" Il presente accordo sarà ratificato dal Presidente degli Stati Uniti d'America, in base al parere e col consenso del Senato degli Stati Uniti e dal Governo di S.M. il Re d'Italia in conformità della sua Costituzione e delle sue legge, e diventerà effetivo alla data dello scambio delle ratifiche, il quale avrà luogo a Washington, al più presto possibile.

" Fatto in doppio, nelle lingue inglese ed italiana, a Washington, il ventotto Maggio, Millenovecentotredici." [1]

[Seals and Signatures.]

At p. 704 of the same volume is a precisely similar " Agreement " between the United States and Spain, denominated in the Spanish text " convenio," and the Convention which it purports to prolong is styled " Tratado " in the Spanish version of Article I.

Similar prolongations of treaties and conventions between States, whose constitutions permit of such a method, are often effected by a mere Exchange of Notes.

The agreement between Bolivia and Chile, signed at la Paz, September 10, 1905, for the purpose of defining more clearly Article 8 of the treaty of October 20, 1904, is styled " Acuerdo sobre exención de derechos aduaneros," and terminates with " En fe de lo cual los infrascriptos firman el Presente Protocolo, en doble ejemplar, y lo sellan con sus sellos respectivos."[2]

§ 552. Accord réglant quelques points concernant le chemin de fer du St.-Gothard ; signé à Berne, le 13 octobre 1909. Original text in French ; the translation into German renders " Accord " by *Übereinkommen*.

This document has a preamble in the same form as that

---

[1] *Nouveau Recueil Général*, etc., viii. 703.   [2] *Ibid.*, vi. 608.

of a convention, with the appointment of plenipotentiaries, the exchange of full-powers, and agreement on the
following stipulations. These consist of four articles,
of which the fourth is—

" L'accord constitué par les dispositions ci-haut sera annexé
à la nouvelle convention internationale concernant le chemin
de fer du St.-Gothard et aura la même valeur que ladite
convention.
" En foi de quoi, les Plénipotentiaires ont signé le présent
accord et y ont apposé leurs cachets.
" Fait à Berne, en double expédition, le 13 octobre 1909.
[*Signatures*.]

To this is attached a *procès-verbal* of October 4, 1913.

" Procès-verbal.
" Au moment de procéder à l'échange des ratifications de
la Convention internationale relative au Chemin de fer du
St.-Gothard conclue par la Suisse, l'Allemagne et l'Italie à
Berne le 13 octobre 1909.
Les Représentants soussignés du Conseil Fédéral Suisse et
du Gouvernement Royal Italien constatent que les Actes de
Suisse et d'Italie portant ratification de la dite Convention
contiennent aussi le texte de l'Accord relatif au Chemin de fer
du St.-Gothard conclu entre la Suisse et l'Italie, à Berne, le
13 octobre 1909, et qui a la même valeur que la Convention
internationale susvisée.
" En foi de quoi, le présent Procès-verbal, etc." [1, 2].

This is equivalent therefore to a ratification of the
Agreement.

§ 553. Other Agreements worth noting are : (1)
Accord provisoire de commerce, etc. entre l'Italie et le
Japon, réalisé par un Echange de notes du 12 juillet 1911
(*Nouv. Rec. Gén.* etc., vi. 571) ; (2) Accord au sujet de la
nationalité des personnes se trouvant dans les terri-
toires échangés, le 4 novembre 1911, par l'Allemagne et la

---

[1] *Nouveau Recueil Général*, etc., 3ème série, viii. 210.
[2] *Ibid.*, 195.

France en Afrique équatoriale, in the German translation of which " Accord " is rendered by " Übereinkunft " (*ibid.*, 330) ; and (3) " Agrèement extending the duration of the Arbitration Convention of April 4, 1908," between Great Britain and the United States of America, which by Article II has to be ratified by and with the consent of the Senate of the United States and by H.M. the King of Great Britain and Ireland. It is sealed as well as signed.

ARRANGEMENT

§ 554. The number of compacts to which this designation is given does not appear to be very numerous. Some of them, especially relating to commercial matters, are effected by a simple exchange of notes. Some are entered into subject to the approval of the governments concerned, others require formal ratification. A few examples will be sufficient.

§ 555. Arrangement de Madrid du 14 avril 1891 pour l'enregistrement international des marques de fabrique ou de commerce révisé à Bruxelles le 14 décembre 1900 et à Washington le 2 juin 1911, conclu entre l'Autriche, la Hongrie, la Belgique, le Brésil, Cuba, l'Espagne, la France, l'Italie, le Mexique, les Pays-Bas, le Portugal, la Suisse et la Tunisie.

Preamble.

" Les Soussignés, dûment autorisés par leurs Gouvernements respectifs, ont, d'un commun accord, arrêté le texte suivant, qui remplacera l'Arrangement signé à Madrid le 14 avril 1891 et l'Acte additional signé à Bruxelles le 14 décembre 1900, savoir :

[Articles 1 to 11]

Article 12

" Le présent Arrangement sera ratifié, et les ratifications en seront déposées à Washington au plus tard le 1er avril 1913.
" Il entrera en vigueur un mois à partir de l'expiration de

ce délai, et aura la même force et durée que la Convention générale.

" En foi de quoi, les Plénipotentiaires respectifs ont signé le présent Arrangement.

" Fait à Washington, en un seule exemplaire, le deux juin 1911." [1]

[*Signatures.*]

556. Arrangement pour l'établissement de câbles télégraphiques reliant les possessions coloniales asiatiques des Pays-Bas et d'Allemagne ; signé à Berlin, le 24 juillet 1901.

Headed " Convention," etc., but in the text spoken of as an " arrangement."

Preamble.

" Dans le but de l'établissement d'une communication télégraphique avec leurs possessions coloniales d'Asie, le Gouvernement royal des Pays-Bas et le Gouvernement impérial d'Allemagne ont conclu l'arrangement ci-après :

. . . .

" En foi de quoi, les soussignés, dûmont autorisés à cet effet, ont conclu cet arrangement, en le revêtant de leur sceaux.

" Fait à Berlin, en double expédition, le 24 juillet 1901, sous réserve de l'approbation du Gouvernement royal néerlandais et du Gouvernement impérial allemand." [2]

[*Signatures.*]

§ 557. Arrangement relatif à la répression de la circulation des publications obscènes.

Preamble.

" Les Gouvernements des Puissances désignées ci-après, également désireux de faciliter, dans la mesure de leurs législations respectives, la communication mutuelle de renseignements en vue de la récherche et de la répression des délits relatifs aux Publications obscènes, ont résolu de conclure un Arrangement [3] à cet effet et ont, en conséquence, désigné leurs Plénipotentiaires qui se sont réunis en Con-

[1] *Nouveau Recueil Général*, etc., viii. 786.   [2] *Ibid.*, vii. 272.
[3] *Abkommen* in the German translation.

férence, à Paris, du 18 avril au 4 mai 1910, et sont convenus des dispositions suivantes ;

[*Articles 1 to 5*]

" *Article* 6.

" Le présent arrangement sera ratifié, et les ratifications seront déposées à Paris dès que six des États contractants seront en mesure de le faire.

" Il sera dressé de tout dépôt de ratifications un procès-verbal, dont une copie, certifiée conforme, sera remise, par la voie diplomatique, à chacun des États contractants.

[Article 7 provides for the case of a Contracting Power desiring to carry out the Arrangement in one or more of its colonies, possessions or consular districts. Also for giving notice of withdrawal for any of such colonies, etc.]

" Fait à Paris, le quatre mai mil neuf cent dix, en un seul exemplaire, dont une copie conforme sera delivrée à chacun des Gouvernements contractants.

" Pour l'Allemagne."

[*Seals and signatures.*]

§ 558. Arrangement entre l'Italie et la France pour la protection réciproque des jeunes ouvriers ; signé à Paris, le 15 juin 1910.[1]

Plenipotentiaries, the Italian Ambassador at Paris, and the Director of the Labour Bureau in the Ministry of Agriculture, Industry and Commerce for Italy, the minister of Foreign Affairs and the minister of Labour and Social Providence for France. They communicated to each other their full-powers, and concluded an arrangement in twelve articles, of which the last provided for ratification. Thus the shape it took was substantially that of a Convention.

[1] *Nouveau Recueil Général*, etc., vii. 528.

CHAPTER XXIX

TREATIES AND OTHER INTERNATIONAL COMPACTS (*contd.*)

PROTOCOL, PROCÈS-VERBAL, EXCHANGE OF NOTES, RÉVERSALES

PROTOCOL

§ 559. THE word protocol is derived from the Low-Latin *protocollum*, Gr. πρωτόκολλον, the " first glued-in " to the book ; originally a register into which public documents were stuck. It then came to mean the form used in drawing up such documents. In diplomacy the register in which the minutes of a conference are kept. It is also employed to signify the forms to be observed in the official correspondence of the Minister for Foreign Affairs and in the drafting of diplomatic documents, such as treaties, conventions, declarations, full-powers, ratifications, letters of credence and other letters addressed by one Head of a State to another. In France *le bureau du protocole* is the sub-department charged with the preparation of such papers and the regulation of ceremonial. In England this is the Treaty Department of the Foreign Office.

Used to denote the form taken by an international compact, the word may be regarded as describing the record of an agreement between the High Contracting Parties, less formal than a treaty or convention.

During a congress or a conference, no matter for what object or purpose, the minutes of meetings of the plenipotentiaries are styled either protocol or *procès-verbal*, indifferently. Perhaps the former word is the more dignified. Obviously protocol in this sense does not mean an agreement ; *procès-verbal* would be better, as it means that and nothing else.

SPECIMEN OF A PROTOCOL IN THE SENSE OF " AGREEMENT "

§ 560. Protocole relatif à l'Article III des Préliminaires de Paix signé à Constantinople par les Plénipotentiaires de la Grèce et de la Turquie, le 7/19 novembre, 1897.

Art. 3 des Préliminaires de la Paix, signés à Constantinople, le 6/18 septembre, 1897.[1]

Sans toucher au principe des immunités et privilèges dont les sujets Hellènes jouissaient avant la guerre sur le même pied que les nationaux des autres Etats, des arrangements spéciaux seront conclus en vue de prévenir l'abus des immunités Consulaires, d'empêcher les entraves au cours régulier de la justice, d'assurer l'exécution des sentences rendues et de sauvegarder les intérêts des sujets Ottomans et étrangers dans leurs différends avec les sujets Hellènes, y compris les cas de faillite.

[1] See § 510 above.

Protocole.

Sur la demande de LL. EE. les Plénipotentiaires Hellènes de connaître les bases principales qui formeront les propositions du Gouvernement Impérial en ce qui concerne les arrangements prévus par l'Article III des Préliminaires de Paix, LL. EE. les Plénipotentiaires acceptent de leur communiquer dès à présent, à titre de renseignements et sans qu'aucune discussion puisse être entamée à ce sujet avant la ratification du Traité de Paix Définitif, les bases principales des dits arrangements, telles qu'elles ont été arrêtées dans la pensée du Gouvernement Impérial et qui consisteront dans les points suivants :—

Fixer les limites de la franchise douanière des Consuls ; assurer l'exécution des jugements rendus par les Tribunaux Ottomans envers les Consuls Hellènes en matière civile et commerciale ; définir le domicile de sujet Hellène et préciser les conditions à observer lors des perquisitions domiciliaires, surtout pour les cas où le Drogman ne se rendrait pas à l'invitation des autorités Ottomanes ; préciser également les conditions à observer pour les cas où les Délégués Consulaires ne se rendraient pas aux Tribunaux compétents en matière mixte ; reconnaître la compétence de la Cour de Cassation Ottomane d'après les lois en vigueur ; déclarer également la compétence des Tribunaux Ottomans pour les cas de faillite des sujets Hellènes, ainsi qu'en matière pénale, soit entre eux, soit avec les sujets des autres Puissances ; régulariser la signification des pièces judiciaires destinées aux sujets Hellènes et assurer l'exécution par les autorités Ottomanes des jugements rendus par les Tribunaux Ottomans dans les procès mixtes.

LL. EE. les Plénipotentiaires Hellènes, prenant acte de cette communication, déclarent faire leurs réserves les plus formelles, soit sur son contenu, au sujet duquel des discussions et négociations ultérieures devront avoir lieu immédiatement après la ratification du Traité de Paix définitif, soit sur le recours en cas de divergence, à l'arbitrage des Représentants des Grandes Puissances à Constantinople, prévu par l'Article 9 des Préliminaires de Paix.

Constantinople, le 7/19 novembre, 1897.[1]

[*Signatures of the plenipotentiaries.*]

§ 561. It not infrequently happens that it is found desirable on the conclusion of a treaty to supply simul-

---

[1] *Brit. and For. State Papers,* xc. 429.

taneously observations, declarations and agreements elucidatory of the text, and these are recorded in a Final Protocol (Protocole Final, Schluss Protokoll, or Protocole de Clôture), which becomes part of the compact. The following are examples :—

§ 562. Protocole de Clôture, annexe à la Convention d'Union de Paris du 22 mars 1883 pour la Protection de la Propriété Industrielle ; révisée à Washington le 6 juin, 1911.

" Au moment de procéder à la signature de l'Acte conclu à la date de ce jour, les Plénipotentiaires soussignés sont convenus de ce qui suit : . . .

" Le présent Protocole de clôture, qui sera ratifie en même temps que l'Acte conclu à la date de ce jour, sera considéré comme faisant partie intégrante de cet Acte, et aura méme force, valeur et durée.

" En foi de quoi, etc."

§ 563. Final Protocol to the Treaty of Commerce between Austria-Hungary and Germany, signed at Berlin, containing observations, declarations and agreements, explanatory of certain articles of the Treaty. (*Translation*) " The Plenipotentiaries have agreed that the present Protocol shall be presented simultaneously with the Treaty of the honourable Contracting Parties, and that in case of the ratification of the latter, the declarations and agreements contained in the former shall be looked upon as accepted without any further formal ratification.

" Upon which the present Protocol was executed in duplicate, Berlin, December 16, 1878." [1]

[*Signatures.*]

§ 564. Similar cases are the protocol attached to the Treaty of Friendship, Commerce and Navigation between Japan and Siam (in the Japanese, English, and Siamese languages, the English text being authoritative in case of discrepancy between the Japanese and Siamese versions), signed at Bangkok, February 25, 1898, *Brit. and For. State Papers*, xc. 70 ; Protocole Final annexé au Traité de Commerce et Navigation conclu le 27 décembre

---

[1] *Nouveau Recueil Général*, 3ème série, viii.

1878 entre l'Autriche-Hongrie et l'Italie, *Brit. and For. State Papers*, lxix. 1297, and " Convention Monétaire conclue à Paris, le 5 novembre, 1878, entre la Belgique, la France, la Grèce, l'Italie et la Suisse," which, besides an " arrangement rélatif à l'exécution de l'article 7," the ratifications of which were to be exchanged at the same time as the Convention, has a Protocol attached, of even date ; with regard to this it was stipulated that " Le présent Protocole, qui sera considéré comme approuvé et sanctionné par les Gouvernements respectifs, sans autre ratification spéciale, par le seul fait de l'échange des ratifications sur l'Arrangement Monétaire auquel il se rapporte, a été dressé en double expédition, à Paris, le 5 novembre, 1878.[1]

[*Signatures.*]

§ 565. Sometimes such an explanatory protocol may be signed at a later date.

Protocole Additionnel à la Convention relative à l'Établissement d'une Cour international des Prises du 18 octobre, 1907, signé à la Haye, le 19 septembre 1910.[2]

Preamble—

L'Allemagne [et trente-deux autres Puissances] signataires de la Convention de la Haye en date du 18 octobre 1907, pour l'établissement d'une Cour internationale des Prises, considérant que, pour certaines d'entre ces Puissances, des difficultés d'ordre constitutionnel s'opposent à l acceptation, sous sa forme actuelle, de ladite Convention, ont jugé utile de s'entendre sur un Protocole additionnel tenant compte de ces difficultés tout en ne compromettant aucun intérêt légitime, et ont, à cette fin, nommé pour leurs Plénipotentiaires, savoir : L'Allemagne, etc. . . . .

Lesquels, après avoir déposé leurs pleins pouvoirs, trouvés en bonne et due forme, sout convenus de ce qui suit :—

Arts. I–VII.

Art. VIII. Le présent Protocole additionnel sera considéré comme faisant partie intégrale de la Convention et sera ratifié en même temps que celle-ci.

[1] *Brit. and For. State Papers*, lxx. 169.　　　[2] *Ibid.*, civ. 258.

Art. IX. L'adhésion à la Convention est subordonnée à l'adhésion au présent Protocole additionnel.

En foi de quoi les Plénipotentiaires ont revêtu le présent Protocole additionnel de leurs signatures.

Fait à la Haye, le 19 septembre, 1910, en un seul exemplaire qui restera déposé dans le archives du Gouvernement des Pays-Bas et dont des copies, certifiées conformes, seront remises par la voie diplomatique aux Puissances, désignées à l'article XV de la Convention rélative à l'établissement d'une Cour internationale des Prises du 18 octobre, 1907, et dans son annexe.

[*Signatures only, no seals.*]

It will be observed that this Protocol is essentially in the same form as a Convention. Most of the plenipotentiaries were diplomatic representatives of their respective countries at the Hague, others were diplomatists on active service in other countries than Holland, one was the Netherlands minister for Foreign Affairs, and one was a distinguished jurisconsult from the United States of America.

§ 566. Protocol between the Argentine Republic and Brazil respecting the interpretation of Article IX of the Treaty of Commerce and Navigation of March 7, 1856 (Surrender of Military and Naval Deserters).—Signed at Rio de Janeiro, October 22, 1878.

Translation—

Whereas it is stipulated by Article IX of the Treaty, etc. . . . And whereas it is expedient to render clear the meaning of these words, etc. . . . it is understood, etc. . . .

In faith whereof the Envoy Extraordinary and Minister Plenipotentiary of the Argentine Republic and the Brazilian Minister and Secretary of State for Foreign Affairs have signed and sealed the present Protocol in duplicate, in Rio de Janeiro, the 22nd of October, 1878.[1]

[*Seals and signatures.*]

Here there is no naming of plenipotentiaries, no men-

---

[1] *Brit. and For. State Papers,* lxx. 1302.

tion of full-powers, nor ratification provided for. A similar Protocol is one signed at Montevideo, August 22, 1882, between Spain and Uruguay, respecting Articles of the Treaty of Peace of July 19, 1870 ; see *Brit. and For. State Papers*, lxxiii. 606.

§ 567. Another example is the " Protocole, additionnel à l'Arrangement Monétaire conclu le 15 novembre, 1893, entre les Gouvernements Français, Belge, Grec, Italien et Suisse.—Signé à Paris, le 15 mars, 1898."

" Le Gouvernement Italien ayant décidé, etc. . . . et ayant, en outre, pris la résolution, etc. . . . les Gouvernements Français, etc., sont convenus avec lui qu'en conséquence l'Italie, etc. . . . Cette obligation, qui, etc. . . . Il est entendu, en outre, qu'à titre de réciprocité, les autres États, qui, etc.

" En foi de quoi les soussignés, dûment autorisés par leurs Gouvernements respectifs, ont, sous réserve de ratification ultérieure, dressé le présent Protocole.

" Fait à Paris en cinq exemplaires, le 15 mars, 1898." [1]

[*Seals and signatures.*]

Here there is no nomination of plenipotentiaries. No full-powers were produced, but a statement is made that the persons who sign are duly authorized by their Governments. And ratification is required.

§ 568. Or a Protocol may be signed by way of fulfilment of a previous compact. For instance—

Protocole relatif à la nomination du Gouverneur du Liban ; signé à Constantinople, le 15 août, 1892.

Preamble : " Par suite du décès de Wassa Pacha, le poste de Gouverneur du Liban étant devenu vacant, S.M.I. le Sultan a daigné nommer Naoum Effendi, Secrétaire Général du Ministère des Affaires Étrangères, Gouverneur du Liban.

" Les Représentants des Puissances signataires du Règlement organique du Liban en date du 9 juin 1861, de celui du 6 septembre 1864, ainsi que des Protocoles des 27 juillet 1868,

---

[1] *Brit. and For. State Papers*, xc. 333.

22 avril 1873, et 8 mai 1883, réunis en conférence chez le Ministre des Affaires Etrangères de S.M. le Sultan, sont unanimes pour constater, par le présent Protocole, l'entente préalable qui, à l'occasion de cette nomination, s'est établie entre eux et la Sublime Porte.

" En foi de quoi les Plénipotentiaires ont signé le présent Protocole et y ont apposé le sceau de leurs armes.

" Fait à Constantinople le quinzième jour du mois d'août de l'an mil huit cent quatre vingt douze.[1]

[Seals and signatures, apparently in order of local seniority, the Turkish Minister for Foreign Affairs signing alone in the place of honour, on the left.]

§ 569. Another is the protocol between Belgium and Germany, for the delimitation of the frontier between the Belgian Congo Colony and German East Africa, signed at Goma, June 25, 1911.

" L'an 1911, 25ᵉ jour du mois de juin.

[Name, office] commissaire du Gouvernement de S.M. le Roi des Belges ;

[Name, office] premier commissaire du Gouvernement de S.M. l'Empereur d'Allemagne ;

[Name, office] second commissaire du Gouvernement de S.M. l'Empereur d'Allemagne ;

" Délégués par leurs Gouvernements respectifs à l'effet de procéder conformément à la Convention du 11 août, 1910, à l'abornement de la frontière entre la colonie du Congo belge et celle de l'Est africain allemand, depuis la rive septentrionale du Kivu, jusqu'au parallèle passant par le sommet septentrional du Héhu, sont convenus d'adopter, sous réserve de ratification, le tracé de frontière indiqué sur la carte annexée au présent protocole.

[Here follows the detailed description of the line.]

' Ainsi fait à Goma aux jour, mois et an que dessus, en deux originaux dressés en langue française et en langue allemande." [2]

[Seals and signatures.]

[1] Nouveau Recueil Général, 3ème série, viii. 651.
[2] Brit. and For. State Papers, civ. 820.

§ 570. A protocol may also be used to record the ratification of an international compact.

Protocol recording the ratification by the United States of America of the General Act of Brussels of July 2, 1890.—Signed at Brussels, February 2, 1892.

" Le 2 février, 1892, conformément à l'Article XCIX de l'Acte Général du 2 juillet, 1890, et à la décision unanime des Puissances qui a prorogé au 2 février, 1892, pour les États-Unis, le terme prévu au même Article XCIX, le Soussigné, Envoyé Extraordinaire et Ministre Plénipotentiaire des États-Unis d'Amérique, a déposé entre les mains de M. le Ministre des Affaires Étrangères de Belgique les ratifications du Président des États-Unis sur le dit Acte Général.

A la demande de S. E., la Résolution suivante, par laquelle le Sénat des États-Unis a consenti à la ratification du Président, a été insérée dans le présent Protocole :—

" Resolved (two-thirds of the Senators present concurring therein) : That the Senate advise and consent to the ratification of the General Act signed at Brussels on the 2nd July, 1890, by the Plenipotentiaries of the United States and other Powers, for the suppression of the African Slave Trade, and for other purposes.

" Resolved further : That the Senate advise and consent to the acceptance of the partial ratification of the said General Act on the part of the French Republic, and to the stipulations relative thereto, as set forth in the Protocol signed at Brussels on January 2, 1892.

" Resolved further, as a part of this act of ratification : That the United States of America, having neither possessions nor Protectorates in Africa, hereby disclaims any intention, in ratifying this Treaty, to indicate any interest whatsoever in the possessions or Protectorates established or claimed on that continent by the other Powers, or any approval of the wisdom, expediency, or lawfulness thereof, and does not join in any expressions in the said General Act which might be construed as such a declaration or acknowledgment ; and, for this reason, that it is desirable that a copy of this Resolution be inserted in the Protocol to be drawn up at the time of the exchange of ratifications of this Treaty on the part of the United States."

Cette résolution du Sénat des États-Unis ayant été préalablement et textuellement portée par le Gouvernement de S.M. le Roi des Belges à la connaissance de toutes les Puissances Signataires de l'Acte Général, celles-ci ont donné leur assentiment à son insertion au présent Protocole, qui demeurera annexé au Protocole du 2 janvier, 1892.

Il en est donné acte à M. le Ministre des Etats-Unis.

Les ratifications du Président des États-Unis ayant été trouvées en bonne et due forme, il est également donné acte de leur dépôt à S.E. Mr. Edwin H. Terrell ; elles seront conservées dans les archives du Ministère des Affaires Etrangères de Belgique.

" Au moment de procéder à la signature du présent Protocole le Ministre des Affaires Etrangères de S.M. le Roi des Belges fait connaître que le Représentant de la Russie, dans la note exprimant l'assentiment de son Gouvernement, a émis l'avis qu'il eût été désirable qu'une traduction en langue Française accompagnât au Protocole le texte Anglais des Résolutions du Sénat des États-Unis d'Amerique, et qu'en tout cas l'absence de cette traduction ne doit pas servir de précédent.

" Une copie certifiée du présent Protocole sera adressée par le Gouvernement Belge aux Puissances Signataires de l'Acte Général."

Fait à Bruxelles, le 2 février, 1892.[1]

[Signatures of the Belgian Minister for Foreign Affairs and of the American Representative.]

The Protocol recording the delivery of the Portuguese ratification of the same General Act is to be found at p. 58 of the same volume. The simple term *procès-verbal* would have sufficed.

§ 571. Protocols recording a refusal to ratify on the part of a signatory to a treaty between several Powers.

1. Protocole de la Conférence tenue au Foreign Office, le 19 février, 1842.

Présens : Les Plénipotentiaires d'Autriche, de France, de la Grande Bretagne, de Prusse et de Russie.

Les Plénipotentiaires des cinq Cours se sont réunis aujourd'hui, à l'échéance du terme fixé pour l'échange des ratifications du Traité conclu à Londres le 20 décembre, 1841, relatif à la suppression de la Traite des Nègres d'Afrique.

A l'ouverture de la Conférence le Plénipotentiaire de France

[1] *Brit. and For. State Papers*, lxxxiv. 57.

a annoncé n'avoir pas encore reçu de sa Cour les ratifications du susdit Traité ; et se référant aux explications qu'il a été chargé d'offrir à cet égard au Cabinet de S.M. Britannique, a demandé que dans l'attente d'une issue mutuellement satisfaisante de ces explications, le Protocole restât ouvert à la France.

Le Plénipotentiaire de la Grande Bretagne, en accédant à cette demande, et en partageant cet espoir, a invité les Plénipotentiaires d'Autriche, de Prusse et de Russie à procéder avec lui à l'échange des actes de ratification envoyés par les dites Cours contre ceux de l'Angleterre.

En se rendant à cette invitation, les Plénipotentiaires des Cours d'Autriche, de Prusse, et de Russie ont effectué avec le Plénipotentiaire de la Grande Bretagne l'échange des dites ratifications.

A la suite de cette échange le Plénipotentiaire d'Autriche a déclaré n'avoir pas encore reçu de sa Cour les instrumens de ratification destinés à être échangés contre ceux des Cours de France, de Prusse, et de Russie,

En conséquence il a demandé et obtenu le délai nécessaire pour mettre sa Cour en mesure d'envoyer à Londres les ratifications jusqu'ici restées en retard ; et le Protocole est resté ouvert pour la France.[1]

  (*Signed*) KOLLER. (*Signed*) BUNSEN.
   ,, STE. AULAIRE. ,, BRUNNOW.
   ,, ABERDEEN.

2. Protocole de la Conférence tenue à Londres, le 11 mai, 1842.

Présens : Les Plénipotentiaires d'Autriche, de France, de la Grande Bretagne, de Prusse, et de Russie.

En exécution du Protocole de la Conférence tenue au Foreign Office le 19 février dernier, le Plénipotentiaire d'Autriche a déclaré avoir reçu de sa Cour les instrumens de ratification du Traité du 20 décembre, 1841, pour être échangés contre ceux des Cours de Prusse et de Russie.

En conséquence, les Plénipotentiaires des Cours d'Autriche, de Prusse, et de Russie ont procédé à l'échange des dites ratifications, et ont constaté cet échange dans les formes usitées.

Ainsi qu'il a été convenu d'un commun accord entre les Plénipotentiaires des cinq Puissances, le Protocole est resté ouvert à la France.

         [*Signatures.*]

[1] *Brit. and For. State Papers*, xxx. 298.

3. Protocole de la Conférence tenue au Foreign Office, Londres, le 9 novembre, 1842.

Présens : Les Plénipotentiaires d'Autriche, de la Grande Bretagne, de Prusse, et de Russie.

Le Principal Secrétaire d'Etat de S.M.B. pour les Affaires Etrangères a invité les Plénipotentiaires des Cours d'Autriche, de Prusse, et de Russie, à se réunir en conférence aujourd'hui pour leur donner connaissance d'une communication qui lui a été adressée par M. l'Ambassadeur de France : elle a pour objet d'annoncer que le Gouvernement de S.M. le Roi des Français a jugé de son devoir de ne point ratifier le Traité conclu à Londres le 20 décembre, 1841, relatif à la suppression de la Traite des Nègres d'Afrique.

Les Plénipotentiaires ont unanimement exprimé le regret que leur fait éprouver cette détermination du Gouvernement Français. Mais en même tems ils ont jugé nécessaire de constater d'un commun accord que, nonobstant le changement survenu dans les intentions du Gouvernement Français, les Cours d'Autriche, de la Grande Bretagne, de Prusse, et de Russie n'en sont pas moins fermement décidées à mettre à exécution les engagemens qu'elles ont contractés par le susdit Traité, qui, pour leur part, restera dans toute sa force et valeur.

En manifestant cette détermination, au nom de leurs Cours, les Plénipotentiaires d'Autriche, de la Grande Bretagne, de Prusse, et de Russie, ont cru devoir la consigner formellement par écrit.

Finalement, ils ont résolu de déclarer, que le Protocole jusqu'ici resté ouvert pour la France, est clos.

(*Signed*) NEUMANN. (*Signed*) BUNSEN.
,, ABERDEEN. ,, BRUNNOW.

[The Note annexed to this protocol is given in Chapter VII, § 100.]

§ 572. Again, protocols are employed to record compacts more or less independent of other international agreements.

Protocol of Agreement between the United States and Spain, embodying the terms on which Negotiations for Peace shall be undertaken.—Signed at Washington, August 12, 1898.

Preamble : [Name] Secretary of State of the United States, and H.E. [name] Ambassador Extraordinary and Plenipotentiary of the Republic of France at Washington, respectively possessing for this purpose full authority from the Government of the United States and the Government of Spain, have concluded and signed the following Articles, embodying the terms on which the two Governments have agreed in respect to the matters hereinafter set forth, having in view the establishment of peace between the two countries, that is to say—

Articles I to V.

Article VI. Upon the conclusion and signing of this Protocol, hostilities between the two countries shall be suspended, and notice to that effect shall be given as soon as possible by each Government to the commanders of its military and naval forces.

Done at Washington, in duplicate, in English and French, by the Undersigned, who have hereunto set their hands and seals, the 12th day of August, 1898.[1]

[*Signatures and seals.*]

[The French and English texts are printed side by side, with the signatures of the plenipotentiaries attached to each, the United States plenipotentiary signing first in each place, from which fact it is evident that the counterpart retained on each side had the two texts in parallel columns. No full-powers were produced and there is no provision for ratification, as in the case of a treaty of preliminaries of peace.]

§ 573. Protocole consulaire entre le Mexique et la Turquie ; signé à Rome, le 23 décembre, 1910.

Somewhat in the same form as a Convention, except that it is stated to be between States, the respective heads thereof not being mentioned. The names and official designations of the persons signing are given, and they are said to be duly authorized by their respective governments. No full powers, therefore, were exhibited. Ratifications were to be exchanged at Rome between the Legation of the United States of Mexico and the Imperial Ottoman Embassy.[2]

---

[1] *Brit. and For. State Papers*, xc. 1049.
[2] *Nouveau Recueil Général*, etc., 3 ème série, viii. 286.

§ 574. Protocole d'arbitrage pour le règlement des réclamations des ressortissants français ; signé à Port-au-Prince, le 10 septembre, 1913.

Preamble: Les Gouvernements de France et de Haïti, animés du désir de maintenir et de resserrer les bonnes relations existant entre les deux pays, sont convenus de régler par l'arbitrage, les réclamations introduites à cette date, contre la république de Haïti pour dommages directs qui ont pu avoir été causés à des ressortissants français.

A cet effet, les soussignés [names and official designations] dûment autorisés par leurs gouvernements respectifs,

Ont arrêté et signé le compromis suivant.

. . . .

En foi de quoi le présent protocole a été signé en double original par les soussignés qui y ont apposé leurs sceaux.

[Place, date.] [1]

[Seals and signatures.]

575. Protocole entre la France et l'Uruguay, remettant en vigueur la Convention de Commerce et de Navigation conclue entre les deux Pays le 4 juillet, 1892 ; signé à Montevideo, le 23 juin, 1898.

Preamble—

Réunis au Ministère des Relations Extérieures de la République Orientale de l'Uruguay,

LL. EE.

M. [name official designation and decoration].

et M. [name. and official designation].

Reconnaissant qu'il n'a pas été, etc. . . . et convaincus de la nécessité, etc. ;

Ont déclaré, dûment autorisés à cet effet, ainsi qu'il résulte de la communication de leurs pleins pouvoirs respectifs trouvés en bonne et due forme, que la Convention de Commerce et de Navigation conclue à Montevideo, le 4 juillet, 1892, entre les deux pays est remise purement et simplement en vigueur à partir du jour de l'échange des ratifications du présent Protocole.

En foi de quoi les susdits Plénipotentiaires ont signé le présent Protocole, et y ont apposé leurs sceaux.

Fait à Montevideo, en double exemplaire, le 23 juin, 1898.[2]

[Seals and signatures.]

[1] *Ibid.*, 345.   [2] *Brit. and For. State Papers*, xc. 339.

In this instance full-powers were produced, and provision was made for ratification.

§ 576. Protocol of submission to arbitration of certain claims of United States citizens against the Government of Mexico.—Signed at Washington, March 2, 1897.

Preamble—

" The United States of America and the United States of Mexico, through their Representatives [names and official designations] have agreed upon and signed the following Protocol :—

" Whereas, etc. . . . it is therefore agreed between the Governments with the consent of [claimants' names] given through their respective attorneys of record—

[Articles I to VI fixing on arbitrators and procedure.]

" Done in duplicate at Washington, this 2nd day of March, 1897." [1]

In this case no full-powers were produced and there was no provision for ratification. Nothing could well be simpler.

§ 577. Protocole entre Suède et Norvège, et l'Italie, sur la procédure à suivre lors de la collation de décorations aux sujets des pays respectifs ; signé à Rome, le 15 mai, 1901.

" Les Soussignés, dûment autorisés à cet effet, prennent au nom de leurs Gouvernements respectifs l'engagement suivant. . . .

" en foi de quoi le présent protocole a été signé.

" Fait à Rome en double expédition le 15 mai, 1901." [2]

[*Signatures ; no seals.*]

§ 578. Protocole en vue de rétablir les relations diplomatiques entre les Pays-Bas et la Vénézuéla ; signé à la Haye, le 19 avril, 1909.

---

[1] *Ibid.*, 1252.   [2] *Nouveau Recueil Général*, 3 ème série, vi. 588.

Protocole.

Preamble—

Le Gouvernement de S.M. la Reine des Pays-Bas et le Gouvernement des États-Unis de Vénézuela, animés du désir sincère de prévenir à l'avenir de nouvelles difficultés pareilles à celles surgies entre les deux pays dans le cours de l'année précédente et de poser une base durable pour une entente cordiale ; considérant que les deux Gouvernements se déclarent satisfaits des explications fournies réciproquement au sujet des incidents qui ont troublé leurs bonnes relations ;

considérant que les intérêts des deux pays demandent la prompte conclusion d'un traité d'amitié, de commerce et de navigation, ainsi que d'une convention consulaire, offrant des garanties nécessaires pour un commerce réel entre les colonies des Antilles néerlandaises et le continent vénézuélien ;

considérant que le rétablissement antérieur des relations diplomatiques est désirable à cet effet ;

sont convenus de ce qui suit.

.   .   .   .

" En foi de quoi les soussignés [names and official designations] dûment autorisés par S.M. la Reine et par le Vice-Président constitutionnellement chargé de la Présidence de la République ont apposé leurs signatures au présent protocole, lequel sera soumis à la ratification des pouvoirs compétents et dont une traduction exacte en hollandais et en espagnol sera faite et signée par les deux plénipotentiaires.

" Fait en double à la Haye, le 19 avril 1909." [1]

[Seals and signatures.]

PROCÈS-VERBAL

These seem to be less used than protocols.

§ 579. Procès-verbal de Clôture.

" Au moment de procéder à la signature du Traité de Commerce conclu à la date de ce jour entre l'Italie et la Suisse, les Plénipotentiaires des Hautes Parties Contractantes sont convenus des déclarations suivantes.

I. *En ce qui concerne le texte du Traité* . . .

II. *En ce qui concerne le Tarif* (A) : *Droits a l'Entrée en Suisse* . . .

[1] *Nouveau Recueil Général,* 3ème série, vi. 507.

III. *En ce qui concerne le Tarif* (B) : *Droits a l'Entrée en Italie* . . .

IV. *En ce qui concerne le Tarif* (D).

" Fait à Zurich, en double expédition, le 19 avril, 1892." [1]

[Signatures, no seals.]

§ 580. Procès-verbal de la Commission Roumaine-Russe pour la Délimitation du Territoire rétrocédé à la Russie en vertu de l'Article XLV du Traité de Berlin :— signé à Bucarest, le 5/17 décembre, 1878.

" Les Soussignés [names] Délégués du Gouvernement Princier de Roumanie, et [name] Délégué du Gouvernement Impérial Russe, en vertu des délégations qu'ils ont [reçues] de leur Gouvernements respectifs, pour procéder au tracé de la ligne-frontière entre les deux États sur le Bas-Danube, se sont constitués en commission le 23 novembre (v.s.). La Commission, après s'être rendue sur les lieux, et vu l'Article XLV du Traité de Berlin, fixe la ligne frontière entre les deux Etats comme il est indiqué sur la Carte annexée au présent procès-verbal, savoir. . . . En ce qui regarde la frontière entre le Tchatal d'Ismail et l'embouchure du Pruth, la Commission, ne pouvant se mettre d'accord, expose comme suit l'opinion de chaque partie, séparément :

" Les Délégués Roumains soutiennent que . . . Le Délégué Russe, sans entrer dans l'examen des Traités, soutient que . . .

" En conséquence, il a été dressé le présent procès-verbal en doubles exemplaires pour être soumis aux Gouvernements respectifs.

" Fait à Bucarest, le 5/17 décembre, 1878." [2]

[Signatures, no seals.]

In vol. lxix., p. 439, there is a *procès-verbal* between Italy and Switzerland of the Demarcation of the Frontier between Pizzo Combolo and Sasso Lughina.—Berne, January 29, Milan, February 4, 1877.

§ 581. *Procès-verbal* of Deposits of Ratifications.— Washington, December 12, 1911.

" The Convention for the Protection of Fur Seals, signed by

---

[1] *Brit. and For. State Papers*, lxxiv. 1128.
[2] *Brit. and For. State Papers*, lxx. 693.

the respective Plenipotentiaries of Great Britain, the United States of America, Japan, and Russia, at Washington on the 7th July, 1911, having been ratified by the four Governments and the ratifications having been found to conform to one another, the undersigned, the Ambassador of Great Britain, the Ambassador of Japan, and the Ambassador of Russia, duly authorized thereto by their respective Governments, do hereby declare that, in conformity with the understanding that has been reached by the Governments signatory of the said Convention as to the form and manner in which the exchange of ratifications provided for in Article XVII of the said Convention shall be effected, they have delivered, and the undersigned Secretary of State of the United States of America hereby declares that he has received, for deposit in the archives of the Government of the United States of America, the respective instruments of ratification by Great Britain, Japan, and Russia, of the said Convention for the Protection of Fur Seals. And the Secretary of State further declares that the instrument of ratification of the said Convention by the President of the United States of America has, in accordance with the understanding above mentioned, been deposited in the archives of the Government of the United States of America, together with the like instruments of ratification of the Sovereigns of Great Britain, Japan, and Russia.

" In faith whereof the undersigned have prepared the present *procès-verbal* in one original, of which a copy, duly certified, will be transmitted by the Government of the United States, through the diplomatic channel, to each of the signatory Governments, together with a certified copy each of the instrument of ratification of the said Convention by H.B.M. the President of the United States of America, H.M. the Emperor of Japan, and H.M. the Emperor of Russia.

" Done at the city of Washington this 12th day of December, 1911." [1]

[*Seals and signatures.*]

(In preparing the certified copies of such a *procès-verbal* as the present, the *alternat* has to be strictly observed.)

§ 582. *Procès-verbal* (Échange des Ratifications).— *Berlin*, le 3 août, 1878.

---

[1] *Brit. and For. State Papers*, civ. 180, where the heading is " Protocol of Deposit," etc., but as in the body of the document it is styled " *procès-verbal*," we place it here.

" Les Soussignés s'étant réunis pour procéder à l'échange des ratifications du Traité conclu à Berlin le 13 juillet, 1878, les instruments de ces ratifications confirmant le dit Traité ont été produits par les Représentants de S.M. la Reine du Royaume Uni de la Grande Bretagne et d'Irlande, Impératrice des Indes ; S.M. l'Empereur d'Allemagne, Roi de Prusse ; S.M. l'Empereur d'Autriche, Roi de Bohême, etc., et Roi Apostolique de Hongrie ; S.E. le Président de la République Française ; S.M. le Roi d'Italie, et S.M. l'Empereur de Toutes les Russies, et ayant été, après examen, trouvés en bonne et due forme, l'échange en a été operé.

" L'Ambassadeur de Turquie, tout en exprimant les regrets de la Sublime Porte de ce que les instruments de ratification Turcs n'ont pu être expédiés à temps, annonce qu'il est autorisé à déclarer que S.M. l'Empereur des Ottomans a également ratifié le Traité du 13 juillet, 1878, et qu'elle le considère comme valable à partir de la date d'aujourd'hui.

" Sadoullah Bey annonce en outre qu'il sera procédé à l'échange des instruments de ratification Turcs dans un délai de quinze jours.

" En foi de quoi les Soussignés ont dressé le présent Procès-Verbal, qu'ils ont revêtu du sceau de leurs armes.

" Fait à Berlin, le 3ᵉ jour du mois d'août, de l'an 1887." [1]

[Seals and signatures.]

(Each diplomatic representative received a copy of this *procès-verbal* in which his sovereign was named first and his own signature attached first, the others being placed in the alphabetical order of the countries represented, according to the French language.)

§ 583. The following forms of *procès-verbal* of an exchange of ratifications are taken from Garcia de la Vega's *Guide Pratique des Agents Politiques*, p. 259, with some slight changes :—

" Les Soussignés s'étant réunis pour procéder à l'échange des ratifications de Sa Majesté . . . et de . . . sur le traité de . . . ., conclu le . . . dernier, entre . . . et . . ., les instruments de ces ratifications ont été produits et ayant été trouvés exacts et concordants [*ou* ,en bonne et due forme], l'échange en a été opéré.

[1] *Brit. and For. State Papers*, lxix. 768.

" En foi quoi, les Soussignés ont dressé le présent procès-verbal qu'ils ont signé [en double expédition] et revêtu de leurs cachets.

" Fait à . . ., le . . . mil neuf cent . . ."

or,

" Les Soussignés s'ètant réunis pour procéder à l'échange des ratifications de Sa Majésté 1 . . . et Sa Majesté 1 . . . sur la Convention concernant . . . conclue et signée à . . . échange qui, d'après l'article . . . de la Convention, aurait dû être effectué, au plus tard, le . . . dernier, mais qui a été retardé par suite de . . ., les instruments de ces ratifications ont été produits, et ayant été trouvés, après collation attentive [*ou*, après examen] en bonne et due forme, le dit échange en a été opéré.

" En foi de quoi, les Soussignés ont dressé le présent procès-verbal, qu'ils ont signé en double expédition et revêtu de leurs cachets [du sceau de leurs armes].

" Fait à . . . le . . . mil neuf cent . . .

" Le Plénipotentiaire   Le Plénipotentiaire
  de S. M. 1 . . .   de S. M. 1 . . ."
  [L. S.] [*Signature.*]   [L.S.] [*Signature.*]

EXCHANGE OF NOTES.

§ 584. Agreements on topics of minor importance which have been arrived at in oral discussion may then be recorded in diplomatic Notes, dated usually on the same day, sometimes with but a short interval between them. When the interval is of longer duration, and it seems likely that discussion has taken place between the date of the first Note and the reply to it, the inference is that the expression " exchange " of Notes is not applicable, but that the term " correspondence " would be more suitable.

The subject of more important exchanges of Notes relates to the establishment or prolongation of a commercial *modus vivendi*, to the renewal of an arbitration convention, the reciprocal protection of trade-marks (in China), sanitary precautions against the introduction of epidemic diseases, reciprocal communication of *actes d'état civil* affecting subjects of the two countries, recognition of rules of tonnage measurement, admission to

U

coasting trade, the labels to be affixed to imported drugs, the analysis of imported olive oil, treatment of commercial travellers' samples, and so forth. Among the second class, to which we give the name of "correspondence," will be included Notes respecting the recognition of the establishment of a protectorate, or the surrender of consular jurisdiction. In the three volumes vi., vii. and viii. of the *Nouveau Recueil Général des Traités*, etc., 3ème série, there are about a hundred sets of these two classes, entitled " Échange de Notes."

It will be observed that the Notes are exchanged between the minister for Foreign Affairs of the one Power and the diplomatic representative of the other.

§ 585. *Renewal of an Arbitration Convention.*

Paris, le 13 juillet, 1910.
M. le Ministre,
J'ai eu l'honneur de faire connaître à votre Excellence que mon Gouvernement était disposé à renouveler pour une période de deux ans la Convention d'Arbitrage conclue à Paris entre la Suisse et la France le 14 decembre, 1904.

V.E. a bien voulu me faire savoir que le Gouvernement de la République est également prêt à accepter dans ces conditions le renouvellement de la Convention du 14 décembre 1904.

Si cette manière de procéder convient à V.E., il sera entendu que la présente note et la réponse que V.E. me fera parvenir serviront à constater l'entente intervenue entre nos deux pays.

Agréez, etc.
[*Official designation and signature.*]

Paris, le 13 Juillet, 1910.
M. le Ministre,
J'ai l'honneur de vous accuser réception de votre note en date de ce jour, par laquelle vous avez bien voulu me faire savoir que le Gouvernement fédéral était prêt, comme le Gouvernement de la République, à renouveler, pour une période de deux ans, la Convention d'Arbitrage conclue entre nos deux Gouvernements, le 14 décembre, 1904, et dont les ratifications ont été échangées le 13 juillet, 1905.

Il reste entendu que le présent échange de notes entre vous

et moi sera considéré comme constatant l'entente intervenue entre nos deux Gouvernements à ce sujet.

Agréez, etc.

[*Signature*.]

§ 586. *Prorogation of a Treaty of Commerce.*

Sophia, le 6 juin, 1911.

Monsieur le Ministre,

En vertu de l'entente verbale qui a eu lieu entre la légation de S.M. le Roi d'Italie et le Gouvernement de S.M, le Tsar des Bulgares, j'ai l'honneur de communiquer à V.E., au nom du Gouvernement du Roi, mon Auguste Souverain. que l'Italie s'oblige de maintenir en vigueur jusqu'au 31 décembre 1917 (n.s.) le traité italo-bulgare de commerce, douane et navigation, signé à Sophia le 32 décembre 1905/13 janvier 1906.

Le traité pourra, par conséquent, aux termes de son article 21, être dénoncé seulement douze mois avant la date sus-indiquée ; demeurant entendu que dans le cas où la dénonciation serait notifiée postérieurement au 31 décembre 1916 (n.s.) le traité continuera à produire ses effets pour une année à partir de la date de la dénonciation.

Je prie V.E. de bien vouloir m'assurer que la Bulgarie accepte ces mêmes obligations et conditions dans ses rapports avec l'Italie.

Veuillez agréer, etc.[1]

[*Signature*.]

Sophia, le 24 mai/6 juin, 1911.

Monsieur le Ministre,

En réponse à votre note en date d'aujourd'hui sous le n. 662, j'ai l'honneur de communiquer à V.E., au nom du Gouvernement du Roi, mon Auguste Souverain, que la Bulgarie s'oblige à maintenir en vigueur jusqu'au 31 décembre 1917 (n.s.) le traité italo-bulgare de commerce, douane et navigation, signé à Sophia le 13 janvier 1906 (31 décembre 1905), sous condition que cet engagement du Gouvernement royal soit soumis à l'approbation du Sobranié.

Le traité pourra par conséquent, aux termes de son article 21, être dénoncé seulement douze mois avant la date sus-indiquée ; demeurant entendu que dans le cas où la dénonciation serait notifieé postérieurement au 31 décembre 1916

---

[1] *Nouveau Recueil Général*, etc., 3ème série, viii. 295.

(n.s.) le traité continuera à produire ses effets pour une année à partir de la date de la dénonciation.

Veuillez agréer, etc.

[*Signature.*]

§ 587. Il Regio Incaricato d'Affari in Petropolis al Ministro brasiliano delle relationi estere.[1]

Petropolis, 15 maggie, 1910.

Essendo ormai troppo breve il lasso di tempo che manca alla scadenza del *modus vivendi* commerciale italo-brasiliano perchè si possa utilmente negoziare e stipulare un definitivo trattato di commercio tra i nostri due paesi, il governo di S.M. il Re, mio Augusto Sovrano, mi ha autorizzato ad informare il governo federale che, per sua parte, è disposto a prorogare sino a tutto il 31 dicembre 1912 l'accordo commerciale provisorio stabilito mediante lo scambio di note del 5 luglio 1900 e protratto sino al 31 dicembre 1910 con le note del 21 e 23 settembre 1908 tra questa regia legazione e codesto ministero delle relazioni estere, accordo per il quale fu stipulato che, in cambio della riduzione dei diritti di entrata del caffè nel regno da 150 a 130 lire per 100 chilogrammi, i prodotti italiani conserverebbero il beneficio delle tasse minime della tariffa brasiliana.

All' accordo in parola verrebbe tosto sostituito il trattato definitivo non appena esso venisse concluso ed approvato.

Sarò grato all' Eccellenza Vostra se vorrà farmi conoscere a tal riguardo le disposizioni del governo federale, e nel caso in cui esse fossero, come credo, conformi a quelle dalle quali è animato il mio governo, propongo che si consideri fin da oggi prorogato per il termine sopra menzionato l'accordo provisorio del 5 luglio 1900.

Colgo, etc.

[*Signature.*]

Il Ministro brasiliano delle relazioni estere al Regio Incaricato d'Affari in Petropolis.

Rio Janeiro, 4 jumho, 1910.

Em resposto á sua nota de 15 maio ultimo, tenho a honra de lhe declarar, devidamente autorisado pelo Presidente da Republica, que o Governo Federal concorda em que tenha vigor até 31 de dezembro de 1912 o Accordo Commercial provisorio resultante das notas trocadas em 5 de julho de 1900

---

[1] *Nouveau Recueil Général*, etc., 3ème série, vi. 543.

entre este Ministerio e a Legação de Sua Majestade o Rei de Italia.

Conseguintemente fica prorogado o Accordo provisorio entre os dois paizes, e em virtude de tal prorogação os productos italianos continuarão a ter até 31 de dezembro de 1912 o beneficio da tarifa minima brasileira, uma vez que o direito de entrada do café brasileiro na Italia não exceda de 130 Liras por 100 kilogrammas.

[*Signature.*]

§ 588.

Lisbonne, le 8 août, 1912.

Monsieur le Ministre,

Le Gouvernement de S.M.I. et R.A. et le Gouvernement de la République Portugaise s'étant entendus sur la date de la mise en vigueur du *modus vivendi*, signé le 8 juillet 1911, j'ai l'honneur de communiquer à V.E. que le traitement de la nation la plus favorisée sera accordé aux produits portugais dans le territoire douanier conventionnel des deux États de la Monarquie Austro-Hongroise dès le 15 août prochain.

Agréez, Monsieur le Ministre, les assurances de ma haute considération.

[*Signature.*]

Monsieur le Ministre,

Le Gouvernement de la République Portugaise et le Gouvernement de S.M.I. et R.A. s'étant entendus sur la date de la mise en vigueur du modus vivendi, signé le 8 juillet 1911, j'ai l'honneur de porter à la connaissance de V.E. que le traitement de la nation la plus favorisée sera accordé en Portugal et aux îles adjacentes, aux produits de l'Autriche et de la Hongrie, dès le 15 août prochain.

Je saisis cette occasion, Monsieur le Ministre, pour renouveler à V.E. les assurances de ma haute considération.

Lisbonne, le 8 août, 1912.[1]

[*Signature.*]

A Monsieur . . . Ministre d'Autriche-Hongrie.

The foregoing is an excellent model of an exchange of Notes. Other examples may be found in the section devoted to *Modus vivendi*.

In all the preceding cases there was reciprocity of benefits, but in those to which the designation is more

[1] *Nouveau Recueil Général*, etc., 3ème série, viii. 187.

properly applied, the advantage is apparently all on one side, though possibly an equivalent may have been stipulated or obtained in some other direction. The answer may perhaps be delayed while this is being negotiated, or there is some other reason for withholding immediate consent. The following are two examples :—

§ 589. L'Ambasciatore di Francia in Roma al Ministro degli affari esteri.

Rome, le 25 décembre, 1912.

Monsieur le Ministre,
J'ai l'honneur de notifier à V.E. d'ordre de mon Gouvernement, le traité de protectorat franco-marocain qui a été signé a Fez le 30 mars 1912, dont le texte est ci-annexé.

Le Gouvernement de la République serait heureux que le Gouvernement du Roi voulût bien donner son adhésion à cet acte, et je me plais à espérer que V.E. sera en mesure de me faire le plus tôt possible une communication en ce sens.

Veuillez agréer, etc.

[*Signature.*]

Il Ministro degli affair esteri all' Ambasciatore di Francia in Roma.

Roma, 12 febbraio, 1913.

Signor Ambasciatore,
Con sua nota del 25 dicembre p. p. l'Eccellenza Vostra, in conformità alle sue instruzioni, mi notificava il trattato di protettorato franco-marocchino firmato à Fez il 30 marzo 1912, il cui testo era annesso alla stessa sua communicazione, e chiedeva che il Governo di S.M. il Re d'Italia desse la propria adhesione al medesimo atto internazionale.

In risposta alla nota succitata, ho l'onore di partecipare alla Eccellenza Vostra che il Governo Italiano formalmente dichiara di riconoscere il protettorato della Francia sul Marocco, sancito dal trattato di Fez del 30 marzo 1912.

Prego l'Eccellenza Vostra di voler portare questa dichiarazione a conoscenza del Governo della Republica.

Gradisca ecc.[1]

[*Signature.*]

---

[1] *Nouveau Recueil Général*, etc., 3ème, série, viii. 658.

RÉVERSALES.

§ 590. These are now explained to be a declaration that an error of etiquette or draughtsmanship shall not serve as a precedent. They are drawn up in this form :—

"The undersigned, in proceeding to the exchange of ratifications of . . . between . . . and . . . declare that having given precedence in drawing up the documents belonging to A [name of the country] the name of [Head of the State] of B over that of [Head of the State] of A, as well as naming the House of [B] before that of [A], contrary to the usage of the A chancery, cannot be invoked as a precedent in similar cases hereafter."[1]

[*Place*, date.]

[*Seals and Signatures.*]

§ 591. *Lettres réversales*, according to the author whose name is given in the footnote, are a declaration made by a Court that an alteration in ceremonial practice is effected without prejudice to the general rule.[2] Calvo, *Dictionaire du Droit International*, s.v., defines *lettres réversales* as "Déclaration par laquelle un État s'engage à ne pas contrevenir à des arrangements convenus antérieurement, ou à un usage établi ; ou acte par lequel un État fait une concession en retour d'une autre ; ordinairement par les lettres réversales une cour reconnait qu'une concession spéciale qui lui est faite par une autre cour ne devra préjudicier en rien aux droits et prérogatives antérieurs de chacune d'elles."

§ 592. Ducange is the original authority for the definition of these terms. He says—

"Reversale, Reversales Literæ, generatim dicuntur Epistolæ quibus quis alterius literis respondet,[3] ut videre est in *Responsali* ann. 1472 apud Ludewig. tom. 5. Reliq. *MSS.*

[1] Castro y Casaleiz, i. 379. [2] Pradier-Fodéré, i, 51*n.*
[3] This definition seems to suggest that what are now called "exchange of notes" is meant. The author remembers to have heard the Spanish equivalent "*cartas reversales*" used to signify "exchange of notes."

pag. 196, et in *Responsalibus literis* Caroli IV. Imper. ad Edwardum III. Angliæ Regem an. 1349, ibidem, p. 462.

" Maxime vero *Reversales* nude vel *Reversales literæ* vocantur Scripta quibus ii, qui munus aliquod suscipiunt, vel in rei alicujus possessionem mittuntur, declarant se servaturos conditiones consuetas vel conuentas. Literæ Johannis, Episc. Argentin. an. 1585, inter Instrum. Novæ Gall. Christ. tom. 5. col. 504. ' Hinc est quod te (Priorem monasterii Marbacensis, qui sese male gesserat, alloquitur) per præsentes hasce patentes litteras ratione præstiti tui iuramenti atque intuitu Reversalium, quæ nobis ea propter dedisti, requirimus, ut primo tempore ad praedictum monasterium in Marbach redeas, administrationis tuæ rationem Conventui ibidem coram à nobis deputandis reddas, abductam pecuniam aliasque res restituas . . . omniaque alia in pristinum statum reponas atque reducas.' "

It appears from this that the Prior, when he received that benefice, had given an undertaking to surrender it when called upon, to render an account of his administration before the Bishop's deputies, and to hand over the funds and all other property as they existed at the time of his taking charge. Evidently the Prior had run away from his monastery and was ordered back to give an account of his stewardship. The point is that he had signed *réversales* in return for his appointment.

An early French reference given by Ducange is from the Consuetudo Lotharingiæ, tit. 5, art. 6.

" Lesdites reprinses (des fiefs) faites, sont données lettres de la part de son Altesse, temoignantes le devoir des vassaux, qui reciprocquement doivent donner Reversales de ce dequoy ils auront reprins, et s'ils ont reprins d'une ou plusieurs seigneuries distinctes et separées, doivent en faire declaration expresse." [1]

Motley, *Dutch Republic*, iii. 535, says :—" In August 1582, [2] William of Orange accepted the countship of

---

[1] Paris edit. of 1734, s.v.

[2] March 26, 1583, is the right date. See Kruit, *Hist. der Holland. Staatsregeering*, i. 451, where the title is Renversaalbrieven van opdracht. Wederbrieven is given as the equivalent of Renversael, p. 450.

Holland and Zealand, for the completion of which letters of ' Renversal ' had to be drawn up and formally delivered. Then the rendering of homage had to take place. All these measures were duly arranged except the last, which was prevented by his assassination."

§ 593. In 1700, when the Elector of Brandenburg was contemplating the assumption of the title of King in Prussia, he entered into a secret negotiation with the Republic of Poland with a view to obtaining their consent. It was given, on his undertaking that the new title should not prejudice the rights of the Republic, in this form :—

" Fredericus Tertius, Dei Gratia, etc. Omnibus quorum interest notum facimus, cum Titulum & Dignitatem Regalem, quibus ante plura sæcula fulgebat Ducalis nostra Prussia, reassumendum meritò censeamus, nihil ex hac Majestatica prærogativa Prussiæ Nostræ quæ nunc Ducalis appellatur, praejudicii inferendum nec inferri posse juri ac possessioni Regalis Prussiæ, quâ Serenissimus Rex & Respublica Poloniæ gaudent, neque ullam in eamdem Prussiam Regalem prætentionem à nobis ac Successoribus Nostris inde vindicandam ; Pacta quoque Bydgostiensia [1] perpetui Fœderis Serenissimam Regiam Majestatem, inclitamque Rempublicam & nos inter, præcipue vero Art. VI. quo cautum est ut deficientibus masculis ex lineâ legitima Divi quondam Parentis Nostri Descendentibus Serenissimis Regibus & Reipublicæ Poloniæ jus suum integrum in altè memoratam Prussiam Ducalem reservetur, planè & sacrosanctè servanda, neque ullatenùs vel in toto vel in parte à Nobis ac Successoribus Nostris infringenda ac violanda, in quorum fidem Dat. Coloniæ ad Spream [2] de 8 Junii 1700." [3]

East Prussia, hitherto a dukedom, and until the Treaty of Wehlau, September 19, 1657, a fief of Poland, was a possession of the Elector of Brandenburg, while

[1] Bydgostia is the Latin name of Bromberg.
[2] Kölln an der Spree, now a part of Berlin.
[3] Lamberty, i. 95. This title was changed in 1773 by Frederick the Great, into König von Preussen (Koch and Schoell, Brussels edit. iv. 313) after the acquisition of West Prussia by the first partition of Poland in 1772.

West Prussia was still Polish and therefore Royal. Hence the Elector Frederick, to dispel any suspicion of his motives for taking the title of King in [East] Prussia, declares that it will not imply any prejudice to the rights of the King and Republic of Poland in West Prussia. And by Article VI of the Treaty referred to under the name of Bydgostiense,[1] the House of Hohenzollern had agreed that in the case of failure of male heirs, East Prussia should revert to Poland, which Treaty is solemnly confirmed by these *Lettres réversales*.[2]

§ 594. At p. 43, n. of Vol. I. will be found the *réversales* given to the King in Prussia in 1722 when he recognized the imperial title of the Tsar of Russia, and at p. 45 that given to France in 1745 when it was recognized by Louis XV. Maria-Theresa gave the title of Empress to the Tsaritsa Elisabeth, on which occasion the latter gave the following *réversales*—

" Demnach Ihro Königliche Mayestät zu Hungarn und Boheimb es vor gut befunden Ihro Kayserl. Mayst. von allen Reussen, Unserer Allergnädigsten Kayserin und Souverainin, den Kayserlichen Titul zu zustehen, zu geben und in Ihren Reichen und Landen festzustellen ; So hat auf Ihro Kayserl. Mayst. Allergnädigsten Befehl hiedurch declariret werden sollen, dass durch selbigen Unserer Allerdurchlauchtigsten Souverainin, von Ihro Königl. Mayst. zugestandenen und festgestelten Kayserlichen Titul in dem unter beyderseits Mayst. Mayst. und Ihren Reichen zu gebrauchenden Ceremoniel und etablirten Egalität, auf keinerley Weise und arth einige Veränderungen gemacht, noch desfals einige Preference pretendiret werden soll.[3]
" Moscau, den 8 July, 1742.
" (*Signed*)   PR. ALEXEI CZERKASKOY.
      „   G. ALEXEI BESTOUGEFF-RUMIN."

---

[1] It was really signed at Wehlau ; but the ratification by the King of Poland, dated November 6, 1657, was signed at Bromberg, *i.e.* Bydgostia. Koch and Schoell, iv. 78.
[2] See J. G. Droysen, *Der Staat des grossen Kurfürsten*, Bd. ii. pp. 256, 257.
[3] F. de Martens, i. 129.

§ 595. *" Projet de Réversales sous serment que les Ad-
ministrateurs des Revenus d'Oost-Frise seront tenus de
donner à L.H.P. les États Généraux des Provinces-
Unies."*[1]

This is an undertaking not to dispose of the revenues
of the real and personal taxes granted by the Estates in
1721, 1722 and 1723 to provide for the interest and repay-
ment of the principal of a sum of 600,000 florins borrowed
on the guarantee of their High Mightinesses, but to
employ the whole proceeds for the payment of the said
interest and principal. Further, to aid their receiver
of taxes to levy the said taxes in preference to all other
imposts, without allowing any arrears. And, lastly, in
case a flood or other calamity should render it impossible
to collect the said taxes to the amount of 50,000 florins
annually, to supplement what is deficient out of the proceeds of other farms, and in particular those of Leer,
Embden and Noorden formerly pledged to their High
Mightinesses.

" We engage ourselves to perform the whole of the
foregoing by solemn oath, so may God and his holy
Gospel help us."

[Enclosed in a *mémoire* from Ammon, Prussian diplomatic agent, dated August 22, 1745. He had succeeded
Podewils as Resident at the Hague. *Ibid.*, 147.]

By a resolution of the States-General of December 9,
1746, the proposed *lettres réversales* were accepted. On
January 18, 1747, the estates of Oost-Frise wrote to the
States-General that they had sent the draft *réversales*
to the King of Prussia to obtain his guarantee, and they
enclosed a duplicate (*Ibid.*, 149.) In a *mémoire* of March
16, 1749, Ammon transmitted the *lettres réversales* and
the *Acte de garantie* of the King of Prussia.

§ 596. *Les Réversales pour l'Exécution des Conditions
des lettres d'Investiture, données à Madrid par le Roi
Louis I, le 28 février, 1724.*

---

[1] Rousset, xix. 145.

[In Rousset, iv. 110 are the Lettres expectatives de l'Investiture éventuelle, pour l'Infant Don Carlos. Philip V in 1724 abdicated in favour of his son Luis, who dying shortly after, he resumed the crown.]

This document refers to the *literæ expectativæ investituram eventualem continentes* received by the undersigned minister plenipotentiary of the Sacred Royal Catholic Majesty in satisfaction of Article V of the treaty of London of August 2, 1718, and acceded to at the Hague, February 16, 1720, by the Catholic King. This was duly delivered to us by the Ministers Plenipotentiary of his Sacred Cæsarian Majesty in proper form in the presence of the Ministers Plenipotentiary of the mediating Kings ; " promittimusque nomine Sacræ Catholicæ Majestatis, omnes & singulas in prædicto diplomate expressas conditiones, juxta tenorem præfati quadruplicis fœderis erga Sacram Cæsaream Majestatem, & Imperium à Sacra Regia Catholica Majestate, prout & à Serenissimo Infante Carolo, ejusque Hæredibus, & Successoribus masculis ibidemque recensitis ejus Fratribus sanctè inviolatè executum & observatum iri, in cujus fidem præsens hoc instrumentum virtute Plenipotentiæ à Sacra Regia Catholica Majestate Nobis concessæ, cujus Apographum ad finem adjunctum est, manu propria, sigilloque nostro firmavimus ; quemadmodum, & in majus robur à Sacra Regia Catholica Majestate ratihabitionibus suis ritè confirmabitur, ratihabitionumque tabulæ intra spatium sex septimanarum à die subscriptionis, aut citiùs, si fieri potest, Sacræ Cæsaræ Majestatis Ministris Plenipotentiariis Cameraci extradentur : Actum Cameraci die vigesima quarta Januarii, Anni millesimi septingentesimi vigesimi quarti.

(L.S.) EL CONTE DE SANTISTEVAN.
(L.S.) EL MARQUES BERETTI LANDI."

[Here follows the King's ratification of February 28, 1724, signed—

(L.S.) Yo El Rey,
(*countersigned*) JOANNES AB ORENDAYN.[1]

It is interesting to observe that the forms used to-day to give validity to a treaty are derived directly from the Latin.

Lettres réversales seem to have become an obsolete form of compact.

[1] Rousset, v. 374.

TREATIES AND OTHER INTERNATIONAL COMPACTS (*contd.*)
COMPROMIS D'ARBITRAGE, MODUS VIVENDI

COMPROMIS D'ARBITRAGE

(Engl. Submission to arbitration.)

§ 597. *Preamble.*

Compromis.

Le Gouvernement de la République Française et le Gouvernement Royal Italien, s'étant mis d'accord le 26 janvier 1912 par application de la Convention d'arbitrage franco-italienne du 25 décembre 1903, renouvelée le 24 décembre 1908, pour confier à un Tribunal d'arbitrage l'examen de la capture et de la saisie momentanée du vapeur postal français " Manouba " par les autorités navales italiennes notamment dans les circonstances spéciales où cet opération a été accomplie et de l'arrestation de vingt-neuf passagers ottomans qui s'y trouvaient embarqués, ainsi que la mission de se prononcer sur les conséquences qui en dérivent,

Les soussignés dûment autorisés à cet effet, sont convenus du Compromis suivant.

[*Articles* 1 *to* 9]

Pour tout ce qui n'est pas prévu par le présent Compromis les dispositions de la Convention de La Haye du 18 octobre 1907 pour le règlement pacifique des conflits internationaux seront applicables au présent Arbitrage.

Fait en double à Paris, le 6 mars 1912.[1]

[*Signatures.*]

[1] *Nouveau Recueil Général*, etc., 3ème série, viii. 170.

§ 598. Also a similar "compromis d'arbitrage" between the same parties of November 8, 1912.[1]

Some such sort of written agreement is a necessary preliminary to arbitration.

An agreement for the reference of certain pecuniary claims to arbitration, concluded August 18, 1910, between Great Britain and the United States of America, is to be found in § 550. In all the arbitration conventions entered into by that Power it is stipulated that in each case there shall be a special agreement made by the President by and with the advice and consent of the Senate.

In 1908 an agreement[2] to refer to arbitration certain occurrences at Casablanca in Morocco was concluded by means of a " Protokoll " of November 10, 1908, and a " Schiedsvertrag " of November 24.

A " compromis d'arbitrage "[3] was signed at Bogotá, October 28, 1909, between Italy and Colombia. It is headed " Convenzione " and " Convención " in the Italian and Spanish texts respectively, signed by the Italian Minister Resident and the minister of Foreign Affairs, duly authorized by their respective Governments. No provision for ratification. [*Seals and Signatures.*]

An agreement to submit to arbitration a difference respecting the delimitation of their respective possessions in the Island of Timor, was signed at the Hague between the Netherlands and Portugal, April 3, 1913.[4] It is in the form of a convention, has a preamble, and was concluded by plenipotentiaries, duly authorized for that purpose, and was subject to ratification.

---

[1] *Nouveau Recueil Général*, etc., 3ème série, viii. 172.
[2] *Rapport du Conseil Administratif de la Cour Permanente d'Arbitrage* . . . pendant l'année 1909.
[3] *Nouveau Recueil Général*, etc., 3ème série, vi. 378.
[4] *Ibid.*, vii. 656.

Modus Vivendi

§ 599. This is the name given to a temporary and provisional agreement, usually intended to be replaced later on, whenever it may prove feasible, by one of a more permanent and detailed character, or, it may be, pending a reference to arbitration. It is, however, not always so designated in the document by which it is established. This sometimes consists of an agreement signed by both parties, or even of a convention, but more often of an exchange of notes. The following are some specimens.

§ 600. Between the Dominican Republic and Hayti.—Signed at Port-au-Prince, May 20, 1910. Substituting for passports, certificates of identity signed by the proper local authority and *visés* by a consular or diplomatic authority.

Preamble.

" M. [name and official designation] représentant le Gouvernement haïtien, et M. [name and official designation] représentant le Gouvernement Dominicain, tous deux dûment autorisés à cet effet, en vue de, etc. . . . ont arrêté et signé le présent *modus vivendi* entre les deux pays :—

[Article I *to* V]

" Le présent *modus vivendi* rentrera en vigueur et sera communiqué aux autorités locales intéressées immédiatement qu'il aura été signé.
" Fait en double exemplaire à Port-au-Prince, le 20 mai, 1910."

[Signatures, no seals.]

§ 601. Exchange of Notes between the Spanish Ambassador at Paris and the French minister for Foreign Affairs (who was also President of the Council) for the purpose of agreeing to respective tariff conditions.

(1)   Paris, le 30 décembre, 1893.
M. LE PRÉSIDENT,
Mon Gouvernement ayant conclu avec plusieurs nations

Européennes des Traités de Commerce dont quelques-uns seront appliqués à partir du 1   janvier, 1894, la nécessité s'imposait, pour la France et l'Espagne, d'examiner à nouveau la question du *modus vivendi* qui règle leurs relations commerciales, par suite de l'échange de notes et de la publication des Décrets respectivement effectués les 27 et 28 mai, 1892.

.   .   .   .

Veuillez agréer, etc.

[Signature.]

(2)   Paris, le 30 décembre, 1893.
M. L'AMBASSADEUR,

Par votre lettre d'aujourd'hui, vous avez bien voulu m'exposer les conditions nouvelles qui résultent pour l'Espagne de l'entrée en vigueur, à la date du 1er janvier prochain, des nouveaux Traités passés par elle avec certaines Puissances étrangères et vous avez attiré l'attention du Gouvernement de la République sur la nécessité qui s'imposait d'examiner, d'un commun accord, la question du *modus vivendi* actuellement existant entre les deux pays. Vous avez bien voulu reconnaître également que, malgré le désir des deux Puissances d'arriver, le plus tôt possible, à un accord durable réglant les relations économiques entre les deux pays, le court délai qui nous sépare du 1er janvier rendait impossible la conclusion d'une pareille entente. Dans ces conditions, vous m'avez fait savoir que vous étiez autorisé par votre Gouvernement à nous proposer l'arrangement suivant :

[Here follows a recapitulation of the Spanish proposals, with one slight reserve.]

" Cette réserve étant acceptée par vous, il serait entendu qú'à partir du 1er janvier prochain les mesures seront prises pour mettre cet arrangement simultanément à exécution dans les deux pays.
" Agréez," etc.

[Signature.]

(3)   Paris, le 30 décembre, 1893.
M. LE PRESIDENT,

J'ai l'honneur de vous accuser réception de votre lettre du 30 courant avec la réserve qu'elle contient au sujet de . . .

Au nom de mon Gouvernement, je déclare adhérer à l'arrangement ainsi conclu entre les deux pays.

Veuillez agréer, etc.[1]

[*Signature.*]

§ 602. Echange de Notes en vue de proroger *sine die*
le Modus vivendi commercial existant entre le France
et l'Espagne.

(*Traducción.*)

El Excmo. Sr. Embajador Extraordinario y Pleni-
potenciario de la República Francesa, al Excmo. Sr.
Ministro de Estado.

Madrid, 29 de Noviembre de 1906.

Sr. Ministro : En las conferencias que hemos celebrado
estos últimos dias hemos reconocido la conveniencia de prorro-
gar *sine die* el *modus vivendi* que rige las relaciones comerciales
entre España y Francia.

Tengo el honor de participarle que estoy autorizado por el
Gobierno de la República para concertar con V. E. la con-
tinuación *sine die* entre los dos Paises del régimen comercial
actual, basado en la concesión de la tarifa de Aduana la más
reducida. Queda entendido que ambas Naciones gozarán
de todas las ventajas que desde esta fecha cada una de ellas
pudiera conceder à una tercera Potencia. Queda igualmente
convenido que en el caso que una de las Partes denunciara
el presente acuerdo, no expirará éste sino tres meses después
de su denuncia.[2]

[*Signature.*]

The reply simply reproduces the language of the
Ambassador's Note.

§ 603. Notes exchanged between Great Britain and
France for the renewal of the *Modus vivendi* in Newfoundland during the Fishery Season of 1892.

---

[1] *Nouveau Recueil Général*, etc., 3ème série, vi. 288.

[2] *Nouveau Recueil Général*, etc., 3 ème série, vi. 292, reprinted from
Olivart, *Tratados de España*, 1906, No. 27.

Foreign Office, April 4, 1892.

M. L'AMBASSADEUR,

In pursuance of verbal communications which have passed between Your Excellency and me, I have the honour to propose that the *modus vivendi* of 1890,[1] relative to the catching and preparation of lobsters, which was renewed purely and simply for the fishing season of last year, should again be renewed for the fishery season of the present year.

I should esteem it a favour if Y.E. would notify to me the consent of your Government to this arrangement, if accepted by them, in which case H.M.G. will consider the exchange of notes as an agreement between the two Governments, and will give the necessary directions to carry it into execution on behalf of Great Britain.

I have, etc.

[*Signature.*]

Londres, le 4 avril, 1892.

M. LE MARQUIS,

J'ai reçu la lettre en date de ce jour par laquelle Votre Seigneurie veut bien me proposer de renouveler purement et simplement pour l'année 1892, ainsi que cela a été fait l'année dernière, le *modus vivendi* de 1890 relatif à la pêche et à la préparation du homard à Terre-Neuve.

Je m'empresse de faire savoir à V.S. que mon Gouvernement consent au renouvellement de cette Convention, et j'accepte en son nom de considérer le présent échange de notes comme une constatation officielle de l'accord des deux Gouvernements à ce sujet.

Veuillez, etc.[2]

[*Signature.*]

[1] The formal part of this negotiation began with a note from Lord Salisbury of March 10, 1890, to M. Waddington, referring to previous verbal communications which had taken place, enclosing the draft of a document styled " *a modus vivendi*," and asking to be informed whether H.E. was authorized to assent to it on behalf of the Government of the French Republic. To this note M. Waddington replied on the following day, accepting the proposed draft in the name of his government (*Brit. and For. State Papers*, lxxxii. 993). On March 11, 1891, an " Agreement " was signed between the two Powers for the submission to arbitration of all the questions of principle concerning the catching and preparation of lobsters on a certain portion of the coasts of Newfoundland. And by Art. 3 of this Agreement the *modus vivendi* of 1890 was renewed for the fishery season of 1891 (*Brit. and For. State Papers*, lxxxiii. 415).

[2] *Brit. and For. State Papers*, lxxxiv. 61.

§ 604. In vol. xc. of the *British and Foreign State Papers*, p. 10, is a series of Notes exchanged between the Belgian minister for Foreign Affairs and the British Diplomatic Representative at Brussels establishing a provisional *modus vivendi* pending the conclusion of a treaty of Commerce and Navigation between the two countries, and for the extension of the arrangement to various British Colonies and Possessions.

§ 605. In February 1892 a treaty (styled Convention in the preamble) was concluded between Great Britain and the United States for the purpose of submitting to arbitration questions which had arisen between the two governments concerning the jurisdictional rights of the United States in the waters of Behring Sea, the preservation of the fur-seals resorting to the said Sea, and the rights of the subjects and citizens of either country as regards the taking of fur-seals in, or habitually resorting to those waters. This was followed in April by a convention respecting restrictive regulations necessary " during the pendency " of such arbitration, which, though the words *modus vivendi* do not occur in the document, was clearly of that character. In accordance with the constitutional requirements of the United States it was necessary for this convention to be ratified by and with the advice and consent of the Senate, and on behalf of Great Britain it was stipulated that it should be ratified by His Britannic Majesty. The ratifications of both the Arbitration Treaty and the *Modus Vivendi* were exchanged on May 7.

[1] *Brit. and For. State Papers*, lxxxiv. 48 and 62.

CHAPTER XXXI

TREATIES AND OTHER INTERNATIONAL COMPACTS (*contd.*)
RATIFICATION, ADHESION AND ACCESSION

RATIFICATION

§ 606. Ratification is a solemn act on the part of a Sovereign or by the President of a Republic, by which he declares that a treaty, convention or other international compact has been submitted to him, and that after examining it he has given his approval thereto, and undertakes its complete and faithful observance. The whole text of the treaty, etc., should be reproduced in the instrument, which is signed by him and sealed with the Great Seal, and is countersigned by the minister for Foreign Affairs. This document is exchanged for a similar one given by the other party to the treaty, and the fact of the exchange having been effected is then recorded in a protocol or in a *procès-verbal*. In some countries the exhibition of special full-powers by the officials who make the exchange is insisted on, but as a general rule this is not held to be necessary, the production of the instruments of ratification by a minister for Foreign Affairs or by an accredited diplomatic representative of the other high contracting party being sufficient evidence that the official who tenders it is duly authorized to proceed to the exchange.

In the case of multilateral treaties where there are more than two high contracting parties, and each signatory Power has received a counterpart, it exchanges a separate instrument of ratification with each of the other parties. But where only one original text has been signed by all the plenipotentiaries, and deposited in the archives of the State where it was signed, the other contracting parties send their instruments of ratification to the government of that State, which then delivers an " acte d'acceptation " and sends to each of the remaining contracting parties a copy of the whole record.

What circumstances may justify a State in declining to ratify a treaty to which it has become a party is not a question of international *law*, although writers on that subject discuss it. It is rather one of morals and policy. Where, as in the United States, it is the President under whose direction the Secretary of State concludes and signs a treaty, but ratification is dependent on the advice and approval of the Senate, the refusal to ratify is sometimes consequent on other than the ordinarily recognized motives. In such a case the ratifying power sometimes adds new proposals, which transform the instrument into a new treaty. The other party is justified in refusing to accept the new conditions, or may accept them. This happened in connection with the treaty of 1794 between Great Britain and the United States. The Senate proposed an Additional Article, which was accepted by the British Government.[1] But in 1807 the United States returned the treaty signed in London on December 31, 1806, unratified, and proposed alterations thereto. Canning, who was then Secretary

---

[1] *Brit. and For. State Papers*, i. 803.

of State for Foreign Affairs, protested against "a practice altogether unusual in the Political Transactions of States," and he announced that the King had no option, under the circumstances, but to acquiesce in the refusal of the President to ratify the treaty in question.[1] More recently, the first Hay-Pauncefote treaty of 1900 was modified by the American Senate in consenting to its ratification, and in consequence it fell through.[2] In countries where the administration is the creation of a parliamentary majority such a contingency is less likely to arise, even when the consent of the legislature is necessary.

In former times it was not the practice to make a reserve of ratification in a full-power. Thus in the British full-power given at p. 118, Vol. I., there is a promise to hold as *grata, rata et accepta* in the fullest manner, and not to suffer anything to be done, in whole or in part contrary to what the plenipotentiary may have agreed to and concluded. The full-power of the King of France similarly undertakes *en foi et parole de Roi, d'avoir agréable, tenir ferme et stable à toujours, accomplir et exécuter ponctuellement, tout ce que le dit Sieur Comte de Vergennes aura stipulé et signé, en vertu du présent plein-pouvoir, sans jamais y contrevenir, ni permettre qu'il y soit contrevenu, pour quelque cause et sous quelque prétexte que ce puisse être, comme aussi d'en faire expédier Nos lettres de ratification en bonne forme, et de les faire délivrer, pour être échangées, dans le tems dont il sera convenu : Car tel est Notre plaisir.* Likewise, the passage at p. 122 of the Emperor's full-power, and on p. 123 in the full-power of the King of Spain, and in the Dutch full-power at p. 125. The modern example of a Belgian full-power at p. 126 also makes no reserve as to ratification, but contains the same undertaking to approve whatever may be stipulated, promised and

---

[1] *Brit. and For. State Papers*, i. 1187.

[2] Mr. J.W. Foster's *Practice of Diplomacy as illustrated in the Foreign Relations of the United States* has an important chapter on this subject.

signed by the plenipotentiary, as the earlier ones already cited, and the Spanish form of full-power at p. 127 is worded in much the same manner, except that it contains no promise to ratify. But the more recent form of a British full-power, as at p. 128, inserts the words, *" subject if necessary to Our Ratification,"* which perhaps may seem to weaken the force of the words " Engaging and Promising on Our Royal Word, that whatsoever things shall be so transacted and concluded by Our said Commissioner, Procurator and Plenipotentiary, shall [subject, if necessary, etc.] be agreed to, acknowledged and accepted by Us in the fullest manner, and that We will never suffer, either in whole or in part, any person whatsoever to infringe the same, or act contrary thereto, as far as it lies in Our power."

Nevertheless, it was from an early time customary, and was recognized by Bynkershoek as forming an established usage, to look upon ratification by the Sovereign as necessary to impart validity to a treaty concluded by his plenipotentiary, and full powers were interpreted as conferring a general power of negotiating subject to instructions received from time to time, and of concluding agreements subject to the ultimate approval or otherwise of the Sovereign. But it should not be capriciously withheld, and its refusal ought to be by solid reasons.[1] Sometimes, however, it is stipulated that a treaty shall come into force without waiting for ratification. An example is the treaty of July 15, 1840, between Austria, Great Britain, Prussia, Russia and Turkey.

The practice of reserving the ratification of the Sovereign had formerly its use when the plenipotentiary of one of the High Contracting Parties was negotiating at such a distance that he might perhaps not have time to refer the text of the instrument agreed upon to his Government before signing. In modern times, however, when all the capitals of the civilized world are in tele-

[1] Oppenheim, 2nd edit., i. 556 ; Hall, 6th edit., 323, 4.

graphic communication, it is the usual practice for plenipotentiaries to submit the precise wording of the proposed treaty to their Governments for approval before signature, so that to withhold ratification can rarely be justified, except where the negotiating and ratifying authorities are distinct. It may be added that the cases of a refusal to ratify are not by any means numerous. They might be counted on the fingers of two hands.

It will be found on reference to the international compacts given in these chapters, other than those specifically denominated " Treaties " or " Conventions," that sometimes ratification is expressly stipulated. Where this is not done, it is to be inferred that ratification is not obligatory, yet it may sometimes take place even in those cases. In the Index to the British Treaty Series for 1915 there are six instances where ratification is stated to be not required. These six were either Declarations, Accessions or Agreements. We hold, therefore, that apart from those compacts which bear the title of Treaty or Convention, ratification is only *required* where it is provided for.

History records the reasons which induced the Cabinet presided over by M. Guizot to refuse ratification of the treaty for the suppression of the Slave Trade in 1841. The documents in which this refusal is recorded are given in §§ 100 and 571.

§ 607. The form of ratification now used by Great Britain is as follows :—

GEORGE, by the Grace of God, of the United Kingdom of Great Britain and Ireland and of the British Dominions beyond the Seas King, Defender of the Faith, Emperor of India, etc., etc., etc., To all and singular to whom these Presents shall come, Greeting !
Whereas, a
between Us and

was concluded and signed at   on the   day of

in the year of Our Lord one thousand nine hundred and
by the Plenipotentiaries of Us and of   duly and
respectively authorized for that purpose, which   is,
word for word, as follows :—
(Inseratur—in   texts—   .)
[And whereas, a   between Us and Our said
was concluded and signed at   on the   day of
in the year of Our Lord one thousand nine hundred
by the Plenipotentiaries of Us and of   duly
and respectively authorized for that purpose, which
is, word for word, as follows :—]
(Inseratur—in   texts—   :)
We, having seen and considered the   aforesaid, have
approved, accepted, and confirmed the same in all and every
one of   Articles and Clauses, as We do by these Presents
approve, accept, confirm, and ratify   for Ourselves, Our
Heirs and Successors; engaging and promising upon Our Royal
Word that We will sincerely and faithfully perform and
observe all and singular the things which are contained and
expressed in the   aforesaid, and that We will never
suffer the same to be violated by any one, or transgressed in
any manner, as far as it lies in Our power.   For the greater
testimony and validity of all which, We have caused the Great
Seal of Our United Kingdom of Great Britain and Ireland to
be affixed to these Presents, which We have signed with Our
Royal Hand.

Given at Our Court of St. James, the   day of
in the year of Our Lord one thousand nine hundred and
in the   year of Our Reign.

(*Signed*)   GEORGE R.I.

§ 608. *A Russian Instrument of Ratification.*

Par La Grace de Dieu
NOUS NICOLAS II,
Empereur et Autocrate
de toutes les Russies,

de Moscou, Kiow, Wladimir, Novogorod ; Tsar de Casan, Tsar
d'Astrakhan, Tsar de Pologne, Tsar de Sibérie, Tsar de la
Chersonese Taurique, Tsar de la Géorgie, Seigneur de Plescow
et Grand Duc de Smolensk, de Lithuanie, Volhynie, Podolie
et de Finlande ; Duc d'Estonie, de Livonie, de Courlande et
Semigalle, de Samogitie, Bialostock, Carelie, Twer, Jugorie,
Perm, Viatka, Bolgarie et d'autres ; Seigneur et Grand Duc de
Novgorod-Inférieur, de Czernigow, Riasan, Polotzk, Rostow,

Jaroslaw, Bélosersk, Oudor, Obdor, Condie, Witepsk, Mstislaw, Dominateur de toute la contrée du Nord ; Seigneur d'Jberie, de la Cartalinie, de la Cabardie et de la province d'Arménie ; Prince Héréditaire et Souverain des Princes de Circassie et d'autres Princes montagnards ; Seigneur du Turkestan ; Successeur de Norvège, Duc de Schleswig-Holstein de Stormarn, de Dithmarsen et d'Oldenbourg, etc., etc., etc. Savoir faisons par les présentes qu'à la suite d'un commun accord entre Nous et Sa Majesté Le Roi des Belges Notre Plénipotentiaire a conclu et signé le 17/30 novembre 1904, une convention d'arbitrage obligatoire ainsi qu'une déclaration additionnelle y annexée, relative au maintien de tous les droits et obligations resultant pour les Hautes Parties contractantes du traité du 19 avril 1839, qui garantit l'indépendence et la neutralité de la Belgique, qui portent mot pour mot ce qui suit :

[Text of the Convention and Declaration.]

A ces causes, après avoir suffisamment examiné ces convention et déclaration. Nous les avons agréées, confirmées et ratifiées, comme par les présentes Nous les agréons, confirmons et ratifions dans toute leur teneur, promettant sur Notre parole Imperiale, pour Nous, Nos Héritiers et Successeurs que tout ce qui a été stipulé dans les Actes sus mentionnés sera observé et exécuté inviolablement. En foi de quoi Nous avons signé de Notre propre main la présente ratification Imperiale et y avons fait apposer le sceau de Notre Empire. Donné à Péterhof, le 27 juillet de l'an de grâce mil neuf cent cinq et de Notre règne la onzième année.
(L.S.) Nicolas.
Contresigné: le Ministre des Affaires Etrangères, Secrétaire d'Etat ; *Comte Lamsdorff.*[1]

§ 609. *A German Example.*

Wir Wilhelm
von Gottes Gnaden
Deutscher Kaiser, Konig von Preussen usw.
Urkunden und bekennen hiermit : Nachdem von Unserem Bevollmächtigten und dem Bevollmächtigten Seiner Majestät des Königs des Vereinigten Königreichs von Grossbritannien und Irland und der Britischen Uberseeischen Lande, Kaisers von Indien, am 17 August 1911 in Berlin ein Vertrag zwischen dem Deutschen Reiche und Grossbritannien über die gegen-

[1] *Traités Généraux d'Arbitrage*, 1ère série. La Haye, 1911, 88.

seitige Auslieferung von Verbrechern zwischen Deutschland und gewissen britischen Protektoraten unterzeichnet worden ist, und nachdem dieser Vertrag, der wörtlich also lautet :

(Text of Treaty.)

Uns vorgelegt und von Uns geprüft und in allen Stücken Unseren Absichten gemäss befunden worden ist, so erklären Wir, dass Wir den vorstehenden Auslieferungsvertrag genehmigen und ratifizieren, auch versprechen, ihn erfüllen und ausführen zu lassen.

Zu Urkund dessen haben Wir die gegenwärtige Ratifikationsurkunde vollzogen und mit Unserem Insiegel versehen lassen.

Gegeben, Neues Palais, den 16 Dezember, 1911.

(Signed) WILHELM I.R.
KIDERLEN.

§ 610. *A French Example.*

RAYMOND POINCARÉ
Président de la Républquie Française.
A tous ceux qui ces présentes Lettres verront,

Salut :

Une Convention Radiotélégraphique Internationale et ses Annexes ayant été arrêtées à Londres, le 5 juillet 1912, Convention et Annexes dont la teneur suit :

(Text of Convention.)

AYANT vu et examiné les dites Convention et Annexes, Nous les avons approuvées et approuvons en vertu des dispositions de la Loi votée par le Sénat et par la Chambre des Députés ; DÉCLARONS qu'elles seront acceptées, ratifiées, et confirmées, et PROMETTONS qu'elles seront inviolablement observées.

EN FOI DE QUOI, Nous avons donné les présentes, revêtues du Sceau de la République.

A PARIS, le 22 janvier 1914.

(L.S.) *(Signed)* POINCARÉ.
Par Le Président de la République : Le Président du Conseil, Ministre des Affaires Etrangères.

(Signed)

§ 611. *An United States Example.*

WILLIAM HOWARD TAFT,
President of the United States of America,

TO ALL TO WHOM THESE PRESENTS SHALL COME, GREETING :

KNOW YE, That whereas a Treaty between the United States of America and the United Kingdom of Great Britain and Ireland providing for the preservation and protection of the fur seals, was concluded and signed by their respective Plenipotentiaries at Washington on the seventh day of February, one thousand nine hundred and eleven, a true copy of which Treaty is word for word as follows :

(Text of Treaty.)

AND WHEREAS, the Senate of the United States by their resolution of February 15, 1911 (two-thirds of the Senators present concurring therein) did advise and consent to the ratification of the said Treaty ;

NOW, THEREFORE, be it known that I, William Howard Taft, President of the United States of America, having seen and considered the said Treaty, do hereby, in pursuance of the aforesaid advice and consent of the Senate, ratify and confirm the same and every article and clause thereof.

IN TESTIMONY WHEREOF, I have caused the seal of the United States to be hereunto affixed.

Given under my hand at the City of Washington this sixth day of March in the year of our Lord one thousand nine hundred and eleven, and of the Independence of the United States of America the one hundred and thirty-fifth.

(L.S.)   *(Signed)* WM. H. TAFT.
By the President—
    HUNTINGTON WILSON,
        Acting-Secretary of State.

§ 612. Form of ratification of an international compact concluded between Governments.

Whereas a . . . between . . . Government and the Government of . . . (or governments therein mentioned) relating to . . . was signed at . . . on the . . . day of . . . 19 . . which . . . is, word for word, as follows—
    (*Inseratur*—in . . . texts—)
H. . . . M. (or the . . .) Government having seen and considered the . . . aforesaid, approve, accept, confirm, and ratify it, engaging and promising sincerely and faithfully to perform and observe all and singular the things which are contained and expressed in the . . . aforesaid.

In witness whereof . . . H. . . . M. (or the . . .) Secretary of State (or, Minister) for Foreign Affairs has signed these Presents and has affixed thereto his seal.

Done at . . . the . . . day of . . . 19 . .

ADHESION AND ACCESSION

§ 613. Only such multilateral treaties and conventions comprise a clause providing for the accession of other Powers, as are intended to become universal, or at any rate general, because of their subject matter. This was the case with the Conventions signed at the Hague Peace Conferences of 1899 and 1907. The form adopted was—

" Les Puissances non-signataires sont admises à adhérer à la présente Convention. La Puissance qui désire adhérer notifie par écrit son intention au Gouvernement des Pays-Bas en lui transmettant l'acte d'adhésion, qui sera déposé dans les archives du dit Gouvernement. Ce Gouvernement transmettra immédiatement à toutes les autres Puissances copie certifiée conforme de la notification ainsi que de l'Acte d'adhésion, en indiquant la date à laquelle il a reçu la notification."

If any theoretical distinction is to be made between *adhésion* and *accession*, then the proper English equvalent of *adhérer* would be " accede."

§ 614. M. Pradier-Fodéré draws a distinction between *adhésion* and *accession* in these terms—

" Il y a certains traités qui tirent de leur caractère général une importance supérieure à l'intérêt même des contractants, et dès lors les États qui n'y ont pas eu de part directe, qui ne les ont pas signés, peuvent non seulement les couvrir de leur approbation, mais encore vouloir y participer d'une manière directe, *ex post-facto*.

" Lorsqu'il en est ainsi, et que les États contractants se sont mis d'accord avec les États qui n'ont pas signé le traité, ces derniers, suivant les circonstances, déclarent, soit qu'ils *adhèrent* à certaines clauses ou à toutes les clauses, soit qu'ils *accèdent* au traité.[1]

" *L'adhésion* marque un degré de plus que l'approbation, mais elle ne constitue pas par elle-même un engagement défini : pour que la déclaration d'adhésion produise des obligations et des droits, il faut que les États adhérents déterminent explicitement le caractère et la portée de leur adhésion.

" *L'effet* de l'*accession* est de placer l'État qui accède au traité dans les mêmes conditions que les États qui l'ont négocié. Elle a lieu, tantôt par un échange de ratifications entre tous les États signataires et tous les États qui accèdent, tantôt par une déclaration officielle faite à tous les États signataires ou à l'un de ces États chargé de recevoir les accessions des États qui n'ont pas signé le traité." [2]

We prefer to this statement the account of the matter given by Professor Oppenheim, where he says—

" But it must be specially observed that the distinction between accession and adhesion is one made in theory, to which practice frequently does not correspond. Often treaties speak of accession of third States where in fact adhesion only is meant, and *vice versa*. Thus article 6 of the Hague Convention with respect to the laws and customs of war on land stipulates the possibility of future *adhesion* of non-signatory *Powers*, although accession is meant." [3]

It may be pointed out, moreover, that so-called " *adhesion* " is not admissible in cases where the clauses of an international compact are declared to be a whole, one and indivisible, as, for instance, the Declaration of Paris of 1856 taken together with the protocol of the 16th April, and in Article 65 of the Declaration of London it is expressly stated that " Les dispositions de la présente Déclaration forment un ensemble indivisible." A method of attaining a purpose similar to that defined as *adhésion* was adopted at the second Hague Peace Con-

---

[1] In 1839 the German Confederation *acceded* to the first seven Articles of the annexe to the Treaties between the five Great Powers, Belgium and the Netherlands, " *en tant qu'elles peuvent concerner la Confédération Germanique.*"

[2] *Cours de Droit Diplomatique*, ii. 445.

[3] *International Law*, i. 569.

ference in 1907, where various reserves were made by different Powers on signing the Conventions in which the results of the Conference were recorded. Out of fifteen conventions only two, the third and the eleventh, were signed without any reservations.

On April 15, 1834, a treaty was concluded in London between Great Britain, Spain and Portugal (but not yet signed), by which the Queens of Spain and Portugal were to join forces for the expulsion from the Peninsula of Don Carlos and Don Miguel, the Spanish and Portuguese pretenders, Great Britain undertaking to support the military operations by the despatch of a naval force to the coast of Portugal.

France was invited by Palmerston to give her accession to this treaty. Talleyrand was instructed to present a counter-draft by which France would become a contracting party on a footing of equality with the other three parties, and the agreement was thus transformed into a quadruple alliance.[1]

§ 615. *Act of Accession of the British Government to the Convention of August 22, 1864, for the Amelioration of the Condition of the Wounded in Armies in the Field— Signed at London, February 18, 1865. And Acceptance thereof by the Swiss Confederation, in the name of all the Contracting Parties.—Signed at Berne, March 3, 1865.*

" The President and Federal Council of the Swiss Confederation having communicated to the Government of H.M. the Queen of the United Kingdom of Great Britain and Ireland a Convention signed at Geneva on the 22nd August, 1864, between . . . which Convention is word for word as follows :—

" And the Swiss Confederation having, in virtue of Article 9 of the said Convention, invited the Government of H.B.M. to accede thereto :

" The undersigned, H.B.M. Principal Secretary of State for Foreign Affairs, duly authorized for that purpose, hereby declares that the Government of H.B.M. fully accedes to the convention aforesaid.

[1] Guizot, *Mém.*, iv. 86.

" In witness whereof he has signed the present Act of
Accession, and has affixed thereto the seal of his arms.

" Done at London, the 18th day of February, in the year
of our Lord 1865." [1]

[*Seal and Signature.*]

Le Conseil Fédéral de la Confédération Suisse :
Vu l'Acté signé à Londres le 18 février, 1865, par lequel
S.S. le Ministre des Affaires Etrangères de S.M. la Reine du
Royaume Uni de la Grande Bretagne et d'Irlande, faisant
usage de la faculté réservée à l'Article IX de la Convention
Internationale conclue à Genéve le 22 août, 1864, pour l'amélioration du sort des militaires blessés dans les armées en
campagne, déclare que le Gouvernement de S.M.B. adhère [2]
entièrement à cette Convention ; acte d'adhésion [2] dont la
teneur suit :

(Here follows the Act of Accession,)

Déclare par les présentes—
En vertu de la disposition finale du procès-verbal d'échange
des ratifications de ladite Convention, signé à Berne le 22
décembre, 1864, accepter cette adhésion tant au nom de la
Confédération Suisse qu'en celui des autres Hauts États
Contractants, auxquels en est donné acte par la présente
Déclaration.
En foi de quoi les présentes ont été signées par le Président
et le Chancellier de la Conféderation, et munies du sceau du
Conseil Fédéral à Berne, le 3 mars, 1865.
Au nom du Conseil Fédéral Suisse.

[*Seal. Office. Signature.*]
[*Office. Signature.*]

§ 616. *Act of Accession of the Sultan, to the Treaty be-
tween Great Britain, France, Russia, and Greece, of
March 29, 1864, for the Union of the Ionian Islands to
Greece ; and Acceptance thereof by the Contracting
Parties to that Treaty.—Signed at Constantinople, April
8, 1865.*

[Ratifications exchanged at Constantinople, June 15,
1865.]

[1] *Brit. and For. State Papers*, lv. 43.
[2] Observe that these words are used to express the " fully accedes "
and " Act of Accession " of the English declaration.

" LL.MM. la Reine du Royaume Uni de la Grande Bretagne et d'Irlande, L'Empereur des Français, et l'Empereur de Toutes les Russies, d'une part, et S.M. le Roi des Hellènes de l'autre part, ayant conclu entre elles le 29 mars, 1864, un Traité pour l'Union des Iles Ioniennes au Royaume de Grèce ; et leurs dites MM., vu l'Acte en date du 24 avril, 1819,[1] par lequel la Sublime Porte Ottomane a reconnu le Protectorat de la Grande Bretagne sur les Iles Ioniennes, ayant proposé a S.M.I. le Sultan d'accéder au susdit Traité ; et S.M.I. ayant accepté cette proposition, les Plénipotentiaires des Hautes Puissance, savoir :

(Here follow the names of the plenipotentiaries of the respective Powers, their official titles and the list of their decorations) ;

" Se sont réunis afin de constater en due forme l'Accession de S.M.I. le Sultan, et l'Acceptation de cette Accession par les quatre Cours Signataires du Traité.

" En conséquence le Plénipotentiaire de S.M. le Sultan déclare, en vertu de ses pleins pouvoirs, que la Sublime Porte accède formellement au susdit Traité signé à Londres le 29 mars, 1864,[2] entre LL. MM. la Reine, etc. . . ., d'une part, et S.M. le Roi des Hellènes, de l'autre part, pour l'Union des Iles Ioniennes au Royaume de Grèce, duquel Traité la teneur suit mot à mot—

" Les Plénipotentiaires de la Grande Bretagne, de France, de Russie et de Grèce, en vertu de leurs pleins pouvoirs, acceptent formellement, au nom de leurs Cours respectives, ladite Accession de la Sublime Porte Ottomane.

" Le présent Acte d'Accession et Acceptation sera ratifié, et les Actes de Ratification en seront échangés à Constantinople dans l'espace de deux mois à dater de ce jour, ou plus tôt si faire se peut.

" En foi de quoi les Plénipotentiaires respectifs l'ont signé, et y ont apposé le sceau de leurs armes.

" Fait à Constantinople, le 8e jour d'avril, l'an de grace 1865."

Seals and signatures in the following positions—

1. Great Britain.	2. Turkey.
3. France.	4. Russia.[3]

---

[1] *Brit. and For. State Papers*, vol. vii.   [2] *Ibid.*, vol. liv. 11.
[3] *Brit. and For. State Papers*, lv. 48.

[The British Plenipotentiary was Chargé d'Affaires, that of France an Ambassador, those of Russia and Greece Envoys Extraordinary and Ministers Plenipotentiary, that of Turkey His Highness Mouhammed Emin Aali Pacha, minister of Foreign Affairs. Each plenipotentiary must have received a counterpart in which the rule of the *alternat* was observed, and that fact explains why in the copy here printed the signature of the British plenipotentiary occupies the first place. It will also be noted that this document partakes of the solemn forms of a treaty, while the preceding one resembles rather an Acte de Ratification.]

§ 617. *Accession of Great Britain to the Convention signed at Paris, March 20, 1883, for the Protection of Industrial Property.—Paris, March 17, 1884.*

1. *Declaration of Accession.*

" The undersigned, Ambassador Extraordinary and Plenipotentiary of H.M. the Queen of the United Kingdom of Great Britain and Ireland to the French Republic, declares that H.B.M. having had the International Convention for the protection of Industrial Property, concluded at Paris on the 20th March, 1883, and the Protocol relating thereto, signed on the same date, laid before her, and availing herself of the right reserved by Article XVI of that Convention to States not parties to the original Convention, accedes, on behalf of the United Kingdom of Great Britain and Ireland, to the said International Convention for the Protection of Industrial Property, and to the said Protocol, which are to be considered as inserted word for word in the present Declaration, and formerly [*sic*] engages, as far as regards the President of the French Republic and the other High Contracting Parties, to co-operate on her part in the execution of the stipulations contained in the Convention and Protocol aforesaid.

" The Undersigned makes this Declaration on the part of H.B.M. with the express understanding that power is reserved to H.B.M. to accede to the Convention on behalf of the Isle of Man and the Channel Islands, and any of H.M.'s possessions, on due notice to that effect being given through H.M.'s Government.

" In witness whereof the Undersigned, duly authorized, has signed the present declaration of Accession, and has affixed thereto the seal of his arms.

" Done at Paris on the 17th day of March, 1884."

[*Seal and Signature.*]

2. *Declaration of Acceptance of Accession.*

" S.M. la Reine du Royaume Uni de la Grande-Bretagne et d'Irlande ayant accédé à la Convention Internationale, relative à la protection de la propriété industrielle, conclue à à Paris le 20 mars, 1883, et suivie d'un Protocole en date du même jour, en vertu de l'Acte d'Accession, délivré par son Ambassadeur Extraordinaire et Plénipotentiaire près le Gouvernement de la République Française ; acte dont la teneur suit ici, mot pour mot :—

[Here is inserted the text of No. 1 in English.]

" Le Président de la République Française a autorisé le Soussigné, Président du Conseil, Ministre des Affaires Étrangères, à accepter formellement la dite accession, y compris les réserves qui y sont contenues, concernant l'Ile de Man, les Iles de la Manche, et toutes autres Possessions de S.M.B., s'engageant, tant en son nom qu'au nom des autres Hautes Parties Contractantes, à concourir à l'accomplissement des obligations stipulées dans la Convention et le Protocole y annexé, qui pourront concerner le Royaume Uni de la Grande Bretagne et d'Irlande.

" En foi de quoi le Soussigné, dûment autorisé, a dressé le présent Acte d'Acceptation et y a fait apposer son cachet.

" Fait à Paris, le 2 avril, 1884." [1]

[*Seal and signature.*]

§ 618. *Accession of the United Kingdom to the International Convention for the prohibition of the use of white phosphorus in the match industry.—Signed at Berne, September 26, 1906.*

1. *H.M. Chargé d'Affaires at Berne to the President of the Swiss Confederation.*

Berne, December 28, 1908.

Monsieur le Président,

In compliance with telegraphic instructions which I have received from H.M.'s Secretary of State for Foreign

[1] *Brit. and For. State Papers,* lxxv. 414.

Affairs, I have the honour to notify to Y.E., as provided in Article V, the accession of the United Kingdom of Great Britain and Ireland to the Convention prohibiting the use of white (yellow) phosphorus in the manufacture of matches, which was signed at Berne on the 26th September, 1906.

I am to point out that the above-mentioned accession applies only to the United Kingdom.

I avail, etc. [*Signature.*]

2. *The President of the Swiss Confederation to H.M.'s Chargé d'Affaires at Berne.*

Berne, le 15 Janvier 1909.

Monsieur le Secrétaire,

Nous avons l'honneur de vous accuser réception de la note du 28 décembre, 1908, nous informant de l'adhésion du Gouvernement Britannique, uniquement pour le territoire restreint du Royaume-Uni de Grande-Bretagne et d'Irlande, à la Convention de Berne du 26 septembre, 1906, concernant l'interdiction de l'emploi du phosphore blanc (jaune) dans l'industrie des allumettes.

Nous avons notifié cette adhésion aux États intéressés par une note circulaire de ce jour, dont ci-joint une copie pour votre information.

Veuillez, etc.,
Au nom du Conseil Fédéral.

[Signature] *Président de la Confédération.*
[Signature] *Chancellier de la Confédération.*

Inclosure.

Berne, le 5 Janvier, 1909.

M. le Ministre,

Par note du 28 décembre, 1908, la Légation Britannique à Berne nous a informé de l'adhésion de son Gouvernement uniquement pour le territoire restreint du Royaume-Uni de Grande-Bretagne et d'Irlande à la Convention de Berne du 26 Septembre, 1906, concernant l'interdiction de l'emploi du phosphore blanc (jaune) dans l'industrie des allumettes.

Nous avons l'honneur par la présente de notifier cette adhésion à V.E. et de lui remettre une copie authentique de la note précitée ,ex exécution de l'Article V de la Convention.[1]

[Signature and counter-signature as before.]

---

[1] *Brit. and For. State Papers*, xcix. 989.

This is as simple a form of giving notice of accession to a treaty as can well be conceived.   It will be observed that the English word " accession " is rendered by " adhésion," as in one of the cases previously noted (§ 615).   In vol. c. of the State Papers, p. 280, there is an " Exchange of Notes between the British and Netherlands Governments respecting the Accession of Great Britain to the Declarations signed at the Hague, July 29, 1899, respecting (1) Expanding bullets ; (2) Asphyxiating gases.—dated August 30 and September 3, 1907. These notes are in the same simple form as in the last-cited case.

CHAPTER XXXII

GOOD OFFICES (BONS OFFICES)

§ 619. In popular language, even in the writings of diplomatists and historians, the term mediation is employed somewhat loosely and is often confounded with good offices, though the two are essentially distinct in character. Thus, Delane, writing from Paris, April 26, 1867, says : " The French profess to be very grateful for our *bons offices* " [in connexion with the Luxemburg affair, see § 481]. Yet, on the following day, he writes to G. W. Dasent, whom he had left as acting editor of the *Times*, " Pray blow the trumpet of the mediator " [apparently meant for Lord Stanley, then Secretary of State for Foreign Affairs].[1] The author referred to in the footnote speaks of the " mediation " of the Foreign Office in the Luxemburg affair in 1867. Many other instances might be quoted.

Good Offices are exerted in order to compose differences between two Powers, either (1) to avoid the exacerbation of hostile feeling threatening a rupture and a possible resort to force, or (2) with the object of restoring peace between belligerents who are thought likely to welcome

---

[1] A. I. Dasent, *John Thaddeus Delane*, ii. 200.

an opportunity of laying down their arms and concluding an honourable peace. They may be offered and refused or accepted, or they may be asked and accorded. In any case the offer can only be made by, or accepted from, a neutral Power, and this should be a Power of whose friendly sentiments towards both parties there cannot be any doubt. The duty of the friendly Power is, in the first place, to bring the contending parties together, and to make such suggestions as may facilitate the removal of causes of disagreement, or, in the second case, the conclusion of peace. It is only in cases where the parties consent to the negotiations being conducted through the channel of the Power which has offered good offices, that the good offices develope into mediation.

§ 620. Part II of the Hague Convention of 1907 for the " Pacific Settlement of International Disputes " runs thus :—

" Art. 2. In case of serious disagreement or dispute, before an appeal to arms, the Contracting Powers agree to have recourse, as far as circumstances allow, to the good offices or mediation of one or more friendly Powers. Art. 3. Independently of this recourse, the Contracting Powers deem it expedient and desirable that one or more Powers, strangers to the dispute, should, on their own initiative and as far as circumstances may allow, offer their good offices or mediation to the States at variance.

" Powers, strangers to the dispute, have the right to offer good offices or mediation, even during the course of hostilities.

" The exercise of this right can never be regarded by either of the parties at variance as an unfriendly act. Art. 4. The part of the mediator consists in reconciling the opposing claims and appeasing the feelings of resentment which may have arisen between the States at variance. Art. 5. The duties of the mediator are at an end when once it is declared, either by one of the contending parties, or by the mediator himself, that the means of reconciliation proposed by him are not accepted. Art. 6. Good offices and mediation, undertaken either at the request of the contending parties or on the initiative of Powers strangers to the dispute, have exclusively the character of advice, and never have binding force. Art. 7. The acceptance of mediation cannot, in default of agreement to the contrary, have the effect of interrupting, delaying or hindering mobilisation or other measures of preparation for war. If mediation takes place after the commencement of hostilities, the military operations in progress are not interrupted, in default of agreement to the contrary. Art. 8. The Contracting Powers are agreed in recommending the application, when circumstances allow, of special mediation in the following form :—In case of a serious difference endangering peace, the contending States choose respectively a Power, to which they entrust the mission of entering into direct communication with the Power chosen on the other side, with the object of preventing the rupture of pacific relations. For the period of this mandate, the term of which, in default of agreement to the contrary, cannot exceed thirty days, the States at variance cease from all direct communication on the subject of the dispute, which is regarded as referred exclusively to the mediating Powers. These Powers shall use their best efforts to settle the dispute. In case of a definite rupture of pacific relations, these Powers remain jointly charged with the task of taking advantage of any opportunity to restore peace." [1]

Dr. Pearce Higgins' comment on this passage is—

" There is, according to many writers on international law, a theoretical difference between mediation and good offices, but this is not observed in the text of the Convention. The difference is, however, more theoretical than practical, and both consist in a friendly interposition of a third Power to adjust differences and lead to a pacific solution of a dispute between two Powers at variance." [2]

§ 621. Against this view may be placed the following—

" Diplomatic practice frequently does not distinguish between good offices and mediation. But although good offices can easily develop into mediation, they must not be confounded with it. The difference between them is that, whereas good offices consist in various kinds of action tending to call negotiations between the conflicting States into existence, mediation consists in a direct conduct of negotiations between the differing parties on the basis of proposals made by the mediator. Good offices seek to induce the conflicting parties,

[1] A. Pearce Higgins, 103. This is a translation from the French original. [2] *Ibid.*, 167.

who are not at all inclined to negotiate with each other or who have negotiated without effecting an understanding, to enter or to re-enter into such negotiaions. Good offices can also consist in advice, in submitting a proposal of one of the parties to the other, and the like, but the Power which offers them does not itself take part in the negotiations. On the other hand, the mediator is the middleman who does take part in the negotiations. He makes certain proposals on the basis of which the States at variance may come to an understanding. He even conducts the negotiations himself, always anxious to reconcile the opposing claims and to appease the feeling of resentment between the parties. All the efforts of the mediator may often, of course, be useless, the differing parties being unable or unwilling to consent to an agreement. But if an understanding is arrived at, the position of the mediator as a party to the negotiation, although not a participator in the difference, frequently becomes apparent either by the drafting of a special act of mediation which is signed by the States at variance and the mediator, or by the fact that in the convention between the conflicting States, which stipulates the terms of their understanding, the mediator is mentioned." [1]

§ 622. " Les *bons offices* sont les démarches, les actes au moyen desquels une tierce Puissance essaye d'ouvrir la voie aux négociations des parties intéressées, ou de renouer ces négociations, quand elles sont interrompues. Ils peuvent être offerts spontanément ou accordés à la suite d'une demande directe ; ils peuvent aussi résulter d'engagements souscrits à titre éventuel.[2] En général, ils n'emportent aucune respon-

---

[1] Oppenheim, *International Law*, ii. § 9, slightly altered.

[2] For instance, see Treaty between Great Britain and Portugal, signed at Lisbon, May 16, 1703. Art. III. " If ever it shall happen that the Kings of Spain and France, either the present or the future, both of them together, or either of them separately, shall make war, or give occasion to suspect that they intend to make war, upon the kingdom of Portugal, either on the continent of Europe or in its Dominions beyond Seas, Her Majesty the Queen of Great Britain, and the Lords the States-General, shall use their friendly offices with the said Kings, or either of them, in order to persuade them to observe the terms of peace towards Portugal, and not to make war upon it. IV. But these good offices not proving successful, but altogether ineffectual, so that war should be made by the aforesaid Kings, or by either of them upon Portugal, the above-mentioned Powers of Great Britain and Holland, shall make war, with all their force, upon the aforesaid Kings or King, who shall carry hostile arms into Portugal, and towards that war which shall be carried on in Europe, they shall supply 12,000 men, whom they shall arm and pay, as well when in quarters as in action ; and the said High Allies shall be obliged to keep that number of men complete, by recruiting it from time to time at their own expense " (*Brit. and For. State Papers*, xiii. 1124).

sabilité, à moins d'une stipulation expresse. La Puissance qui prête ses bons offices fait usage de son autorité et de son influence morales, en donnant de bienveillants conseils pour apaiser les ressentiments, pour amener la concorde ; elle propose des moyens pour arriver à une transaction, afin d'empêcher de prendre les armes, ou d'obtenir qu'on les dépose."

" Les notes échangées pour l'interposition des bons offices doivent être rédigées avec une très-grande prudence avec beaucoup de modération, afin de montrer qu'on n'agit que par bienveillance, par amitié, sans aucune arrière-pensée d'intérêt propre et particulier. Le grand soin du rédacteur doit être d'éviter d'éveiller les susceptibilités. Le secret le plus absolu doit être gardé ; la démarche ne doit pas être ébruitée. L'initiative de la publication des documents diplomatiques relatifs à l'interposition des bons offices doit être laissée au gouvernement auquel les conseils sont adressés."

§ 623. " Two methods of amicable settlement are generally invoked before there is an appeal to arbitration. In case of conflict contending States are expected to resort in the first instance to diplomatic negotiations in the hope of adjusting by mutual concession and compromise pending differences. In that way Great Britain and the United States settled their notable boundary controversies, and the prolonged disputes as to the rights of fishery on the banks of Newfoundland and in the Gulf of St. Lawrence, in the treaties of 1818, 1854 and 1871. When the parties themselves cannot agree, some common friend often interposes his good offices in the spirit of mediation so as to bring about a friendly understanding by reconciling conflicting claims and opinions. In the hope of promoting that method of settlement the plenipotentiaries who united in the making of the Protocol of the Treaty of Paris, 1856, declared that they did " not hesitate to express, in the name of their governments, the wish that States between which any serious misunderstanding may arise should, before appealing to arms, have recourse, as far as circumstances might allow, to the good offices of a friendly power." [2]

§ 624. *Protocol of the Treaty of Paris*, 1856, *passage relating to " good offices."* The French text is—

" MM. les Plénipotentiaires n'hésitent pas à exprimer, au nom de leurs Gouvernements, le vœu [3] que les Etats entre

---

[1] Pradier-Fodéré, ii. 466.   [2] Hannis Taylor, § 359.
[3] A stronger word than " wish."

lesquels s'élèverait un dissentiment sérieux, avant d'en appeler aux armes, eussent recours, en tant que les circonstances l'admettraient, aux bons offices d'une Puissance amie. MM. les Plénipotentiaires espèrent que les Gouvernements non représentés au Congrès s'associeront à la pensée qui a inspiré le vœu consigné au présent Protocole."

Lord Clarendon, in introducing this subject, referred to Article 8 of the Treaty concluded a fortnight earlier, which was worded—

" S'il survenait, entre la Sublime Porte et l'une ou plusieurs des autres Puissances signataires, un dissentiment qui menaçât le maintien de leurs relations, la Sublime Porte et chacune de ces Puissances, avant de recourir à l'emploi de la force, mettront les autres Parties Contractantes en mesure de prévenir cette extrémité par leur action médiatrice."

He proposed that the Congress should give a wider application to this principle, by agreeing to a resolution conducive to ensuring this chance of maintenance of peace in the future.

Count Walewski, on behalf of France, gave his support to this idea.

Count Buol " could not undertake in the name of his Court an absolute engagement which would be of a nature to limit the independence of the Austrian Cabinet."

Baron Manteuffel (for Prussia) declared that his august master shared the ideas put forward by Lord Clarendon.

Count Orloff (for Russia), while recognizing the wisdom of the proposal, felt bound to refer home for instructions.

Count Cavour inquired whether the *vœu* would extend to military intervention against a *de facto* government, such as that undertaken by Austria in 1821 in regard to Naples.

Lord Clarendon replied that the *vœu* would admit of a more general application. For instance, if the good offices of another Power had resulted in inducing Greece to respect the laws of neutrality, Great Britain and France would probably have refrained from occupying the Piræus (which had been done during the Crimean War).

Count Walewski stated that there was no question of stipulating for a right or of taking an engagement ; the *vœu* would not limit the liberty of individual judgment of any power in questions touching its dignity.

Count Buol replied to Count Cavour that in speaking of the Austrian occupation of the kingdom of Naples in 1821, he had forgotten that the measures in question was the result of an understanding between the Five Great Powers who met at Laybach. That being the case, it came within the category of ideas put forward by Lord Clarendon. Similar instances might occur again, and he did not admit that an intervention which took place in consequence of an agreement between the Five Great Powers could be protested against by a Power of secondary[1] class. He applauded the proposal presented by Lord Clarendon, as having a humane object, but he could not assent to it, if it were desired to give to it too great an extension, or to deduce from it couse-quences favourable to *de 'facto* governments and to doctrines which he could not admit. He desired that the Conference should not find itself compelled to discuss irritating questions, calculated to disturb the perfect harmony which had not ceased to prevail among the plenipotentiaries.

Count Cavour rejoined that he was entirely satisfied with the explanations which he had elicited, and he acceded to the proposal submitted to the Congress.

Thereupon the paragraph above quoted was added to the protocol.

§ 625. It was invoked in 1864 with reference to the

---

[1] This assertion was untrue. The agreement was limited to the three autocratic Powers, Russia, Austria and Prussia. See § 464.

Conference on Danish affairs,[1] and in 1866 by Lord Clarendon on the eve of the Seven Weeks War, but without success.[2]   Again in 1876 an attempt was made to settle the disputes between Russia and Turkey (see § 487, Conference of Constantinople).

§ 626. During the Franco-Prussian war of 1870-1 a constant correspondence went on between the Foreign Offices of the Great Powers, both neutral and belligerent, in which *bons offices* and *médiation* were mentioned.   At first Great Britain was requested by France to use her " influence " to adjust the difficulty that had arisen in respect of the offer of the Spanish crown to Prince Leopold of Hohenzollern.   Next, the " good offices " of Her Majesty's government were asked for.   Then we begin to find " good offices " and " mediation " spoken of as if they were more or less of an identical character. Two days before the French declaration of war was despatched to Berlin, Lord Granville telegraphed recommending to both France and Prussia that before proceeding to extremities they should have recourse to the good offices of some friendly Power or Powers acceptable to both.   He quoted Protocol 23 of the Treaty of Paris, and declared that Her Majesty's government were ready to take any part in the matter that might be desired. This last phrase seems to amount virtually to an offer of mediation, and it was so regarded by the French government.   For in a despatch dated July 17, the day on which the British proposal was received, the Duc de Grammont, writing to the French ambassador in London said : " Le Cabinet de Londres, se référant au 23me Protocole du Congrès de Paris, a offert au Gouvernement de l'Empereur d'interposer entre la France et la Prusse son *action médiatrice* " ; but further on he added : " Quelle que pût être d'ailleurs en ce moment notre disposition à accepter les *bons offices* d'une Puissance

[1] *Brit. and For. State Papers*, liv. 173.   [2] *Ibid.*, lvii. 380.

amie, et en particulier de l'Angleterre, nous ne saurions
accéder aujourd'hui à l'offre du Cabinet de Londres."
And yet on the previous day he spoke to the Chamber
of having immediately commenced " des négotiations
avec les Puissances étrangères, afin d'obtenir leurs
bons offices auprès de la Prusse afin qu'elle reconnût la
légitimité de nos griefs," whereas up to July 13 he had
only asked Her Majesty's Government to "use influence";
so that he seems to have regarded this expression as
synonymous with " good offices."   A similar identifica-
tion of good offices and mediation is found in a despatch
from the British Ambassador at Berlin,[1] and in a despatch of Lord Granville's to the British Ambassador in
Paris.[2] In consequence of the French refusal—which was
emphasized by the Prince de la Tour d'Auvergne,[3]
after the defeats of Wissembourg and Wörth, informing
Lord Lyons that " France under present circumstances
could listen to no offer of mediation from any quarter "
—Lord Granville announced on August 17[4] that Her
Majesty's Government " have no intention or desire to
obtrude their mediation on either France or Prussia,
but if at any time recourse should be had to their good
offices, they will be freely given, and zealously exerted
for the restoration of peace between the two countries."
From this date onwards Lord Granville constantly
maintained that the time had not yet arrived for
mediation.   Yet he was not quite clear as to the relative
value of the two expressions ; for on August 31[5] he
informed the British ambassador at Petersburg that :
" France declares formally that she does not need the
good offices of others, or wish for them," the word used
by M. de la Tour d'Auvergne having been mediation.[6]
After the disaster of Sedan M. Jules Favre told Lord
Lyons [7] that France would be glad that an offer of

---

[1] *Brit. and For. State Papers*, lx. 855.   [2] *Ibid.*, 559.
[3] He had succeeded Grammont as Minister for Foreign Affairs.
[4] *Brit. and For. State Papers*, lx. 683.   [5] *Ibid.*, 713.
[6] *Ibid.*, 686.   [7] *Ibid.*, 725.

mediation, on the basis of the integrity of French territory, should be made by a neutral Power to Prussia. To this Lord Granville replied that it would do more harm than good if Her Majesty's government attempted mediation, unless they had reason to believe that both parties would receive their mediation, and that there was a basis of negotiation which both would accept. Her Majesty's government, just as they had been the *channel of communication* in minor matters, would be happy to be the channel of any communication that was likely to lead to peace.[1]

That was as much as to say : " Mediation is impossible, we will confine ourselves to good offices." And, in fact, the good offices of the British government were used in arranging an interview between Jules Favre and Bismarck.

Even M. Thiers, an historian by profession, at the time of his celebrated tour of Europe, did not distinguish between the two terms ; or, at least, as his language was repeated by Count Beust. He requested that the Austrian Government " se joignit aux tentatives de *médiation* qui seraient faites par d'autres Puissances, et particulièrement par la Russie," but also said that : " Il croyait que les intérêts de l'humanité aussi bien que ceux de la politique engagerait la Cour de Russie à interposer ses *bons offices*." (Underneath these appeals for good offices and strong " moral support " there lay a desire, not obscurely intimated, for something in the nature of an " armed mediation.")

At a later period[2] Lord Granville evidently endeavoured to make a distinction. In writing to Lord A. Loftus, the British Ambassador at Berlin, he said: " Offers of mediation *or* of good offices would not have been wanting if Her Majesty's government had at any time believed that such offers would have been acceptable to both the belligerents." And he then instructed

[1] *Brit. and For. State Papers*, 180.
[2] October 20, *ibid.*, 866.

him to urge on the Berlin Government the propriety of
" exhausting every attempt for peace before orders for
the attack on Paris were given, and that the conditions
of peace were just, moderate, and in accordance with
true policy and the sentiments of the age." This
despatch, clearly intended for communication to the
Prussian government, was certainly an exertion of good
offices.

In a despatch of October 28,[1] addressed to the Prussian
Ambassador in London, and intended as a reply to the
despatch to Lord A. Loftus just quoted, Count Bismarck spoke of " proposals " for the convocation of an
assembly, " which were made to the members of the
Paris government with our consent, on the 9th of this
month, met with such a reception from them that even
the mediating personages declared that they must now
give up the hopes which they had entertained " ; and
further on in the same despatch he said : " In the humane
sympathy which has occasioned the *intervention*, the
illusion may be found of support from the neutral
Powers, and thereby encouragement to further resistance,
which might produce just the contrary to what Lord
Granville intended." It must be remembered, however,
that we have not here an original document, but only a
translation from the German.

M. Jules Favre, in a circular of November 21, said :
" la proposition d'armistice appartient aux Puissances
neutres, et l'une d'elles a bien voulu faire auprès de la
Prusse la démarche qui a donné à notre négociateur
l'occasion d'entrer en pour-parlers. Ce *bon office* n'était
point un fait isolé. Dès le 20 octobre Lord Granville
adressait à Lord Augustus Loftus une dépêche com-
muniquée au Cabinet de Berlin, et dans laquelle il
exposait, avec une grande autorité, les raisons d'intérêt
Européen qui devaient amener la cessation de la guerre."

Towards the end of February 1871[2] Lord Granville
informed the British Ambassador at Berlin that Her

---

[1] *Brit. and For. State Papers*, 919.   [2] Feb. 26, *ibid.*, 661.

Majesty's government were willing to tender their *good offices* to Germany, under the conviction that it was in the interest of Germany, as well as of France, that the amount of the indemnity should not be greater than it was reasonable to expect could be paid. Count Bismarck had already, on the 23rd, announced to MM. Thiers and Jules Favre that he had induced the king of reduce the indemnity to five milliards of francs from the six which had at first been demanded.[1]

The conclusion to be drawn from the foregoing summary is that *mediation* cannot take place unless it is accepted by both the parties to a dispute or conflict, but that it is possible to exert *good offices* at the request of one of them, since the essential character of such a step is the presentation to the other party of reasons for a particular course of action which he is invited to take into consideration and adopt.

§ 627. In 1898, after war had lasted for three months between the United States and Spain, with the result that the latter Power found it impossible to continue the contest with any hope of ultimate success, the Ministro de Estado, on July 22, addressed a telegraphic message to the President of the United States asking on what terms the conflict could be terminated. It was delivered to the President on the 26th by the French Ambassador, whose good offices in the matter had been invoked through the French government.

The President's reply of the 30th was telegraphed back to Madrid by the French Ambassador. It stated the terms required, and undertook that if they were accepted commissioners would be named by the United States to meet similarly authorized commissioners on the part of Spain for the purpose of settling the details of the Treaty of Peace, and signing and delivering it on the terms previously mentioned. On August 7 the Spanish acceptance was telegraphed from Madrid to the French

[1] Sorel, *Hist. Dipl. de la guerre franco-allemande*, ii. 237.

ambassador, who left a copy of the telegram with the President on the 9th.   As its wording, " doubtless owing to the various transformations which it had undergone in the course of its circuitous transmission by telegraph and in cypher was not entirely explicit," in the form in which it reached the President, the Secretary of State drafted a protocol embodying the terms offered, and sent it to the ambassador on August 10.   The text was, no doubt, telegraphed by the ambassador to Madrid by way of Paris, and on the 11th a full-power to sign the protocol, which had been previously discussed between the Secretary of State and the ambassador, reached the latter.   Full-powers in the usual documentary form were to be subsequently sent to him.   Consequently on the 12th, this information having been communicated by the ambassador to the Secretary of State, the President addressed to him the following authorization—

" William R. Day, *Secretary of State.*
" You are hereby authorized to sign, on the part of the United States, the Protocol of this date embodying the terms on which the United States and Spain have agreed to treat of peace.
" WILLIAM MCKINLEY." [1]

A summary of the protocol signed on this occasion will be found in chap. xxix, § 572.

§ 628. *Mr. Roosevelt's good offices between Japan and Russia.*

On June 8, 1905, the Acting Secretary of State of the United States telegraphed to the Ambassador at Petersburg and the Minister at Tokyo, that the time had come when, in the interest of all mankind, he must endeavour to see whether it were not possible to bring to an end the terrible and lamentable conflict then being

---

[1] W. F. Johnson, *America's Foreign Relations*, ii. 263 gives a more detailed account of the negotiations.   Compare with papers presented to Congress.

waged. He, therefore, urged both governments to open direct negotiations for peace, and he suggested that the negotiations should be conducted directly and exclusively between Russian and Japanese plenipotentiaries or delegates without any intermediary. If the two Powers concerned felt that his services would be helpful in arranging the preliminaries as to time and place of meeting, he was willing to do what he properly could ; but if those preliminaries could be arranged directly between the two Powers, or in any other way, he would be glad, as his sole purpose was to bring about a meeting which the whole civilized world would pray might result in peace.

The answer of Japan was that the Imperial government, desiring in the interest of the world, as well as in the interest of Japan, the re-establishment of peace on terms that would fully guarantee its stability, would in response to the suggestion of the President, appoint plenipotentiaries to meet plenipotentiaries of Russia at such time and place as might be found mutually agreeable and convenient, for the purpose of negotiating and concluding terms of peace directly and exclusively between the two belligerents.

Russia replied that with regard to the eventual meeting of Russian and Japanese plenipotentiaries " in order to see if it were not possible for the two Powers to agree to terms of peace," the Imperial Government had no objection in principle to this endeavour if the Japanese government expressed a like desire.

On that it was proposed that the meeting-place should be Washington, which was accepted by both belligerents. This was followed on the part of the President by a suggestion that each belligerent should communicate to him the names of the plenipotentiaries, and that at the time of the appointment of the Russian plenipotentiaries it should be stated that they were named to negotiate and conclude a treaty of peace, as the wording of the Russian reply had evidently made Japan feel doubtful whether they would really be appointed to conclude a treaty of peace. The names having been stated on both sides were then confidentially communicated by the President to the respective belligerents, and Japan proposed through the same channel for the time of meeting the first ten days of August. This was accepted by the Emperor of Russia, who, however, thought it rather distant. This point having been arranged, the President on July 1 telegraphed to Petersburg that on the following Monday he would publicly announce the names of the plenipotentiaries, and state that they would be clothed with full-powers to conclude a treaty of peace, subject to ratification by the respective governments.

Ultimately the negotiations were carried on at Portsmouth in New Hampshire, and the treaty of peace was concluded there on September 5. It was arranged that the ratification of the treaty by the Emperors of Japan and Russia should be announced through the American Embassy at Petersburg and the French Legation at Tokyo. Both sovereigns signed their respective instruments of ratification on the same day : namely, the 14th October. Both expressed their gratitude to the President for his exertions in co-operating in the establishment of peace.[1]

It seems natural to suppose that if, during the progress of negotiations any difficulties occur between the plenipotentiaries, the Head of the State, who has succeeded by the exercise of good offices in bringing the belligerents together, would also, if appealed to confidentially by either party, give such advice as might tend to facilitate the removal of such difficulties.

Some further details as to this particular instance of the interposition of good offices follow :—

November 17, 1904. Mr. Hay, the Secretary of State, received a telegram from Petersburg : " I am requested

---

[1] *Papers Relating to the Foreign Relations of the United States.* Washington, 1906, p. 807. W. F. Johnson, *America's Foreign Relations,* ii. 295.

to inform you that the Emperor earnestly desires to accept the President's proposal, but will be prevented by existing conditions."[1] The author adds : " It required further defeats—at the Hun river and Mukden on land, and in the Sea of Japan—to bring Russia to terms." It is clear, therefore, that Mr. Roosevelt had begun to offer his good offices in November 1904.

1905, January 3, Diary. " The air is still full of rumours of peace by our intervention. I gave the newspapers to understand that we were doing nothing and had no intention of interfering in a matter where our intervention is not wanted."

February 13. " Sternberg [German ambassador] says the British Ambassador in Petersburg has pointed out to Ct. Lamsdorff the advantages to Russia of a speedy conclusion of peace. The Ambassador stated that Lamsdorff seemed to agree with him. Benckendorff [Russian ambassador in London] has had similar interview with Lansdowne."

February 15. " The President keeps warning Japan not to be exorbitant in her terms of peace."

Ibid., p. 406, June 15. " Hay landed in New York [after a holiday in Europe] and went to Washington, where he learnt that President Roosevelt was on the point of bringing about peace negotiations between Japan and Russia."

June 19, 1905. " The President gave me an interesting account of the peace negotiations—which he undertook at the suggestion of Japan. He was struck with the vacillation and weakness of purpose shown by Russia ; and was not well pleased that Japan refused to go to the Hague."

It seems evident that the *Papers Relating to the Foreign Relations*, and the allusions contained in the *Life and Letters of John Hay*, do not by any means give the whole story. What is worth noting for the present

[1] W. R. Thayer, *Life and Letters of John Hay*, ii. 384.

purpose is the clearness of President Roosevelt's intention to confine himself to " good offices," and not to obtrude his mediation on the belligerents. He knew well where to draw the line.

§ 629. Three cases which occurred in the eighteenth century show that at that period the distinction between good offices and mediation was well understood. The first of these was with reference to the dispute between Great Britain and Frederick the Great over his sequestration of the remaining instalment of the Silesian loan. The British Government had asked the King of France to interpose his good offices with his ally, the King of Prussia, and the French Ministry tried to convert this request into an application for French mediation.[1]

During the winter of 1741–2 France offered her mediation between Russia and Sweden. In the spring of 1742 the brothers Bestucheff prevailed on the Empress Elisabeth to decline it, and to inform the French Minister, La Chêtardie, that while appreciating the King's good offices, she preferred to treat with Sweden without any intermediary.[2]

The third is found in a letter from the Empress Catherine to Frederick the Great, of October 9, 1770. His Envoy at Petersburg had conveyed to her an offer to mediate between herself and the Turks. She wrote : " il faut éviter le mot et la forme de la médiation. Je suis prête à accepter les bons offices de la Cour de Vienne. Je réclame ceux de votre Majesté." The words " et la forme " show that she was perfectly alive to the possible disadvantages of a mediation, in which the negotiations are carried on through the plenipotentiaries of the mediating Powers. It was her intention to treat directly with the Turks. If Austria and Prussia would employ their good offices in the way of persuasion applied to Turkey, she would accept that kind of assistance towards the restoration of peace. She persisted in this view to

---

[1] Satow, chap. xiv., and app. 64–100 ; 101–8.
[2] A. Vandal, *Louis XV et Élisabeth de Russie*, 174.

the end, as is shown by the treaty of July 25, 1772, between the two Empresses' enumerating their respective shares in the partition of Poland (Article 4), in which the Empress Maria-Theresa " promet de continuer à S'employer sincèrement au succès désirable des Négociations du Congrès, consequemment aux bons offices auxquels Elle s'est engagée envers les deux Parties belligérantes." [1]

§ 630. Finally, let us quote another distinguished international jurist on this matter.

" Les anciens auteurs établissaient une distinction nette entre l'interposition des bons offices et la médiation. ' L'interpositeur ' ou ' pacificateur ' était le tiers qui s'interposait sans que son intervention eût été admise expressément par toutes les parties intéressées ; le ' médiateur ' était celui qui avait reçu un véritable mandat. Actuellement encore les deux institutions diffèrent et c'est même à tort qu'à la conférence de la Haye le project rédigé par la délégation russe a prétendu ramener la distinction à une portée exclusivement théorique.

" ' Les bons offices, dit Alexandre Mérignac, se traduisent par des conseils, des actes, des négociations ayant pour but d'amener la paix, sans que la puissance de laquelle ils émanent s'éngage dans l'examen approfondi du litige.'

" ' Le médiateur, dit Rivier, s'interpose entre les États en conflit ; il prend part aux négociations et même il les dirige. C'est par son intermédiaire que sont échangées les déclarations des parties. Il s'efforce de moyenner un arrangement amiable ; s'il y a guerre, d'amener la paix, sans toutefois avoir qualité pour l'imposer. Les États en conflit restent libres de ne pas accepter ses conseils. Son action s'exerce soit par des négociations d'État, soit dans des congrès ou conférences où le rôle principal lui est dévolu.' " [2]

[1] F. de Martens, ii. 28.
[2] E. Nys, *Le Droit International*, 1906, iii. 59.

CHAPTER XXXIII

MEDIATION

§ 631. FOR a definition of mediation, refer to the last paragraph of the immediately preceding chapter.

The procedure in mediation is partly to be gathered from the accounts in chapter xxv of Congresses, such as Westphalia, Oliva, Nijmegen, Rijswijk, Carlowitz, Cambray, Teschen and Prague.

Possibly it might be held that the Great Powers acted as joint mediators in the Conference on the Affairs of Greece, in 1827–32 (§ 470), but if so, it is evident that the formalities consecrated by previous practice were not observed on that occasion. The Conference on the Affairs of Belgium in 1830–3 (§ 471) may be regarded as having ended in the " armed mediation " of Great Britain and France.

It would appear that in 1856 Austria acted the part of a mediator in bringing about the Congress of Paris, but her mediation went no farther.

In 1897 the mediation of the Great Powers, exercised through their Ambassadors at Constantinople, was accepted by Turkey and Greece.

The cases of mediation quoted in § 73 of Wheaton's *Elements of International Law* (edit. J. B. Atlay, 1904) seem to be of the nature of intervention in the domestic affairs of States, with a view to bringing about a reconciliation between contending political parties. In 1862 France proposed to Great Britain and Russia to offer mediation in the Civil War in America, but both Great Britain and Russia declined to be a party to any such transaction.

During the seventeenth, eighteenth and nineteenth centuries, several important treaties of peace, besides those mentioned in the chapter on Congresses, were negotiated with the assistance of mediators.

Vattel, speaking of mediation, says—

" Cette fonction exige autant de droiture, que de prudence et dextérité. Le Médiateur doit garder une exacte impartialité ; il doit adoucir les reproches, calmer les ressentimens, raprocher les esprits. Son devoir est bien de favoriser le bon droit, de faire rendre à chacun ce qui lui appartient : Mais il ne doit point insister scrupuleusement sur une justice rigoureuse. Il est Conciliateur, & non pas Juge : Sa vocation est de procurer la paix ; et il doit porter celui qui a le droit de son côté, à relâcher quelque chose, s'il est nécessaire, dans la vüe d'un si grand bien." [1]

Of difficulties which a mediator sometimes encounters in the performance of his task instructive examples are presented by the *Repnin Papers*, which throw so much light upon the proceedings at the Congress of Teschen,[2] and the account of Sir Charles Stuart's negotiations at Rio de Janeiro and Lisbon in connexion with the mediation between Portugal and Brazil.[3] The latter can be studied more in detail in the two volumes of *Stuart Papers* preserved at the Public Record Office. In such cases it is found that the principal obstacle to a settlement arises from the *amour propre* of the parties.

[1] *Le droit des Gens*, etc. Leide, 1758, i. § 328.
[2] *Sbornik*, etc., lxv.
[3] Stapleton, *Political Life of Geo. Canning*, ii. 341–72, esp. 349–58.

§ 632. *Mediation of Great Britain between Spain and Portugal, ending in the Treaty of Lisbon, February 3, 1668.*

In 1640 the Portuguese threw off the yoke of Spain, and the Duke of Bragança was proclaimed king with the title of John IV. He entered into alliances with France and the Dutch Republic. But the Dutch signed peace with Spain on January 30, 1648, and eleven years later, at the Peace of the Pyrenees (§ 443), France undertook to abandon her Portuguese allies, unless within three months she was able to bring about such an arrangement between Spain and Portugal as would be satisfactory to the former. John IV had died in 1656, being succeeded by his son, Affonso VI, a boy of thirteen, in whose name the government was carried on by his mother. The peace of the Pyrenees had not enabled Spain so to reorganize her forces as to succeed in reconquering Portugal, which continued to receive secret assistance from Louis XIV. The Regent still further strengthened herself by marrying her daughter Catherine to Charles II, and concluding an alliance by which England agreed to furnish 3000 troops and ten ships of war.[1]

In January 1663/4 Sir Richard Fanshawe (who had negotiated the Portuguese marriage) was appointed Ambassador to the King of Spain. In the instructions given to him on this occasion he was directed to aim at improving commercial relations by negotiating a treaty. He was, however, on no account to listen to any suggestion that the English alliance with Portugal should be renounced. On the contrary, he was to offer the King's mediation for the conclusion of a peace, or a truce of considerable duration between the two countries. If he found the Spanish Court disposed to approve of such an

---

[1] The statement in a letter of Sir Robt. Southwell to the Duke of Ormond, in Carte's *History of the Revolutions of Portugal*, p. 184, that Charles II had " engaged by his articles of marriage to mediate the agreement of these two crowns," has been disproved by an examination of the treaty of marriage. In a secret article annexed to the marriage treaty it is stipulated that Charles II shall mediate a peace between Portugal and Holland (*Brit. and For. State Papers*, xiii. 1123).

arrangement, he was to say that the King of England was ready to prosecute it " with all the fair terms of convenience and honour that could be expected." In that case he was to act in accordance with the power given to him, and take on himself to be instrumental for setting a treaty on foot. On behalf of the Portuguese he was to make use of the encouragements given to him from them. Anything he might require in the shape of further instructions for the prosecution of these overtures would be dispatched to him immediately on the receipt of his application therefor. If the Court of Spain should consent to enter on a negotiation with Portugal he was to send a messenger to Lisbon to convey the information, and if further progress should successfully be made he might proceed either to the frontier, or to Lisbon, to " perform such farther offices therein as shall be requisite." [1]

A whole year elapsed before Fanshawe was enabled to take any steps towards a negotiation between Spain and Portugal. On February 22, 1665 (n.s.) he had to report that the Spaniards refused any accommodation with the Duke of Bragança (as they called him), except on the terms of his surrendering the whole of the kingdoms of Portugal and Algarve.

Philip IV of Spain died September 17, 1665, leaving a son aged four years (Charles II) under the tutelage of the Queen Doña Ana de Austria aided by a council. Louis XIV at once claimed the greater portion of the Spanish Netherlands in right of his wife,[2] and the Spanish regent, alarmed at the menace of an attack on the Low Countries, became willing not only to conclude a commercial treaty with England, but also to agree to articles of adjustment with Portugal, by which a truce was to be made for thirty years. These terms were, however,

---

[1] *Original Letters of His Ex. Sir Rd. Fanshawe*, etc. London, 1702, 11 and 19.

[2] See § 445, Congress of Aix-la-Chapelle in 1668.

not approved by the English cabinet, who sent out Lord Sandwich to supersede Fanshawe.

He arrived at Madrid May 17, 1666,[1] accompanied by William Godolphin as secretary, and shortly afterwards a Spanish *Junta* or commission was appointed to negotiate with him, consisting of the Duque de Medina de las Torres, the Conde de Peñaranda, and an Austrian ecclesiastic named Everard Nithard, the Queen-Regent's confessor. The first conference with them was held on June 29. Medina spoke Spanish, Sandwich a mixture of French, Latin and Spanish, Peñaranda, Nithard and Godolphin Latin. There was some discussion about Portugal, but no definite result was attained. During the negotiation the method of proceeding seems to have been that Sandwich submitted a suggestion, which was discussed by the members of the *Junta*. They then reported to the Council of State, who debated the point and issued a decree. . This was announced to the *Junta*, who then communicated it to Sandwich.

During 1666 several conferences took place, and the results were discussed at about a dozen sittings of the Council. What Portugal demanded was a permanent peace, and the recognition of Don Affonso's kingly title. On September 17 Southwell arrived at Madrid from Portugal with an offer of the foregoing terms. If they were refused, Portugal would break off and enter into a treaty with France.

On October 23 Sandwich presented a draft stipulating for a truce of sixty years ; in this document, instead of Affonso being styled king, he was described as Corona Portugalliæ and Lusitanica Majestas. These proposals he despatched to Lisbon on November 6, with instructions for Southwell and letters for the King containing the proposals, but his messenger returned without any acceptance. During the absence of his messenger, Sandwich had suggested the immediate signature of a new commercial treaty to take the place of that signed

[1] His full-power was dated Feb. 16, 1665, o.s.

by Fanshawe, of which ratification had been refused by the English ministers, coupled with a postponement of the Portuguese question. During November he paid private visits to the members of the *Junta,* and conferences were held nearly every day. These efforts appeared to promise success, for on January 3, 1667, he obtained their consent to a Spanish-Portuguese Treaty being drafted, and they seemed willing to concede the title of king in return for the duration of the truce being limited to fifty years. Then they took a step backward, and produced a new draft commercial treaty, which would have the effect of transferring the English alliance from Portugal to Spain. This he refused to accept. At last, on March 18, it was arranged at a conference with the *Junta* that a fresh draft should be prepared. In the meantime the French were busy with offers to Portugal, and a league between those two countries was actually signed on March 21. This news acted as a spur to the unwilling Spaniards. The commercial treaty with England was drafted on April 19, and there was added a secret article respecting the rendering of assistance to the enemies of the contracting parties. On May 1 Sandwich met the *Junta* and settled all points in dispute, the exact wording of every article, of the truce with Portugal and of the secret article, the whole being put into Latin by Godolphin ; six fair copies being made. The whole were signed on May 13. The French demands on Spain had been presented on May 7 by the Archbishop of Embrun, French Ambassador, and this event hastened the signature.

A messenger was now sent off to Lisbon with the offer of a forty-five years' truce. He did not, however, arrive there till July 6, having been instructed not to use unnecessary speed on his journey, so as to afford time for further concessions from Spain. On July 21 the Treaty of Breda was signed, putting an end to the naval war between England, and France and Holland. The news of this event, which set free the hands of England and

France, induced the Queen-Regent to grant to Portugal the title of king and to make a perpetual peace instead of the truce first offered. It was not until nearly the end of November that Sandwich, after prolonged wrangling with the Spaniards, obtained from them full-powers for the marqués del Carpio (who was a prisoner of war in Portugal), a commission empowering himself to treat, and the draft treaty of peace in thirteen articles. Armed with these papers he at last got away from Madrid on December 26, and arrived at Lisbon on January 12, 1668.

On the 25th January he and del Carpio met the Portuguese commissioners, to whom they exhibited their full-powers and credentials, and the articles of peace. These were substantially the same as those offered by Fanshawe and Southwell two years previously, with the addition of the title of king. The next meetings were on January 29 and three succeeding days, on February 1 the text was agreed to and the fair copies engrossed. Signature took place on February 3.[1] There is a duplicate of the original document at the Public Record Office.

In this instance the mediating Power's representative received a commission or full-power from one of the parties, to enable him to discharge his function effectually, and the same arrangement will be found to have been made on other occasions when there was only one mediator, as at the peace of Belgrade in 1739 (§ 634) and the British mediation between Portugal and Brazil in 1825 (§ 635). But where there were *two* mediating Powers, as was usually the case, we do not find that the mediators received full-powers except from their own sovereigns, *e.g.* as at Teschen (§ 455).[2]

[1] This date is o.s. In the Spanish version, printed in Dumont, vii. part i. 73, the date given is Feb. 13.

[2] The materials used for the account in this § of Sandwich's negotiations are derived exclusively from vol. ii. of F. R. Harris, *The Life of Edward Mountagu, K.G., First Earl of Sandwich.* For the rest of the §, from Dyer's *Modern Europe*, vol. iii., *Original Letters of H.E. Sir Richard Fanshawe*, and *Memoirs of Lady Fanshawe*, edited by Beatrice Marshall. Spanish text of the treaty, with the full-powers given by the Queen-mother of Spain, the King of Portugal and the King of England, as also the Queen-Mother's ratification, in Dumont, vii. p. i. 70–74.

§ 633. What is known to historians as the " Northern War," broke out in 1700, before the war of the Spanish Succession, and lasted beyond its termination.

In 1717 Peter the Great, being at Amsterdam, concluded an alliance with Louis XV and Frederick William I of Prussia. By Article IV it was agreed that the contracting parties mutually reserved their existing treaties and alliances, which were not to be derogated from, in so far as they were not contrary to the present treaty, and especially on the part of the Most Christian King, the alliance signed at the Hague on January 4 of the same year between the King's ministers and those of the King of Great Britain and of the Republic of Holland.

There were three " separate and secret articles," of which the first stipulated that if any Power whatsoever should attempt anything to the prejudice of the contracting parties or of the guarantees they had entered into with regard to the treaties of Utrecht and Baden and those future treaties which should re-establish peace in the North, they would interpose their *offices* to procure satisfaction for the injured party, and oblige the aggressor to abstain from all sort of hostilities. By the second it was agreed that in case these *bons offices* should fail of the desired effect within a period of four months, an agreement should then be arrived at respecting the succours in men or money to be afforded by those contracting parties, who have not been attacked, to their ally. The third states that the Most Christian King, having ever since his succession to the throne persisted in his *offices* to induce the Powers concerned in the Northern War to return to sentiments of peace, and being disposed to continue them, the King of Prussia and the Tsar of all Russia engage to admit the mediation of the Most Christian King in the negotiation which will be undertaken in order to restore peace between them and the King of Sweden.

" Bien entendu que S.M. très Chrétienne bornera à des offices et à des insinuations, ce qu'elle fera en la dite qualité de médiateur, sans jamais employer les voyes de fait directement ny indirectement contre aucune des parties qui sont présentement en guerre pour les obliger à accepter les propositions qui seront faites et quand même ces propositions de paix ne seroient point acceptées, la dite médiation sera pourtant continuée, jusqu'à la fin de la guerre du Nord ; et S. dite M. très Chrétienne, voulant conserver l'exacte impartialité qui convient à la qualité de médiateur et d'amy commun de toutes les parties intéressées, promet et s'engage de ne prendre après l'expiration du traité qui subsiste entre sa couronne et celle de Suède et qui finira au mois d'avril prochain, aucun nouvel engagement avec la dite couronne, sous quelque nom et quelque manière que ce soit qui puisse être, directement ny indirectement contraire aux intérêts de Leurs dites Majestés le Roi de Prusse et le Tsar de toute la Russie, et qu'Elle ne donnera aussy à la dite couronne après le dit terme aucun secours de trouppes ny d'argent sous quelque nom que ce puisse être." [1]

The course of events delayed action from being taken on these articles, and it was not till February 1, 1720, that a peace was signed at Stockholm between Sweden and Prussia, under the joint mediation of France and England.[2] The treaty of peace between Sweden and Russia was negotiated at Nystad in Finland, and signed Aug. 30/Sept. 10, 1721, through the mediation of France, which had been claimed by the Swedish King.[3] Besides these two treaties, peace was signed between Sweden and Denmark June 3/14, 1720, at Stockholm, Campredon and Carteret, for France and Great Britain respectively, being the mediators.

§ 634. *Mediation of France in the Negotiation of the Treaties of Belgrade*, 1739.

The Treaty of Passarowitz, in 1718, gave to Austria Belgrade and the surrounding districts, constituting nearly two-thirds of the territory of Serbia, besides

---

[1] F. de Martens, v. 167.
[2] Koch and Schoell, xiii. 294. Brussels edit., iv. 227.
[3] *Ibid.*, 306. Brussels edit., iv. 232.

Wallachia west of the R. Aluta, and a strip of land on the south bank of the Save to its junction with the Danube.

The next important date is August 6, 1726, that of the signature of a treaty between Russia and Austria, by which it was agreed that if either Power should be at war with Turkey, the other should come to its assistance with all its own available forces.[1]

In the winter of 1735 Russia was preparing for war against Turkey, and called upon the Emperor to act in fulfilment of the alliance of 1726. In March 1736 the Porte sounded Villeneuve (French Ambassador since 1728) as to the desirability of French mediation in what they regarded as a mere quarrel between the Tartars of the Crimea and the Cossacks. Towards the end of March the Russians attacked and took Azov, and marched an army into the Crimea, events which caused the Porte to declare war on May 28, 1736. But the Turks were not prepared, and they appealed to Prince Eugene, Cardinal Fleury, the States-General and the Republic of Venice against the proceedings of the Russians. Austria thereupon offered her mediation, which was temporarily accepted. The British and Dutch envoys, Fawkener and Calkoen also offered their good offices, while Villeneuve maintained a reserved attitude. In the autumn the French Government warned the Emperor not to allow Russia to gain too great an extension of territory, and on the other hand encouraged the Turks to hope that France would lend them diplomatic assistance. January 9, 1737, an offensive alliance against Turkey was concluded between Austria and Russia, followed by a military convention, March 18/29.[2] Not until after the capture of Otchakov, later in the year, did Austria reluctantly take the field. She then invaded Wallachia, took Bukharest, and, marching out from Belgrade, invested Nish, which was forced to capitulate. About the same time Otchakov fell into

---

[1] F. de Martens, i. 32.   [2] F. de Martens, i. 69.

the hands of the Russians. Thereupon the plenipotentiaries of the allies assembled at Nemirow made known their conditions of peace to Turkey. Seriously alarmed at last, the Turks resolved to invite the mediation of France. France accepted the proposal, without consulting Austria and Russia, but urged the Turks to exert themselves in their own defence. This appeal aroused them from their torpor. A new Vizir was appointed and a Holy War was preached throughout the Ottoman dominions. In November 1737 they abandoned operations against their Russian enemy, and bore with all their strength against the Austrians, gradually pushing them back on Belgrade. The Russians on their side, unable to advance across the wastes of Bessarabia, retired behind their frontier into the Ukhraine. On December 7 Villeneuve received instructions to persuade the victorous Turks that now was the time to treat, while the French government endeavoured to induce the allies to accept French mediation, *i.e.* to leave to France the care of composing the differences between the belligerents. Villeneuve, avoiding assumption of the part of an official mediator, maintained that of a well-wishing intermediary. His task was to bring the Vizir to prefer the advantages of peace to the uncertain chances of war.

May 24, 1736, the Vizir left for Adrianople to preside over the preparations for the coming campaign. He was accompanied by a young French secretary disguised as a Turk. Austria had already accepted French mediation, and early in the year had sent to Villeneuve full-powers, with a statement of her conditions, while Russia still remained unwilling to place herself in the hands of France, with whom diplomatic relations had not been renewed since the War of the Polish Succession. The Tsaritsa declared that she would not accept the good offices of Louis XV unless the Maritime Powers took part in the mediation. But the Vizir would not hear of this, and was resolved not to consent to a collective mediation.

She then tried to negotiate directly with the Turks, but
this, too, failed. Finally she officially accepted French
mediation, furnished Villeneuve with full-powers
modelled on those sent to him from Vienna, and authorized him to represent her in the negotiations. These
reached him only in the summer of 1738. In 1739, in
view of the menace of a possible attack from the side of
Sweden, the despatch of fresh powers was announced to
Villeneuve by the two imperial Courts. Those of the
Emperor Charles VI offered sacrifices of territory in
Serbia. The Sultan appointed a new Grand Vizir,
who left Constantinople at once to take command of
the army, and invited Villeneuve to join him at his
headquarters. On May 9 Villeneuve was received in
solemn audience by the Sultan to present his credentials
as Ambassador Extraordinary charged with the functions of mediator, and started a few days later, hoping
to reach his destination before the renewal of active
hostilities. In this expectation he was disappointed;
a fiercely contested battle near Belgrade had been
followed by the retreat of the Imperial forces under
Marshal Wallis, and on July 27 the Turks laid siege
to that fortress. Hereupon the Emperor resolved to
treat for peace apart from his ally, and despatched full-
powers to Wallis, who was shortly after superseded by
Count Neipperg provided with still ampler instructions.
These empowered him to give up the whole of Serbia and
Wallachia, retaining only Belgrade. Neipperg rashly
betook himself on August 18 to the Turkish camp, where
he saw Villeneuve, and asked him to repeat to the Vizir,
on behalf of the Emperor, the proposal to cede Serbia
minus Belgrade, and to demolish the fortress. The
Vizir replied that he would have Belgrade, and would
listen to nothing until the keys were delivered to him.
Villeneuve then brought Neipperg over to his own
quarters, as there was reason to fear that the Turks would
treat him as their prisoner in defiance of the Law of
Nations; and he asked him whether, in offering to

demolish the fortress, he had not intended to say that the
town, when dismantled as a fortress, would remain in the
possession of Turkey.　On the 22nd a solemn conference
was held under the presidence of Villeneuve, with
Neipperg at his right, the Vizir's delegates, Mustapha and
Said, at his left.　But no agreement was arrived at.
Finally, at a meeting on the 29th, a compromise was
reached, by which the Austrians were to raze the modern
fortifications constructed since the peace of Passarowitz
and hand the city over with only its ancient walls.
Accordingly, on September 1, the preliminaries of peace
were signed by the Vizir and Neipperg and countersigned
by Villeneuve.　It was provided that five days after
the suspension of hostilities one of the gates of Belgrade
should be handed over to the Turks, and that the garrison
should commence the work of demolition.

At this moment the Russians were pursuing a vic-
torious career in Moldavia.　As soon as Villeneuve heard
the news, he hastened to make use of the full-powers
given to him by the Tsaritsa.　Though not authorized
to restore Azov to the Turks, he consented to its
neutralization, subject to her ratification, and on
September 18 the treaty was signed, as well as the
definitive treaty with Austria.　The desertion of her
Imperial ally and internal troubles which had broken
out in Russia induced her to ratify the treaty concluded
by Villeneuve, though it fell short of what she had
desired.　The ratifications of both treaties were exchanged at Constantinople December 1, 1739.　Austria
sacrificed all that she had gained by the Treaty of
Passarowitz, and Russia restored all her recent conquests.

Authority: A. Vandal, *Une Ambassade en Orient sous Louis
XV.* As to the language in which these treaties were drawn
up, see § 93.

§ 635. *Mediation of Great Britain between Portugal and
Brazil in* 1825.

In 1807 the Regent Dom João of Portugal, with the whole of the Royal Family, including his mother the insane Queen Maria I, sailed for Brazil to escape the French forces under Junot. After the restoration of peace in 1815 he remained there. His mother having died March 20, 1816, he succeeded to the throne as João VI of Portugal, Brazil and the Algarves, and to secure his position brought over 4500 veteran troops to garrison Rio de Janeiro and Bahia.

In 1820 discontent in Portugal led to a revolt at Oporto, and a revolutionary *Junta* was formed. The Cortes met and proceeded to frame a constitution of the most democratic character. Yielding to pressure from public opinion in Portugal and Brazil, and to the advice of the British government, Dom João in 1821 sailed for Lisbon, leaving the Prince Royal Dom Pedro Regent and Lieutenant of Brazil. The Portuguese Cortes hastily decreed the abolition of all the institutions created by João VI in Brazil, and ordered Dom Pedro to lay down his office and return to Portugal.

Brazilian patriots resolved to resist the decrees of the Cortes. Dom Pedro was persuaded to remain in the country, and the troops at Rio were shipped back to Lisbon in February 1822. A council of representatives of the different provinces was called together, and on May 13 Dom Pedro assumed the title of " Perpetual Protector and Defender of Brazil." The Portuguese troops at Pernambuco were induced to leave the country, but the garrison of Bahia, being reinforced from Lisbon, continued to resist the attacks of the Brazilian forces which were besieging them. This was practically war between Portugal and Brazil. On September 22 the Prince declared Brazil to be independent, and on October 12 he was proclaimed Constitutional Emperor of Brazil at Rio. Bahia was blockaded, and on July 2, 1823, the garrison was forced to capitulate and embark for Portugal. Maranham and Pará were reduced, followed by Montevideo, which had been conquered by a Portuguese expedition in 1817. By the end of the year Brazil had become *de* ʿ*facto* independent.

Internal troubles had broken out in Portugal. The Infante Dom Miguel (a younger son), as leader of the Absolutist party, seized the Palace April 30, 1824, and carried on the government in the name of his father, who took refuge on board a British man-of-war in the Tagus. The diplomatic representatives of the Powers, headed by Sir Edward Thornton, the British Minister, intervened. The minister Palmella, who had been banished by Dom Miguel, was reinstated in office, and Dom Miguel himself was forced to leave the kingdom.

As early as September 1823 the mediation of Great Britain had been invoked by Portugal in order to induce Brazil to remain subject to the mother country, and in April 1824 Marshal Brandt arrived in London with a commission to negotiate " an arrangement of the differences unhappily subsisting between Portugal and Brazil."[1] Eventually the British Government, in March 1825, took the step of sending to Lisbon Sir Charles Stuart, who had previously been British Envoy there from 1810 to 1814, provided with full-powers as Commissioner, Mediator and Plenipotentiary of King George IV. After some discussion of a proposal made by Sir Charles Stuart that the King of Portugal should establish the principle of the dissolution of the administrative and legislative union of the two countries, the king was induced to issue on May 13 a " Carta Patente " (styled *Diploma* in the preamble to the treaty subsequently concluded), by which he ceded and transferred to his son, Dom Pedro, the full exercise of sovereignty over the kingdom of Brazil, with the title of King of Brazil and Prince Royal of Portugal and the Algarves, reserving to himself the titles of King of Brazil and of King of Portugal and the Algarves, with full sovereignty over

[1] Canning to Sir Edwd. Thornton, April 17, 1824, P.R.O., F.O., 63.

Portugal and the Algarves and their dominions. Natives of Portugal and its dominions to be considered as Brazilians in Brazil, and natives of the kingdom of Brazil to be considered as Portuguese in the kingdom of Portugal and its dominions.[1]

The political separation of Brazil from Portugal having thus been attained, full-powers as Commissioner and Plenipotentiary were conferred on Stuart by the King, to treat, conclude and sign with such plenipotentiary or plenipotentiaries as might be named by Dom Pedro, any agreement that might tend to promote the re-establishment of good harmony between the two kingdoms. This full-power specifically acknowledged that Dom Pedro had been compelled by circumstances to assume the style of Emperor of Brazil.

The instructions given to Stuart by the Portuguese Government enumerated the conditions agreed upon between them and himself as necessary to be accepted by Brazil in return for the delivery of the " Carta Patente " to Dom Pedro. They were : (1) the immediate cessation of hostilities, and the restoration to all Portuguese subjects of the full exercise of their rights, properties and *acções* (shares in companies) ; (2) the restitution of the prizes made on the Portuguese trade, and the establishment of a mixed commission, composed of equal numbers of Portuguese and Brazilian members, for the liquidation of the losses incurred, the commission to sit at Lisbon, with the British diplomatic agent as arbitrator in case of disagreement ; (3) the removal of the sequestration placed upon Portuguese properties in Brazil, and the appointment of a similar commission to meet at Rio de Janeiro, to ascertain the rents accrued during the period of sequestration, the arbitrator in cases of disagreement to be the British diplomatic agent at Rio ; (4) the payment of £3,000,000 sterling by Brazil to Portugal, to cover the Brazilian share of the common public debt, as well as all other government

[1] P.R.O., F.O., 13/3.

claims. If Brazil should not agree to this sum, then a similar commission to be set up, the place of assembly to be wherever was found most convenient; but in this case Brazil to pay down at once a sum of £1,500,000 the remainder to be liquidated and the form of its payment to be determined within one year; (5) the indemnification of the Lords Proprietors of the different Brazilian provinces, whose rights had been purchased by the King of Portugal by means of annuities, or by borrowing money to pay for them, all of which contracts being for the advantage of Brazil, ought to remain at the charge of the latter from the moment of the complete separation of the two kingdoms; (6) the establishment of trade relations between Portugal and Brazil pending the conclusion of a definitive treaty of commerce; if possible on the footing on which they stood at the time of the King's departure from Rio de Janeiro, with mutually exclusive privileges in favour of specified Brazilian goods and Portuguese salt. Two other points were to be insisted on: (1) the continuance of life-pensions granted by the King before his departure from Brazil, in the full and lawful exercise of his prerogative, or else the indemnification of the holders; (2) the establishment and maintenance in Brazil of the form of government best adapted to secure the integrity of the Empire and most conformable to the principles of monarchy.

Armed with these powers and instructions, Sir Charles Stuart arrived at Rio de Janeiro on July 18, and without loss of time entered with Dom Pedro on the discussion of the conditions he was empowered to offer. On the 24th, three Brazilian plenipotentiaries were appointed, with whom he exchanged full-powers on the following day. They offered strenuous objections to the wording of the Carta Regia, but he rejoined that it was the basis of the whole negotiation. The conditions were then examined, and most of them accepted with but slight modifications. The result of this conference was recorded in a protocol, signed by all the plenipotentiaries.[1] The pecuniary sacrifices demanded of Brazil proved to be the thorniest part of the whole negotiation ; finally, it was agreed to reduce the amount payable to two millions sterling, which was to cover all pecuniary claims of whatever sort. The private claims of the King of Portugal, representing property estimated to be worth nearly £500,000, the accounts of the Portuguese war department amounting to £150,000, and landed property and movables amounting in value to nearly £350,000 more, which Dom Pedro was to make good to his father, almost brought the total up to the three millions originally demanded. The texts of the treaty of friendship and alliance and of the convention for the settlement of the pecuniary claims were finally settled on August 27, and their signature was effected on the 29th.[2]

The preamble of the treaty, which is headed *Em Nome da Santissima e Indivisivel Trindade*, says :—

Sua Magestade Fidelissima . . . por Seo Diploma de treze de Maio do corrente anno, reconheceo o Brasil na Cathegoria de Imperio Independente, e separado dos Reinos de Portugal e Algarves, e a Seo sobre Todos muito Amado e Prezado Filho Dom Pedro por Imperador, cedendo e transferindo de Sua livre Vontade a Soberania do dito Imperio ao Mesmo Seo Filho, e Seos Legitimos Successores, e tomando sómente, e reservando para a Sua Pessoa o mesmo Titulo.

E Estes Augustos Senhores, acceitando a Mediação de Sua Magestade Britannica para o ajuste de toda a questão incidente à separação dos dous Estados, tem nomeado Plenipotenciarios, a saber—

[By H.M.F. Majesty, Sir Charles Stuart, etc., and by His Imperial Majesty, Luis José de Carvalho e Mello, Barão de Santo Amaro, and Francisco Vilella Barbosa.]

[1] P.R.O., Stuart's report of July 27, in F.O. 13/4.
[2] P.R.O., F.O., 13/4, desp. no. 65, from Sir Charles Stuart of August 30.

E vistos e trocados os Seos Plenos Poderes, convierão em que, na conformidade dos principios expressados neste Preambulo se formasse o presente Tratado.

Art. I recognizes Brazil as an Empire independent and separate from the kingdoms of Portugal and the Algarves, and Dom Pedro as Emperor, H.M.F.M. reserving for his own person the same title.

By Art. II Dom Pedro agrees to his father assuming the personal title of Emperor.

By Art. III he undertakes not to accept the offer of any Portuguese Colony to be united to the Empire of Brazil.

Art. IV stipulates for peace, alliance and perfect friendship between the kingdoms of Portugal and the Algarves and the Empire of Brazil.

Art. V provides for the reciprocal treatment of subjects of Portugal and Brazil as subjects of the most favoured and friendly nation.

Art. VI agrees to the immediate restoration of all real and personal property and all shares (*acções*) sequestrated or confiscated belonging to subjects of either sovereign and all mesne profits, or, failing restoration, indemnification in the manner set forth in Article 8.

Art. VII stipulates that all vessels and cargoes captured are to be reciprocally restored, or the owners indemnified.

Art. VIII. Huma Commissão nomeada por ambos os Governos, composta de Portuguezes e Brasileiros em numero igual, e estabelecida onde os respectivos Governos julgarem por mais conveniente, será encaregada de examinar a materia dos Artigos VI e VII; entendendose que as reclamações deverão ser feitas dentro do prazo de hum anno, depois de formada a Commissão, e que, no caso de empate nos votos, será decidida a questão pelo Representante do Soberano Mediador. Ambos os Governos indicarão os fundos por onde se hão de pagar as primeiras reclamações liquidadas.

Art. IX. Todas as reclamações publicas de Governo a

Governo serão reciprocamente recebidas e decididas, ou com a restituição dos objectos reclamados, ou com huma indemnisação do seo justo valor. Para o ajuste destas reclamações, Ambas as Altas Partes Contractantes convierão em fazer huma Convenção directa e especial.[1]

Art. X. Commercial relations to be at once re-established.

Art. XI. Ratifications to be exchanged at Lisbon within five months, or sooner, if possible.

Sir Charles Stuart signed the Portuguese counterpart first, but whether as Portuguese plenipotentiary or in virtue of his position as mediator does not appear. The Brazilian ratification was despatched to Lisbon together with the treaty, without delay, and the exchange having been completed there, the Portuguese King's ratification was received in Brazil early in January.

This case of mediation presents another instance of the plenipotentiary of the mediating Power having a full-power from one of the contracting parties.

Authorities : *Cambridge Modern History*, vol. x. chap. x.; A. G. Stapleton, *Political Life of the Rt. Hon. George Canning*, vol. ii. chap. xi. ; Portuguese text of the treaty, with an English translation, in *Brit. and For. State Papers*, xii. 674. Other papers at the Public Record Office as cited in the footnotes.

§ 636. *Mediation of France between Great Britain and the Kingdom of the Two Sicilies, in the matter of the Sulphur Monopoly.*

In 1836, certain French speculators, headed by a M. Taix, laid before the Neapolitan government a proposal for the establishment of a company which should have the sole right of purchasing at fixed prices all the sulphur produced in Sicily and the exclusive privilege of exporting it, for ten years.

[1] This was signed the same day.

The British government held that the grant of such a monopoly would be an infringement of the treaty of 1816, while the French Chargé d'Affaires, M. Tallenay, was ordered by his government to protest against the measure, as an infringement of the treaty between France and Naples.

Some of the resident British merchants owned sulphur mines, and restrictions on working them and on the free disposal of the product would result from this exclusive grant.

On May 29, 1838, Mr. Temple, by instructions from his government, addressed a formal protest to the Neapolitan minister for Foreign Affairs, and informed various members of the government that compensation would be demanded for British subjects. Nevertheless, as he reported in his despatch of July 4, the monopoly was granted.

On October 12 Palmerston wrote to the Neapolitan minister in London that his government would be held responsible for all losses and injuries suffered by British subjects in consequence of the monopoly, and the Neapolitan government was urged to take steps for its annulment. After a lapse of time, employed in negotiation, Mr. Kennedy reported on August 29, 1839, that the King of Naples had decided to set aside the contract with Taix, Aycard and Co. Nevertheless, its cancellation was delayed.

On January 28, 1840, Palmerston instructed Kennedy to inform the Neapolitan government that unless Her Majesty's Government were enabled without further delay to announce the termination of the monopoly, they would have to take measures little in accordance with the friendly relations which they wished to see subsisting between the two countries. Again, on March 12 he instructed Mr. Temple to present a Note demanding immediate abolition, with compensation for losses, and to ask for an answer within a week ; failing the receipt of a satisfactory answer, he was to inform the

Commander-in-Chief at Malta in order that he might proceed at once to make reprisals. These were to take the shape of seizing and detaining all Neapolitan and Sicilian ships he might meet with in Neapolitan or Sicilian waters. Accordingly, on March 25, Temple presented an ultimatum, and on April 3 informed the minister for Foreign Affairs that instructions had been sent to Malta.[1]

On April 10 M. Guizot, the French Ambassador in London, inquired of Palmerston whether the French government could be of any use in this affair, and was informed in reply that H.M. Government would be willing to suspend active measures if the French government would exert its good offices with the King of Naples, as H.M. Government would rather owe a success to the friendly interposition of France than to any extreme measures at their disposal.

Three days later M. Thiers offered to Lord Granville, the British Ambassador in Paris, the mediation of France. Palmerston, in a despatch of April 10 recording his interview with Guizot, had said that England would prefer the interposition of France to the use of compulsory measures ; that if " the mediation of France meant its intervention to obtain the abolition of the sulphur monopoly and the indemnity due to H.M. subjects for the loss they had sustained, there could be no doubt of its being readily and thankfully accepted ; that, of course, mediation was not understood to be arbitration." On Granville reading this despatch to Thiers, the latter responded that when he proposed mediation, he did not mean arbitration.

Palmerston, in reply to Granville's despatch reporting his conversation with Thiers wrote on the 17th : " H.M. Government accepts with great pleasure the good offices of the government of France." On this being made known to Thiers, he telegraphed to the Vicomte d'Haussonville, the French diplomatic agent at Naples, to make

[1] *Brit. and For. State Papers*, xxviii. 1163–1240 ; xxix. 176–97.

a similar offer to the Neapolitan government. Palmerston, in his reply to Granville, who had reported Thiers' last step, spoke of the " good offices " of France, but in later despatches to Granville, of June 15, July 14 and 20, he used the expression " the mediation of France."

On June 27 Thiers gave to Granville the draft of a Note which he proposed to address to him, if its terms were approved by Palmerston. This draft having been transmitted to London, Palmerston returned it to Paris, where by this time Mr. Henry B. Lytton was in charge. Then the amended draft was written out, signed by Thiers, and sent to Granville. To make assurance doubly sure, the Note was sent over to Guizot, to show to Palmerston, who returned it to him, stating that H.M. Government were satisfied with and willing to agree to the arrangement therein contained.[1]

The text of the Note thus agreed on was as follows—

A Son Excellence,
  Lord Granville,
Monsieur l'Ambassadeur,
    Le gouvernement du Roi mon auguste Souverain, justement préoccupé des intérêts de la paix générale et animé des sentiments les plus bienveillants pour deux Cours qui lui sont unies par des liens étroits, avait cru devoir offrir sa médiation, dans le but de faciliter l'accommodement du différend survenu entre les Cabinets de Londres et de Naples, relativement à l'exploitation des soufres de Sicile.
    Cette médiation a été acceptée. Ce témoignage de confiance qui, de la part d'un Etat aussi puissant que la Grande Bretagne, atteste l'honorable volonté de chercher, dans les voies de conciliation, plûtôt que dans un appel à la force, la satisfaction à laquelle il croit avoir droit, a vivement touché le cœur du Roi. Le Gouvernement de Sa Majesté, dans son empressement à s'acquitter de la haute mission qui lui était ainsi déférée, a examiné avec l'attention la plus scrupuleuse tous les éléments de la question. Il s'est attaché à apprécier avec une équitable impartialité, les prétensions et les droits respectifs, et cette appréciation consciencieuse lui a suggéré les propositions que je vais énoncer à Votre Excellence comme

[1] Palmerston to Guizot, July 7, 1840, P.R.O., F.O., 27/613.

les plus propres, dans notre manière de voir, à amener une transaction vraiment acceptable pour les deux parties.

Le contrat passé, le 9 juillet 1838, entre le gouvernement Napolitain et la compagnie Taix, pour l'exploitation des soufres de Sicile, serait résilié. L'objet que Sa Majesté Sicilienne s'était proposé , en souscrivant cette convention, pouvant, comme on l'a reconnu, être atteint par d'autres moyens qui concilient, avec le bien-être de ses sujets, les intérêts des étrangers établis ou trafiquant dans ses Etats, la résiliation ne fait plus une difficulté sérieuse ; et il reste seulement à déterminer le moment où elle aurait lieu. Nous pensons qu'elle devrait étre dénoncée, à Naples et en Sicile, aussitôt que le gouvernement Napolitain serait officiellement informé de l'approbation donnée par Votre Excellence, au nom de son gouvernement, au projet d'arrangement développé dans la présente dépêche.

Cette mesure ne saurait être interprétée comme impliquant de la part de Sa Majesté Sicilienne, l'abandon de son droit souverain d'imposer les soufres et d'en réglementer l'exploitation. Il est presque superflu d'ajouter que le gouvernement Britannique n'entend pas souscrire d'avance à des règlements qui violeraient les droits de ses sujets ou qui tendraient à rétablir, sous une autre forme, le contrat que Sa Majesté le Roi de Naples consent aujourd'hui à révoquer.

Après avoir ainsi pourvu à l'avenir, voici ce que le gouvernement du Roi croit pouvoir proposer pour régler le passé.

Sa Majesté Sicilienne, animée d'un sentiment d'équité bienveillante, consentirait à écouter les réclamations de ceux des sujets anglais, qui prétendent avoir éprouvé des pertes par suite du privilège concédé en 1838 à la compagnie Taix. Une commission de liquidation serait immédiatement instituée à cette effet. Elle siégerait à Naples, et serait composée de deux commissaires anglais, deux commissaires Napolitains et d'un commissaire sur-arbitre, désigné d'avance par le gouvernement français, avec l'agrément des deux Cours intéressées, pour départager, dans l'occasion, les quatre autres Commissaires.

Cette Commission ne pourrait accueillir que les demandes d'indemnité formées par les sujets anglais dans les catégories suivantes :

1. Ceux qui, avant le 9 juillet 1838, époque du marché passé avec la compagnie Taix, étant devenus ou propriétaires ou fermiers de mines, auraient essuyé des empêchements dans l'extraction ou l'exportation des soufres, et auraient fait, en conséquence de ces empêchements, des pertes constatées.

2. Ceux qui, avant la même époque, ayant passé des marchés à livrer, auraient été mis dans l'impossibilité d'accomplir leurs engagements, ou privés du bénéfice convenu de leurs transactions.

3. Enfin, ceux qui, ayant acheté des soufres dont l'exportation aurait été, soit interdite, soit limitée, soit soumise à des conditions plus onéreuses, auraient fait des pertes appréciables d'une manière certaine.

La Commission de liquidation une fois instituée, un délai de trois mois serait accordé aux réclamants pour produire devant elle les titres justificatifs de leurs demandes en indemnité ; un second terme de six mois serait assigné pour la conclusion de ses travaux, et les indemnités dont elle reconnaîtrait la justice seraient soldées dans l'année qui suivrait le jour de sa dissolution.

Telles sont, Monsieur l'Ambassadeur, les propositions que le gouvernement du Roi croit devoir présenter simultanément aux deux Puissances qui ont accepté sa médiation. J'ai la conviction qu'elles vous paraîtront reposer sur des bases satisfaisantes et j'attends avec confiance l'adhésion que vous vous jugerez sans doute en mesure d'y donner.

Agréez, Monsieur l'Ambassadeur, les assurances de la haute considération avec laquelle j'ai l'honneur d'être.

de Votre Excellence,
le très humble et très
obéissant serviteur,
A. THIERS.

Paris, le 5 juillet 1840.[1]

It is very clear from this Note that Thiers regarded his action as having the character of a mediation. And that Palmerston, while sometimes using the term good offices, really took the same view, appears from a Note he addressed to Prince Castelcicala, Neapolitan Envoy in London, on May 18, 1840, in which he told him that he could not enter into communication with him respecting the differences between the two governments, inasmuch as France had offered her good offices, which had been accepted by Her Majesty the Queen. This was quite the correct attitude to assume under the circumstances, because, while good offices do not involve a cessation of

[1] From the draft corrected by Palmerston, at P.R.O., F.O., 27/603.

direct negotiations between the parties, the acceptance of mediation necessarily has that consequence.

On July 7 Palmerston wrote to Bulwer enclosing a copy of Thiers' Note and his answer [to Guizot], stating that H.M. Government were satisfied with the arrangements, and two days later authorized him to sign any instrument in the words of M. Thiers' Note. To Mr. Temple he wrote on July 13, informing him of the arrangements made " through the mediation of France," and on the 20th instructed Bulwer to present the thanks of H.M. Government to that of France " for its successful mediation."

Yet on November 17, 1840, we find him stating to the British commissioners that " The Government of His Majesty the King of the French having tendered its good offices to the Government of Her Majesty for the settlement of certain differences which had arisen between H.M. Government and the Government of Naples on the subject of a monopoly of the sulphur trade of Sicily . . . and Her Majesty's Government having accepted the offers thus made by the Government of France, a plan of arrangement proposed by the French Government was consented to by the Government of Her Majesty and by that of His Majesty the King of the Two Sicilies."

The French Government appointed Count de Lurde as *sur-arbitre*.

The minute of the installation of the Commission, dated March 23, 1841, begins—

" La Commission établie en conséquence de l'arrangement fait entre S.M. la Reine du Royaume Uni de la Grande Bretagne et d'Irlande, et S.M. le Roi du Royaume des Deux Siciles, sous la médiation de S.M. le Roi des Français, pour la liquidation des demandes d'indemnité formées par les sujets anglais, s'étant réunie aujourd'hui, le 23 mars, 1841, dans le Palais du Ministère des Finances à Naples ; les membres qui la composent, après s'être communiqué leurs Pleins Pouvoirs et Lettres de Nomination, ont déclaré que la Commission était légalement instituée dès ce jour même.

[Signatures of the four commissioners and the *sur-arbitre*.]

The minute of the closing of the commission, dated December 24, 1841, also speaks of the *médiation* of the King of the French.

The British Commissioners, in reporting on December 29, stated that they would have had to appeal to the arbitrator in one case only, and in that case the reference was withdrawn, as his good offices sufficed to induce the Neapolitan Commissioner to accede to the proposals of the British Commissioners.

The proceedings terminated by the exchange of complimentary letters between the commissioners and the arbitrator.[1]

§ 637. An arrangement intended to settle by mutual agreement certain questions pending between Italy and Colombia was concluded at Paris May 24, 1886, through the friendly mediation of Spain. The Italian Ambassador and the Colombian Envoy signed a protocol, which, after being approved by their respective governments, was to be submitted to that of Spain. It provided (1) that certain real property taken from the Italian subject Cerruti by the Colombian authorities during the last civil war, should be restored to him; (2) that all other claims of Cerruti or other Italian subjects were to be submitted to the mediation of the Spanish government, to whom all proofs and documents were to be presented; (3) the questions to be decided by the mediator were enumerated; (4) if the result of the mediation was that Colombia had to pay indemnities, the amounts, modes, terms and guarantees for payment were to be submitted to the arbitration of a mixed commission, consisting of the Italian diplomatic agent at Bogotá, a delegate of the Colombian government and the Spanish diplomatic agent at Bogotá. This mixed commission was also to fix the extent, if disputed, of the real property to be restored to Cerruti under paragraph 1.[2]

[1] *Brit. and For. State Papers*, xxx. 111–15.
[2] *Nouveau Recueil Général*, 2ème série, xviii. 659.

This so-called mediation, in its second stage at least, is in reality an arbitration left, on questions of principle, to the Spanish government, and on points of detailed fact to the mixed commission. It resembles in this particular the mixed commission appointed to fix the indemnities payable under the plan of French mediation between Great Britain and Naples, where in case of dispute the French member was to have the deciding voice.

W. F. Johnson, *America's Foreign Relations*, ii. 188, states that the decision of the Spanish Government was in favour of Cerruti on all the points. Colombia accepted it, but a further dispute arose over the question of indemnity, concerning the amount of his losses. In 1890 Blaine offered friendly offices to the Italian Government, in consequence of which it was decided to submit the case to the President of the United States. On March 2, 1897, President Cleveland gave his award, disallowing some of Cerruti's claims and confirming others. Colombia paid the indemnity, but protested against the award on six separate grounds. The reply was given by John Sherman, Secretary of State, under President McKinley, to the effect that the President could not re-open the case or reconsider the award, save at the request of both parties for a new submission or new arbitration. Such request was not made, and the United States was not further concerned in the case.

§ 638. Besides the instances already given of successful mediation, there are many others in which it was offered but not accepted, as well as others in which, after negotiations had been carried on for that purpose, these proved failures. We select an example of each.

On the news reaching Mexico and South America of the trickery by which Napoleon had obtained control of the persons of Charles IV and his son Ferdinand VII, and of the revolt of the population of Madrid on May 2, 1808, great excitement arose in all the provinces. Local governments, some of a royalist, others of a revolutionary and separatist character, were set up, and from this time onwards for many years the southern continent was a scene of sanguinary civil wars and political chaos.

The Central Junta, which had fled to Cadiz, pending the election of representatives by the Colonies, admitted to its ranks such Americanos as happened to be present there. The policy it pursued was directed towards retaining the connexion of the Colonies with the Mother-country on the old footing, and the monopoly of commercial intercourse on which the wealth of Cadiz depended. In America the movement in favour of separation continued to grow. Both parties were willing to obtain the support of Great Britain, the one for the purpose of consolidating their autonomy, the other for maintaining the ancient system of domination.

In a despatch of Canning's of January 30, 1814, it is stated that in 1810 Spain asked the mediation of Great Britain in order to arrive at a conciliation with her Colonies. But the evidence furnished by earlier correspondence is the other way, and points to the proposal for mediation having originated with the British Government. It is true that in a Note of the Duque de Alburquerque of July 28 of that year, in reply to a communication of intelligence received from Caracas, he urged that " the British Government should, as well towards the city of Caracas as towards her deputies, make use of all the means of conciliation which may occur." In his *Relaciones entre España é Inglaterra durante la Guerra de la Independencia*, the late Spanish ambassador in London speaks of " la mediación ofrecida por Inglaterra para la pacificatión de las Américas," and in a Note from Canning to the Chevalier de los Rios of March 25, 1825, the language used by the former is " the repeated offers of Great Britain to mediate between Spain and her Colonies," and " in 1812, when our Mediation was offered to the Cortes." This much, however, is evident from the correspondence preserved at the Public Record

Office, that negotiations proceeded for several years between the respective Cabinets directed towards this object.

In July 1810 an application was addressed to the British Government by a deputation, headed by Bolivar, which had arrived from Caracas. They informed Marquess Wellesley that Venezuela was far from aspiring to sever the bonds which had united her to the Metropolis, but merely desired to provide against the dangers which threatened the province. Though it was independent of the Council of Regency, it was no less faithful to its King, and interested in the holy struggle in which Spain was engaged. But the resolution adopted by Venezuela might become a source of unpleasant discussion with other provinces, which had recognized the Regency, and the Central Government would perhaps attempt direct hostilities or the disturbance of its domestic peace by fomenting faction. The inhabitants of Venezuela, therefore, solicited the mediation of His Britannic Majesty in order to preserve peace and friendship with its brethren of both hemispheres. The continuance of relations of amity, commerce and mutual support between Venezuela and the Mother-country would require stipulations to be entered into between the respective governments, and that of Venezuela would lend itself to them with perfect confidence under the guarantee of His Britannic Majesty. The deputies begged that instructions might be despatched to the commanders of squadrons and governors of colonies in the West Indies to facilitate the aims stated, and undertook that British subjects should enjoy most-favoured-nation treatment in respect of trade.

In a memorandum on the situation Marquess Wellesley concluded that by skilful use of Ferdinand's title as sovereign, it would be possible for England to prevent a sudden and complete emancipation of the Spanish colonies and yet compel Spain to modify her colonial system ; but that it was chimerical to suppose that the Mother-country could preserve her colonies otherwise than as allied states under a common sovereign.

The Secretary of State, in replying to the Venezuelan deputation, said that the province was earnestly recommended to aim at immediate reconciliation with the central government actually recognized in Spain. The good offices of England were offered for this purpose, and she was willing to use her friendly interposition to prevent war between the province and the Mother-country. The deputies answered that they could not depart from the refusal to recognize the sovereignty of the Council of Regency.

A copy of the reply and of a memorandum on the conferences held with the Venezuelan deputation was delivered to Apodaca, the Spanish Envoy, and Alburquerque, the Special Ambassador. These papers having been transmitted to Cadiz, the former wrote on October 8 that " his orders were to express pain at the turn affairs had taken, after His Majesty's generous declaration respecting the integrity and independence of the Spanish monarchy." No proposals could be admitted from those deputies, since they refused to acknowledge the Regency, and they were expected to return to their allegiance. " Hence H.M. (*i.e.* the Cortes) is disposed willingly to admit the good offices of Great Britain in favour of the inhabitants of Caracas, with a view to their reconciliation with the Mother-country. From these considerations, the Council of Regency flatter themselves that H.B.M. will listen to their just representations, and that, far from establishing relations with the revolters of America, His Majesty will assist the Spanish Government to re-establish in Caracas the ancient order of things, in which England is likewise interested, if, as may be presumed, she desires the peaceful preservation of her own Colonies and establishment, as well as of those of H.M. her faithful ally."

Marquess Wellesley had, on July 13, written to his

brother Henry, British diplomatic representative at Cadiz, that if Venezuela continued to refuse recognition of the Regency's authority, His Majesty's Government was, nevertheless, not disposed to renounce friendly relations with the Colony, much less to contribute to the use of force in order to compel it to admit that authority. He instructed him in another despatch to propose a commercial treaty for the duration of the war, including a mitigation in favour of England of the laws which prohibited trade with America, seeing that the war could only be maintained by the resources furnished from the Colonies: of which Spain could not avail herself, while England could not continue to supply Spain with money unless facilities for obtaining it were given to English merchants by the traffic with America.

On August 16, 1810, Wellesley accordingly presented a sketch of a commercial treaty, containing the proposed clause relative to the trade with America, to the Foreign Minister. Bardaxí replied on the 24th that all possible facilities had already been conceded without the formality of a treaty. Direct trade with the Colonies had always been prohibited, and at no time had that sacred rule been departed from. Spain could not surrender her only source of wealth, even for a short time.

In a despatch of August 29 he reported that the reception accorded in England to the deputation from Caracas had caused such irritation that it was advisable to postpone pushing proposals for trade with the American Colonies. The Regency seemed disposed to accept the offer of mediation, if the insurgents began by submitting to the Spanish authorities; that was the indispensable condition of their past errors being pardoned. The government would adopt such measures as it judged necessary to enforce obedience, endeavouring on all occasions to conciliate clemency with the rigour prescribed by its obligations, and going so far in its paternal solicitude as to invite them to name deputies to the Congress which was about to meet.

Several months passed without either the government or the Cortes coming to a decision on pending questions. At last Marquess Wellesley addressed a despatch to his brother on May 4, 1811, in which he spoke of " the offer of His Majesty's mediation being directed to the object of reconciling the Spanish possessions in America to whatever government, acting in the name and on behalf of Ferdinand VII, might be acknowledged in Spain." A conciliatory policy towards the Colonies was advised. Great Britain must be admitted to participate in the South American trade if her efforts on behalf of Spain were to be continued. The ambassador was to " renew and urge the offer of the mediation of Great Britain for the purpose of checking the progress of this unfortunate civil war, and of effecting at least such a temporary adjustment as may prevent, during the existing contest with France, so ruinous a waste of the general strength of the Spanish Empire." A week later the ambassador received a paper entitled " Heads of Articles of Adjustment between Spain and Spanish America," intended to serve as a basis for the proposed mediation.

1. A cessation of Hostilities, including Blockades and every other Act of mutual injury between the Parties.

2. A general amnesty, pardon and oblivion of all acts of hostility committed by the Spanish Americans against the parent State, or the Authorities therein, or against its officers in America.

3. A confirmation of the concession already made to the Colonies respecting their admission to a full, fair and free representation in the Cortes, and that the elections of the Spanish American deputies should be immediately made in America.

4. A free trade, with a proper degree of preference to Old Spain and her Colonies.

5. The admission of native Americans indifferently with Spaniards to the office of Viceroys or Governors in Spanish America.

6. The internal or provincial administration of Spanish

America (under the Viceroys or Governors) to be conducted by the Cabildos and Ayuntamientos of Spanish America, into which Assemblies native Spanish Americans shall be eligible, as well as natives of Old Spain, and all judgments as given in Spanish America shall be final, and appeal to European Spain (as heretofore allowed) shall be abolished.[1]

7. Spanish America to recognize the supremacy of the general representative body or Cortes residing in Spain, in which an adequate share of representation shall have been granted to the Spanish American Deputies.

9. Spanish America to engage to establish a regular communication of succours with the parent State.

10. Spanish America to engage to co-operate with the allies in the prosecution of the present war against France.

11. Spanish America to furnish a certain proportion of resources to the Mother-country for the purpose of maintaining the present contest against France.

12. These Articles to be guaranteed by England.

These Articles were accompanied by a memorandum on the whole question from the beginning. When the Venezuelan deputies arrived in England in the summer of 1810 they were told that as long as they continued their allegiance to Ferdinand VII and their hostility to France they should receive as against that Power the maritime protection of England ; and reconciliation with Spain was urged upon them. An offer of mediation between the Colonies and the parent State was made to both parties and received with greater satisfaction by the former than by the latter. Hence all the representations of England for the past three years in favour of free trade and measures of conciliation had been received by Spain with coldness. In Mexico alone the Spaniards possessed a party of any consequence. In all the other Colonies the leading persons were decided enemies of

---

[1] Pencil addition in margin of draft at P.R.O.

Spain, and the prevailing spirit tended towards absolute independence. England was consequently regarded there as the only nation from which they had much to hope or fear. Every representation from England would certainly be received with the greatest deference by the colonists, who without the intervention of British commissioners would probably refuse to a Spanish commission leave to land. They had declined to acknowledge the Regency of Cadiz, and through the Cortes alone could any plan of accommodation be verified (sic). Unless Spain was prepared to concede something in the internal government of her Colonies and in the system of trade, no adjustment could be attempted with advantage to either party or to England. If the Spanish commissioners were to leave Cadiz without precise instructions on these points, their mission would only provoke further dissension. Without the guarantee of England the Colonies would listen to no conditions.

On May 27 Wellesley sent to Bardaxí a copy of his instructions of the 4th, mentioning at the same time the desirability of admitting England to a share of the trade with the Colonies. It seems probable that he also communicated the " Heads of Articles," for on June 14 Bardaxí informed him in conversation that he believed four points would be accepted by the Cortes : namely, (1) the cessation of hostilities during the negotiations and a general amnesty for the past : (2) the trade to continue with Great Britain during the negotiation, measures to be adopted for the future being left to the Cortes to decide ; (3) the Colonies to state what concessions would satisfy them, and (4) the Colonies to send deputies to the Cortes and to undertake to accept whatever the constitution might lay down with respect to America. He believed the Cortes to be unanimous in regard to the advantage of mediation, but he wished to learn what course the British Government would take if the Colonies rejected the proposed measures of conciliation. Wellesley replied that if the Spanish government lent itself to the liberal concessions which the circumstances rendered indispensable, he had no doubt of the success of mediation, but the British Government would not be induced to commit acts of hostility against the Colonies on the ground of a refusal to recognize the constituted government in the Peninsula, because such a course would merely drive them into the arms of the enemy. He added that mediation had not been proposed by Great Britain for her own benefit, but in order to reconcile the Colonies with the Mother-country and maintain the integrity and independence of the Spanish monarchy; there was no reason why, if the mediation failed, England should quarrel with countries that had been foremost in claiming her protection and offering her the advantage of their trade.

The British government from the outset had taken care to make it clear that England would not help Spain to subjugate the insurgent Colonies, nor renounce the trade they offered. Nevertheless, in the bases of mediation voted by the Cortes, after confining the mediation to the Rio de la Plata, Venezuela, Santa Fé de Bogotá and Cartagena, and limiting the duration of British trade with the provinces to which the English mediators were to proceed, to fifteen months, they added a seventh article in the following terms : " Whereas the mediation of Great Britain would be entirely illusory if the negotiation failed because the dissentient provinces would not lend themselves to the just and moderate conditions which have been set forth, it must be agreed between the two nations that, if reconciliation is not attained within fifteen months, Great Britain will suspend all communication with the said provinces, and will, moreover, aid the Metropolis with her forces in order to bring them back to their duty."

Wellesley at once informed Bardaxí that the Prince Regent would not accept this article. Bardaxí then proposed to convert it into a " separate and secret article," to which Wellesley rejoined that this was useless, as he was certain that it would not be accepted, no matter what form it might assume. Another objectionable point was the exclusion of Mexico from the scope of the mediation.

Notwithstanding this warning, Bardaxí communicated the bases officially in a Note of June 29, in which he also complained that the reception accorded to the Venezuelan deputies had encouraged the insurgents in believing that they could count on the support of England. He also enclosed Article 7 as a "separate and secret article."

Wellesley replied sharply to the complaints about the treatment of the deputies from Caracas, and declared emphatically that England would not carry out Article 7.

On January 21, 1812, a new Regency was elected by the Cortes, consisting of the Duque de Infantado, Admiral Villavicencio, and General O'Donnell for Spain, with D. Joaquin Mosquera and D. Ignacio Rodriguez de Rivas for America. Their first act was to send for Wellesley, and tell him that they desired to act in complete agreement with England. This encouraged Wellesley to write again on January 30 to Bardaxí that Article 7 must be suppressed if an agreement was to be arrived at. A few days later Bardaxí was replaced by José Garcia de Leon y Pizarro, who being violently anti-English, did all he could to wreck the negotiation. On April 4 Wellesley reminded him that his Note of January 30 had remained without an answer, and as he received none to this fresh communication, he went to see Mosquera, who was president of the Regency pending Infantado's arrival from England. The commissioners for the mediation were momentarily expected from England, having been appointed in the previous October, and he urged the advisability of withdrawing Article 7 without delay, and proceeding to discuss the other bases and the instructions for the commissioners.

On April 24 the Cortes held a secret session, and agreed

to send the two pending questions to the committee which had framed the bases. They took three weeks to draw up their report, which left the suppression of Article 7 at the discretion of the Regency.

Marquess Wellesley had been replaced on March 4 by Castlereagh, who proceeded on April 1, 1812, to send fresh instructions to the Ambassador, transmitting a copy of the instructions to the British commissioners. Their head was Charles Stuart, Minister Plenipotentiary at Lisbon, where he had been since 1810. In these instructions were contained the terms proposed by Great Britain, liberty being left to Wellesley to modify them by agreement with the Spanish government.

The points of importance remaining for discussion between the two governments were—

(1) The proposed secret article ; (2) the exclusion of certain provinces, and especially of Mexico ; (3) the total silence of the Spanish government upon the commercial rights which those provinces were hereafter to enjoy. What Wellesley had said to Bardaxí on the first point was entirely approved. The British Government could not bind themselves to make a refusal on the part of the Colonies a cause of war, because the consequence might be, instead of replacing those provinces under the authority of Spain, to drive them into a connexion with the common enemy. The Spanish government must at once desist from any such expectation, if it wished the mediation to proceed. As to point No. 2, the despatch observed that Mexico was not only the first object in the scale of importance, but its settlement was an indispensable preliminary to success elsewhere. If Spain was prepared to relinquish the hated colonial system for a better one, and was disposed to tender such a system under the mediation of Great Britain to the provinces in revolt, she could not ultimately mean to withhold it from Mexico. Why then not begin by granting it to that province whose allegiance had been least shaken ? Wellesley was to press this object to the

utmost, short of making it a *sine quâ non* of the mediation, and he might acquaint the Spanish government that the Prince Regent's best hope of success depended on being empowered to commence the work of pacification in Mexico. In general, provinces of such magnitude as those of South America would not longer submit to be treated as mere Colonies. They had not only, in point of fact, outgrown that relation, but they had been acknowledged by the Cortes to be no longer Colonies, but integral parts of the Spanish monarchy, equal in rights and admissible on that principle to an equal share in the national representation. It was, therefore, a departure from the principles established by the Cortes themselves, any longer to apply to those provinces the restrictions of the colonial system. Spanish America must now be governed on other principles, or the inhabitants would assume the direction of their own affairs. The despatch went on to point out the advantage of the system applied to the British-Indian possessions, where commerce was thrown open to all neutral nations, and Great Britain as sovereign claimed nothing but a commercial preference. In regard to the Spanish American possessions, Great Britain had neither the right nor the wish to propose that a due preference should not be reserved to the European and American dominions of Spain in their intercourse with each other. She had no other desire than that of being admitted to share in that commerce, not on the same footing of advantage as Old Spain, but on that of the most-favoured-nation.

Wellesley, in replying on April 24, reported that before Bardaxí's removal from the Foreign Department he had represented the necessity of withdrawing the " secret article ." He had repeatedly urged it on Pizarro, but without effect, even putting it before him in a Note, to which no answer was received. In that Note, dated April 4, he stated to Pizarro that Article 7 was entirely inadmissible, and could not be acceded to by the government of the Prince Regent. He therefore sought an interview with Mosquera (the result of which has already been stated).   Wellesley also represented that no success was to be expected, unless the commissioners were allowed to proceed, in the first instance, to Mexico. He advised that this should be made a *sine quâ non* of engaging in the mediation, and apprehended that neither party would be satisfied with anything short of the guarantee of Great Britain to any arrangement which might be agreed upon.

Pizarro had impressed on the Regency the inadvisability of acceding to the English demands, and as that body took no heed of his remonstrances he presented his resignation, which was accepted on May 12.   His place was taken temporarily by D. Ignacio de la Pezuela.

Pezuela began by writing to Wellesley on the 14th, that the Regency had suppressed the latter paragraph of Article 7.   To this he rejoined that unless the other part, relating to the cessation of English relations with the disaffected provinces, were also suppressed, the commissioners, who had now been waiting a whole month at Cadiz, would return to England.   On this the whole of the article was withdrawn, " provided that the communications of England with the Colonies were no obstacle to the measures which the Mother-country had the right of taking after having tried in vain all means of conciliation."

Wellesley, assuming that the principal obstacle to an agreement had now been removed, proceeded in a Note of May 21 to state his views on the two questions which he held to be necessary to solve : namely, the inclusion of Mexico and the grant of commercial facilities.   He supported his arguments in a long conference with Pezuela, maintaining that there were only two alternatives open to the Spanish Government : either to confer extensive powers on the commissioners, or to reject the proposed mediation altogether.   In the latter case the British Government would communicate the whole correspondence to Parliament.

Pezuela replied on the 26th that, Article 7 having been suppressed, it became necessary to add to No. 6 a paragraph stating that if the mediation failed, things would remain as before, and he repeated his arguments justifying the exclusion of Mexico. As to the question of trade, Spain was disposed to concede it by way of payment for the assistance already rendered and still to be afforded, as the Regency had explained in the course of their negotiations for a loan and a treaty of subsidy. But that was a separate question from the mediation offered by Great Britain for the reconciliation of the disaffected provinces, in accordance with bases already determined. To mix up the two matters would complicate a very simple question, and its salutary effect would be delayed if it became necessary to obtain fresh resolutions from the Cortes.

Wellesley rejected the proposed addition to Article 6, insisted on the necessity of mediation in the case of Mexico, and as regarded the trade, explained that it was no question of a privilege desired by Great Britain, but of advantages and rights which must be conceded to the Americanos, in order that they might trade freely with everybody like the inhabitants of the Peninsula.

In reply, Pezuela delivered a gigantic Note, a great portion of which was devoted to arguing that as the Spanish government possessed the means of putting an end to the internal dissensions of the monarchy, it would be incompatible with its responsibilities and sense of decency to take advantage of the intervention of a foreign Power. He considered it unnecessary to assure to the inhabitants of America the liberty to make use of the advantages that nature had conferred on them in respect of commercial liberties. The Regency consented, however, to withdraw the addition to Article 6. Finally, he said that, in accordance with the expressed wish of the Ambassador, he was communicating the correspondence to the Cortes.

Whilst the discussion was proceeding in the Cortes, a lively interchange of Notes took place between Wellesley and Pezuela, which ended in the former sending in a somewhat stiff Note on July 4, declaring that the mediation was at an end and that the commissioners would return to England without delay. They accordingly took formal leave on the 9th, but Pezuela begged that their departure might be postponed until the resolution of the Cortes was known. On the 16th the vote was taken, when by a large majority it was decided to declare that the Cortes " was informed." Nothing more. This put an end to the proposal for mediation. The correspondence between the Ambassador and Don Pedro Labrador (who had succeeded to Pezuela) nevertheless continued for some time longer, until the month of February 1813, when Wellesley reported to Castlereagh, in repetition of what he had said in a recent despatch, that he considered it inexpedient to renew the subject with the Spanish government.

Authorities : *Cambridge Modern History*, vol. x. chap. ix.; Villa-Urrutia, *Relaciones entre España é Inglaterra durante la Guerra de la Independencia*, vol. ii. ; correspondence preserved at the Public Record Office.

§ 639. *Subsequent Attempts to establish Mediation between Spain and her American Colonies.*

In 1815 Spain asked for the mediation of Great Britain, but refused to state the terms to which she was willing to agree. Again in 1818, at Aix-la-Chapelle, the question of an arrangement between Spain and her Americas was discussed between the Five Great Powers.[1]

It appears from the reports on this subject addressed by Castlereagh to the British Cabinet, that it was discussed by the conference during two days. There was a

[1] Canning to De los Rios, March 25, 1825, in *Brit. and For. State Papers*, xii. 911.

c c

general concurrence of opinion that under no circumstances could force be employed, and that Spain must,
as a preliminary measure, confer upon her American
provinces which had remained faithful the full extent of
advantage which the mediating Powers were to be
authorized to propose to the provinces in revolt. The
only difference of opinion on these two points seemed
to be whether the intention of not using force should be
explicitly declared to both parties, or only to Spain.
The latter was the view held by the Russian and French
plenipotentiaries. This divergence of opinion appeared
to Castlereagh of such material importance that he
judged it necessary to lay before the other members
a statement of the considerations which it involved.
No further discussion took place for between two
and three weeks, probably owing to the receipt of
a report from Tatischeff, the Russian diplomatic
representative at Madrid, that Spain did not any
longer propose to avail herself of the mediation of
the Five Powers, which was confirmed by similar
language held by the Duque de Fernan Nuñez, Spanish
Ambassador in Paris. But after that lapse of time, the
Duc de Richelieu produced a memoir, prepared by him
in concert with the Russian plenipotentiaries. It proposed among other things to open a communication with
the United States which was supposed to be on the point
of recognizing the republic of Buenos Ayres ; and also
that an intimation should be made to Spain that if she
were liberal in her terms, and if the Colonies refused the
terms of pacification which the mediating Powers
approved and tendered to them, the Powers would, in
that event, break off all communication with them,
commercial or otherwise. This was read to the conference, and having been taken *ad referendum*, was
discussed at great length in another meeting. The
Russian plenipotentiaries supported the Duc de Richelieu's views, while the British and Austrian plenipotentiaries argued strongly on the opposite side ; the

Prussians (owing in a great measure to Hardenberg's deafness) took little or no part. The conference broke up without coming to any decision or even approximation of opinion. As Castlereagh explained to the Emperor Alexander after the meeting was over, the English view was that the mediating Powers were not entitled to *arbitrate* or to *judge* between the King of Spain and his subjects, and consequently were not competent to enforce any such judgment directly or indirectly. They could only mediate and facilitate, but not compel or menace. Adverting to the particular means of coercion which had been considered in conference, and which were principally of a commercial description, force being admitted to be out of the question, Castlereagh stated to the Emperor that it was a species of hostility which Great Britain was not in the practice of using against her bitterest enemy, that in the latter years of the great war she had had a large direct trade with the ports of France, and suffered the French armies to be clothed by her manufacturers. If she had tolerated commerce with France in war, how could she deny it to her subjects at peace with South America after they had been accustomed to this commerce for ten years with the acquiescence of Spain ? After this conversation between Castlereagh and the Emperor Alexander the tone of the Russian plenipotentiaries changed, for when the Duc de Richelieu brought forward the question for re-discussion, they no longer supported him, and after a very short conversation he said that, finding his propositions did not meet the general sentiment, he withdrew them ; but that supposing the Duke of Wellington were invited to Madrid by the Spanish government, he would wish him to state what description of instructions could be with advantage given to him by the mediating Powers. That same evening, at an adjourned conference, Wellington produced memoranda of his views, but the sovereigns having already taken their departure, the plenipotentiaries could only take them *ad rèferendum.* Nothing further seems to have resulted from these conversations.[1]

Rush's *A Residence at the Court of London,* i. 1, relates a conversation with Castlereagh on February 12, 1919, respecting the affairs of Spanish America. Rush read to him a despatch received from his government. The latter hoped that the British Government and the European Powers in general would before long come to see the desirability of "such a recognition as would bring them within the pale of nations." The President had resolved to grant *exequatur* to a consul-general for Buenos Ayres appointed by the government of that state in the previous May. Castlereagh said that Great Britain had done her best to bring the controversy between Spain and her colonies to an end on the basis of a continued Spanish supremacy. She had always opposed the employment of force to that end. How far that plan was practicable was not for him to say.

In May 1822, Spain, then ruled by the Liberals who had forced the King to accept the constitution of 1812, spontaneously announced that she had measures in contemplation for the pacification of her Americas on an entirely new basis, which basis, however, was not explicitly described. But in November it was made known that the Cortes meditated opening negotiations with the colonies on the basis of colonial independence. Such negotiations were subsequently opened and carried to a successful termination with Buenos Ayres ; but they were afterwards disavowed by the King.[2]

The idea of a conference of the Powers was mooted in 1823, as appears from the record of a conversation between Canning and the Prince de Polignac on October 9.[3] The latter, in reply to Canning's statement that the British Government would countenance any negotiation between Spain and her colonies, provided it were founded

[1] See P.R.O., F.O., 139/45, 48, despatches Castlereagh to Bathurst of Nov. 2 and 24, 1818. There is a very short account in F. de Martens, vii. 297. As no protocols have been published, it is probable that no record was kept. [2] *Brit. and For. State Papers,* xii. 911.

[3] In a report to Chateaubriand of January 30, 1824, from Polignac

on a basis which appeared to them to be practicable, but that England could not go into a joint deliberation upon the subject of Spanish America, upon an equal footing with other Powers, whose interests were less implicated in the decision of it ;—in reply to these observations Polignac said that when the King of Spain was once more a free agent, the French Government would be ready to enter upon the subject of an arrangement between Spain and her colonies, in concert with their allies ; he saw no difficulty, he said, which should prevent England from taking part in the Conference.[1] The substance of this conversation was communicated to Spain [2] as well as to Austria, Russia, Prussia, Portugal, the Netherlands and the United States (xi. 61 *n*).

In December of the same year Count Ofalia, the Spanish minister for Foreign Affairs, addressed an instruction to the Spanish Ambassador at Paris, and to the Ministers Plenipotentiary at Petersburg and Vienna, stating that the King of Spain invited his allies to hold a Conference at Paris, for the purpose of aiding Spain to adjust the affairs of the revolted countries of America (*el arreglo de los negocios de America en los Paises disidentes*). He would in conjunction with them consider the relations which, during the disorders, had

---

occurs the following passage : " M. Canning saisit favorablement la distinction que j'avais faite et pour me le prouver, me dit en propres termes, *Des Plénipotentiaires dans un Congrès sont des arbitres, et dans des Conférences peuvent n'être que des conseillers*, or *M. le Vicomte, la note que vous* m'avez transmise porte, au contraire : " *L'Espagne ne demande pas des Conseillers mais des arbitres*, et plus *loin*, que dans la médiation proposée *L'Angleterre serait appelée à juger un différend*.

In consequence of this the word *Conference* was substituted for *Congress* in the memorandum published as a Parliamentary Paper, March 16, 1824, and republished in *British and Foreign State Papers*, xi, 49, by agreement between Polignac and Canning according to a further report of Polignac to Chateaubriand of March 5.

For the material of the foregoing note the author is indebted to Mr. H. W. V. Temperley. But the distinction said to have been drawn by Canning between a Congress and a Conference does not appear to be well-founded.

[1] *Ibid*, xi. 49–53. See also Stapleton, *The Political Life of George Canning*, ii. 26.
[2] *Ibid*., xii. 911.

been formed with commercial nations, in order to adopt the most proper measures for reconciling the rights and just interests of the Crown of Spain and its sovereignty with those which circumstances might have occasioned with respect to other nations. His Majesty hoped they would aid him in re-establishing peace between him and his colonies (*la paz entre ella* [1] *y sus Colonias*). The despatch ended with an instruction to endeavour to dispose the government to which the recipient was accredited to decide upon the desired co-operation for which the events of the Peninsula had paved the way (*se decida á la deseada cooperación que los acontecimientos de la Peninsula han preparado;* i.e. the overthrow of the Liberal party by the French Expeditionary Force, and the restoration of the King's autocratic power).[2]

No direct invitation was sent to Great Britain to take part in the proposed Conference, as there was no Spanish representative in London, but a copy of these instructions was enclosed in a Note of December 26 to Sir William A'Court, the British Minister at Madrid, with a request that he would transmit it to his government. For a similar reason, a copy was also furnished to the Prussian Minister.

Canning's reply of January 30 to Sir William A'Court explained at great length the reasons for which the British Government did not regard it as necessary to go into a Conference. At the same time he said frankly that in their opinion it was vain to hope that any mediation not founded on the basis of independence could now be successful. But if the Court of Madrid desired it, the British Government would willingly afford their countenance and aid to a negotiation commenced on the only basis which appeared to them to be now practicable, and would see, without reluctance, the conclusion, through a negotiation on that basis, of an arrangement by which the Mother-country should be

---

[1] Appears to refer to *Su Majestad* at the beginning of the sentence in the original Spanish.

[2] *Brit. and For. State Papers*, xi. 56–7.

secured in the enjoyment of commercial advantages superior to those conceded to other nations.[1]

In reply to this despatch, of which a copy had been furnished to him, Count Ofalia informed the British Minister in a further Note of April 30, that the other Four Powers had acceded to the proposal to take part in a Conference at Paris, and he again invited and requested the Government of His Britannic Majesty to consent to and take part in the proposed Conference.[2]

Towards the latter end of August Canning had sounded Mr. Rush, the United States Minister, as to whether the two Governments might not come to an understanding on the subject of the Spanish American colonies, and whether it would not be expedient for themselves and beneficial for the world, that its principles should be clearly settled and plainly avowed ; he added that the British Government conceived the recovery of the Colonies by Spain to be hopeless, and the question of recognizing their independence to be one of time and circumstances, but were not disposed to put any impediment in the way of an arrangement between them and the Mother-country by amicable negotiation. They did not aim at the possession of any portion of them for Great Britain, but could not see any part of them transferred to any other Power with indifference. Mr. Rush, however, did not feel authorized to put on paper any such agreement, whether in the form of a convention or an exchange of Notes,[3] but he would have neglected his duty as a diplomatic agent if he had not reported the conversation to the Secretary of State at Washington.[4]

The United States had already in 1822 appointed Ministers to Colombia and Buenos Ayres, and in his

<hr/>

[1] *Brit. and For. State Papers*, xi. 58–63.　　[2] *Ibid.*, xii. 958.
[3] Stapleton, ii. 23.
[4] Despatches from Bagot, minister at Washington, of October 7 and 31, 1818, and January 4 and April 7, 1819, show that Castlereagh was discussing the affairs of the Spanish-American Colonies with the United States confidentially during those years, and in particular that in February 1819 he had conversed with Rush on this subject (*Castlereagh Correspondence*, 3rd series, vol. iv.).

message of December 2, 1823, President Monroe announced that diplomatic relations were being established
with the more important South American Republics.
But more important in its effect was the passage in this
message to the effect that the United States owed it to
candour and to the amicable relations existing between
them and the European Powers to declare that " we
should consider any attempt, on their part, to extend
their system to any portion of this hemisphere, as
dangerous to our peace and safety. With the existing
colonies or dependencies of any European Power, we
have not interfered, and shall not interfere. But with
the Governments who have declared their independence,
and maintained it, and whose independence we have,
on great consideration and on just principles, acknowledged, we could not view any interposition for the
purpose of oppressing them, or controlling, in any other
manner, their destiny, by any European Power, in any
other light than the manifestation of an unfriendly
disposition towards the United States." [1]

The Conferences in Paris were held, but were composed only of the resident diplomatic representatives of
the Powers who had agreed to take part. " The object
of those conferences never clearly transpired." [2]

§ 640. *Rejection of British Mediation by France between
her and Spain.*

Wellington, on his way back from Verona (see § 465),
arrived in Paris in December 1822, where he found instructions awaiting him to offer the mediation of George
IV between France and Spain before the despatches
drafted at Verona were transmitted to Madrid, and
having learnt that they had not yet been forwarded, he
addressed the following Note to the French Government :

---

[1] *Brit. and For. State Papers*, xi. 17–18. *American State Papers*,
Washington, 1858, v. 250 ; W. F. Johnson, *America's Foreign Relations*,
i. 329.
[2] Stapleton, ii. 60.

Paris,
December, 17 1822.

The Undersigned, His Britannic Majesty's Plenipotentiary, has explained and recorded at the conferences of Verona the Sentiments of his Government upon the present critical State of Affairs between France and Spain ; and the earnest solicitude of The King, His Master, to avert a War of which no human foresight can calculate the consequences.

Upon his arrival at Paris the Undersigned found instructions from his Government to offer to H.M.C. Majesty the Mediation of the King, his Master, before the decisive Step should have been taken of transmitting to Madrid the despatches written at Verona.

The Undersigned rejoiced at the delay which had been interposed to the transmission of those despatches to Madrid by the reference to Verona, and his Government have learnt with the liveliest satisfaction the determination of the French Government to reconsider a measure, which The Undersigned had so anxiously deprecated.

It is the sincere hope of His Majesty that this salutary Reconsideration may prevent recourse to Arms. But as the issue of the reference to Verona may still be doubtful, the Undersigned is instructed to declare that if the Answer to that reference should not be such as to preclude all danger of hostilities His Majesty will be ready to accept the office of Mediator between the French and Spanish Governments, and to employ His most strenuous Endeavours for the Adjustment of their differences, and for the preservation of the Peace of the World.[1]

The reply of the duc de Montmorency, French minister for Foreign Affairs, to the foregoing, was worded as follows :—

Paris, le 26 décembre, 1822.

Le soussigné, ministre des affaires étrangères, a reçu et mis sous les yeux du roi la note que S. Exc. le duc de Wellington lui a fait l'honneur de lui adresser le 17 de ce mois.

S.M. a apprécié les sentimens qui ont engagé le roi d'Angleterre à offrir sa médiation à S.M., afin de prévenir une rupture entre elle et le gouvernement espagnol ; mais S.M. n'a pu s'empêcher de voir que la situation de la France à l'égard de l'Espagne n'était pas de nature à appeler une médiation entre les deux cours.

[1] From a copy at the P.R.O., F.O., 179/23. A French translation in Garden, *Traité Complet*, iii. 336.

En fait, il n'existe aucun différend entre elles, aucun point spécial de discussion par l'arrangement duquel leurs relations pourraient être rétablies dans l'état où elles devraient être. L'Espagne, par la nature de sa révolution et par les circonstances qui l'ont accompagnée, a excité les craintes de plusieurs grandes puissances ; l'Angleterre a partagé ces craintes, car, même en 1820, elle prévoyait des circonstances dans lesquelles il serait impossible de conserver avec l'Espagne des relations de paix et de bonne intelligence.

La France est plus intéressée qu'aucune autre puissance aux événemens qui peuvent résulter de la situation actuelle de cette monarchie. Mais ce ne sont pas seulement ses intérêts qui sont compromis, et qu'elle doit surveiller dans les circonstances actuelles ; le repos de l'Europe et la conservation de ces principes qui le garantissent se trouvent compromis.

Le duc de Wellington sait que tels sont les sentimens qui ont dicté la conduite de la France à Verone, et que les cours qui les ont approuvés ont regardé les conséquences de la révolution et de l'état actuel de l'Espagne comme communes à elles toutes ; qu'elles n'ont jamais eu l'idée que c'était entre la France et l'Espagne seules qu'il fallait aplanir les difficultés existantes ; qu'elles regardaient la question comme entièrement européenne ; et que c'est en conséquence de cette opinion que les mesures qui avaient pour objet de faire, s'il était possible, une amélioration dans l'état d'un pays si intéressant pour l'Europe, ont été connues et proposées ; mesures dont le succès aurait été certain si l'Angleterre avait jugé qu'elle pouvait y concourir.

S.M.T.C., qui était obligée de peser mûrement ces considérations, a donc cru qu'elle ne pouvait accepter la médiation qu'il a plu à S.M.B. de lui proposer ; elle voit cependant avec plaisir dans cette proposition un nouveau gage de la disposition conciliatrice du gouvernement anglais, et elle pense qu'avec de tels sentimens, ce gouvernement peut rendre un service essentiel à l'Europe, en offrant, de la même manière au gouvernement de l'Espagne des conseils qui, en lui inspirant des idées plus calmes, pourraient produire une heureuse influence sur la situation intérieure de ce pays.

S.M. apprendrait avec la plus vive satisfaction le succès de pareils efforts. Elle y verrait une juste raison d'espérer la conservation de la paix, dont les gouvernemens et les peuples d'Europe ne peuvent trop apprécier le prix.

Le soussigné saisit avec empressement l'occasion de renouveler à S. Exc. le duc de Wellington les assurances de sa haute considération.

(Signé) MONTMORENCY.[1]

De Martens says : " La médiation différant essentielle-ment de l'interposition des bons offices, on peut accepter ceux-ci et rejeter la médiation." [2]   This is what was done by the Note just cited.   The French Minister refuses mediation, but suggests moderating counsels being offered by Great Britain to the Spanish Government in power.   Chateaubriand, in communicating through the French Chargé d'affaires a copy of the King's speech delivered to the Chambers on January 28, 1823, an-nouncing the preparations made for the invasion of Spain, nevertheless accompanied it with a declaration of his desire for the good offices of the British Govern-ment, and Canning in February instructed Sir William A'Court to urge upon the Spanish Government to avert the threatened invasion by modifying in some way the Constitution.   Unfortunately the tone of speeches in the French Chamber nullified any effect which the counsels of the British Government might possibly have produced, and rendered it a point of honour not to entertain the question of modifications.[3]

---

[1] Garden, *Traité complet*, iii. 337.   In the copy in that work the general practice as to use of capital initials and abbreviation of titles has been disregarded.

[2] *Précis du Droit des Gens*, edit. Pinheiro-Ferreira, ii. 20 n.

[3] Stapleton, *Political Li e of George Canning*, i. 280.

CHAPTER XXXIV

ARBITRATION

§ 641. As will be seen from what has been said in the last two chapters, " good offices " are often confused with " mediation," and sometimes assume that form, while a mediation may now and then involve an arbitration. In fact, arbitration may be regarded essentially as an agreement to confer on a mediator, in place of a commission to negotiate terms of settlement, the more extended power of pronouncing a judgment on the matters at issue between the parties. A commission *d'enquête*, such as was held in connexion with the Dogger Bank affair, may have almost the same effect as an arbitration.

When a Power is resolved on war, neither the tender of good offices nor of mediation will avail to prevent the peace of the world from being broken. On the whole, arbitration will only be resorted to where a desire exists on both sides to settle a dispute amicably, and where the subject-matter of the controversy is of comparative unimportance. Nearly all the existing arbitration treaties or conventions accordingly except questions affecting the vital interests, independence or honour of the two contracting States.

The literature of the subject is enormous, much of it produced by persons who regard arbitration as the panacea for the bellicose passions of nations and a means of checkmating the ambitious schemes of governments and autocrats.

The following works may be recommended to students who desire to pursue this subject further :—

Lammasch, *Die Lehre von der Schiedsgerichtbarkeit in ihrem ganzen Umfang*, 1914.

Mérignac, *Traité théorique et pratique de l'Arbitrage*, 1897.

Moore, J. B., *History and Digest of the Arbitrations to which the United States has been a Party*. Six vols. Washington, 1898.

Morris, R. C., *International Arbitration and Procedure*. New York, 1911.

W. Evans Darby, *International Arbitration*, 4th edit., London, 1904, which, besides the subject indicated on the title-page, contains information respecting various famous projects for establishing a perpetual state of peace between nations

APPENDIX I

LIST OF WORKS REFERRED TO

ADAMS, Henry. History of the United States. 9 vols. New York, 1889–91.

Adams, J. Q., Life of. Philadelphia, 1871.

Almanach de Gotha for 1914.

Alt, Dr. L. Handbuch des Europäischen Gesandschafts-Rechtes, etc. Berlin, 1870.

Alvarez, Alex. Le Droit International Américain. Paris, 1910.

Angeberg (*cte* d').[1] Le Congrès de Vienne et les Traités de 1815. Paris, 1864.

—— Recueil des Traités, Conventions, Actes, Notes, Capitulations et Pièces Diplomatiques concernant la Guerre Franco-Allemande. 5 vols. Paris, 1873.

Anson, Sir Wm. The Law and Custom of the Constitution. Oxford, 1907.

Ashley, Evelyn. Life of Lord Palmerston. London, 1876.

Baruch, B. M. The Making of the Reparation and Economic Sections of the Treaty. New York and London, 1920.

Bath, Marq. of. Calendar of MSS. Hist. MSS. Commission, 1908.

Blok, Geschiedenis van het Nederlandsche Volk, tweede druk. Leiden, 1912–15.

Bologna, Giacomo. Nozze Busnelli-Ballarin. Schio, 1884.

Brewer, J. S. Reign of Henry VIII to the Death of Wolsey. London, 1884.

British and Foreign State Papers.

Broglie (J. B. Albert, *duc* de). Maurice de Saxe et le Marq. d'Argenson. Paris, 1891.

—— La paix d'Aix-la-Chapelle. Paris, 1892.

—— (A. L. V. C., *duc* de). Souvenirs du feu, etc. Paris, 1886.

Browning, O. The Despatches of Earl Gower. Cambridge, 1885.

Bryce, James. The Holy Roman Empire. London, 1889.

[1] Pseudonym of Jákob Leonard Chodzko.

Bulwer, Sir Henry Lytton. Life of Henry John Temple, *Visct*. Palmerston. 3 vols. London, 1870–74.
Busch, Moritz. Bismarck und Seine Leute während des Kriegs mit Frankreich, 4th edit. Leipzig, 1878.
—— Bismarck, Some Secret Pages of his History. 3 vols. London, 1898.

Callières, François de. De la manière de négocier avec les souverains, etc., Paris, also Amsterdam, 1716. Translation by A. F. Whyte, London, 1919.
Calvo, Carlos. Le Droit international théorique et pratique, 4ᵉ édit. 6 vols. Paris and Berlin, 1877-86.
Cambridge Modern History.
Camden, William. Annales rerum Anglicarum et Hibernicarum regnante Elizabetha. Lugd. Bat., 1639. Translation by T. R., 3rd edit. folio, 1635.
Cantlie, J. Sun Yat Sen and the awakening of China. 1912.
Carte, Th. History of the Revolutions of Portugal. London, 1740.
Castlereagh. Memoirs and Correspondence, 3rd series, vol. iv. London, 1853.
Castro y Casaleiz, de. Guía práctica del diplomático Español, 2nd edit. 2 vols. Madrid, 1886.
Chateaubriand, *vte* de. Mémoires d'Outretombe, édit. E. Biré, 1880.
Cobbett, Pitt. Cases and Opinions on International Law, 3rd edit., 1900–13.
Cobbett, W. Parliamentary History. 12 vols. London, 1806–12.
Coleridge, S. T. Table Talk. Several editions.
Collier, Price. Germany and the Germans. London, 1918.
Conférence Internationale de la Paix, 1899. Nouvelle édition. La Haye, 1907.
Conférence Internationale d'Algeciras, Protocoles, Comptes Rendus. Paris, 1906.
Correspondence relating to the Affairs of the Levant. 1841.
Cottoni Posthuma. London, 1651.
Crandall Treaties and their Making and Enforcement. 1916.
Croker, J. W. Correspondence and Diaries. 3 vols. London, 1884.
Cussy, *baron* Ferd. de. Dictionnaire du diplomate et du Consul. Leipzig, 1846.

Dasent, A. I. John Thaddeus Delane. 2 vols. London, 1908.

Debidour, Antoine. Histoire Diplomatique de l'Europe, 1814–78. 2 vols. Paris, 1891.
—— ditto, depuis le Congrès de Berlin jusqu'a nos jours, 2 vols. Paris, 1917–18.
Deuxième Conférence de la Haye, Actes et documents, 3 vols. La Haye, 1907.
Die Urkunden der Friedenschlüsse zu Osnabrück und Münster. Zürich, 1848.
Droysen, J. G. Friedrich der Grosse. 1886.
—— Der Staat des Grossen Kurfürsten. Berlin, 1865–71.
Du Casse, A. Mémoires et correspondance du roi Joseph. Paris, 1853–4.
Dumont, J. Corps universel diplomatique. Paris, 1725–31.
Dupuis, Ch. Le droit des gens. Paris, 1920.
Dyer, Thomas Henry. Modern Europe, 2nd edit. London, 1877.

Ellis, G. E. Memoir of Count Rumford. Boston, 1871.
Evelyn, John. Diary, edit. by H. B. Wheatley. 4 vols. London, 1906.

Fain, baron A. J. F. MS. de 1813 pour servir à l'histoire de Napoléon. Paris, 1824.
Fanshawe, Sir Rd. Original Letters during his embassies in Spain and Portugal. 1702.
Ferraris. Prompta Bibliotheca, canonica, juridica, etc. Lutetiæ Par., 1852–7.
Finett, Sir John. Finetti Philoxenis : observations of Sir John Finett, etc. London, 1656.
Flassan (G. de R. de). Histoire de la diplomatie française, 2e éd., 7 vols. Paris, 1811.
Foreign Office List for 1869.
Foreign Relations of the United States.
Foster, J. W. The Practice of Diplomacy as illustrated in the Foreign Relations of the United States. Boston and New York, 1906.
—— Diplomatic Memoirs. 1910.
—— A Century of American Diplomacy. Boston, 1900.
Fournier, A. Der Congress von Châtillon. Wien, 1900.
Friedrich der Grosse. Politische Correspondenz. 35 vols. Berlin, 1879–1912.

Gachard, L. P. Relations des ambassadeurs Vénétiens sur Charles V et Philippe II. Bruxelles, 1855.
García de la Vega, D. Guide Pratique des Agents Politiques, etc. Bruxelles et Paris, 1873.

Garden, le cte G. de. Traité complet de diplomatie. 3 vols. Paris, 1883.
—— Histoire Générale des traités de paix, 15 vols. Paris, 1848–87.
Gardiner, S. R. History of the Commonwealth and Protectorate. 3 vols. London, 1894–1901.
Geffcken, H. Zur Geschichte des Orientalischen Krieges. Berlin, 1881.
Gentz. Dépêches inédites aux Hospodars de Valachie. 3 vols. Paris, 1876–7.
—— Oesterreichs Theilnahme an den Befreiungskriegen. Vienna, 1877. (This work is also catalogued under Metternich, and under Klinkowstrom.
—— Briefe an Pilat. 2 vols. 1848–68. Leipzig.
Gérin, in Révue des Questions Historiques.
Grimblot, P. Letters of William III and Louis XIV, and of their Ministers, 1697–1700. London, 1848.
Grotius. De Jure Belli et Pacis. Translated by Dr. Whewell. 3 vols. Cambridge and London, 1853.
Guizot, F. P. G. Mémoires pour servir à l'histoire de mon temps. 8 vols. Paris, 1858–67.
—— Histoire de la République d'Angleterre et de Cromwell. 2 vols. Paris, 1856.

Hall, W. E. A treatise on International Law. Oxford, 5th edit., 1904; 6th edit., 1909.
Halleck, H. W. International Law. 2 vols. New edition. London, 1878.
Hammer, J. v. Geschichte des Osmanischen Reiches. Pesth, 1827–35.
Harris, F. R. Life of the First Earl of Sandwich. 2 vols. London, 1912.
Haskins and Lord. Some Problems of the Peace Conference. Cambridge, Harvard University Press, and Oxford University Press, 1920.
Haussonville, J. O. B. de Cléron, cte. d'. Histoire de la politique extérieure du gouvernement français, 1830–48. Paris, 1850.
Hearings before the Committee on Foreign Relations of the United States Senate, Document No. 106, 66th Congress, 1st Session. Washington, 1919.
Heffter, A. W. Das europäische Völkerrecht der Gegenwart. 7th edition. Berlin, 1882.
Hertslet, Sir Edw. Recollections of the Old Foreign Office. London, 1901.
—— Commercial Treaties.

Higgins, A. Pearce. The Hague Peace Conferences, etc. Cambridge, 1909.
Hill, D. J. A History of Diplomacy in the International Development of Europe. 3 vols. New York and London, 1911–14.
Holtzendorff, F. v. Handbuch des Völkerrechts. Leipzig, 1885–89.
Hübner, J. A. Graf v. Neuf ans de souvenirs d'un Ambassadeur, etc. Paris, 1904–5.

International Naval Conference, London. Proceedings, le 14 Novembre, 1908.
—— Correspondence and Documents respecting [Cd. 4554]. London, 1909.

Jenkinson, Rt. Hon. C. A Collection of all the Treaties, etc. between Great Britain and other Powers. 3 vols. London, 1785.
Johnson, W. F. American Foreign Relations. 2 vols. London, 1916.

Kinglake, A. W. The Invasion of the Crimea. London, 1863–87.
King's Regulations and Admiralty Instructions.
Klüber, Acten des Wiener Congresses, 2nd edition. Erlangen 1817–35.
Koch, C. G. de. Histoire abrégée des traités de Paix, continuée jusqu'à 1815 par F. Schoell. 1817–18. Brussels edit. 1837.
Krauske, Otto. Entwickelung der ständigen Diplomatie, etc. Leipzig, 1885.

Langlois et Stein. Les Archives de l'Histoire de France Paris, 1891.
Lefèvre-Pontalis. Jean de Witt. Paris, 1884.
Legrelle, A. Notes et documents sur la paix de Ryswyk, etc. Lille, 1894.
Lamberty, G. de. Mémoires pour servir à l'histoire du 18 siècle, etc. Amsterdam, 1733–40.
Lecomte et Lévi. Neutralité Belge et Invasion Allemande. Paris et Bruxelles, 1914.
Legg, L. G. Wickham. List of Diplomatic Representatives, England and France, 1689–1763. Oxford and London, 1909.
Leyes Usuales de la República Oriental del Uruguay.

Macaulay, T. B. History of England. 5 vols. London, 1849–61.

Malmesbury, 1st Earl. Diaries and Correspondence. 4 vols. London, 1844.

Malmesbury, Lord. Memoirs of an Ex-Minister. London, 1884.

Marshall, Beatrice. Memoirs of Lady Fanshawe. London, 1905.

Martens, Ch. de. Causes Célèbres du droit des Gens. Leipzig, 1827.

——, Ch. de. Le Guide Diplomatique, 5ᵉ édit., par M. F. H. Geffcken. Leipzig, 1866.

—— F. de. Recueil des Traités, etc., conclus par la Russie, 1874–1909.

—— G. F. Précis du Droit des Gens. Berlin, 1831.

—— Recueil des principaux traités, etc., 1791–1801.

—— Nouveau Recueil général (three series).

Martin, Sir Theodore. Life of the Prince Consort. 5 vols London, 1877–80.

Masson, F. Le Département des Affaires Etrangères pendant la Révolution. Paris, 1877.

Maulde-la-Clavière, R. de. Histoire de Louis XII, 2ème partie. Paris, 1893.

Mazarin, Cardinal. Lettres où l'on voit de Secret de la Négociation de la Paix des Pyrenées. Amsterdam, 1745.

Metternich, *Fürst* C. W. N. L. von. Mémoires, documents et écrits divers. 8 vols. Paris, 1880–4.

Michaud & Poujoulat. Nouvelle Collection de Mémoires, etc., 1850.

Miruss, A. Europäisches Gesandschaftsrecht. 1847.

Montagu, Lady Mary Wortley, edit. Lord Wharncliffe, with additions, etc., by W. M. Thomas, new edit. 2 vols London, 1887.

Moore, J. B. Digest of International Law, etc. Washington, 1906.

Motley. The Rise of the Dutch Republic. Many editions.

Nouveau Recueil Général des Traités. See G. F. de Martens.

Nys, E. Le Droit International, 2 édit. 3 vols. Bruxelles et Paris, 1904–6.

—— Les Origines du Droit international. Bruxelles et Paris, 1894.

Ollivier, E. L'Empire Libéral, 1895–1915. 16 vols. Paris, 1895–1912.

Oncken, W.   Oesterreich und Preussen im Befreiungs Kriege.
    Berlin, 1876–9.
Oxford Dictionary.

Papers relating to the negotiations with France, 1806.
Pasquier, E. D. *duc*. Histoire de mon temps.   6 vols.   Paris,
    1893–5.
Peace Proposals and War Aims, Documents and Statements
    relating to.   London, 1919.
Pearsall Smith, L.   Life and Letters of Sir Henry Wotton.
    2 vols.   London, 1907.
Pepys, Samuel.   Diary.
Phillimore, Sir Robt.   Commentaries on International Law.
    1854–61.   There is a 3rd edit., 1879–89.
Phillips, W. Alison.   Modern Europe.   1815–1899.   London,
    1901.
Politische Correspondenz Friedrichs des Grossen.
Poole, Stanley Lane.   Life of the Rt. Hon. Stratford Canning.
    2 vols.   London, 1888.
Pradier-Fodéré, P.   Cours de Droit Diplomatique.   Paris,
    1881.
Prescott, W. H.   History of the Reign of Philip II.   1855.
—— and Robertson.   History of the Reign of Charles V.
    1857.
—— Ferdinand and Isabella, 8th edition.   3 vols.   London,
    1854.
P.R.O. = Public Record Office.
Prokesch-Osten.   Geschichte des Abfalls der Griechen.   6 vols.
    Wien, 1867.

Rapport du Conseil Administratif de la Cour Permanente
    d'Arbitrage pendant l'année 1909.
Recueil des Instructions données aux Ambassadeurs et
    Ministres de France, etc.   Paris, 1884–92.
Redesdale, Lord.   The Garter Mission to Japan.   London,
    1906.
Reid, Stuart J.   Life and Letters of the First Earl of Durham.
    2 vols.   London, 1906.
Reliquiæ Wottonianæ, 4th edit.   London, 1685.
Révue Générale du Droit International Public.
Révue des Questions Historiques.
Rivier, A.   Principes du Droit des Gens.   1896.
Robertson, C. Grant.   Bismarck.   London, 1908.
Roederer.   De l'application des immunités de l'Ambassadeur
    au Personnel de l'Ambassade.   Paris, 1904.

Rose, J. Holland. Life of Napoleon I. 2 vols. London, 1902.

Rousset. Recueil historique d'Actes, etc. La Haye, 1752.

Russell, Lord John. Memoir and Correspondence of Charles James Fox. 3 vols. London, 1853–7.

Rush, Rd. Residence at the Court of London. London, 1883, and 2 other editions.

Ruville, A. v. William Pitt, Earl of Chatham. 3 vols. London and New York, 1907.

Rymer, T. Foedera. 20 vols. London, 1704–32.

Satow, Sir E. The Silesian Loan and Frederick the Great. Oxford, 1915.

Sbornik. Imperat. Russ. Istorie. Obshchestva, t. 65. Petersburg, 1888.

Schäfer, A. D. Geschichte des Sieben-jährigen Krieges, 2 vols. Berlin, 1867–74.

Schmalz, T. Europäisches Völkerrecht. Berlin, 1817.

Schmelzing, J. Systematischer Grundriss des Völkerrechts. Rudolstadt, 1818–20. References in footnotes are to Band. ii. only.

Scott, J. B. The Hague Peace Conferences of 1899 and 1907. Baltimore, 1909.

—— Cases on International Law.

Ségur, cte. Ph. P. de. Mémoires et Souvenirs, 2nd edit. 1873.

Shilder. Alexander 1, evo zhuzn i tsarstvovanie (in Russian). St. Petersburg, 1904–5.

Sismondi, J. C. L. de. Histoire des Français. Bruxelles, 1836–46.

Smith, Logan Pearsall. The Life and Letters of Sir H. Wotton. Oxford, 1907.

Sorel, Albert. La Question d'Orient au 18° siècle, 2° édit. Paris, 1889.

—— Histoire diplomatique de la Guerre Franco-Allemande. 2 vols. Paris, 1875.

—— l'Europe et la Révolution Française. 8 vols. Paris, 1885–1904.

—— Essais d'histoire et de critique. 2 vols. Paris, 1894.

S.P.O. = State Paper Office.

Spectator, The. London, 1712.

Stapleton, A. G. Political Life of Rt. Hon. George Canning. 3 vols. London, 1831.

—— George Canning and his Times. London, 1859.

State Trials. London, 1809–28.

Stephens, Sir J. F. Digest of the Criminal Law, 5th edit. London, 1883.
Sun Yat Sen. Kidnapped in London.
Syveton, G. Une Cour et un aventurier au 18e siècle : le baron de Ripperda. Paris, 1896.

Talleyrand. Mémoires. Édités par le Duc de Broglie. 5 vols. Paris, 1891–2.
Tardieu, A. La Paix. Paris, 1921.
Taylor, Hannis. A treatise on Public International Law. Boston, 1902.
Temperley, Harold. Frederick the Great and Kaiser Joseph. London, 1915.
—— History of the Peace Conference of Paris, 5 vols. London, 1920–.
Thayer, W. R. Life and Letters of John Hay. London, 1915.
Thompson. The Peace Conference Day by Day. New York, 1920
Thurloe's State Papers, 7 vols., folio, 1742.

Ullmann, E. v. Völkerrecht, new edit. Tübingen, 1908.

Valfrey, Jules. Hugues de Lionne, Ses Ambassades, etc. Paris, 1881. (Also entitled La Diplomatie Française au 17 ème Siècle.
Vandal, A. Une Ambassade Française en Orient sous Louis XV. Paris, 1887.
—— Louis XV et Elisabeth de Russie. Paris, 1882.
—— Napoléon et Alexandre Ier, 3 vols. Paris, 1891–4.
Vast, H. Les Grands Traités du Règne de Louis XIV. Paris, 1893–9.
Vattel. Le Droit des Gens. Nouvelle édition, 3 vols. Paris, 1835.
Villa-Urrutia, W. R. de. Relaciones entre España é Inglaterra durante la Guerra de la Independencia. 3 vols. Madrid, 1911–14.

Waddington, A. Le Grand Electeur Frédéric Guillaume de Brandebourg : Sa politique extérieure, 1640–88. Paris, 1905–8.
Waddington, R. Louis XV et le Renversement des Alliances. Paris, 1896.
Walton, Izaak. Lives.
Weber, Ottocar. Der Friede von Utrecht. Gotha, 1891.
Webster, C. K. British Diplomacy, 1813–15. London, 1921.

Welschinger, H. La Guerre de 1870. 2 vols. Paris, 1910.
Wheaton, Henry. Elements of International Law, edit. J. B. Atlay. London, 1904.
Whewell's Grotius. Cambridge and London, 1853.
Wicquefort. L'Ambassadeur et ses Fonctions Amsterdam, 1730.
Wortley Montague, Lady Mary. Letters and Works. New edition, 2 vols. London, 1887.

Zinkeisen, J. W. Geschichte des Osmanischen Reiches in Europa. Gotha, 1857.

APPENDIX II

THE importance of Grotius, whose work *De Jure Belli et Pacis, libri tres*, appeared in 1625 and is still frequently quoted, renders it advisable that every Mission should possses a copy. There are several English translations, of which the most recent is by Whewell (Cambridge), 1853. Barbeyrac's translation into French (Amsterdam, 1724) is much used by continental writers. A new English translation by Dr. John D. Maguire, Professor of Latin at the Catholic University of America, will be published shortly by the Carnegie Institution at Washington.

Of the books which were published in the eighteenth century, Vattel's *Le Droit des Gens, ou Principes de la Loi Naturelle appliqués à la Conduite et aux Affaires des Nations et des Souverains* (Leyden, 1758) is of importance and continues to be referred to as an authority. The author was a Swiss of Neuchâtel who entered the diplomatic service of Saxony, and became Saxon Minister at Berne. There is an excellent edition by Pradier-Fodéré (Paris, 1863); and an English translation by Chitty (London, 1834).

Of less importance than Vattel, but also frequently quoted, is G. F. de Martens, *Précis du Droit des Gens moderne de l'Europe*, 1789. The last edition was by Vergé (Paris, 1864) The author, who was professor of law at Göttingen, must not be confounded with his nephew Charles, author of the *Guide Diplomatique*, or with the Russian Professor F. de Martens, author of a general treatise on International Law mentioned below. G. F. de Martens began the important collection of treaties which goes by the name of " Martens, Recueil de Traités, etc.," and is still being continued.

Likewise of importance—although only a fragment—is Ward, *A Treatise of the Relative Rights and Duties of Belligerent and Neutral Powers in Maritime Affairs*, and *An Essay on Contraband*, both published in 1801. The first of these was reprinted in 1875 with a preface by Lord Stanley of Alderley. Ward also wrote *An Enquiry into the Foundation and History of the Law of Nations from the time of the Greeks and Romans to the Age of Grotius*. London, 1795.

As regards nineteenth and twentieth century literature, the following general treatises are the most considerable :

BRITISH

Manning, W. O., Commentaries on the Law of Nations, 1839, new edition by Sheldon Amos, 1875. Manning's is the first English treatise which attempts a survey of the British practice regarding maritime warfare based on the judgments of Sir William Scott (Lord Stowell).

Phillimore, Commentaries upon International Law, 4 vols., 1854–61, 3rd edit. 1879–89. Phillimore's work comprises a vast amount of material ; vol. iv treats of Private International Law.

Twiss, The Law of Nations, 2 vols., 1861–63, 2nd edit., vol. i (Peace), 1884, vol. ii (War), 1875. A French translation brought up to date, appeared in 1887–89. This is a necessary book for the student.

Hall, A Treatise on International Law, 1880, 6th edit., 1909 (out of print) ; a 7th edition by Pearce Higgins was published in 1917. This is an excellent work, distinguished by the sound judgment of the author.

Lawrence, Rev. T. J., The Principles of International Law, 4th edit., 1910. This is a justly appreciated work, which has attained a wide circulation ; its value consists in its inclusion of moral and political considerations.

Oppenheim, International Law, 2 vols., 1905–6, 2nd edit., 1912 ; third edition, 1920–21, vol. i., revised by A. Pearce Higgins, vol. ii., revised by R. F. Roxburgh.

Westlake, International Law, 2 vols., 1904–7, 2nd edit., 1910–13. Not a complete treatise, it supplies very valuable information on the principal questions of International Law.

Phillipson, Coleman. Termination of War and Treaties of Peace. London, 1916.

AMERICAN

Kent, Commentary on International Law, 1826. English edition by Abdy, 1878.

Wheaton, Elements of International Law, 1836. Wheaton was at first American Chargé d'affaires at Copenhagen and afterwards Minister Plenipotentiary in Berlin, and although his work is in many points antiquated, it is still of value, and is often consulted. Many editions have appeared, of which the best is by Dana, Boston, 1866. English edition by J. B. Atlay, 1904. Wheaton is also author of the best history of International Law, which appeared first in French in 1841, but an enlarged English edition was brought out at Washington in 1846. A new edition of Wheaton, by C. Phillipson, appeared in 1916. The editor has made no distinction between Wheaton's original text and his own additions to it.

Taylor, Hannis, A Treatise on International Public Law, 1902. The author was for some time American Minister Plenipotentiary at Madrid, and his work is a good compilation of the rules of modern public International Law.

Moore, J. B., A Digest of International Law, 8 vols., 1908. Not a general treatise, but a digest of the international practice of the United States from her first appearance as a member of the Family of Nations up to 1906. This is an important and valuable work, and should be constantly consulted. It is more exhaustive than the similar work of Francis Wharton, 3 vols, 1886, which it has practically superseded.

The best of the small American maunals is by Wilson and Tucker, International Law, 1901, 5th edit., 1910.

FRENCH

Calvo, Le Droit International, 1868, 5th edit., 6 vols., 1896. The author was born at Buenos Ayres, and represented the Argentine Republic at Petersburg, Vienna, Berlin and Paris. The first edition appeared in Spanish in 1868, but the following ones are in French. It is a storehouse of facts and opinions, but requires to be consulted with caution, as its juristic basis is not at all exact.

Pradier-Fodéré, Traité de Droit International Public, 8 vols., 1885–1906. The same observation applies as to Calvo.

Bonfils, Manuel de Droit International Public, 1894, 7th edit., by Fauchille, 1914.

Despagnet, Cours de Droit International Public, 1894, 4th edit., by De Boeck, 1910.

Rivier, Principes du Droit des Gens, 2 vols, 1896.. The author was a Swiss who was a professor of law at the University of Brussels and at the same time diplomatic representative of Switzerland at the Belgian Court. This is an excellent work.

Nys, Le Droit International, 3 vols., 1904–6, new edit., 1912. A general treatise on an historical basis by a Belgian jurist of repute.

Mérignac, Traité de Droit Public International, 3 vols., 1905–12, to be completed by a 4th volume.

German

The German treatises, which saw the light during the first half of the nineteenth century, are now regarded as antiquated, but Klüber and Heffter are nevertheless still consulted and frequently quoted.

Klüber, Droit des Gens moderne, 1819, German edition under the title of Europäisches Völkerrecht, 1821. Last German edit. by Morstadt, 1851, last French edit. by Ott, 1874.

Heffter, Das Europäische Völkerrecht der Gegenwart, 1844, 8th edit. by Geffcken in 1888, French translation by Bergson, 1851, and by Geffcken, 1883. This and the preceding work must not be neglected, as they are frequently cited as authorities.

Bluntschli, Das moderne Völkerrecht der civilizirten Staaten als Rechtbuch dargestellt. Born at Zurich, was professor there, from 1848 at München, and in 1861 at Heidelberg. This is not a general treatise, but a kind of code. On account of the author's great reputation, his work is frequently quoted, but it should be consulted with caution, since the rules it gives are not infrequently in disaccord with the existing rules of positive international law.

Holtzendorff, Handbuch des Völkerrechts, 4 vols., 1885–89. This work is the joint composition of several authors ; Holtzendorff is one of the chief contributors and also general editor.

Ullmann, Völkerrecht, 1898, 2nd edit., 1908.

Liszt, Das Völkerrecht, 1898, 10th edit., 1914. This is a short, but well-written manual, and the author being professor at the University of Berlin, it is much used and consulted in Germany.

Italian

Fiore, Trattato di diritto internazionale pubblico, 1865, 4th edit., in 3 vols., 1904. French translation of the 2nd edit. by Antoine, 1885. Fiore was professor at the University of Naples (he died in 1914), and his work is the leading Italian general treatise on international law. He also published in 1911 " Le Droit International Codifié," of which an English translation is about to appear under the auspices of the Carnegie Institution at Washington. Both these works must be consulted with caution, because the author frequently enunciates rules which are more based on the Law of Nature than on the actual practice of States.

Diena, Principi di Diritto Internazionale, parte prima, Diritto Internazionale Pubblica, 1908, 2nd edit., 1914, is a valuable manual.

SPANISH AND SPANISH-AMERICAN

Calvo's work has been already mentioned amongst the French works.

Olivart, Tratados y Notas de Derecho Internacional Público, 2 vols., 1887 ; 4th edit. in 4 vols., 1903–4 ; 5th edit. abridged, in 1 vol. 1906.

Campos, Elementos de Derecho Internacional Público, 3rd edit., 1912.

Suarez, S. P. Tratado de Derecho Internacional Público. Madrid, 1916. Vol. I, Peace.

DUTCH

De Louter, Het Stellig Volkenrecht, 2 vols., 1910.

De Louter, French version by the author. Le Droit International Public Positif. 2 vols. Oxford, 1920.

RUSSIAN

De Martens, F. The Russian original reached a 5th edit. in 1905. A French translation by Léo of the first edit., 3 vols., 1883–7, a German edit. by Bergbohm in 2 vols., 1883–6. This is a work of great value and importance.

PORTUGUESE

Vilela, Alvaro, Direito Internacional. The author is a professor at the University of Coimbra.

BRAZIL

Bevilacqua, Direito publico Internacional, 1911. Rio de Janeiro.

APPENDIX III

MEMOIRS OF BRITISH STATESMEN.

Bulwer, Sir Henry Lytton. Life of Henry John Temple,
Visct. Palmerston, 3 vols. London, 1870.

Evelyn Ashley. Life of Lord Palmerston, in continuation.
2 vols. London, 1876.

Malmesbury, First Earl. Diaries and Correspondence, 4 vols.
London, 1844.

Poole, Stanley Lane. Life of the Rt. Hon. Stratford Canning,
2 vols. London, 1888.

Reid, Stuart J. Life and Letters of the First Earl of Durham,
2 vols. London, 1906.

Russell, Lord John. Memoir and Correspondence of Charles
James Fox, 3 vols. London, 1853–7.

Ruville, A. v. William Pitt, Earl of Chatham, 3 vols. London
and Berlin, 1905; New York, 1907, also in German.

Stapleton, A.G. Political Life of Rt. Hon. George Canning,
3 vols. London, 1831.

—— George Canning and His Times. London, 1859.

Ballantyne, A. Lord Carteret. London, 1887.

Edwards, H. G. Sir William White, His Life and Correspondence. London, 1902.

Lord Edmund Fitzmaurice. Life of the 2nd Earl Granville,
2 vols. 1905.

Lord Fitzmaurice. Life of William, Earl of Shelburne.
Revised edition, 2 vols. London, 1902.

Maxwell, Sir Herbert. Life and Letters of Lord Clarendon
(4th Earl), 2 vols. London, 1913.

Newton, Lord. Lord Lyons, A Record of British Diplomacy,
2 vols. London, 1913.

Walpole, Spencer. Life of Lord John Russell, 2 vols.
London, 1889.

Wemyss, Mrs. Memoirs and Letters of Sir Robert Morier,
2 vols. London, 1911.

Williams, Basil. Life of W. Pitt, Earl of Chatham, 2 vols. London, 1913.

Lady Gwendolen Cecil. Life of Lord Salisbury, up to 1880, 2 vols. London, 1922.

Disraeli, B., Life of, Earl of Beaconsfield. By Monypenny and Buckle, 6 vols. London, 1910–20.

Lord Stanmore. The Earl of Aberdeen. London, 1893.

French Statesmen.

Pasquier, E. D. *duc*. Histoire de mon temps, 6 vols. Paris, 1893-5.

Pallain, G. Correspondence de Talleyrand et du roi Louis XVIII. pendant le Congrès de Vienne. Paris, 1881.

—— Ambassade de Talleyrand à Londres, 1830–4. Paris 1891.

Le Duc de Broglie. Mémoires de Talleyrand, 5 vols. Paris, 1891–2.

Guizot, F. P. G. Mémoires pour servir à l'histoire de mon temps, 8 vols. Paris, 1856.

Ollivier, E. L'Empire Libéral, 16 vols. Paris, 1895–1915.

Major John Hall. England and the Orleans Monarchy. London, 1912.

Le Vassor, Michel. Histoire de Louis XIII, 7 vols. Amsterdam, 1700–13.

Hanotaux, Gabriel. Histoire de Cardinal de Richelieu, 2 vols. Paris, 1893–1903.

Grant, A. J. The French Monarchy, 2 vols. Cambridge University Press, 1914.

German Statesmen.

Busch, Moritz. Bismarck und seine Leute während des Kriegs mit Frankreich, 4th edit. Leipzig, 1878.

Bismarck, Otto Fürst v. Gedanken und Erinnerungen, 2 vols. Stuttgart, 1898 ; vol. 3. 1921.

Busch, Moritz. Bismarck, Some Secret Pages of His History, 3 vols. London, 1898.

Matter, P. Bismarck et son temps, 3 vols. Berlin, 1905–8.

C. Grant Robertson. Bismarck. London. 1918.

Hohenlohe, Denkwürdigkeiten, 2 vols. Berlin, 1906. English translation, 2 vols. London, 1906.

Italian Statesmen.

Chiala L. Lettere di Camillo Cavour, 7 vols. Torino, 1883–7. (But a later edition is fuller.)

Mazade, Charles de. Le Comte de Cavour. Paris, 1877.
Trevelyan, George Macaulay. Garibaldi and the Making of
  Italy. London, 1911.
Ollivier, Emile. See Empire Libéral, vol. iv. for Cavour and
  Napoléon III.
Bianchi, Nicomede. Diplomazia Europea in Italia, 8 vols.
  Napoli, 1865–72.
Martinengo Cesaresco, Countess E. Cavour. London, 1898.
La Rive (W. de). Récits et Souvenirs. Paris, 1862. Remin-
  iscences of Cavour. Translated by E. Romilly. London,
  1862.
Marriott, J. A. R. The Makers of Modern Italy. London,
  1889.
Cavour. Ouvrages politiques-économiques. 5 vols. Coni,
  1855–7.

Austrian Statesmen.

Metternich. Mémoires, documents et écrits divers, 8 vols.
  Paris, 1880–4.
Vivenot. Thugut und sein politisches System. Wien, 1870.

American Statesmen.

Abraham Lincoln. By Nicolay, J. G., and J. Hay, 10 vols.
  New York, 1890.
W. R. Thayer. Life and Letters of John Hay. London, 1915.

French Revolution and Napoleon I.

Sorel, A. l'Europe et la Révolution Française, 8 vols. Paris,
  1885–1911.
J. Holland Rose. Life of Napoleon I. 2 vols. London,
  1914.
Angeberg. Le Congrès de Vienne et les Traités de 1815
  2 parts. Paris, 1864.
The Cambridge History of British Foreign Policy. Edited by
  Sir A. W. Ward and G. P. Gooch, vol. i. 1783 1815.
  Cambridge, 1922.
Webster, C. K. British Diplomacy, 1813–5. London, 1921.
—— The Congress of Vienna, 1814–5. Oxford, 1919.
—— England and the Polish-Saxon Problem at the Congress
  of Vienna. London, 1913.
Weil, M. H. Les dessous du Congrès de Vienne, 2 vols. Paris,
  1917.
Méneval. Mémoires pour servir à l'Histoire de Napoléon 1er,
  3 vols. Paris, 1894.

Vandal, A.   Napoléon et Alexandre 1ᵉʳ, 3 vols.   Paris, 1898–1900.

General Works on History.

W. Alison Phillips.   The Confederation of Europe, 2ud edit. London, 1920.
—— Modern Europe, 1815–99.   London, 1901.
Marriott, J. A. R.   The European Commonwealth.   Oxford, 1918.
—— The Eastern Question.   Oxford, 1917.
Ramsay Muir.   The Expansion of Europe, 3rd edit.   London, 1922.
Elliott, Hon. Arthur D.   Traditions of British Statesmanship. London, 1918.
Debidour.   Histoire diplomatique de l'Europe, 1814–78, 2 vols.   Paris, 1891.   Continuation from 1878 to 1916, La Paix Armée, 1917, and Vers la Grand Guerre, 1918.
G. M. Trevelyan.   British History in the Nineteenth Century. London, 1922.
Bourgeois, E.   Manuel Historique de Politique Étrangère, 3 vols.   Paris, 1901–6.
Dunning, W. A.   The British Empire and the United States. New York, 1914.
Seeley, John Robert.   The Expansion of England.   London, 1883.
—— Growth of British Policy.   Cambridge, 1895.
Taine, H.   Les origines de la France contemporaine, various editions.
Bryce, James.   The Holy Roman Empire, various editions.
—— The American Commonwealth, 2 vols.   New edition. New York, 1911.
Vander Linden and Hamelius.   Anglo-Belgian Relations. Past and Present.   London, 1918.
Acton, Lord.   Lectures on Modern History.   London, 1906.
—— Lectures on the French Revolution.   London, 1910.
Immich, Max.   Geschichte des Europäischen Staatensystems von 1660 bis 1789.   München und Berlin, 1905.

Germany.

von Sybel, Heinrich.   Die Begründung des Deutschen Reiches, 7 vols.   München u. Berlin, 1913.
Barker, J. Ellis.   The Foundations of Germany.   London, 1916.

Rose, J. H. Hereford, C. H., Gonner, E. C. K., and Sadler, M. E. Germany in the Nineteenth Century. An Introductory Note by Viscount Haldane. Manchester University Press, 1912.

Ward, Sir A. W. Germany, 3 vols. Cambridge University Press, vol. i., 1916 ; vol. ii., 1917 ; vol. iii., 1918.

WAR OF 1914.

Collected Diplomatic Documents relating to the outbreak of the European War. London, 1915. [Cd. 7860.]

Bülow, Prince von. Imperial Germany. 1st edit. London. January, 1914. New and revised edit. November, 1916.

Loreburn, Earl. How the War came about. London, 1919.

Haldane, Visct. Before the War. London, 1920.

Oman, C. The Outbreak of the War of 1914–18. London Stationery Office, 1919.

PEACE NEGOTIATIONS.

Temperley, H. W. V., Editor. A History of the Peace Conference of Paris, vols. i. to v. London, 1920–1.

Tardieu, A. La Paix. Paris, 1921.

Mermeix. Les Négociations Secrètes et les Quatre Armistices. Paris, 1921.

—— Le Combat des Trois. Paris, 1922.

Hammann, Otto. 1. Der Neue Kurs ; 2. Um den Kaiser 3. Zur Vorgeschichte des Weltkrieges. Berlin, 1918–19.

—— Der Missverstandene Bismarck, Berlin. 1921.

Pribram, Dr. Alfred Francis. Die politischen Geheimverträge Oesterreich-Ungarns, 1879–1914. Wien u. Leipzig, 1920 (English translation. The Secret Treaties of Austria-Hungary, 1879–1914. Cambridge Harvard University Press, 1920.)

Kautsky. Die deutschen Documente zum Kriegsausbruch, 4 vols. Charlottenburg, 1919.

Keynes, J. M. The Economic Consequences of the Peace. London, Dec. 1919.

—— A Revision of the Treaty. London, 1922.

Nitti, F. l'Europa Senza Pace. Firenze, 1921.

Baruch, B. M. The Making of the Reparation and Economic Sections of the Treaty. New York and London, 1920.

Haskins, C. H. and Lord, R. H. Some Problems of the Peace Conference. Cambridge, Harvard University Press and Oxford University Press, 1920.

E E

Texts of the Treaties of Versailles, Saint-Germain-en-Laye, Neuilly-Sur-Seine, Trianon and Sèvres, *i.e.*, with Germany, Austria, Bulgaria, Hungary and Turkey. Best editions of the Treaties with Germany and Austria, together with other Treaties and documents relevant thereto, published by H.M. Stationery Office, 1920 and 1921 respectively. Others in the Treaty Series.

INDEX

[For the compilation of this index, the author is indebted to Mr. Gaselee, Librarian and Keeper of the Papers at the Foreign Office.]

A

ABERDEEN, LORD, at Congress of Châtillon, ii, 72 ; at 1830 London conference on Belgian affairs, 113

Ablegatus, i, 241

Absence of diplomatist from court ceremony, i, 375

Acceptance of accession, ii, 319, 323, 324

Accession, ii, 317 ; distinguished from adhesion, *ibid.*; British forms, 319, 322 *sq.*; Turkish form, 320

A'Court, Sir William, i, 349 ; ii, 390, 395

Acte, i, 178 ; special, at 1863 Brussels conference for redemption of Scheldt dues, ii, 129

Acte authentique, i, 172

Acte final, ii, 246 ; of Vienna, 81, 246 ; of Hague Peace Conference, 247. *See also* Final Act.

Acte général, ii, 246 ; of Berlin, 248 ; of Algeciras, 170

Ad deliberandum, ii, 76

Additional articles (to a convention), ii, 245

Address of sovereigns, i, 52

Adhesion, ii, 317

Ad referendum, i, 171, 172 ; ii, 74, 76, 115, 388

Adrianople, peace between Russia and Turkey signed at (1829), ii, 112

Africa, conference on affairs of (Berlin, 1884), ii, 152

Agent and consul general, i, 246 ; local diplomatic titles of, 247

Agent can be accredited to more than one State, i, 194

Agent, diplomatic, *see* Diplomatic agent

Agents deputed to congress or conference, i, 194

Agréation, i, 203 ; American usage, 207–212

Agreement, ii, 259 *sqq.* ; for preliminaries of peace, 261 ; for settlement of claims, 264

Aix-la-Chapelle, Congress of 1668, ii, 17 ; treaty drafted, 19 ; proposed Congress of 1728, 45 ; —— Congress of 1748, 47 *sqq.* ; treaty of, 51 ; —— Congress of 1818, 82, 385 ; its protocol as to maritime honours, i, 62

Alabama claim, Catacazy's intrigue to prevent a settlement, i, 386

Alburquerque, duque de, ii, 372, 374

Alexis, grand-duke, proposed visit to United States in 1871, i, 385

Algeciras, conference of, 1906, ii, 165

Alliance, treaties of, ii, 231

Almodovar y Rio, duque de, president of conference of Algeciras, ii, 167

Alsace, French sovereign rights under treaty of Westphalia, ii, 23

Alt, Dr, on languages of London Treaty of 11 May, 1867, i, 75

Alternat, i, 31–35 ; ii, 61, 63

Ambassador, accredited by great Powers, i, 194 ; an honourable spy, 133, 183 ; derivation of word, 237 ; —— ordinary, 240 ; —— extraordinary, 241 ; formal entry of, 27 *n.*, 218 ; reception at court, 225 ; official reception after presentation of credentials, 225, 233 ; precedence of, 226 ; entitled to place of honour at festivities, 374 ; refusal to receive, 203 *sqq.*

Amiens, Congress of, ii, 67

"Anne, Statute of," i, 262, 271 ;

419

E

East India Company, power to appoint diplomatic agent, i, 193

Egan, United States minister in Chile, i, 309

Elector Palatine and Congress of Teschen (1779), ii, 56 *sqq.*

Elizabeth, Queen, and acceptance of foreign Orders by British subjects, i, 368 *sq.*

Embassy, special, i, 59

Embrun, Archbishop of, French Ambassador at Madrid 1667–8, ii, 18, 349

Eminence, title of, i. 94 *n.*

Emperor of Germany, title of, i, 39 *n.*

Enemy subjects, time granted for withdrawal in case of war, ii, 14, 22, 30

Envoyé, i, 241

Envoy Extraordinary, i, 241 ; and Minister Plenipotentiary, 241, 242 ; reception at Court, 226, 227

Equality between sovereign states, i, 35

Erlaucht, i, 40

Estrades, Count d', French Ambassador in London, 1661 : fight for precedence with Spanish Ambassador, i, 26 ; French plenipotentiary at Nijmegen, ii, 20

Evidence of diplomatic agent, how procured, i, 281 ; United States regulation, 282

Examining committee, ii, 176

Excellency, title of, who are entitled to, i, 365 ; dispute between France and Portugal in 1737, 367 ; dispute at Rijswijk, ii, 26

Exchange of Notes, ii, 289 ; for renewal of arbitration convention, 290 ; for prolongation of commercial treaty or *modus vivendi,* 291

Explosive bullets, conference on (Petersburg, 1868), ii, 137

Exposé de motifs, i, 87

Extradition, treaties of, ii, 236

" Extraordinary," as title of Ambassadors, i, 241

Extra territoriality, i, 249 ; — of ships, 250 *n.*

F

Faisans, Isle des, scene of Congress of the Pyrenees (1659), ii, 13

Fane, Julian, protocollist of 1867 London Conference respecting Luxembourg, ii, 135

Fanshawe, Sir Richard, and mediation by Great Britain between Spain and Portugal (1665–8), ii, 346

Ferdinand VII and Spanish colonies in America, ii, 376 *sq.*

Fersen, objected to by French as Swedish delegate at Rastadt (1797) because friend of Marie-Antoinette, ii, 64

Filitti, joint secretary at conference of Bucharest (1913), ii, 179

Final Act, copy for each power ; signed by plenipotentiaries ; deposit of — ; ii, 158

Final protocol, ii, 147, 148, 163

Fin de non-recevoir, i, 177

Fish, United States Secretary of State, and Catacazy case, i, 385

Fishing boats in time of war, ii, 67

Flag flown on diplomatic house, i, 375

Fleury, Cardinal, at Congress of Soissons (1728–9), ii, 44 *sqq.*

Fokchany, Congress of, ii, 54

Foreign department in England, i, 11 ; in other countries, 13

Foreign language, use of by diplomatist, i, 148

Foreign Office dinner to diplomatists, i, 59

" Four points " at Conference of Vienna (1855), ii, 121

Four Power Treaty (Washington Conference, 1920–1), ii, 204

Fox and Talleyrand, i, 362 ; forms of correspondence between, 95

Franchise du quartier, i, 315 ; French case in 1660, *ibid.* ; in 1688, 322 ; case at Genoa, 324

Frankfort, Congress of, ii, 23

Frederick the Great on *ultimatum,* i, 162, 163, 165 ; on duties of ambassador, 183, 248 ; dismissal of Comte de Broglie from Dresden, 341 ; and Congress of Teschen, ii, 56 *sqq.* ; presents there given by, i, 374

liminary to Congress of Münster) ii, 5

Hanover, Alliance of, ii, 44 ; conference at (for redemption of Stade toll, 1861), 125 ; Elector's title, 35

Haro, Don Luis Mendez de, at Congress and Peace of Pyrenees, ii, 12 sq.

Hawkesbury, Lord, signs articles preliminary to Congress of Amiens (1801), ii, 67.

Hay, John, American Secretary of State and good offices between Russia and Japan (1904-5), ii, 340 sq.

Head of Mission, duties, i, 145 sq., 155

Henry IV, King of France, bestowal of Orders on British subjects, i, 368

Héron, Marquis de, French envoy to Poland, kidnapped in Prussia 1702, i, 337

Historical works recommended for diplomatist's reading, ii, 413 sqq.

Hoey, van, his case, i, 339

Hoheit, i, 40

Hohenlohe, Cardinal, refused as Envoy by Pope on account of his ecclesiastical rank, i, 213

Holdernesse, Lord, arrest of, i, 336

Holland, style of the States-General of, i, 125 ; French declaration of war in 1747, ii, 47, 52 ; separation of Belgium from —, 113 sqq.

" Holy League," ii, 31

Holy Roman Empire, dissolution of, ii, 2

Holy See, British diplomatic relations with, i, 191 ; possesses right of legation, 194

Hostages given by Great Britain to France in 1748, ii, 52

Hubertusburg, i, 33 ; Congress of, ii, 4 ; treaty of (1763), confirmed at Congress of Teschen (1779), 61

Hübner, Baron (afterwards Count) on trials of a diplomatist, i, 156

I

Immunities of diplomatic agents, i,

251 sqq. ; from local civil jurisdiction, 261 ; as to property, 262 ; laws of different countries, 263 sqq. ; from local criminal jurisdiction, 259 ; case of Italian secretary, 260 ; offences committed by members of the suite, 278; from taxation, 284 sqq.; from customs duties, confined to heads of missions, 286, 289 ; Callières on abuse of privilege, 284 ; practice of various countries, 288 sqq. ; from parochial rates, 290 sqq. ; violation of French Embassy at Venice in 1540, 310 ; in a third State, 329 sqq. ; of diplomatists accredited to the Holy See, 331 ; — immunities extend to diplomatists' wives and children, 292 ; to his suite, 292, 294 ; —Immunities of sovereigns and heads of States, 5-7, 249 ; of officials of League of Nations, ii, 196

India, right of legation of Governor, i, 193

Infanta of Spain sent home, ii, 43

Inojosa, i, 405

Inscription, i, 93

Instructions, i, 153, 217 ; French collection of, 153

International compacts, varieties of, ii, 212

Internonce apostolique, i, 243

Internuncius, i, 243 ; Austrian — at Constantinople, *ibid.* and 357

Inviolability, i, 251

Isturíz, dismissal of by Palmerston i, 391

J

Jackson, F. J., British Minister at Washington in 1809, recall of, i, 382

Java, right of legation of Governor, i, 193

Jean Casimir, King of Poland, ii, 16, 17, *n.*

Jenikalé, cession demanded by Russia from Turkey, 1773, ii, 55

Jenkins, mediator at Nijmegen (1676), ii, 21

Jewett, i, 383

João, Dom, Regent of Portugal in 1807, King João VI in 1816, ii, 357

INDEX

437

actions against dismissed in New York and London, i, 333 *sq.*

Venice first institutes permanent diplomatic missions, i, 240

Verona, Congress of, ii, 90

Versailles, treaty of (1919), ii, 193

Victor-Amadeus of Savoy, ii, 41

Victoria, Queen, and acceptance of foreign orders by British subjects, i, 369 *sq.*; endings of letters, 53 *sq.*; Jubilee, precedence at, 58

Vienna, Congress of, ii, 78 *sqq.*; Conference of (1855), 120; Second Treaty of (1731), 46

" Vienna Note," i, 167

Villars, Marquis de, French ambassador in Madrid in 1679, and *franchise du quartier*, i, 320 *sq.*

Ville, Abbé de la, ii, 52

Villiers, Viscount, British plenipotentiary at Congress of Rijswijk, ii, 25

Vion, French consul at Lima in 1865, and right of asylum, i, 302

Visits, first, i, 357 *sq.*

Vivâ voce conferences, ii, 17

Vœu, ii, 144, 155, 160, 164, 169

Vossem, peace of, ii, 20

Voting at a conference, ii, 172

W

Waddington, Carlos, i, 272

Walewski, Count, president of 1856 Congress of Paris, ii, 92; French plenipotentiary at 1858 Paris conference on Danubian principalities, 123

Wall, General, Spanish envoy in London 1748–62, though a British subject by birth, i, 213

Wartensleben, Dutch envoy, arrested by Landgrave of Hesse-Cassel for fraud as trustee, i, 267, 275

War-time, conduct of diplomatists in, i, 361

Washburne, i, 345

Washington, audience at, to present credentials, i, 226; conference of (limitation of armaments, 1921), ii, 197

Watteville, de, Spanish Ambassador in London, 1661; fight for precedence with French ambassador, i, 26

Webster, Daniel, and Marcoleta case, i, 394

Wellesley offers mediation between Spain and her American colonies (1810), ii, 373 *sqq.*

Wellington, British plenipotentiary at Congress of Vienna, ii, 79; at Verona (1822), 90; at Petersburg (1826), 109; endeavours to mediate between France and Spain (1822), 392

Westmorland, Lord, British plenipotentiary at 1855 Conference of Vienna, ii, 120

Westphalen, Count von: refused as envoy in 1847 by King of Hanover because a Roman Catholic, i, 212

Westphalia, Congress of, ii, 5; Treaties of, confirmed at Congress of Teschen (1779), ii, 61

Wheaton, United States minister at Berlin in 1839, i, 269

Whitworth, Lord, ordered by Queen Anne to apologise to Peter the Great for the arrest of his ambassador, i, 43, 300; British plenipotentiary at Conress of Cambray (1722), ii, 41

Wicquefort on right of religious service limited to language of ambassador, i, 327

Wildshut, Braunau, etc., ceded by Elector Palatine to Maria-Theresa, ii, 61

William of Orange, ii, 20; opposition to treaty of Nijmegen, 22; recognition as King of England, 24; at Rijswijk, 27, 31

Williams, Sir Charles Hanbury, instructions on mission to Berlin in 1750, i, 218

Williamson, Sir Joseph, British plenipotentiary at Congress of Rijswijk, ii, 25

Windelheim, ii, 61

Wise, United States minister to Brazil; recall requested, 1847, i, 389

Wittelsbach family, ii, 56

Witzendorff, protocollist at 1861 Hanover Conference on redemption of Stade Toll, ii, 126

Printed by Fox, Jones & Co., Kemp Hall Press,
High Street, Oxford

SD - #0013 - 070122 - C0 - 229/152/24 - PB - 9781332133864 - Gloss Lamination